GRE® EXAM

Strategies, Practice, and Review

2010 Edition

KAPLAN)

PUBLISHING

New York

©2009 Kaplan, Inc.

Published by Kaplan Publishing, a division of Kaplan, Inc.
1 Liberty Plaza
New York, NY 10006

Printed in the United States of America

10 9 8 7 6 5 4 3 2

ISBN-13: 978-1-4195-5296-0

Kaplan Publishing books are available at special quantity discounts to use for sales promotions, employee premiums, or educational purposes. Please email our Special Sales Department to order or for more information at *kaplanpublishing@kaplan.com*, or write to Kaplan Publishing, 1 Liberty Plaza, 24th Floor, New York, NY 10006

TABLE OF CONTENTS

Chapter 4: Quantitative Section

Chapter 5: Analytical Writing Section

Chapter 6: Take Control of the Test

PART THREE: FULL-LENGTH PRACTICE TEST

PART FOUR: PRACTICE TEST ANSWERS AND EXPLANATIONS

PART FIVE: GETTING INTO GRAD SCHOOL

Chapter 7: Where and When to Apply

Chapter 8: How to Apply

GRE RESOURCES

kaptest.com/publishing

The material in this book is up-to-date at the time of publication. However, the Educational Testing Service may have instituted changes in the tests or test registration process after this book was published. Be sure to carefully read the materials you receive when you register for the test.

If there are any important late-breaking developments—or changes or corrections to the Kaplan test preparation materials in this book—we will post that information online at **kaptest.com/publishing.** Check to see if there is any information posted there regarding this book.

kaplansurveys.com/books

What did you think of this book? We'd love to hear your comments and suggestions. We invite you to fill out our online survey form at *kaplansurveys.com/books*.

Your feedback is extremely helpful as we continue to develop high-quality resources to meet your needs.

ABOUT THE EXPERTS

Eric Goodman has been teaching the Kaplan GRE, GMAT, and LSAT courses for over a decade and also works for Kaplan Test Prep and Admissions as a product consultant. When not teaching or writing for Kaplan, Eric works as a composer and musician in New York City.

Anna Gratz is a classroom teacher in New York City. She is a former GRE product manager for Kaplan and has authored and edited many of Kaplan's GRE classroom materials. She has also tutored and taught GRE students extensively. She is the author of the *Score! Mountain Challenge* Grade 5 Language Arts Workbook. She holds a B. S. from Indiana University in Education and a master's degree from Columbia University Teachers College in Literacy. She is the 2008 winner of Columbia University Teachers College After Ed TV's School ReDesign Green Classroom Challenge.

Ray Ojserkis has researched the GRE extensively, written a slew of GRE preparation materials, and taught numerous GRE students in the New York City area. He holds a B.A. in Economics from Lehigh University, and an M.A. and Ph.D. in International History, both from the London School of Economics and Political Science. He recently published a book on the beginning of the Cold War arms race.

Bob Verini is currently the National Director of Academics for Kaplan Test Prep and Admissions. Since joining Kaplan in 1980, he has taught thousands of students how to ace the GRE and other standardized tests. Bob also trains new Kaplan instructors nationally, contributes to course development, and works with individual students as part of Kaplan's Admissions Consulting program. He is in national demand as a speaker and panel moderator on a wide range of educational issues. Bob holds a B.A. from SUNY Albany and an MFA from Indiana University. In his spare time, he is a writer, actor, and director, with several films, books, and extensive stage experience to his credit. He was also a five-time winner on the game show Jeopardy™ and won its 1987 Tournament of Champions.

UPDATES TO THE GRE

Instead of one major overhaul as originally planned, ETS will introduce revisions to the GRE gradually, beginning with two new question types—one math, one verbal—that were introduced into the computer-based GRE in November 2007. **For the time being, these new question types do not count toward your score.**

On Test Day, you may see just one sample of the new math question type, just one sample of the new verbal question type, OR you may not see either question at all.

As of this printing, ETS has not announced a time line for when these new types will count toward your score.

NEW QUESTION TYPES

The new verbal question type, Text Completion, is a revised Sentence Completion that requires you to fill in two or three blanks within a passage. The answer choices appear in separate multiple-choice lists, one for each blank. Although the two or three answers must be selected independently of the others, there's no partial credit. You will find more details on the new question types, as well as a sample question with a detailed answer explanation, on page 28 in chapter 3.

The new math question type, Numeric Entry, has no answer choices. Instead, it requires you to manually enter a numerical answer into an empty answer box. You will find more details on the new question types, as well as a sample question with a detailed answer explanation, on page 150 in chapter 4.

You will also find practice sets with these new question types in your Online Companion, in case you'd like to become more familiar with them, but again, these questions do not count toward your score.

REFORMATTED QUESTION TYPE

ETS has announced one reformatted question type, highlighted Reading Comprehension passages. Some of the passages will not have line numbers and line numbers will not be referenced in the questions. Instead, when a question references a specific part of the text, that part will be highlighted in the passage. ETS believes the highlighting will make it easier for test takers to locate referenced information in the passage. You will see some Reading Comprehension passages that contain line references and some that contain highlighting. For more on this reformatted question type, see the Reading Comprehension section in chapter 3.

STAYING ON TOP OF THE LATEST DEVELOPMENTS

ETS is still working out the remaining planned updates and time lines, and will announce changes as they are finalized. As ETS makes further announcements, you can depend on Kaplan to provide you with the most accurate, up-to-the-minute information. Late-breaking details will be posted to your online companion, so be sure to check it frequently. You can also get updates by visiting us at Kaptest.com/ NEWGRE.

HOW TO USE THIS BOOK

More people get into graduate school with a Kaplan course than any other major test prep company. The techniques and approaches from Kaplan's classroom and tutoring programs are distilled in this book in a clear, easy-to-grasp format. Here's the plan to get you started!

TAKE A PRACTICE TEST TO IDENTIFY YOUR STRENGTHS AND OPPORTUNITIES

You have one test in this book, and free, exclusive access to one test online. To take the online test that comes with this book, follow these three easy steps:

(1) Locate your serial number in the book. It's on the inside back cover.

(2) Go to Kaptest.com/GREBooksOnline.

(3) Enter your serial number. Make sure to enter it exactly as it appears in the book.

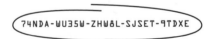

To return to your test results, enter www.Kaptest.com in any Internet browser and select the "My Page" link. Based on your performance on a practice test, you'll be able to focus and customize your study time.

HOW TO EVALUATE YOUR TEST RESULTS

First look at the summary of your performance at the end of the test to get a sense of:

- The number of questions you got right, wrong, skipped, or didn't answer—overall and by section
- How long it took you to answer each question
- How much you changed your mind

Next, read the answer explanations for each questions. Make a list of your personal strengths and opportunities by identifying whether or not:

- You know and understand the concepts being tested
- You find certain GRE question types especially challenging
- You are answering questions quickly enough

You can also go to Kaptest.com/GRE, and take the free practice test provided there.

GET TO KNOW THE GRE, AND CREATE YOUR STUDY PLAN

First, read chapter 1 of your book, "Introduction to the GRE" to get familiar with important details about the test, including structure, scoring, and registration info. Next, choose a test date and register! This will secure your spot in the test center.

At that point you can work back from your test date to figure out much time you have to prepare.

Divide that preparation time in half. Start with the key concepts and GRE question types you need to focus on. Go through the lessons in this book, take the practice sets, and read the answer explanations.

Once you've improved on those, devote time to reinforcing your strengths through lesson reviews and practice sets. Also, plan time to practice with the essay prompts, even if writing is your best subject. Understanding the essay requirements and practicing periodically will help you deliver the right paragraphs on Test Day, when it really counts.

As soon as you are comfortable with the question types and Kaplan Methods, take another full-length practice test.

MORE GRE PRACTICE

If you're looking for more practice, pick up a copy of Kaplan's *GRE Exam Math Workbook or GRE Exam Verbal Workbook*. You'll get a review of core concepts, as well as additional test-like practice questions to help build speed and accuracy.

Good luck!

Part One

THE GRE

CHAPTER 1: INTRODUCTION TO THE GRE

- Understand how the GRE is constructed
- Get registration and score reporting information
- Learn about the various GRE Subject Tests

This book will explain more than just a few basic strategies. It will prepare you for practically everything that's ever on the GRE.

We know this sounds too good to be true, but we mean it. We are able to do this because we don't explain questions in isolation or focus on particular problems. Instead, we explain the underlying principles behind *all* of the questions on the GRE. We give you the big picture.

UNDERSTANDING THE GRE

Let's take a look at how the current GRE is constructed. As someone famous once said, "Know thine enemy." And you need to know firsthand the way this test is put together if you want to take it apart. Before you begin, though, remember that the test makers sometimes change the content, administration, and scheduling of the GRE too quickly for a published guide to keep up with. For the latest, up-to-the-minute news about the GRE, visit Kaplan's website at **kaptest.com**.

THE PURPOSES OF THE GRE

The GRE is a test that is designed to assess readiness for graduate school for a wide variety of programs. The ways in which graduate schools use GRE scores vary. Scores are often used as part of the application packet for entrance into a program, but they also can be used to grant fellowships or financial aid.

Each section of the GRE is designed to assess general skills necessary for graduate school. Some of these skills include the ability to read complex informational text and understand high-level vocabulary words in the Verbal section, the ability to respond to an issue in written form in the Analytical Writing section, and the ability to apply general mathematical concepts to a variety of problem types in the Quantitative section. Not all graduate students will find that these skills are necessary for success in their chosen programs. Nonetheless, graduate school admissions officers often view the score as an important indictor of readiness. In addition, graduate school admissions officers are comparing hundreds or even thousands of applications, and having a quantitative factor such as a GRE score makes the job of comparing so many applicants much easier. Just by purchasing this book and making a commitment to yourself to be as well prepared as possible for this exam, you've already taken the crucial first step toward making your graduate school application as competitive as possible.

THE SECRET CODE

Doing well on the GRE requires breaking down the "secret code" upon which each and every test is constructed. The GRE, like all of the tests ETS creates, is based on psychometrics, the peculiar science concerned with creating "standardized" tests. For a test to be "standardized," it must successfully do three things. First, the test must be "reliable"; in other words, a test taker who takes the GRE should get approximately the same score if he or she takes a second GRE (assuming, of course, that he or she doesn't study with Kaplan materials during the intervening period). Second—and this is closely related to our first point—it must test the same concepts on each test. Third, it must be able to create a "bell curve" when a pool of test takers' scores are plotted; in other words, some people will do very well on the test, and some will do very poorly, but the great majority will score somewhere in the middle.

What all this boils down to is that in order to be a standardized test, the GRE has to be extremely predictable. And this is what makes the GRE and other standardized tests so coachable. Because ETS has to test the same concepts in each and every test, certain vocabulary words appear over and over again, as do variations of the same exact math questions. Moreover, the GRE has to create some questions that most test takers will get wrong—otherwise, it wouldn't be able to create its bell curve. This means that hard questions will usually contain "traps"—wrong answer choices that will be more appealing than the correct answer to a large percentage of test takers. Fortunately, these traps are predictable (this is what we mean by the secret code), and we can teach you how to recognize and avoid them. The goal of this comprehensive program is to help you break the code.

PLAY THE GAME

Too many people think of standardized tests as cruel exercises in futility, as the oppressive instruments of a faceless societal machine. People who think this way usually don't do very well on these tests.

The key discovery that people who ace standardized tests have made is that raging against the machine doesn't hurt it. If that's what you choose to do, you will just waste your energy. What these high scorers choose to do instead is to think of the test as a game—not an instrument of punishment, but an opportunity for reward. And like any game, if you play it enough times, you get really good at it.

ACQUIRE THE SKILLS

You may think that the GRE isn't a fair or decent predictor of skills—but that attitude won't help you get into graduate school.

None of the GRE experts who work at Kaplan were *born* acing the GRE. No one is. That's because these tests do not measure innate skills; they measure *acquired* skills. People who are good at standardized tests are simply people who've already acquired these skills, maybe in math class, or by reading a lot, or by studying logic in college, or perhaps the easiest way—in one of Kaplan's GRE courses. But they have, perhaps without realizing it, acquired the skills that spell success on tests like the GRE. And if *you* haven't, you have nothing whatsoever to feel bad about. You just have to acquire them now.

SAME PROBLEMS—BUT DIFFERENT

As we noted, the test makers use the same problems on every GRE. We know it sounds incredible, but it's true—only the words and numbers change. They test the same principles over and over.

Here's an example. This is a type of math problem known as a Quantitative 數量上的 Comparison. (Look familiar? It should, if you've ever taken an SAT. This question type used to appear on the SAT, although ETS decided to drop this question type from the SAT starting in 2005.) Your job is to examine the relationship and pick **(A)** if the term in Column A is bigger, **(B)** if the term in Column B is bigger, **(C)** if they're equal, or **(D)** if there is not enough information given to solve the problem.

Column A	Column B

$$2x^2 = 32$$

x	4

Most people answer **(C)**, that they're equal. They divide both sides of the centered equation by 2 and then take the square root of both sides to get $x = 4$.
方程式,相等
Wrong. The answer isn't **(C)**, because x doesn't have to be 4. It could be 4 *or* -4. Both work, so the answer is **(D)** because the answer cannot be determined from the information given. If you just solve for 4 you'll get this problem—and every one like it—wrong. ETS figures that if you get burned here, you'll get burned again next time. Only next time it won't be $2x^2 = 32$; it will be $y^2 = 36$ or $s^4 = 81$.

The concepts that are tested on any particular GRE—Pythagorean triangles, simple logic, word relationships, and so forth—are the underlying concepts at the heart of *every* GRE.

ETS makes changes only after testing them exhaustively. This process is called *norming,* which means taking a normal test and a changed test and administering them to a random group of students. As long as the group is large enough for the purposes of statistical validity and the students get consistent scores from one test to the next, then the revised test is just as valid and consistent as any other GRE.

That may sound technical, but norming is actually quite an easy process. We do it at Kaplan all the time—for the tests that we write for our students. The test at the back of this book, for instance, is a normed exam. While the interactive, computer-based test experience of the GRE is impossible to reproduce on paper, the paper-based test in our book is a normed exam that will produce an equivalent score.

HOW THE GRE IS ORGANIZED

The Graduate Record Examination (GRE) is administered on computer and is between two and three-quarters and three and a quarter hours long, depending on which question type you get on your experimental section (more on this in a bit). The exam consists of three scored sections, with different amounts of time allotted for you to complete each section.

Verbal	
Time	30 minutes
Length	30 multiple-choice questions
Format	Sentence Completion, Analogy, Reading Comprehension, and Antonym
Content	Tests vocabulary, verbal reasoning skills, and the ability to read complex passages with understanding and insight

Quantitative	
Time	45 minutes
Length	28 multiple-choice questions
Format	Quantitative Comparison, Word Problems, and Data Interpretation (graph questions)
Content	Tests basic mathematical skills, ability to understand and apply mathematical concepts, and quantitative reasoning skills

בלתא בלתך

Analytical Writing	
Time	75 minutes
Length	2 essay prompts
Format	Perspective on an Issue and Analyze an Argument
Content	Tests ability to understand and analyze arguments, to understand and draw logical conclusions, and to write clearly and succinctly

Your test will also contain an experimental section—a second Verbal or Quantitative section that the test makers put on the test so that they can norm the new questions they create for use on future GREs. That means that if you could identify the experimental section, you could doodle for half an hour, guess in a random pattern, or daydream and still get exactly the same score on the GRE. However, the experimental section is disguised to look like a real section—there is no way to identify it. All you will really know on the day of the test is that one of the subject areas will have two sections instead of one. Naturally, many people try to figure out which section is experimental. But because ETS really wants you to try hard on it, they do their best to keep you guessing. If you guess wrong, you could blow the whole test, so we urge you to treat all sections as scored unless you are told otherwise.

After you have completed the four test-like sections, you may get a fifth "research" section, which ETS includes on the GRE to find the answers to such vital questions as how best to market its own test prep materials. The research section is also unscored, and is not always included in the GRE. If you see a research section on Test Day, ETS will be kind enough to tell you when it appears. So there is no reason whatsoever for you to complete it, unless you feel like doing ETS a favor, or unless they offer you some reward (which they have been known to do).

SCORING

The Analytical Writing section is scored on a scale of 0–6 in half-point increments. (See chapter 5 for details on this scoring rubric.) The Verbal and Quantitative sections each yield a scaled score within a range of 200 to 800. These scaled scores are like the scores that you received if you took the SAT. You cannot score higher than 800 on either section, no matter how hard you try. Similarly, it's impossible (again, no matter how hard you try) to get a score lower than 200 on either section.

But you don't receive *only* scaled scores. You will also receive a percentile rank, which will place your performance relative to those of a large sample population of other GRE takers. Percentile scores tell graduate schools just what your scaled scores are worth. For instance, even if everyone got very high scaled scores, universities would still be able to differentiate candidates by their percentile score.

Percentile ranks match with scaled scores differently, depending on the measure. Let's imagine that you took the GRE this year, and that you scored a perfect 800 on each measure type. Your scaled score would be the same in each section, but that would translate into different percentile ranks. In Verbal, you'd be scoring above 99 percent of the population, so that would be your percentile rank. But in the Quantitative section, many other people will score very high as well. Difficult as this section may seem, so many people score so well on it that high scaled scores are more common. Your percentile rank for Quantitative, even if you don't miss a single question, would be in only the 96th percentile. So many other people are scoring that high in Quantitative that no one can score above the 96th percentile!

What this means is that it's pretty easy to get good scaled scores on the GRE and much harder to get good percentile ranks. A Quantitative score of 600, for example, might be okay if you're applying to a humanities program; but if you're applying to science or engineering programs, it would be a handicap at most schools. Even a score of 700 in Quantitative is relatively low for many very selective programs in the sciences or engineering—after all, it's only the 79th or 80th percentile.

The relative frequency of high scaled scores means that universities pay great attention to percentile rank. What you need to realize is that scores that seemed good to you when you took the SAT might not be all that good on the GRE. It's important that you do some real research into the programs you're thinking about. Many schools have cut-off scores below which they don't even consider applicants. But be careful! If a school tells you they look for applicants scoring 600 average per section, that doesn't mean they think those are good scores. That 600 may be the baseline. You owe it to yourself to find out what kinds of scores *impress* the schools you're interested in and work hard until you get those scores. You can definitely get there if you want to and if you work hard enough. We see it every day.

A final note about percentile rank: the sample population that you are compared against in order to determine your percentile is not everyone else who takes the test the same day as you do. ETS doesn't want to penalize an unlucky candidate who takes the GRE on a date when everyone else happens to be a rocket scientist. So they compare your performance with those of a random three-year population of recent GRE test takers. Your score will not in any way be affected by the other people who take the exam on the same day as you. We often tell our students, "Your only competition in this classroom is yourself."

Cancellation and Multiple Scores Policy

Unlike many things in life, the GRE allows you a second chance. If, at the end of the test, you feel that you've definitely not done as well as you can, you have the option to cancel your score. The trick is, you must decide whether you want to keep your scores before the computer shows them to you. If you cancel, your scores will be disregarded.

(You also won't get to see them.) Canceling a test means that it won't be scored. It will just appear on your score report as a canceled test. No one will know how well or poorly you really did—not even you.

Two legitimate reasons to cancel your test are illness and personal circumstances that cause you to perform unusually poorly on that particular day. Also, if you feel that you didn't prepare sufficiently, then it may be acceptable to cancel your score and approach your test preparation a little more seriously the next time.

But keep in mind that test-takers historically underestimate their performance, especially immediately following the test. (This underestimation is especially true on the CAT, which is designed to give you questions at the limits of your abilities.) They tend to forget about all of the things that went right and focus on everything that went wrong. So unless your performance is terribly marred by unforeseen circumstances, don't cancel your test.

If you do cancel, your future score reports will indicate that you've canceled a previous score. But since the canceled test was never scored, you don't have to worry about bad numbers showing up on any subsequent score report. If you take more than one test without canceling, then all the scores will show up on each score report, so the graduate schools will see them all. Requested score reports are sent to schools within 10–15 days after the exam. All GRE testing administrations will be listed (and usable) in your ETS record for five years. Most grad schools average GRE scores, although there are a few exceptions. Check with individual schools for their policies on multiple scores.

TEST REGISTRATION

You should first obtain a copy of the *GRE Registration Bulletin*. This booklet contains information on scheduling, pricing, repeat testing, cancellation policies, and more. You can receive the booklet by calling the Educational Testing Service at (609) 771-7670, or by downloading it from **gre.org.**

The computer-based GRE General Test is offered year-round. To register for and schedule your GRE, use one of the options below. (If you live outside the United States, Canada, American Samoa, Guam, the U.S. Virgin Islands, or Puerto Rico, visit **gre.org** for instructions on how to register.)

Register Online

You can register online (if you are paying with a credit card) at **gre.org.** Once the registration process is complete, you can print out your voucher immediately (and can reprint it if it is lost).

READ MORE

To learn more about how schools use your score, go to **gre.org** and click on "Scores and Score Reporting."

Register by Phone

Call 1-800-GRE-CALL or 1-800-529-3590 (TTY). A confirmation number, reporting time, and test center location will be given to you when you call. Though you can register by phone up to two days before the exam, registering earlier is strongly recommended since spaces often fill quickly. Payments can be made with a Visa, MasterCard, or American Express card.

Register by Mail

Complete the Authorization Voucher Request Form found in the *GRE Registration Bulletin*. Mail the fee and signed voucher request form in the envelope provided to the address printed on the voucher.

ETS advises that you allow up to four weeks for processing before you receive your voucher in the mail. When you receive your voucher, call to schedule an appointment. Vouchers are valid for one year from the date of issue.

When you register, make sure you list a first- and second-choice test center. If you register online, you can confirm test center availability in real time.

GRE CHECKLIST

BEFORE THE TEST

- ☐ Choose a test date.

- ☐ Register online at gre.org or by phone at phone at 1-800-GRE-CALL.

- ☐ Receive your admission voucher.

- ☐ Check out your test center.

    - ☐ Know the kind of workstation you'll be using and whether the room is likely to be hot or cold.

    - ☐ Know the directions to the building and room where you'll be tested.

- ☐ Create a test-prep calendar to ensure that you're ready by the day of the test.

    - ☐ If you skipped it, go back and read "How to Use the This Book."

    - ☐ On a calendar, block out the weeks you have to prepare for the test.

    - ☐ Based on your strengths and weaknesses, establish a detailed plan of study and select appropriate lessons and practice. (Don't forget to include some days off!)

☐ Stick to the plan; as with any practice, little is gained if it isn't methodical. Skills can't be "crammed" in the last minutes.

☐ Reevaluate your strengths and weaknesses from time to time and revise your plan accordingly.

☐ Print out your downloadable Study Plan to bring with you on Test Day.

THE DAY OF THE TEST

☐ Make sure you have your GRE admission voucher and acceptable ID.

☐ Leave yourself plenty of time to arrive at the test site stress-free.

☐ Arrive at the test site at least 30 minutes early for the check-in procedures.

☐ Don't stress; you're going to do great!

GRE SUBJECT TESTS

Subject Tests are designed to test the fundamental knowledge most important for successful graduate study in a particular subject area. In order to do well on a GRE Subject Test, you need to have an extensive background in the particular subject area—the sort of background you would be expected to have if you majored in the subject. Subject Tests enable admissions officers to compare students from different colleges with different standards and curricula. Not every graduate school or program requires Subject Tests, so check admissions requirements at those schools in which you're interested.

ORGANIZATION, SCORING, AND TEST DATES

All Subject Tests are administered in paper-and-pencil format and consist exclusively of multiple-choice questions that are designed to assess knowledge of the areas of the subject that are included in the typical undergraduate curriculum.

On Subject Tests, you'll earn one point for each multiple-choice question that you answer correctly but lose one-quarter point for each incorrectly answered question. Unanswered questions aren't counted in the scoring. Your raw score is the number of correctly answered questions minus one-quarter of the incorrectly answered questions. This raw score is then converted into a scaled score, which can range from 200 to 900. The range varies from test to test.

Some Subject Tests also contain subtests, which provide more specific information about your strengths and weaknesses. The same questions that contribute to your subtest scores also contribute to your overall score. Subtest scores, which range from 20 to 99, are reported along with the overall score. For further information on scoring, you should consult the relevant Subject Test Descriptive Booklet, available from ETS.

Subject Tests are offered three times a year: in October, November, and April. Note that not all of the Subject Tests are offered on every test date; consult **gre.org** for upcoming test dates and registration deadlines.

SUBJECTS

Currently, eight Subject Tests are offered. A list of them follows, along with a brief description of each.

Biochemistry, Cell, and Molecular Biology

This test consists of 180 questions and is divided among three subscore areas: biochemistry, cell biology, and molecular biology and genetics.

Biology

This test consists of about 200 questions divided among three subscore areas: cellular and molecular biology, organismal biology, and ecology and evolution.

Chemistry

This test consists of about 136 questions. There are no subscores, and the questions cover the following topics: analytical chemistry, inorganic chemistry, organic chemistry, and physical chemistry.

Computer Science

This test consists of approximately 70 questions. There are no subscores, and the questions cover the following topics: software systems and methodology, computer organization and architecture, theory and mathematical background, and other, more advanced topics, such as numerical analysis, graphics, and artificial intelligence.

Literature in English

This test consists of 230 questions on literature in the English language. There are two basic types of questions: factual questions that test the student's knowledge of writers typically covered in the undergraduate curriculum, and interpretive questions that test the student's ability to read various types of literature critically.

Mathematics

This test consists of 66 questions on the content of various undergraduate courses in mathematics. Most of the test assesses the student's knowledge of calculus, abstract algebra, linear algebra, and real analysis. About a quarter of the test, however, requires knowledge in other areas of math.

Physics

This test consists of 100 questions covering mostly material covered in the first three years of undergraduate physics. Topics include classical mechanics, electromagnetism, atomic physics, optics and wave phenomena, quantum mechanics, thermodynamics and statistical mechanics, special relativity, and laboratory methods. About 9 percent of the test covers advanced topics, such as nuclear and particle physics, condensed matter physics, and astrophysics.

Psychology

This test consists of 210 questions drawn from courses most commonly included in the undergraduate curriculum. Questions fall into three categories. The experimental or natural science-oriented category includes questions in learning, cognitive psychology, sensation and perception, ethology and comparative psychology, and physiological psychology. The social or social science-oriented category includes questions in abnormal psychology, developmental psychology, social psychology, and personality. Together, these make up about 85 percent of the test, and each of the two categories provides its own subscore. The other 15 percent or so of the questions fall under the "general" category, which includes the history of psychology, tests and measurements, research design and statistics, and applied psychology.

For more information, you should consult ETS's Subject Test section at **gre.org.** You can also visit the Kaplan website **(kaptest.com)** for a more detailed description of each Subject Test and some free sample questions.

 READ MORE

To prepare for the Biology and Psychology Subject Tests, see Kaplan's prep guides for those tests.

CHAPTER 2: CAT TEST MECHANICS

- Understand how the GRE CAT works and how it affects you
- Learn how to navigate through the test on the computer easily
- Study Kaplan's CAT-specific test-taking strategies

The first year of graduate school is a frenzied experience for many students. It's no surprise, then, that the GRE, the test specifically designed to predict success in the first year of graduate school, is a speed-intensive test that demands good time-management skills.

So when you're comfortable with the content of the test, namely, the type of material discussed in the previous chapter, your next challenge will be to take it to the next level—test mechanics—which will enable you to manage an entire section at a time.

On most of the tests you take in school, you wouldn't dream of not making at least a try at every single one of the questions. If a question seems particularly difficult, you spend significantly more time on it, because you'll probably be given more points for answering a hard question correctly. Not so on the GRE.

You've got to develop a way of handling the test sections to make sure you get as many points as you can as quickly and easily as you can. The following principles will help you do just that.

CAT MECHANICS

A CAT, or *computer-adaptive test*, is a computer-based test that you take at a special test center at a time you schedule. A CAT "adapts" to your performance. The GRE CAT is in some ways quite different from the traditional paper-and-pencil tests you've probably taken in the past. In fact, it's pretty unusual at first. Here's how it works. You will only see one question at a time. Instead of having a predetermined mixture of basic, medium, and hard questions, the computer will select questions for you based on how well you are doing. The first question will be of medium difficulty. If you get it right, the second question will be a little harder; if you get the first question wrong, the second will be a little more basic.

If you keep getting questions right, the test will get harder and harder; if you slip and make some mistakes, the test will adjust and start giving you easier problems, but if you answer them correctly, it will go back to the hard ones. Ideally, the test gives you enough questions to ensure that scores are not based on luck. If you get one hard question right you might just have been lucky, but if you get 10 hard questions right, then luck has little to do with it. So the test is self-adjusting and self-correcting.

Because of this format, the CAT is very different structurally from a paper-and-pencil test. After the first problem, every problem that you see is based on how you answered the prior problem. That means you cannot return to a question once you've answered it, because that would throw off the sequence. Once you answer a question, it's part of your score, for better or worse. That means you can't skip around within a section and do questions in the order that you like.

Another major consequence is that hard problems count more than easy ones. It has to be this way, because the very purpose of this adaptive format is to find out at what level you reliably get about *half* the questions right; that's your scoring level. It actually makes a lot of sense. Imagine two students—one who does 10 basic questions, half of which she gets right and half of which she gets wrong, and one who does 10 very difficult questions, half of which she gets right and half of which she gets wrong. The same number of questions have been answered correctly in each case, but this does not reflect an equal ability on the part of the two students.

In fact, the student who answered five out of ten very difficult questions incorrectly could still get a very high score on the CAT GRE. But in order to get to these hard questions, she first had to get medium-difficulty questions right. So, no matter how much more comfortable you might be sticking to the basic questions, you definitely want to get to the hard questions if you can, because that's where the points are.

FIRST IMPRESSIONS COUNT

One of the most important things to know is that the early questions are vital for a good score on the CAT. As in life, first impressions make a big difference. Why? Because the computer doesn't have information about you at the start of the test, and its goal is to get an accurate estimate of your score as quickly as possible. In order to do that, the computer has to make large jumps in the estimation of your score for each of the first few questions.

It's a lot like how you would act if you were trying to guess which number a person had picked from one to ten, and the only thing you could be told was whether the number was higher, lower, or the same as what you guessed. To do this most efficiently, you'd guess five first, since if the right number were higher or lower you could eliminate about half the choices. If you were told the actual number was lower than five, you'd guess three next, since that cuts the possibilities down the most. If the number were higher than three, it would have to be four. If it were lower, it would have to be one or two. Using this method, at most you would have to take three guesses before you knew the answer, whereas if you just started guessing randomly, or started from one and worked your way up, you could guess as many as ten times before getting the right answer.

Like the efficient guesser, the computer doesn't use intuition to find the right answer, but uses the most effective method. Instead of using numbers to "guess" your score, though, the computer gives you questions that have a precise difficulty level assigned to them. In effect, you tell it whether your score is higher or lower than this difficulty level by getting the question right or wrong.

What's the upshot of all this? Simple: *pay extra attention to the first few questions, and do all that you can to get them right.* Feel free to spend a little extra time double-checking the first five problems or so, and make sure you try every elimination technique you know before guessing on one of these problems if you don't know the answer.

MORE SECTION MANAGEMENT TECHNIQUES

First, if you get a lot of mileage from the strategy of eliminating answer choices based on difficulty level, you can apply it on the CAT, though in a different and limited way. It won't be spelled out for you as it would be on a paper-based test, but as you progress through the questions, you should have a good idea of how you're doing. If you've practiced a lot on real questions, it's fairly easy to maintain a pretty clear sense of the difficulty level of your questions and to eliminate answer choices accordingly. For instance, if you're confident that you've been answering most of the questions correctly, then you should be seeing harder and harder questions. If that seems to be the case, you can safely eliminate answer choices that look too obvious or basic for a difficult question.

Secondly, if crossing off answer choices on paper tests really helps to clarify your thinking (using a process of elimination), you may want to consider making a grid on your scratch paper before you begin the CAT. Use it to mark off answer choices that you have eliminated, as shown below. That way you can tell at a glance which answer choices are still in the running. If you end up using it often, it will be worth the 10 seconds it takes to draw a simple grid, like this one:

	Q1	Q2	Q3	Q4	Q5	Q6	Q7	Q8	Q9	Q10	Q11	Q12	Q13
A	X	X		X		X			X		X		
B		X	X	X			X	X	X	X		X	
C					X				X				X
D	X		X		X			X		X		X	
E	X	X		X			X			X			

Finally, the timer in the corner can work to your advantage, but if you find yourself looking at it so frequently that it becomes a distraction, you should turn it off for 10 or 15 minutes and try to refocus your attention on the test, even if you lose track of time somewhat. *The CAT rewards focus and accuracy more than it does raw speed.*

 KAPLAN STRATEGY ————————————————————

CAT basics:

When you start a section, the computer:

- Assumes you have an average score.
- Gives you a medium-difficulty question. About half the people who take the test would get this question right, and half would get it wrong.

What happens next depends on whether you answer the question correctly.

If you answer the question correctly:

- Your score goes up.
- You are given a slightly harder question.

If you answer the question incorrectly:

- Your score goes down.
- You are given a slightly easier question.

This continues for the rest of the test. Every time you get the question right, the computer raises your score, then gives you a slightly harder question. Every time you get a question wrong, the computer lowers your score, then gives you a slightly easier question. In this way, the computer is able to "hone in" on your score.

NAVIGATING THE GRE CAT: COMPUTER BASICS

Let's preview the primary computer functions that you will use to move around on the CAT. ETS calls them "testing tools," but they're basically just boxes that you can click with your mouse. The following screen is typical for an adaptive test.

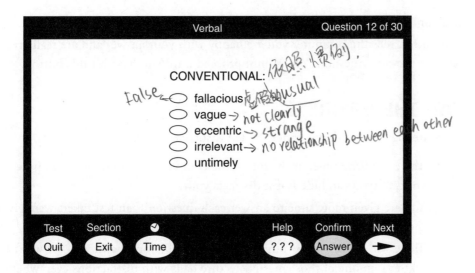

Here's what the various buttons do.

The Scroll Bar

Similar to that on a windows-style computer display, this is a thin, vertical column with up and down arrows at the top and bottom. Clicking on the arrows moves you up or down the page you're reading.

The Time Button

Clicking on this button turns the time display at the top of the screen on and off. When you have five minutes left in a section, the clock flashes and the display changes from Hours/Minutes to Hours/Minutes/Seconds.

The Section Exit Button

This allows you to exit the section before the time is up. If you budget your time wisely you should never have to use this button—time will run out just as you are finishing the section.

The Test Quit Button

Hitting this button ends the test prematurely. *Do not* use this button unless you want all of your scores canceled and your test invalidated.

The Help Button

This one leads to directions and other stuff from the tutorial. But beware: the test clock won't pause just because you click on Help.

The Next Button

Hit this when you want to move on to the next question. After you press Next, you must hit Confirm.

The Confirm Answer Button

This button tells the computer you are happy with your answer and are really ready to move to the next question. You cannot proceed until you have hit this button.

CAT: THE UPSIDE

There are many good things about the CAT, such as:

- There is a little timer at the top of the computer screen to help you pace yourself (you can hide it if it distracts you).
- You are given more time to answer each question than test takers were given on the old pencil-and-paper exam.
- There will be only a few other test takers in the room with you—it won't be like taking it in one of those massive lecture halls with distractions everywhere.
- You get a pause of one minute between each section. The pause is optional, but you should always use it to relax and stretch.
- You can sign up for the GRE just two days before the test (though we recommend signing up much earlier!), and registration is very easy.
- The CAT is convenient to schedule. It's offered at more than 175 centers three to five days a week (depending on the center) all year long.
- You don't have to take it on the same day as a Subject Test, which can greatly reduce fatigue.
- Perhaps the CAT's best feature is that it gives you your Verbal and Quantitative scores immediately and will send them to schools just 10 to 15 days later.

CAT: THE DOWNSIDE

There are also not-so-good things about the CAT.

- You cannot skip around on this test; you must answer the questions one at a time in the order the computer gives them to you.
- If you realize later that you answered a question incorrectly, you can't go back and change your answer.
- You can't cross off an answer choice and never look at it again, so you have to be more disciplined and use your scratch paper to avoid reconsidering choices you've already eliminated.
- You may have to scroll through long Reading Comprehension passages and graphs, which means you won't be able to see the whole thing on the screen at once.

- You can't write on your computer screen the way you can on a paper test (though some have tried), so you have to use scratch paper they give you, which will be inconveniently located away from the computer screen.
- Lastly, many people find that computer screens tire them and cause eyestrain—especially after three hours.

KAPLAN'S CAT STRATEGIES

Using certain CAT-specific strategies can have a direct, positive impact on your score:

- Use the computer tutorial to your advantage. Spend as much time as you need to make yourself comfortable with the computer before you begin the actual test. Once the test is underway, if you click on Help to review the directions or a summary of the tutorial, it will count against your allotted time for that section of the test.
- At the beginning of the section, each question you get right or wrong will rapidly move the computer's estimate of your score up or down. A key strategy for doing well on the CAT is to get the computer's estimate of your score up to where you are handling the hard questions, because getting a hard question right will help your score a lot, but getting a hard question wrong will hurt your score only slightly. Thus it pays to spend more time on those early questions, double-checking each answer before you confirm it. Getting to the hard questions as quickly as possible can only help your final score.
- As you progress through the middle part of the section, try to avoid getting several questions in a row wrong, as this will sink your score on the CAT. If you know that the previous question you answered was a blind guess, spend a little extra time trying to get the next question right.
- The CAT will switch from one question type to another within a section (going from Reading Comp to Antonyms, for example) WITHOUT automatically showing the directions for each new question type. Knowing the format and directions of each GRE question type beforehand will save you a lot of time and avoid possible confusion during the exam. For example, we've seen many students taking a Kaplan GRE practice test for the first time answer all of the antonym questions incorrectly because they thought they were looking for synonyms. Practicing with each question type will help you avoid these mistakes.
- The CAT does not begin with really easy questions that gradually get harder, as do many paper-based tests. Because the order of difficulty will not be predictable, always be on the lookout for traps.
- Because each right or wrong answer directly affects the next question you get, the CAT does not allow you to go back to questions you've already answered to

double-check your work. So be as certain as possible that you have answered a question correctly before moving on.

- The CAT does not allow you to skip questions. So if you are given a question you cannot answer, you'll have to guess. Guess intelligently and strategically—eliminating any wrong answer choices that you can spot and guessing among those remaining.

- Sometimes it's necessary to give up on a tough, time-consuming question. It's difficult to do, but let it go and move on to the next question. That's how you score points on the GRE, not by agonizing over one question.

- Don't get rattled if you keep seeing really, really difficult questions. It just means you're doing very well on that section. Keep it up!

- Conversely, don't get rattled if the questions seem easy. Chances are, you're just very well prepared for that question type.

- At the end of the section, you are penalized more heavily for not getting to a question at all than for answering it wrong. So if you only have a minute or two left and several questions remaining, you should guess at random rather than leave anything unanswered. If you have a few minutes left, it's best to spend more time on every other question and guess at random in between. This keeps your score in a higher range. And if you're down to the very last question and have almost no time left, make sure to click on a response first and then attempt to answer the question. You can always change your answer, and you're allowed to confirm whatever answer you've clicked after the time has run out.

PAPER-AND-PENCIL STRATEGIES

If you are located outside of the United States, Canada, American Samoa, Guam, the U.S. Virgin Islands, or Puerto Rico, you will take the paper-and-pencil version of the GRE test (check **gre.org** for test dates). It is comprised of five sections: Analytical Writing, two Verbal sections, and two Quantitative sections.

You have a total of three hours and 45 minutes to complete the entire test. The test-taking strategies for the paper-based test are different from those for the CAT. One strategy we recommend is to keep track of your answers—particularly ones you've eliminated—by crossing out wrong answer choices. This will also help you grid your answers more accurately. You can also say the question number and answer choice (silently, of course) to yourself as you grid, to help make sure you're gridding carefully.

Here are some targeted strategies for each section of the paper-based GRE.

VERBAL SECTION

Before you start a Verbal section, glance over it completely, but quickly, to familiarize yourself with it. With Reading Comprehension, you can preview question stems to help guide your reading, but don't try to memorize them or answer the questions without reading the passages. We recommend that you do the questions you're most comfortable with first. Make sure you set aside about 15 minutes in each Verbal section for Reading Comprehension.

The short Verbal questions are in ascending order of difficulty, so always try to be aware of where you are in a set. If you find yourself running into trouble with a particular group of questions, move on and come back to them if you have time. Don't get hung up on hard questions. On the GRE, quantity counts. The easy questions are worth as many points as the hard questions, so rack up as many points as you can.

QUANTITATIVE SECTION

Like short Verbal questions, Quantitative questions are arranged in ascending order of difficulty, so try to be aware of the level of each question. This will help you determine how much time you should be spending on the question, and whether or not it's a question that should have an obvious answer.

In addition, calculators are not permitted on the GRE, so don't forget to utilize that scratch paper. Feel free to skip around within this section as well, and do all the problems you can do; then come back to the harder ones.

ANALYTICAL WRITING

For the Analytical Writing section, you will have to handwrite your essay so we suggest you write clearly and legibly. For more tips and strategies for conquering the Analytical Writing section, refer to chapter 5.

Now you have an understanding of the GRE CAT format. Let's now turn to the test sections and get you ready for each one.

Part Two

STRATEGIES AND PRACTICE

CHAPTER 3: **VERBAL SECTION**

- Get to know the 52 Most Common GRE Words
- Learn the basic principles for success on the Verbal section
- Complete the 125-Question Verbal Practice Set

INTRODUCTION

In this chapter and the two chapters that follow, we'll give you the nuts and bolts of GRE preparation—the strategies and techniques for each of the individual question types on the test. For each of the multiple-choice sections—Verbal and Quantitative— we'll present you with the following:

- **Directions and General Information**
  The specific directions for each section will introduce you to the question types. We'll also give you some ground rules for each question type.

- **Basic Principles**
  General rules-of-thumb that you need to follow to succeed on each section.

- **Kaplan's Methods**
  A step-by-step way of organizing your work on every question in each section, Kaplan's Methods will allow you to orchestrate all of the individual strategies and techniques into a flexible, powerful way of attacking the questions.

Now let's begin with an important part of the GRE, the Verbal section. You'll have 30 minutes to complete 30 questions, which are broken down into four types: Sentence Completion, Analogy, Reading Comprehension, and Antonym. The following chart shows roughly how many questions correspond to each question type and how much time you should spend on each question type.

	Sentence Completion	Analogy	Reading Comprehension	Antonym
Number of Questions	approx. 6	approx. 7	approx. 8	approx. 9
Time per Question	20 to 45 seconds	30 to 45 seconds	> 1 minute	30 seconds

Remember, the computer determines the sequence and difficulty of the questions, so you will not be able to tell what sort of question you will get next, or how hard it will be.

There are two basic things that the Verbal section tests: your vocabulary and your ability to read a particular kind of passage quickly and efficiently. You may have wondered how the material we covered earlier about test construction is going to help you in the GRE Verbal sections. Well, just like the math questions, which are the same from test to test (just with different numbers), the Verbal questions are the same (just with different words).

THE NEW VERBAL SECTION QUESTION TYPE—TEXT COMPLETION

Although Sentence Completion questions with more than one blank space are found in the GRE exam, the new verbal question type—Text Completion—is a more complex version.

In this new Text Completion question type, you will be asked to select one entry for each blank from the corresponding column of choices, and it may include as many as three blanks within one question.

Just as with the Sentence Completion questions, this new question type tests your vocabulary and your ability to understand the context in which words are used. The principles and strategies you use for the Sentence Completion questions can be applied to this Text Completion question type. Here is sample question:

> As a result of the (i) _____ pace of life, urban living (ii) _____
> many young professionals the opportunity to (iii) _____ their
> lives with a sense of constant excitement.

Blank (i)	Blank (ii)	Blank (iii)
(A) intrinsic	(D) instigates	(G) eschew
(B) ephemeral	(E) affords	(H) inter
(C) frenetic	(F) arrogates	(I) imbue

Answer: C, E, and I

Use the clues given in the sentence to determine which word belongs in each blank. Starting with the first, you are looking for an adjective that would best describe urban living and that is similar to constant excitement.

Choice (A) means inherent, which doesn't fit the context of the phrase, and (B) means fleeting or brief—again, an inapt description of the pace of urban life; therefore, choice (C) is correct. The second blank requires a word that means to be made available or to give the opportunity. Therefore, choice (E) is correct. One meaning of afford is to offer or impart. The final blank requires a word that tells what young professionals have the opportunity to do. Choice (G) means to avoid and choice (H) means to bury, so they are incorrect. Young professionals are not likely to choose urban living to avoid constant excitement, therefore (I), which means to permeate is the correct answer.

A practice set for this question type can be found in your Online Companion.

VOCABULARY—THE MOST BASIC PRINCIPLE FOR VERBAL SUCCESS

Have you ever heard the expression, "That's an SAT word?" It's a commonly used phrase among high school students, and it refers to any member of a very particular class of prefixed and suffixed words derived from Latin or Greek. For instance, *profligate*, an adjective meaning "immoral" or "excessive," is a great SAT word. It's also a great GRE word. Many of the same kinds of words that show up on the SAT are likely to show up on the GRE as well, though GRE words tend to be harder.

The GRE tests the same kinds of words over and over again. We'll call these words "GRE words," and we're going to make a point of including them in the rest of this chapter. That way, you can get a feel for what they look and sound like, and you can see them used in context. The GRE words used in context in this vocabulary section will appear in **boldface.** So if you see a word in this book that's unfamiliar, take a moment to look it up in the dictionary and reread the sentence with the word's definition in mind.

Word Groups

The GRE does not test whether you know *exactly* what a particular word means. If you have only an idea of what a word means, you have as good of a chance of correctly answering a question as you would if you know the precise dictionary definition of the word. ETS isn't interested in finding out whether you're a walking dictionary. They want to see if you have a broad and diverse (but classically based) vocabulary.

The words in the list below all mean nearly the same thing. They all have something to do with the concept of criticism, a concept often tested on the GRE.

CRITICIZE/CRITICISM

aspersion	impugn
belittle	inveigh
berate	lambaste
calumny	objurgate
castigate	obloquy
decry	opprobrium
defamation	pillory
denounce	rebuke
deride/derisive	remonstrate
diatribe	reprehend
disparage	reprove
excoriate	revile
gainsay	tirade
harangue	vituperate

On the test, for instance, you might see an Antonym question like this:

REMONSTRATE:

- show
- atone
- vouchsafe
- laud
- undo

Or an Analogy question that looks something like this:

DIATRIBE : VITUPERATIVE ::

- flattery : sincere
- parody : lamentable
- equivocation : evasive
- dissertation : unassailable
- cliché : original

The correct answer to the Antonym question is *laud* (**D**)—if you know that REMONSTRATE means something like CRITICIZE, that should be enough to come up with "laud" (which means "praise") as the closest Antonym. The correct answer to the Analogy question is (**C**)—just knowing that the stem words are closely related should have been enough to allow you to eliminate the other choices.

A Thesaurus—Your New Best Friend

The *criticize* group is not the only group of synonyms whose members appear frequently on the GRE. There are plenty of others. And lists of synonyms are much easier to learn than many words in isolation. So don't learn words with a dictionary; learn them with a thesaurus. Make synonym index cards based on the common groups of GRE words and **peruse** those lists periodically. It's like weight-lifting for vocabulary; pretty soon you will start to see results.

If you think this suggestion might be **fallacious,** then check this out: the words in the following list all have something to do with the concept of falsehood. Their precise meanings vary: *erroneous* means "incorrect," whereas ***mendacious*** means "lying." But the majority of test questions won't require you to know the exact meanings of these words. You will most likely get the question right if you simply know that these words have something to do with the concept of falsehood.

FALSEHOOD

apocryphal	fallacious
canard	feigned
chicanery	guile
dissemble	mendacious/mendacity
duplicity	perfidy
equivocate	prevaricate
erroneous	specious
ersatz	spurious

If you get an Antonym question such as:

HONESTY:

⬯ displeasure

⬯ mendacity

⬯ disrepute

⬯ resolution

⬯ failure

You might not know exactly what **mendacity** means, but you'll know that it's "one of those *false* words," which will be enough to get the question right. Your subconscious mind will have done most of the work for you!

KNOW YOUR ROOTS

Another good way to improve your vocabulary, and in turn, do well on the Verbal section, is to become familiar with the meanings of word parts—their "roots" or etymology. Because GRE words are so heavily drawn from Latin and Greek, roots can be extremely useful, both in deciphering words with obscure meanings and in guessing intelligently.

You'll learn more words in less time if you learn them in groups. Once you know, for example, that the root PLAC means "to please," you have a hook for remembering the meanings of several words: **placate, implacable, placid, placebo,** and **complacent.**

Sometimes you can use roots to figure out the meaning of an unfamiliar word. Suppose, for example, you come across the word *circumnavigate* and don't know what it means. If you know that the root CIRCUM means "around" and that the root NAV means "ship, sail," then you can guess that **circumnavigate** means "to sail around," as in "**circumnavigate** the globe."

But don't get too excited. Roots offer the common heritage of words thousands of years old—but things have changed a lot. Roots don't *always* point to the right way to go.

READ MORE

Read the newspaper daily, concentrating on articles covering topics with which you are unfamiliar. Jot down each article's main idea and the author's tone and purpose. This way, you can practice overcoming the hurdle of reading unfamiliar or difficult material.

Example: **Affinity** is of the root FIN, meaning end. But **affinity** means a kinship, or attractive force.

Sometimes, the meaning is close, but the spelling has gone haywire.

Example: **Cogent** is actually of the root, ACT/AG (to do, to drive to lead). **Cogent** means "convincing" or "having the power to compel." These two are somewhat close in meaning, but you can see what we mean about the spelling.

There are other problems with using roots to pinpoint a definition. Looking at the etymology of a word is a great trick if you know Greek, Latin, or French. For example, DEM in Greek means "people." **Democracy** essentially means government of the people. Neat and tidy. Right? Sure, but you do have to know the meaning of the root cold. And there are exceptions.

Example: The word **venal.** The root VEN/VENT means "to come" or "to move toward." But **venal** means "corrupt or capable of being bought." **Adventure, convene, event, avenue, advent,** and **circumvent** clearly spring from the root meaning. **Venal** is a bit of a stretch.

Example: The word **pediatrician** has PED for a root. PED has to do with the foot. But a **pediatrician** is a children's doctor. A **podiatrist** is a foot doctor. It turns out PED in regards to feet is a Latin root, but PED in regards to children is a Greek root.

To sum up, the etymology of a word is merely a good trick. But it won't work every time, and it certainly can't provide the basic definition of a word. In some cases, it may even put you on the wrong track.

So why bother? Because if you don't have a clue what a word means, you have to start somewhere. Roots are an **efficacious** place to begin (FIC: to do, to make).

Use Kaplan's Root List in the back of this book to pick up the most valuable GRE roots. Target these words in your vocabulary prep. Learn a few new roots a day, familiarizing yourself with their meanings.

Words in Context

Learning words in context is one of the best ways for the brain to retain their meanings. In Appendix B at the back of this book, we've not only listed the top 200 GRE words with their definitions, but we've also used all of these words *in context* to help you to remember them.

Reading is ultimately the best way to increase your vocabulary, although it also takes the most time. Of course, some types of reading material contain more GRE vocabulary words than others. You should get into the habit of reading high-level publications, such as *The Wall Street Journal* and *The New York Times*. And because you'll have to read from the computer screen on Test Day, we recommend that you start reading these publications online, if possible.

 READ MORE

Need vocabulary to go? Kaplan's *GRE Exam Vocabulary in a Box* is the perfect size for portable studying.

ETS's Favorite GRE Words

The research team at Kaplan works hard to keep tabs on GRE vocabulary words and to find out which words appear more frequently than others. The following words all turn up time and again on the GRE, so it makes sense to memorize these words if you don't already know them. Of course, some words appear on the GRE more frequently than others.

The top 12 words on the GRE:

anomaly
assuage
enigma
equivocal
erudite
fervid
lucid
opaque
placate
precipitate
prodigal
zeal

The next 20 most popular words:

abstain
adulterate
apathy
audacious
capricious
corroborate
desiccate
engender
ephemeral
gullible
homogenous
laconic

laudable
loquacious
mitigate
pedant
pragmatic
propriety
vacillate
volatile

The next 20 most popular words:

advocate
antipathy
bolster
cacophony
deride
dissonance
enervate
eulogy
garrulous
ingenuous
lethargic
malleable

misanthrope
obdurate
ostentation
paradox
philanthropic
prevaricate
venerate
waver

The Top GRE Words in Context section at the end of this book reviews these and 150 other top GRE words. Make sure you spend the time to get to know these words. At least some of them are bound to appear on the GRE you take.

VOCABULARY WRAP-UP

In review, the best ways to improve your GRE vocabulary are:

- Study word groups
- Learn word roots
- Learn words in context
- Memorize the top GRE words

A broader vocabulary will serve you well on all four GRE Verbal question types (and will also be extremely helpful in the Analytical Writing section). Now let's look at each of the four Verbal question types, starting with Sentence Completions.

SENTENCE COMPLETIONS

You will find about six Sentence Completions per Verbal section. In each of them, one or two words from the sentence will be missing. This question type tests your ability to recognize the point of the sentence and find the best word(s) to fit this meaning.

The directions for Sentence Completions will look something like this:

> Each sentence below has one or two blanks, each blank indicating that something has been omitted. Beneath the sentence are five words or sets of words. Choose the word or set of words for each blank that best fits the meaning of the sentence as a whole.

The difficulty of the Sentence Completions you will see on the CAT depends on how many questions you get right.

THE 7 BASIC PRINCIPLES OF SENTENCE COMPLETIONS

Principle 1. Every Clue Is Right in Front of You.

Each sentence contains a few crucial clues that determine the answer. In order for a sentence to be used on the GRE, the answer must already be in the sentence. Clues *in the sentence* limit the possible answers, and finding these clues will guide you to the correct answer.

For example, could the following sentence be on the GRE?

> The student thought the test was quite _____.
>
> ◯ long
>
> ◯ unpleasant
>
> ◯ predictable
>
> ◯ ridiculous
>
> ◯ indelible

No. Because nothing in the sentence hints at which word to choose, it would be a terrible test question. You would *never* see a question like this on the GRE.

Now let's change the sentence to get a question that *could* be answered:

> Since the student knew the form and content of the questions in advance, the test was quite _____ for her.
>
> ◯ long
>
> ◯ unpleasant
>
> ◯ predictable
>
> ◯ ridiculous
>
> ◯ indelible

What are the important clues in this question? Well, the word *since* is a great structural clue. It indicates that the missing word follows logically from part of the sentence. Specifically, the missing word must follow from "knew the form and content . . . in advance." That means the test was predictable.

Principle 2. Look for What's Directly Implied and Expect Clichés.

We're not dealing with poetry here. These sentences aren't excerpted from the works of Toni Morrison or William Faulkner. The correct answer is the one most directly implied by the meanings of the words in the sentence.

Principle 3. Don't Imagine Strange Scenarios.

Read the sentence literally, not imaginatively. Pay attention to the meaning of the words, not associations or feelings that you have.

Principle 4. Look for Structural Road Signs.

Structural road signs are key words that will point you to the right answer, such as *since*. The missing words in Sentence Completions will usually have a relationship similar or opposite to other words in the sentence. Key words, such as *and* or *but*, will tell you which it is.

On the GRE, a semicolon by itself always connects two closely related clauses. If a semicolon is followed by another road sign, then that road sign determines the direction. Just like on the highway, there are road signs on the GRE that tell you to go ahead and that tell you to take a detour.

"Straight-ahead" signs are used to make one part of the sentence support or elaborate another part. They continue the sentence in the same direction. The positive or negative charge of what follows is not changed by these clues. Straight-ahead clues include: *and, similarly, in addition, consequently, since, also, thus, because, ; (semicolon), likewise,* and *moreover*.

"Detour" signs change the direction of the sentence. They make one part of the sentence contradict or qualify another part. The positive or negative charge of an answer is changed by these clues. Detour signs include: *but, despite, yet, however, unless, rather, although, while, on the other hand, unfortunately, nonetheless,* and *conversely*.

Knowing the following lists of road signs will help you to determine which way the sentence is going and to predict what words will best complete the blank(s).

Straight-ahead signs:	Detour signs:
And	*But*
Similarly	*Despite*
In addition	*Yet*
Consequently	*However*
Since	*Unless*
Also	*Rather*
Thus	*Although*
Because	*While*
; (semicolon)	*On the other hand*
Likewise	*Unfortunately*
Moreover	*Nonetheless*
	Conversely

In the following examples, test your knowledge of Sentence Completion road signs by choosing the right answers (in the parentheses):

(1) The winning argument was _____ *and* persuasive. (cogent, flawed)

(2) The winning argument was _____ *but* persuasive. (cogent, flawed)

(3) The play's script lacked depth and maturity; *likewise,* the acting was altogether _____. (sublime, amateurish)

(4) The populace _____ the introduction of the new taxes, *since* they had voted for them overwhelmingly. (applauded, despised)

(5) *Despite* your impressive qualifications, I am _____ to offer you a position with our firm. (unable, willing)

(6) Scientists have claimed that the dinosaurs became extinct in a single, dramatic event; *yet* new evidence suggests a _____ decline. (headlong, gradual)

(7) The first wave of avant-gardists elicited _____ from the general population, *while* the second was completely ignored. (indifference, shock)

By concentrating on the road signs, it's easier to find your way through each question and arrive at the right answers (1. cogent, 2. flawed, 3. amateurish, 4. applauded, 5. unable, 6. gradual, 7. shock). Now that you understand road signs, let's look at Kaplan's Method for Sentence Completions and try it out on some practice questions.

Principle 5. Look for Key Words.

Key words are descriptive words or phrases that clue you in to the missing words in a sentence. Unlike road signs, where a small set of words tells you a sentence's direction, key words can be any words in a sentence that reflect its theme, give you a sense of its logic, or provide clues to the author's intent. Let's look at this example.

> During their famous clash, Jung was ambivalent about Freud, so he attacked the father of modern psychoanalysis even as he _____ him.
>
> A. enlightened
> B. chastened
> C. revered
> D. despised
> E. understood

The key word in this sentence is "ambivalent." An ambivalent attitude reflects both positive and negative feelings. You know the negative side of Jung's attitude resulted in his attacking Freud. However, even as he attacked Freud, Jung must have done something positive in order to display "ambivalence." You can immediately eliminate (B) and (D) since they're negative words. Choice (C) looks good since revered is a positive word. You can rule out (A) since it doesn't make sense gramatically in the context of the sentence. Choice (E) doesn't work because understood doesn't contrast with "attacked."

Principle 6. Paraphrase Long or Complex Sentences.

You may encounter a sentence that, because of its length or structure, is hard to get a handle on. Here's an example:

> Museum directors understand the need to establish the provenance of every work of art they acquire, from its creation to its most recent owner; such establishment can be hindered, however, by a number of obstacles, including disingenuous dealers who attempt to _____ the truth.

- ⬭ impede
- ⬭ reveal
- ⬭ overshadow
- ⬭ ascertain
- ⬭ obscure

When faced with a complex sentence like this, put it in your own words. We can sum up the 44 words above in 14: "It can be difficult to establish provenance because insincere dealers try to _____ the truth."

If dealers are "disingenuous," or insincere, what would they try to do with the truth? They'd try to hide it. The word overshadow has to do with hiding, but it means "to take attention away from something by appearing more important." Obscure is the better fit in context. Notice, too, that when we simplified the sentence above, we introduced the straight-ahead road sign "because"—restating sentences in simpler terms can help clarify their direction.

Principle 7. Use Word Roots.

If you can't figure out the meaning of a word, take a look at its root to try to get close to its meaning. (In the resource section of this book, you can learn the Latin and Greek roots of many common GRE words.) Etymology can often provide clues to meaning, especially when you couple a root definition with the word in context.

> ### ♟ KAPLAN STRATEGY ─────────────────
>
> Kaplan's basic principles for success on Sentence Completions are:
>
> - Look for clues in the sentence.
> - Focus on what's directly implied.
> - Pay attention to the meanings of the words.
> - Keep an eye out for structural road signs.
> - Paraphrase long or wordy sentences.
> - Make a prediction before going on to the answer choices.

SENTENCE COMPLETIONS PRACTICE SET

Try the following Sentence Completions using Kaplan's strategy above. They are more difficult than the ones you have encountered up to this point, but you should be able to handle them. Time yourself; you only have 30–45 seconds to do each question.

1. The yearly financial statement of a large corporation may seem _____ at first, but the persistent reader soon finds its pages of facts and figures easy to decipher.

   ⬭ bewildering

   ⬭ surprising

   ⬭ inviting

   ⬭ misguided

   ⬭ uncoordinated

2. The giant squid's massive body, adapted for deep-sea life, breaks apart in the reduced pressures of higher ocean elevations, making the search for an intact specimen one of the most _____ quests in all of marine biology.

   ⬭ controversial

   ⬭ meaningful

   ⬭ elusive

   ⬭ popular

   ⬭ expensive

3. Organic farming is more labor intensive and thus initially more _____, but its long-term costs may be less than those of conventional farming.

   ◯ uncommon

   ◯ stylish

   ◯ restrained

   ◯ expensive

   ◯ difficult

4. Unfortunately, there are some among us who equate tolerance with immorality; they feel that the _____ of moral values in a permissive society is not only likely, but _____.

   ◯ decline . . . possible

   ◯ upsurge . . . predictable

   ◯ disappearance . . . desirable

   ◯ improvement . . . commendable

   ◯ deterioration . . . inevitable

SENTENCE COMPLETIONS PRACTICE SET ANSWERS AND EXPLANATIONS

1. A

If you use the Kaplan Method, you will first look for road signs in the sentence. You should recognize the detour road sign *but,* which indicates that the correct answer will mean the opposite of how the financial statement is described at the conclusion of the sentence in the key phrase, "easy to decipher." In your own words, that opposite may be "difficult to understand." Choice (**A**), *bewildering,* is your answer. None of the other choices is an opposite of "easy to decipher," and can be eliminated.

2. C

This is a pretty straightforward Sentence Completion. The key word here is the word *intact,* which means that, although specimens have been collected, they have often (if not always) not been intact when recovered. You can fairly assert that recovering an intact specimen is difficult. When you look for a synonym for *difficult* in the answer choices, you should recognize *elusive* (**C**) as your answer.

3. D

The detour road sign in this sentence is, again, *but.* You also get a big clue with the key phrase "long-term costs" in the second half of the sentence. Your answer, expensive (**D**), is the only answer that has anything to do with costs.

4. E

The road signs in this question are *unfortunately* in the first half of the sentence and *not only* in the second half. *Unfortunately* tells you that the answer will match the key words "equate tolerance with immorality" and "moral values in a permissive society." Further, the second part of the road sign, *not only,* tells us that the second part of the sentence will be a continuation of the first. Paraphrasing the sentence is a good strategy here, and might sound something like this: many think being tolerant is the same thing as being immoral, so they think that the _____ of values in a society that is tolerant is not only likely but_____. A good prediction for the blanks might be "decrease" in the first blank and "certain" in the second, because those who think that tolerance is the same as immorality would think that values would decrease in a permissive society. Choice (**E**) is the closest match and makes sense when read into the sentence.

How'd you do? Now let's look at the next question type: Analogies.

ANALOGIES

You will find about eight Analogies per Verbal section. In each of them, you are given a pair of words. You must determine the relationship between them and choose the pair of words from the answer choices that shares the same relationship. This question type tests your vocabulary to some extent, but really tests your ability to make strong connections between words.

The directions for Analogies look like this:

> This question consists of a pair of words or phrases that are separated by a colon and followed by five answer choices. Choose the pair of words or phrases in the answer choices that best expresses a relationship similar to that expressed in the original pair.

On the GRE, the more questions you get right, the harder the Analogies you will see.

THE 4 BASIC PRINCIPLES OF ANALOGIES

Principle 1. Every Analogy Question Consists of Two Words, Called the Stem Pair, that Are Separated by a Colon.

Below the stem pair are five answer choices. Analogy questions look like this:

MAP : ATLAS ::

- key : lock
- street : sign
- ingredient : cookbook
- word : dictionary
- theory : hypothesis

Principle 2. There will Always be a Direct and Necessary Relationship Between the Words in the Stem Pair.

You express this relationship by making a short sentence that we call a *bridge*. A bridge is whatever simple sentence you come up with to relate the two words. Your goals when you build your bridge should be to keep it as short and as clear as possible.

A weak bridge expresses a relationship that isn't necessary or direct. For the sample Analogy question above, weak bridges include:

- Some maps are put in atlases.
- A map is usually smaller than an atlas.
- Maps and atlases have to do with geography.
- A page in an atlas is usually a map.

You know you have a weak bridge if it contains such words as *usually, can, might, seldom, may or may not, some,* or *sometimes.*

A strong bridge expresses a direct and necessary relationship. You know you have a strong bridge if you can stick the phrase "by definition" into your sentence. For the Analogy above, strong bridges include:

- Maps [by definition] are what an atlas contains.
- Maps [by definition] are the unit of reference in an atlas.
- An atlas [by definition] collects and organizes maps.

Strong bridges express a definite relationship and can contain an unequivocal word, such as *always, never,* or *must.* The best bridge is a strong bridge that fits exactly one answer choice. You might think that the words TRUMPET and JAZZ have a strong bridge. Don't be fooled. Though the words are related, you can play many types of music other than jazz on trumpets. You can also play jazz on instruments other than trumpets. Therefore building a strong bridge is impossible. TRUMPET and INSTRUMENT have a strong bridge; a trumpet is a type of instrument. That fact is always true and is therefore a strong, definite relationship.

Principle 3. Always Try to Make a Bridge Before Looking at the Answer Choices.

ETS uses certain kinds of bridges over and over on the GRE. Of these we have identified five classic bridges. Exposing yourself to them now will give you a feel for the sort of bridge that will get you the right answer. Try to answer these questions as you go through them.

Bridge 1. Definition (is always or is never)

PLATITUDE : TRITE ::

◯ riddle : unsolvable

◯ axiom : geometric

◯ omen : portentous

◯ syllogism : wise

◯ circumlocution : concise

Bridge 2. Function/purpose

AIRPLANE : HANGAR ::

◯ music : orchestra

◯ money : vault

◯ finger : hand

◯ tree : farm

◯ insect : ecosystem

Bridge 3. Lack

LUCID : OBSCURITY ::

◯ ambiguous : doubt

◯ provident : planning

◯ furtive : legality

◯ economical : extravagance

◯ secure : violence

Bridge 4. Characteristic actions/items

PARRY : FENCER ::

◯ sonnet : poet

◯ pirouette : dancer

◯ building : architect

◯ sword : dueler

◯ dress : seamstress

Bridge 5. Degree (often going to an extreme)

ATTENTIVE : RAPT ::

○ ecstatic : happy

○ critical : derisive

○ inventive : innovative

○ jealous : envious

○ kind : considerate

So there you have them, the five classic bridges. Keep them in mind as you practice for the Analogy section of the GRE. (Answers: 1. C, 2. B, 3. D, 4. B, 5. B)

Principle 4. Don't Fall for Classic Analogy Traps.

The right answer to an Analogy question will have the same strong bridge as the stem pair. Wrong answer choices, on the other hand, come in two principal varieties: many will contain weak bridges, others will contain strong but wrong bridges. Some of these wrong answers are designed to be tempting traps. Here are four classic traps often found on GRE Analogy questions:

- *The Both Are trap:* the words aren't directly related to each other, but they are both related to a third word. Examples: *turquoise : jade* are both types of gems; *biography : novel* are both types of books.

- *The Same Subject trap:* the words are in the same subject area as the stem words, but they don't share the same bridge.

- *The Cliché trap:* the words sound natural together, but don't actually have a clear and logical relationship. Examples: *compulsive : gambler, faithful : servant.*

- *The Reverse Direction trap*: this strong but wrong bridge would be right if the order of the words were reversed. For an example, take a look at choice **(A)** in question 5 on the previous page.

 KAPLAN STRATEGY ⎯⎯⎯⎯⎯⎯⎯⎯⎯⎯⎯⎯⎯⎯⎯⎯⎯

Kaplan's basic principles for success on Analogies are:

- There will always be a direct and necessary relationship between the words in the stem pair; the word pair in the correct answer choice will share this relationship.

- Learn the five classic bridges and how to adjust them if necessary.

- Recognize traps to save time and increase your chances of guessing correctly.

KAPLAN'S 4-STEP METHOD FOR ANALOGIES

Step 1. Find a strong bridge between the stem words.

Be flexible: sometimes it's easier to use the second word first.

Step 2. Plug the answer choices into the bridge.

Make sure to keep the same word order that you used with the stem pair.

Step 3. Adjust the bridge as necessary.

You want your bridge to be simple and somewhat general, but if more than one answer choice fits into your bridge, it is too general. Make it a little more specific and try the answer choices again.

Step 4. If you are stuck, eliminate all answer choices with weak bridges.

If two choices have the same bridge—for example, *trumpet* : *instrument* and *screwdriver* : *tool*—eliminate them both. Don't fall for classic traps. Work backward from remaining choices to the stem pair and make your best guess.

Let's try an example to learn how to use the 4-Step Method.

AIMLESS : DIRECTION ::

- ⭕ enthusiastic : motivation
- ⭕ wary : trust
- ⭕ unhealthy : happiness
- ⭕ lazy : effort
- ⭕ silly : adventure

For this question, a good bridge is: "Someone *aimless* lacks *direction.*" Now plug that into the answer choices. Only **(B)** fits. If you were stuck, you should have eliminated **(A)**, **(C)**, and **(E)**, because their bridges are weak. Remember: if an answer choice has a weak bridge it cannot be correct, because no stem pair that you'll find on the GRE will ever have a weak bridge. To be correct, an answer choice must have a strong, clear relationship.

WORKING BACKWARD ON ANALOGIES

If you can't build a good bridge because you don't know the definition of one or both stem words, all is not lost. Even when you can't figure out the bridge for the words in the stem pair, you can guess intelligently by eliminating answer choices. In the following questions, there are no stem words. How are you supposed to do them, you ask? Eliminate all answer choices that have a weak bridge. Also, if two choices in the same problem have the same bridge, you can eliminate them both (because if one of them were correct the other would have to be also). You'll find that you are left with the correct answers.

1. _ _ _ _ : _ _ _ _ ::

    ○ pliant : yield

    ○ sinister : doubt

    ○ trivial : defend

    ○ irksome : annoy

    ○ estimable : admire

2. _ _ _ _ : _ _ _ _ ::

    ○ eavesdrop : listen

    ○ hire : promote

    ○ hint : declare

    ○ attempt : succeed

    ○ endanger : enlighten

3. _ _ _ _ : _ _ _ _ ::

    ○ congratulate : success

    ○ amputate : crime

    ○ annotate : consultation

    ○ deface : falsehood

    ○ cogitate : habit

4. _ _ _ _ : _ _ _ _ ::

    ○ fervent : passionate

    ○ important : momentous

    ○ attractive : exquisite

    ○ pedantic : scholarly

    ○ unique : popular

WORKING BACKWARD ANSWERS AND EXPLANATIONS

1. E

Eliminate **(A)** and **(D)** because they have the same bridge. Eliminate **(B)** and **(C)** because they have weak bridges. Choice **(E)** is correct.

2. A

Eliminate **(B)**, **(D)**, and **(E)** because they have weak bridges. You're left with **(A)** and **(C)**, which gives you 50/50 odds of guessing the correct answer. Choice **(A)** is correct.

3. A

Eliminate **(B)**, **(C)**, **(D)**, and **(E)** because they have weak bridges. Choice **(A)** is correct.

4. D

Eliminate **(B)** and **(C)** because they have the same bridge. Eliminate **(E)** because it has a weak bridge. Eliminate **(A)** because the words are exact synonyms. Choice **(D)** is correct.

ANTONYMS

You will find about nine Antonyms per Verbal section. In each of them, you are given a word and must choose its opposite from the answer choices. This question type mainly tests your vocabulary skills.

The directions for Antonyms look like this:

> Each question below consists of a word printed in capital letters, followed by five words or phrases. Choose the word or phrase that is most nearly opposite in meaning to the word in capital letters.
>
> Since some of the questions require you to distinguish fine shades of meaning, be sure to consider all the choices before deciding which one is best.

On the GRE, the more questions you get right, the harder the Antonym questions you'll see.

THE 6 BASIC PRINCIPLES OF ANTONYMS

Principle 1. Think of a Context in Which You've Heard the Word Before.

For example, you might be able to figure out the meaning of the italicized words in the following phrases from their context: "*travesty* of justice," "crimes and *misdemeanors*," "*mitigating* circumstances," and "*abject* poverty."

Principle 2. Look at Word Roots, Stems, and Suffixes.

Even if you don't know what *benediction* means, its prefix (BENE, which means good) tells you that its opposite is likely to be something bad. Perhaps the answer will begin with MAL (which means bad), as in *malefaction*.

Principle 3. Use Your Knowledge of Romance Languages.

For example, you might guess at the meaning of *credulous* from the Italian, *credere; moratorium* from the French, *morte;* and *lachrimose* from the Spanish, *lagrima*.

Principle 4. Use the Positive or Negative Charges of the Words to Help You.

Use your scratch paper to make + signs for words with positive connotations, – signs for those with negative connotations, and = signs for neutral words. This strategy can work wonders. Look at the example below.

PERDITION :   –

○ deterrent   –

○ rearrangement   =

○ reflection   =

○ salvation   +

○ rejection   –

By looking at the charges of these Antonym answer choices, it is clear that *salvation* (**D**) is the correct choice.

Principle 5. On Hard Antonym Questions, Watch out for Trick Choices and Eliminate Them.

Can you guess the trick in this next example?

RESTIVE :

○ crucial

○ content

○ active

○ rousing

○ striated

ETS loves words like *restive*, that don't necessarily sound like what they mean. You might see the word *rest* in *restive* and think that *restive* means *resting* and pick *active* as the antonym, or think *restive* means *restful* and pick *rousing* as the antonym. *Restive* actually means *restless* or *uneasy*, so its most logical opposite would be (**B**), *content*. As you study GRE vocabulary words, be on the lookout for words that don't mean what they sound like to your ear. It pays to really study these definitions, because ETS will often throw trick choices into questions. People tend to guess wrong on hard Antonyms for a reason.

Principle 6. Work Backward from the Answer Choices When You Don't Know the Meaning of the Root Word.

When you just don't know the meaning of the root word, you should work backward from the answer choices. Begin by making opposites of all the answer choices. If you are having trouble coming up with an opposite, don't waste more than five seconds trying. Many words don't have clear opposites, so you can just get rid of these choices. For instance, in the previous example (**E**), *striated*, means *striped*, and there is no clear opposite for *striped*, so you can eliminate (**E**). Make opposites for the words you can, and then ask yourself which opposite is most likely to be the definition of the root word. If you are totally stuck, pick the answer choice that has the clearest opposite.

 KAPLAN STRATEGY

Kaplan's basic principles for success on Antonyms are:

- Think of a context in which you've heard the root word before.
- Use your knowledge of word roots, stems, and suffixes to arrive at a definition for the root word.
- Pull from your knowledge of romance languages to try to decipher word meanings.
- Take note of the positive or negative connotations of words to help you find the answer.
- Work backward from the answer choices when you just don't know the meaning of the root word.

KAPLAN'S 4-STEP METHOD FOR ANTONYMS

Step 1. Define the root word.

Step 2. Reverse it by thinking about the word's opposite.

Step 3. Go to the answer choices and find the opposite—that is, the choice that matches your prediction.

Step 4. If you are stuck, work backward from the answer choices.

ANTONYMS PRACTICE SET

Now try the following Antonym questions using Kaplan's 4-Step Method. Some of them are tough, but by using our method you should at least be able to make a solid, educated guess on each. Try not to spend more than 30 seconds on each question.

1. PARTISAN :
   ○ clear-cut
   ○ unyielding
   ○ disinterested
   ○ sentimental
   ○ placid

2. DISSEMINATE :
   ○ gather together
   ○ hold down
   ○ move about
   ○ decide against
   ○ distinguish between

3. INSULAR :

   ⭕ fanatical

   ⭕ cosmopolitan

   ⭕ vulnerable

   ⭕ considerate

   ⭕ archaic

4. CRAVEN :

   ⭕ nonchalant

   ⭕ arrogant

   ⭕ petulant

   ⭕ fastidious

   ⭕ plucky

5. SEDULITY :

   ⭕ insolence

   ⭕ verbosity

   ⭕ perfidy

   ⭕ carelessness

   ⭕ futility

ANTONYMS PRACTICE SET ANSWERS AND EXPLANATIONS

1. C

Partisan means "one who is a member of a party," so its opposite would be something like "someone without strong affiliations." As you look through the choices, you'll see that the choice closest in meaning to your opposite is *disinterested* (**C**).

2. A

Disseminate means "to disperse," so its opposite would be something like "to keep together." You'll immediately recognize *gather together* (**A**) as your correct choice.

3. B

Insular means "isolated," so its opposite is something like *cosmopolitan* (**B**), which means "to have a worldwide, rather than limited, scope or bearing."

4. E

Craven means "cowardly," so its opposite is something like "brave." Choice (**E**), *plucky*, means just that, and is your correct answer.

5. D

Sedulity means "diligence." Its opposite would be something like "laziness." *Carelessness* (**D**) is your best answer.

READING COMPREHENSION

Reading Comprehension is the only question type that appears on all major standardized tests, and the reason isn't too surprising. No matter what academic area you pursue, you'll have to make sense of some dense, unfamiliar material and, since you'll be working so hard in graduate school, you'll usually have a limited amount of time to make sense of all the material you'll need to cover. The topics for GRE Reading Comprehension passages are taken from four areas: social sciences, biological sciences, physical sciences, and arts and humanities. These topics will be distributed evenly on the passages you'll see on the exam, although you may not see each topic on your exam.

Reading Comp passages tend to be wordy and dull, and you may find yourself wondering where the test makers get them. Actually, the test makers go out and collect the most boring and confusing essays available, then chop them up beyond all recognition or coherence. The people behind the GRE know that you'll have to read passages like these in graduate school, so they choose test material accordingly. In a way, Reading Comprehension is the most realistic of all the question types on the test. And right now is a good time to start shoring up your critical reading skills, both for the test and for future study in your chosen field.

In the Verbal section, you will find two or three Reading Comprehension passages (each approximately 200–300 words) with two to four questions based on each. The questions test your ability to assess the author's purpose and meaning, to consider what inferences can properly be drawn from the passage, and to research details in the text.

The directions for Reading Comprehension items look like this:

> Each passage in this group is followed by questions based on its content. After reading a passage, choose the best answer to each question. Answer all questions following a passage on the basis of what is stated or implied in that passage.

THE 7 BASIC PRINCIPLES OF READING COMPREHENSION

To improve your Reading Comprehension skills, you'll need a lot of practice—and patience. You may not see dramatic improvement after only one drill. But with ongoing practice, the seven basic principles will help to increase your skill and confidence on this section. After reviewing the following principles, you'll find your first opportunity to apply them by working on a sample passage.

Principle 1. Pay Special Attention to the First Third of the Passage.

The first third of a Reading Comprehension passage usually introduces its topic and scope, the author's main idea or primary purpose, and the author's tone. It almost always hints at the structure that the passage will follow. Let's take a closer look at these important elements of a Reading Comprehension passage.

Topic and Scope. *Topic* and *scope* are both objective terms—that means they include no specific reference to the author's point of view. The difference between them is that the topic is broader; the scope narrows the topic. Scope is particularly important because the answer choices that depart from it will always be wrong. The broad topic of "The Battle of Gettysburg," for example, would be a lot to cover in 450 words. So if you encountered this passage, you should ask yourself, "What aspect of the battle does the author take up?" Because of length limitations, it's likely to be a pretty small aspect. Whatever that aspect is—the pre-battle scouting, how the battle was fought—that will be the passage's scope. Answer choices that deal with anything outside of this narrowly defined aspect will be wrong.

Author's Purpose. The distinction between topic and scope ties into another important issue: the author's purpose. In writing the passage, the author has deliberately chosen to narrow the scope by including certain aspects of the broader topic and excluding others. Why the author makes those choices gives us an important clue as to why the passage is being written. From the objective and broadly stated topic (for instance, a passage's topic might be *solving world hunger*) you should zoom in on the objective but narrower scope (*a new technology for solving world hunger*), and the scope quickly leads you to the author's subjective purpose (*the author is writing in order to describe a new technology and its promising uses*). The author's purpose is what turns into the author's main idea, which will be discussed at greater length in the next principle.

So don't just "read" the passage; instead, try to do the following three things:

(1) Identify the topic.

(2) Narrow it down to the precise scope.

(3) Make a hypothesis about why the author is writing and where he or she is going with it.

Structure and Tone. In an effort to understand what the author is saying, test takers often ignore the less glamorous but important structural side of the passage—namely, how the author chooses to present his ideas. One of the keys to success on this section is to understand not only the passage's purpose but also the structure of each passage. Why? Because the questions about the passage ask both what the author says *and* how he or she says it. Here's a list of the classic GRE passage structures:

- Passages arguing a position (often a social sciences passage)
- Passages discussing something specific within a field of study (for instance, a passage about Shakespearean sonnets in literature)

- Passages explaining some significant new findings or research (often a science passage)

Most passages that you'll encounter will feature one of these classic structures, or a variation thereof. Your job is to actively seek them out as you begin to read a passage. Usually, the structure is announced within the first third of the passage. Let these classic structures act as a jumpstart in your search for the passage's "big picture" and purpose.

As for how the author makes his or her point, try to note the author's position within these structures, usually indicated by the author's tone. For example, in passages that explain some significant new findings or research, the author is likely to be clinical in description. In passages that argue a position, the author's tone may be opinionated or argumentative and use such verbs as *argue for, propose,* or *demonstrate.* On the other hand, the author could simply be describing the strongly held opinions of someone else. In this case, the author's writing style would be more descriptive, factual, and even-handed and use such verbs as *describe* or *discuss.* In either case, remember that the correct answer choice will use verbs similar to those found in the passage.

Principle 2. Focus on the Main Idea.

Every passage boils down to one big idea. Your job is to cut through the fancy wording and focus on this big idea. Very often, the main idea will be presented in the first third of the passage, but occasionally the author will build up to it gradually.

In any case, the main idea always appears somewhere in the passage, and when it does, you must take note of it. For one thing, the purpose of everything else in the passage will be to support this idea. Furthermore, many of the questions—not only "main idea" questions, but all kinds of questions—are easier to handle when you have the main idea in the forefront of your mind. Always look for choices that sound consistent with the main idea. Wrong choices often sound inconsistent with it.

Principle 3. Get the Gist of Each Paragraph.

It will come as no surprise that the paragraph is the main structural unit of any passage. After you've read the first third of the passage carefully, you need to find the gist, or general purpose, of each paragraph and then try to relate each paragraph back to the passage as a whole. To find the gist of each paragraph, ask yourself:

- Why did the author include this paragraph?
- What shift did the author have in mind when moving on to this paragraph?
- What bearing does this paragraph have on the author's main idea?

Principle 4. Don't Obsess over Details.

There are differences between the reading skills required in an academic environment and those that are useful on standardized tests. In school, you probably read to memorize information for an exam. But this isn't the type of reading that's good for racking up points on the GRE Reading Comprehension section. On the test, you'll need to read for short-term retention. When you finish the questions on a certain passage, that passage is over, gone, done with. What's more, there's no need to waste your time memorizing details. The passage will be right there in front of you as you work through the questions.

📖 **READ MORE**

Read the newspaper daily, concentrating on articles covering topics with which you are unfamiliar. Try to jot down each article's main idea and the author's tone and purpose. This way, you can practice overcoming the hurdle of reading unfamiliar or difficult material, which will help you do well on the Reading Comp sections.

Principle 5. Attack the Passages, Don't Just Read Them.

Remember when you took the SAT? Like some of us, did you celebrate when you finally finished the passage and then treat the questions as an afterthought? If so, we suggest that you readjust your thinking. Remember: you get no points for just getting through the passage.

When we read most materials, a newspaper, for example, we start with the first sentence and read the article straight through. The words wash over us and are the only things we hear in our minds. This is typical of a passive approach to reading, and this approach won't cut it on the GRE.

To do well on this test you'll need to do more than just read the words on the page. You'll need to read actively. Active reading involves keeping your mind working at all times while trying to anticipate where the author's points are leading. It means thinking about what you're reading as you read it. It means paraphrasing the complicated-sounding ideas and jargon. It means asking yourself questions as you read:

- What's the author's main point here?
- What's the purpose of this paragraph? Of this sentence?

While reading actively you keep a running commentary in your mind as you jot down notes on your scratch paper. When you read actively you don't absorb the passage, you attack it!

Principle 6. Beware of Classic Wrong Answer Choices.

Knowing the most common wrong answer types can help you to eliminate wrong choices quickly, which can save you a lot of time. Ideally, you want to have phrased an answer in your mind before looking at the choices. When that technique doesn't work, you'll have to go to the choices and eliminate the bad ones to find the correct one. If this happens, you should always be on the lookout for choices that:

- Contradict the facts or the main idea
- Distort or twist the facts or the main idea
- Mention true points not relevant to the question (often from the wrong paragraph)

- Raise a topic that's never mentioned in the passage, or raise an aspect of the topic that is outside the scope of the passage
- Are too strongly worded
- Sound bizarre or have the wrong tone

Being sensitive to these classic wrong choices will make it that much easier to zero in on the correct choice quickly and efficiently.

Principle 7. Use Outside Knowledge Carefully.

You can answer all the questions correctly even if you don't know anything about the topics covered in the passages. Everything you'll need to answer every question is included in the passages themselves. However, you'll have to be able to make basic inferences and extract relevant details from the texts. Using outside knowledge that you may have about a particular topic can be beneficial to your cause, but watch out—it can also confuse your thinking. If you use your knowledge of a topic to help you understand the author's points, then you're taking advantage of your knowledge in a useful way. But if you use it to *answer* the questions, then you may run into trouble. Remember, the questions test your understanding of the author's points, not your previous understanding or personal point of view on the topic.

 KAPLAN STRATEGY

Kaplan's basic principles for success on Reading Comprehension are:

- Read the first third of the passage very carefully.
- Focus on the main idea.
- Get the gist of each paragraph.
- Don't obsess over details.
- Attack the passages; don't just read them.
- Beware of classic wrong answer choices.
- Use outside knowledge carefully.

Reading Comprehension Test Run

Here's a chance to become familiar with a short Reading Comprehension passage and question set. You'll have more opportunities to practice later, under timed conditions. For now, we want you to take the time to read actively, to give the seven basic principles and the Kaplan Method a test run.

The questions in this group are based on the content of the passage. After reading the passage, choose the best answer to each question. Answer each question based upon what's stated or implied in the passage.

Migration of animal populations from one region to another is called faunal interchange. Concentrations of species across regional boundaries vary, however, prompting zoologists to classify routes along which penetrations of new regions occur.

(5)   A corridor, like the vast stretch of land from Alaska to the south-eastern United States, is equivalent to a path of least resistance. Relative ease of migration often results in the presence of related species along the entire length of a corridor; bear populations, unknown in South America, occur throughout the North American

(10)   corridor. A desert or other barrier creates a filter route, allowing only a segment of a faunal group to pass. A sweepstakes route presents so formidable a barrier that penetration is unlikely. It differs from other routes, which may be crossed by species with sufficient adaptive capability. As the name suggests, negotiation of a sweepstakes route

(15)   depends almost exclusively on chance, rather than on physical attributes and adaptability.

1. It can be inferred from the passage that studies of faunal interchange would probably

   ◯ fail to explain how similar species can inhabit widely separated areas.

   ◯ be unreliable because of the difficulty of observing long-range migrations.

   ◯ focus most directly on the seasonal movements of a species within a specific geographic region.

   ◯ concentrate on correlating the migratory patterns of species that are biologically dissimilar.

   ◯ help to explain how present-day distributions of animal populations might have arisen.

2. The author's primary purpose is to show that the classification of migratory routes

   ○ is based on the probability that migration will occur along a given route.

   ○ reflects the important role played by chance in the distribution of most species.

   ○ is unreliable because further study is needed.

   ○ is too arbitrary, because the regional boundaries cited by zoologists frequently change.

   ○ is based primarily on geographic and climactic differences between adjoining regions.

3. The author's description of the distribution of bear populations (lines 8–10) suggests which of the following conclusions?

   I.   The distribution patterns of most other North American faunal species populations are probably identical to those of bears.

   II. There are relatively few barriers to faunal interchange in North America.

   III. The geographic area that links North America to South America would probably be classified as either a filter or a sweepstakes route.

   ○ I only

   ○ II only

   ○ III only

   ○ I and II only

   ○ II and III only

4. According to the passage, in order to negotiate a sweepstakes route an animal species

   ○ has to spend at least part of the year in a desert environment.

   ○ is obliged to move long distances in short periods of time.

   ○ must sacrifice many of its young to wandering pastures.

   ○ must have the capacity to adapt to a very wide variety of climates.

   ○ does not need to possess any special physical capabilities.

How Did You Do?

Were you able to zoom in from the broad topic (migration) to the scope (classification of migration routes)? Did the author's tone and purpose become clear, then, as explanatory rather than argumentative? And were you able to focus on the correct answers (1. E, 2. A, 3. E, 4. E) and not get distracted by outside knowledge or misleading details? You'll be able to assess your performance and skills as you review the next section, where we'll explore the strategies for dealing with the three Reading Comp question types and how these strategies apply to the above questions.

THE 3 COMMON READING COMP QUESTION TYPES

We find it useful to break the Reading Comprehension section down into the three main question types that accompany each passage: global, explicit detail, and inference. Most test takers find explicit detail questions to be the easiest type in the Reading Comprehension section, because they're the most concrete. Unlike inferences, which hide somewhere between the lines, explicit details sit out in the open—in the lines themselves. That's good news for you, because when you see an explicit detail question you'll know that the correct answer requires only recall, and not analysis. Let's look at each of these question types more closely, using the sample questions you just dealt with for illustration.

1. Global Questions

A global question will ask you to sum up the author's overall intentions, ideas, or passage structure. It's basically a question whose scope is the entire passage. Global questions account for 25 to 30 percent of all Reading Comprehension questions. Question 2 in the preceding sample is a global question because it asks you to identify the author's primary purpose.

Strategy. In general, any global question choice that grabs onto a small detail—or zeroes in on the content of only one paragraph—will be wrong. Often, scanning the verbs in the global question choices is a good way to take a first cut at the question. The verbs must agree with the author's tone and the way in which he or she structures the passage, so scanning the verbs and adjectives can narrow down the options quickly. The correct answer must be consistent with the overall tone and structure of the passage, whereas common wrong answer choices associated with this type of question are those that are too broad or narrow in scope and those that are inconsistent with the author's tone. You'll often find global questions at the beginning of question sets, and often one of the wrong choices will play on some side issue discussed at the tail end of the passage.

Take a closer look at the global question (Question 2). You've already articulated the passage's topic (migration), scope (the classification of migration routes), and tone (explanatory). The author mentions three different classifications of migration routes—corridors, filter routes, and sweepstakes routes. And what distinguishes one kind of route from another? The likelihood of migration, from the most likely (corridors, with no barriers to migration) to the least likely (sweepstakes routes, with barriers that species can cross only by chance). So the author's primary purpose here is to show how the classifications are defined according to how likely migration is along each type of route. That should have led you directly to choice **(A)**.

A scan of verbs and adjectives is enough to eliminate choices **(C)** and **(D)**; both imply that the author is making judgments about the classification, but the tone of the passage is objective and explanatory. Meanwhile, **(B)** focuses too much on one part of the passage—the explanation of sweepstakes routes—where the role of chance is mentioned only in relation to that one classification. And **(E)** is a distortion, because the author nowhere mentions climatic and geographic differences between adjoining regions.

Main Idea and Primary Purpose Questions. The two main types of global questions are main idea and primary purpose questions. We discussed these types a little earlier, noting that main idea and purpose are inextricably linked, because the author's purpose is to convey his or her main idea. The formats of these question types are pretty self-evident:

> Which one of the following best expresses the main idea of the passage?

or

> The author's primary purpose is to . . .

Title Questions. A very similar form of global question is one that's looking for a title that best fits the passage. A title, in effect, is the main idea summed up in a brief, catchy way. This question stem may look like this:

> Which of the following titles best describes the content of the passage as a whole?

Be sure not to go with a choice that aptly describes only the latter half of the passage. A valid title, much like a main idea and primary purpose, must cover the entire passage.

Structure Questions. Another type of global question is one that asks you to recognize a passage's overall structure. Here's what this type of question might sound like:

> Which of the following best describes the organization of the passage?

Answer choices to this kind of global question are usually worded very generally; they force you to recognize the broad layout of the passage as opposed to the specific content. For example, here are a few possible ways that a passage could be organized:

- A hypothesis is stated and then analyzed.
- A proposal is evaluated and alternatives are explored.
- A viewpoint is set forth and then subsequently defended.

When picking among these choices, ask yourself, "Was there a hypothesis here? Was there an evaluation of a proposal or a defense of a viewpoint?" These terms may all sound similar but, in fact, they're very different things. Learn to recognize the difference between a proposal, a viewpoint, and so on. Try to keep a constant eye on what the author is doing as well as what the author is saying, and you'll have an easier time with this type of question.

Tone Questions. Finally, one last type of global question is the tone question, which asks you to evaluate the style of the writing or how the author sounds. Is the author passionate, fiery, neutral, angry, hostile, opinionated, low-key? Here's an example:

> The author's tone in the passage can best be
> characterized as . . .

Make sure not to confuse the nature of the content with the tone in which the author presents the ideas: a social science passage based on trends in the 20 century's grisliest murders may be presented in a cool, detached, strictly informative way. Once again, it's up to you to separate what the author says from how he or she says it.

2. Explicit Detail Questions

The second major category of Reading Comprehension questions is the explicit detail question. As the name implies, an explicit detail question is one whose answer can be directly pinpointed and found in the passage. Question 4 in the sample is an explicit detail question because it asks you to go back to the passage and examine the description of a sweepstakes route. This type makes up roughly 20 to 30 percent of the Reading Comprehension questions.

Strategy. Often, these questions provide very direct clues as to where an answer may be found, such as a line reference or some text that links up with the passage structure. (Just be careful with line references; they'll bring you to the right area, but usually the actual answer will be found in the lines immediately before or after the referenced line.)

Now, you may recall that we advised you to skim over details in Reading Comprehension passages in favor of focusing on the big idea, topic, and scope. But now here's a question type that's specifically concerned with details, so what's the deal?

The fact is that most of the details that appear in a typical passage aren't tested in the questions. Of the few that are, you'll either:

- Remember them from your reading
- Be given a line reference to bring you right to them
- Simply have to find them on your own in order to track down the answer

In the third case, if your understanding of the purpose of each paragraph is in the forefront of your mind, it shouldn't take long at all to locate the details in question and then choose an answer. The winning strategy for this question type is to note the *purpose* of details in each paragraph's argument but not to attempt to memorize the details themselves.

Take a closer look at the explicit detail question in the sample (Question 4). When an explicit detail question directs you to a specific place in the passage (as Question 4 does to the discussion of sweepstakes routes), your first job is to go right to that spot in the passage and reread it. And if you do that here, you read that negotiation of a sweepstakes route depends "almost entirely on chance, rather than on physical attributes and adaptability." The discounting of physical attributes here should have led you directly to choice **(E)**.

Choice **(A)**'s mention of a desert environment sinks that choice, because the desert was mentioned by the author in the discussion of filter routes. As for the other choices, "short periods of time," "wandering pastures," and "a wide variety of climates" aren't mentioned in the passage with regard to sweepstakes routes.

3. Inference Questions

An inference is something that is almost certainly true, based on the passage. Inferences require you to draw conclusions about the text based on what is implied or indirectly stated. Questions 1 and 3 in the preceding sample are inference questions. Question 1 specifically asks you what can be "inferred from the passage" and Question 3 asks you to glean possible conclusions based on what is presented.

Strategy. The answer to an inference question is something that the author strongly implies or hints at but does not state directly. Furthermore, the right answer, if denied, will contradict or significantly weaken the passage.

Extracting valid inferences from Reading Comprehension passages requires the ability to recognize that information in the passage can be expressed in different ways. The ability to bridge the gap between the way information is presented in the passage and the way it's presented in the correct answer choice is vital. In fact, inference questions often boil down to an exercise in translation. A good inference:

- Stays in line with the gist of the passage
- Stays in line with the author's tone

- Stays in line with the author's point of view
- Stays within the scope of the passage and its main idea
- Is neither denied by, nor irrelevant to, the ideas stated in the passage
- Always makes more sense than its opposite

Take a closer look at the sample inference questions (1 and 3). Question 1 asks you to select a possible application of the migration study, based only on what you know from the passage. Because the different concentrations of animals prompted the zoologists to classify the migration routes in the first place (line 3), it would make sense that the migration study would help explain how these different concentrations, or distributions, would have arisen. So choice (**E**) is correct.

Choice (**A**) contradicts the purpose of the passage, which we discussed for Question 2, and unless we're told in the passage that the study was a failure (which we are not), we can't guess that it would be one. Choice (**B**) is outside of the passage's scope because the passage never touches on the reliability of the study or on any difficulties in observing long-range migrations. The answer must be based on the passage. Choices (**C**) and (**D**) are misleading distortions. The study does focus on movements of species, but there's no mention of a seasonal influence, and the study does focus on route comparisons but not on species comparisons.

Question 3 asks you to look back to the passage for the example of the bears and decide what conclusion(s) could be drawn based on this example. We read that bear populations occur throughout North America because North America is a "path of least resistance," meaning there are relatively few barriers. The bears did not continue to migrate further south, however, because they're "unknown in South America." This suggests that South America is either a filter or a sweepstakes route. Nowhere are the bears compared with other species, because the focus isn't the bears but the routes. So Statement I can be eliminated, and Statements II and III are accurate. This should have led you, then, to choice (**E**).

KAPLAN'S 4-STEP METHOD FOR READING COMPREHENSION

Now that you've got the basics of GRE Reading Comprehension under your belt, you'll want to learn our 4-step method that allows you to put it all together into a single aggressive and energetic *modus operandi*.

Step 1. Attack the First Third of the Passage.

As outlined in the basic principles section, read the first third of the passage with care, thinking about what you're reading, paraphrasing the complicated parts, and identifying the main idea and author's purpose in writing the passage. Two caveats, however: first, in some passages, the author's main idea won't become clear until the end of the passage. Second, some passages don't contain a main idea, being purely descriptive, with an evenhanded tone and no strong opinions. Bottom line: don't panic if you can't immediately pin down the author's main idea and purpose.

Step 2. Create a Road Map.

As you quickly read through the rest of the passage, take note of each paragraph, reading for the gist and not the details. Try to get a sense of what's covered in each paragraph and how it fits into the overall structure of the passage. This will help you get a fix on the passage as a whole, and will help you locate specific details later on.

Step 3. Stop to Sum Up.

Before answering the questions, take a few seconds to summarize your mental road map and rephrase the main idea of the passage in your own words.

Step 4. Attack the Questions.

Answer the questions based upon your mental road map. As necessary, go back into the passage to locate answers to specific questions. Eliminate wrong answers aggressively, and select the choice that best paraphrases the answer you've found.

READING COMP PRACTICE

Now let's apply the Kaplan 4-Step Method to an actual GRE-strength Reading Comp passage.

> The questions in this group are based on the content of the passage. After reading the passage, choose the best answer to each question. Answer each question based upon what's <u>stated</u> or <u>implied</u> in the passage.

The search for an explanation of the frequency, as well as the weakness, of U.S. third-party movements is illuminated by examining the conditions that have favored the growth of a strong two-party system. Different interests and voting blocs predominate in

(5)   different regions, so that the electorate is geographically fragmented. This heterogeneity is complemented by a federal political structure that forces the major parties to find voter support at state and local levels in separate regions. Historically, for example, the Democratic Party drew support simultaneously from northern Black urban voters

(10)   and segregationists. Such pressures encourage the major parties to avoid political programs that are too narrowly or sharply defined. Instead, they seek broad appeal, supported by sometimes competing promises made to sectional interests. The nondoctrinal character of U.S. politics means that important new issues and voting blocs tend to

(15)   be initially ignored by the major parties. Such issues—opposition

to immigration and the abolition of slavery are two historic
examples—tend to gain political prominence through third parties.

Ironically, the same factors that lead to the emergence of third
parties contribute to the explanation of their failure to gain national

(20)   political power. Parties based on narrow or ephemeral issues remain
isolated or fade rapidly. At the same time, those that raise increasingly
urgent social issues also face inherent limits to growth. Long before a
third party can begin to substantially broaden its base of voter support,
the major parties are able to move to attract the minority of voters

(25)   that it represents. The Democratic Party, for instance, appropriated the
agrarian platform of the Populist Party in 1896, and enacted Socialist
welfare proposals in the 1930s, in both cases winning much of the
popular bases of these parties. Except for the Republican Party, which
gained national prominence as the Whigs were declining in the 1850s,

(30)   no third party has ever achieved national major party status. Only at
state and local levels have a handful of third parties been sustained by a
stable voting bloc that remains unrepresented by a major party.

1. The main concern of the author of this passage is to

    ◯ examine the appeal of U.S. third parties at state and local levels.

    ◯ trace the historical rise and decline of third party movements in the
    United States.

    ◯ explain why most U.S. third-party movements have failed to gain major
    party status.

    ◯ demonstrate the nonideological character of U.S. politics.

    ◯ suggest a model to explain why certain U. S. third-party movements have
    succeeded while others have failed.

2. According to the author, the major factor responsible for the rise of third parties
    in the United States has been the

    ◯ domination of major parties by powerful economic interests.

    ◯ inability of major parties to bring about broad consensus among a variety
    of voters and interest groups.

    ◯ slow response of major parties to new issues and voting groups.

    ◯ exclusion of immigrants and minorities from the mainstream of
    U.S. politics.

    ◯ variety of motivations held by voting blocs in different regions.

3. It can be inferred that which of the following contributed to the "nondoctrinal character of U.S. politics" (lines 13–14).

    I.   The regional diversity of the country

    II. The national political structure

    III. The avoidance of divisive ideological programs by the major parties

    ○ I only

    ○ III only

    ○ I and II only

    ○ II and III only

    ○ I, II, and III

4. Which of the following does the author suggest was an important factor in the establishment of the Republican Party as a major national party?

    ○ The polarization of national opinion at the time of a major social crisis

    ○ The unique appeal of its program to significant sectional interests

    ○ The acceptance of its program by a large bloc of voters unrepresented by a major party

    ○ The simultaneous decline of an established major party

    ○ The inability of the major parties of the era to appeal to all sectional interests

Here's how the Kaplan Method works with this passage.

Step 1. Attack the First Third of the Passage.

The very first sentence introduces the topic—third-party movements—as well as the scope and author's purpose—understanding the factors hindering their success and favoring the two-party system. The author then quickly proceeds to enumerate these factors. So just from reading this first part of the passage closely, you have a strong sense of its overall structure and purpose.

Step 2. Create a Road Map.

Notice how paragraph two also opens with a topic sentence that neatly announces what will be covered therein, which is the failure of third parties to gain national political power. Make note of the author's point-by-point examination, but don't try to memorize details. You can always refer to the passage to answer questions.

Step 3. Stop to Sum Up.

Now it's time to sum up your road map—from the gists of the paragraphs you should be able to quickly paraphrase the main idea of the entire passage. You might have paraphrased the main idea like this: "Factors that lead to the emergence of third parties also lead to their eventual downfall, at least on the national level." Armed with this recap, you should be able to move confidently through the questions. You may not be able to answer every question on sight, but you'll know where to locate the details for those questions, which means quick, correct answers.

Step 4. Attack the Questions.

Work the questions as they appear. Most of the questions should be easy to crack after checking the details, an easy matter with your roadmap.

PRACTICE ANSWERS AND EXPLANATIONS

1. C

Choice (C) is the only choice that fits the topic (third-party movements), scope (how they fare on the national level) and the author's purpose (explaining why they have failed to gain national power). Choices (A) and (D) clearly misrepresent all of these, and (E) is out because no model is suggested, particularly one explaining why some third-party movements have succeeded. Choice (B) might seem tempting at first, but beware of verbs such as *trace,* which are too ambitious for a GRE-length passage—there's certainly no attempt made to *trace* these movements throughout U.S. history.

2. C

This detail question asks for a factor responsible for the *rise* of third parties, so you'll probably want to research the passage for the answer. You'll find the relevant discussion at the end of paragraph one, which is neatly paraphrased in (C).

3. E

Again, you'll probably want to research the relevant part of the passage, a task which in this case is facilitated by the line reference, although here you'll need to read most of paragraph one for the answer. You'll find that Statement I is confirmed on line 4, Statement II on line 6, and Statement III on line 11. The lesson to be learned here is that even on so-called "inference" questions, the answers are very often paraphrases of information found in the passage.

4. D

Once again, this detail question seems to ask for an inference, but if you look for the relevant discussion of the Republican Party (which is easily found by scanning for the word *Republican*), you'll find (on lines 28–29) that (D) directly paraphrases what you find there.

READING COMP STRATEGY REVIEW EXERCISES

Because the Reading Comprehension questions primarily test your ability to read actively, paraphrase as you read and pay attention to purpose and structure, let's spend some time practicing those critical reading skills.

Big Ideas and Details

It's important that you're able to pull out the main idea and supporting details quickly and easily on Test Day. Read the following mini-passages. As you read, jot down their big ideas in the margin and underline details. Then compare your answers with ours.

Mini-passage 1

Few historians would contest the idea that Gutenberg's invention of the printing press revolutionized the production of literature. Before the press became widely available in the late 1400s, every book published had to be individually copied by a scribe working from a master manuscript. With Gutenberg's system of moveable type, however, books could be reproduced in almost limitless quantities once the laborious process of typesetting was complete . . .

Mini-passage 2

Plate tectonics, the study of the interaction of the earth's plates, is generally accepted as the best framework for understanding how the continents formed. New research suggests, however, that the eruption of mantle plumes from beneath the plate layer may be responsible for the formation of specific phenomena in areas distant from plate boundaries. A model of mantle plumes appears to explain a wide range of observations relating to both ocean island chains and flood basalt provinces, for example . . .

Mini-passage 3

Most of the developed countries are now agreed on the need to take international measures to reduce the emission of carbons into the atmosphere. Despite this consensus, a wide disagreement among economists as to how much emission reduction will actually cost continues to forestall policy making. Analysts who believe the energy market is efficient predict that countries that reduce carbon emission by as little as 20 percent will experience a significant depreciation in their national product. Those that hold that the market is inefficient, however, estimate much greater long-term savings in conservation and arrive at lower costs for reducing emissions . . .

Big Ideas and Details Answers

Mini-passage 1

Big idea: Gutenberg revolutionized book publishing.

Details: late 1400s, moveable type, limitless quantities, typesetting

Mini-passage 2

Bid idea: Mantle plume eruptions, not plate tectonics, may explain certain phenomena.

Details: ocean island chains, flood basalt provinces

Mini-passage 3

Big idea: Economists disagree on the cost of emission reduction.

Details: international measures, carbon emission, greater savings, conservation

Paraphrasing

Many people have a hard time paraphrasing passages. Taking dense, academic prose and turning it into everyday English isn't easy under the pressure of time constraints. Yet, this is the most important skill in Reading Comprehension. If you are having trouble with paraphrasing, spend some time with the following exercise.

1. For centuries, the Roman Empire ruled large parts of Europe, Asia, and Africa. Rome had two assets that made continued domination possible. First, its highly trained army was superior to those of its potential adversaries. Second, and more important, Rome built a sophisticated transportation network linking together all of the provinces of its far flung empire. When necessary, it could deploy powerful military forces to any part of the empire with unmatched speed.

   Summarize these lines in your own words:

   _____

   _____

   _____

   Now find the best paraphrase from the choices below:

   ○ Rome's army defeated its opponents because it could move quickly along the empire's excellent transportation network.

   ○ Rome had a big empire, a powerful army, and a good transportation system.

   ○ Rome was able to maintain a large empire because it had an excellent transportation system that allowed its efficient army to move quickly from place to place.

◯ Rome ruled large parts of Europe, Asia, and Africa for centuries because its army was always better than those of its adversaries.

◯ Because it built a sophisticated transportation system, Rome was able to build a big empire in parts of Europe, Asia, and Africa.

2. Despite overwhelming evidence to the contrary, many people think that flying is more dangerous than driving. Different standards of media coverage account for this erroneous belief. Although extremely rare, aircraft accidents receive a lot of media attention because they are very destructive. Hundreds of people have been killed in extreme cases. Automobile accidents, on the other hand, occur with alarming frequency, but attract little media coverage because few, if any, people are killed or seriously injured in any particular mishap.

Summarize these lines in your own words:

_____

_____

_____

Now find the best paraphrase from the choices below:

◯ Compared to rare but destructive aircraft accidents, car accidents are frequent but relatively minor.

◯ Because aircraft accidents get a lot of media attention, while car accidents get much less, many people wrongly believe that flying is more dangerous than driving.

◯ Driving is more dangerous than flying because different standards of media coverage have forced airlines to improve their safety standards.

◯ Many people believe that flying is more dangerous than driving, even though overwhelming evidence points to the opposite conclusion.

◯ Media coverage is responsible for the belief that flying is more dangerous than driving, even though every year more people are killed on the roads than in the air.

Paraphrasing Answers

1. **C**

2. **B**

Key Words

Remember these? Kaplan key words are words in Reading Comprehension passages that link the text together structurally and thematically. Paying attention to key words will help you understand the passage better, and will also help you get some easy points. Here are some key words that you should look for when reading a passage:

Contradiction	Support	Emphasis
however	for example	of primary importance
but	one reason that	especially important
yet	in addition	of particular interest
on the other hand	also	crucial
rather	moreover	critical
instead	consequently	remarkable

Take a moment and circle the structural signal words in this short Reading Comprehension passage:

> Gettysburg is considered by most historians to be a turning point in the American Civil War. Before Gettysburg, Confederate forces under General Robert E. Lee had defeated their Union counterparts—sometimes by considerable margins—in a string of major battles. In this
>
> (5) engagement, however, the Confederate army was defeated and driven back. Even more important than their material losses, though, was the Confederacy's loss of momentum. Union forces took the initiative, finally defeating the Confederacy less than two years later. By invading Union territory, the Confederate leadership had sought to shatter the
>
> (10) Union's will to continue the war and to convince European nations to recognize the Confederacy as an independent nation. Instead, the Union's willingness to fight was strengthened and the Confederacy squandered its last chance for foreign support.

Words of emphasis, though rare, are the most important category of Kaplan key words. Why? Because if you see an emphasis keyword in a sentence, you will always get a question about that sentence. Think about it—if the author thinks something is "of primary importance," it would be remiss of the test-maker not to ask you about it.

In the Gettysburg passage, did you circle *even more important* (line 6)? You should have. You were bound to get a question about it.

You can also get the gist of this paragraph by paying close attention to the contrast words, beginning on line 5: "In the engagement, *however*, the Confederate army was defeated and driven back." Ah, so they weren't doing so well anymore. Contrast words signal a change in direction, and for this reason they often introduce thematically important information. In fact, if a paragraph contains a contrast word, the topic sentence will almost always be that sentence or the next. And the next sentence, which is indeed the topic sentence, contains another contrast word: "Even more important than their material losses, *though*, was the Confederacy's loss of momentum." Finally, the last sentence contains one more contrast word and introduces one more important idea: "*Instead*, the Union's willingness to fight was strengthened and the Confederacy squandered its last chance of foreign support."

The moral of this story is that by paying attention to key words, you can be sure that you won't lose sight of the most important information that the author is trying to convey.

By using all of the techniques discussed above, you will be able to tackle the most difficult Reading Comprehension questions. And now that you have the tools to handle the Verbal section of the GRE, take a swing at the set of practice questions that follow. Then we'll move on and take a look at the Quantitative section of the test.

SUMMARY

Kaplan's 4-Step Method for Sentence Completions is:

Step 1. Read the sentence, looking for structural road signs and other clues to where the sentence is heading.

Step 2. In your own words, predict the answer.

Step 3. Select the choice that most closely matches your prediction.

Step 4. Read your choice back into the sentence to make sure it fits.

Kaplan's 4-Step Method for Analogies is:

Step 1. Find a strong bridge between the stem words. Be flexible: sometimes it's easier to use the second word first.

Step 2. Plug the answer choices into the bridge. Make sure to keep the same word order that you used with the stem pair.

Step 3. Adjust the bridge as necessary. You want your bridge to be simple and somewhat general, but if more than one answer choice fits into your bridge, it is too general. Make it a little more specific and try the answer choices again.

Step 4. If you are stuck, eliminate all answer choices with weak bridges. If two choices have the same bridge—for example, *trumpet : instrument* and *screwdriver : tool*—eliminate them both. Don't fall for classic traps. Work backward from remaining choices to the stem pair and make your best guess.

Kaplan's 4-Step Method for Antonyms is:

Step 1. Define the root word.

Step 2. Reverse it by thinking about the word's opposite.

Step 3. Now go to the answer choices and find the opposite—that is, the choice that matches your preconceived notion of the choice.

Step 4. If you are stuck, work backward from the answer choices.

Kaplan's 4-Step Method for Reading Comprehension questions is:

Step 1. Attack the first third of the passage.

Step 2. Create a mental road map.

Step 3. Stop to sum up.

Step 4. Attack the questions.

VERBAL PRACTICE SET

Directions: Each sentence below has one or two blanks, each blank indicating that something has been omitted. Beneath the sentence are five lettered words or sets of words. Choose the word or set of words for each blank that best fits the meaning of the sentence as a whole.

1. The _____ of the desert explains why so many Egyptian mummies are still intact, whereas the humidity of the tombs in tropical rain forests supports the agents of decay so that few Aztec mummies have _____.

   ○ heat . . . survived

   ○ aridity . . . endured

   ○ dehydration . . . decayed

   ○ barrenness . . . proliferated

   ○ seclusion . . . surfaced

2. They _____ until there was no recourse but to _____ a desperate, last-minute solution to the problem.

   ○ berated . . . try

   ○ delayed . . . envision

   ○ procrastinated . . . implement

   ○ debated . . . maintain

   ○ filibustered . . . reject

3. The Wankel Rotary Engine was an engineering marvel that substantially reduced automobile exhaust emissions, but because it was less fuel-efficient than the standard piston-cylinder engine, it was _____ in the early 1970s when _____ pollution gave way to panic over fuel shortages.

   ○ needed . . . disillusionment with

   ○ conceived . . . attention on

   ○ modified . . . opinion on

   ○ abandoned . . . preoccupation with

   ○ discarded . . . interest in

4. Friendship, no matter how _____, has its boundaries; _____ advice, when thrust insistently upon one, is rarely an act of friendship, regardless of the adviser's intent.

   ○ cool . . . contradictory

   ○ enjoyable . . . obverse

   ○ intimate . . . unsolicited

   ○ distant . . . marital

   ○ special . . . desired

5. Despite generous helpings of _____ from a group of _____ critics, this iconoclastic poet's three volumes have sold steadily.

   ○ zeal . . . hidebound

   ○ mockery . . . obscure

   ○ tedium . . . respected

   ○ abuse . . . ineffectual

   ○ vitriol . . . influential

6. Because the different components of the film industry were "vertically" oriented—arranged so that all _____, from production to projection, were held by one company—it was _____ that monopolistic practices would arise.

   ⚪ opportunities for control . . . inevitable

   ⚪ burdens of business . . . understandable

   ⚪ exercises of power . . . appropriate

   ⚪ means of solicitation . . . predictable

   ⚪ perquisites of commerce . . . unsavory

7. From the _____ that the peasants tried to conceal as they knelt before the body of the dictator's son, I concluded that, far from affection, it was _____ that had brought them to the wake.

   ⚪ hatred . . . sarcasm

   ⚪ reticence . . . violence

   ⚪ diligence . . . adulation

   ⚪ trepidation . . . fear

   ⚪ sorrow . . . patriotism

8. Despite the increased attention _____ juvenile delinquency, there has been a _____ in crimes committed by juveniles.

   ⚪ allotted to . . . dip

   ⚪ offered to . . . development

   ⚪ given to . . . rise

   ⚪ spent on . . . decrease

   ⚪ withdrawn from . . . growth

9. Much of the Beatles' music, as evidenced by "All You Need Is Love," was characterized by a superficial _____ subtly contradicted by an inherent, deeper cynicism.

   ⚪ competence

   ⚪ world-weariness

   ⚪ liveliness

   ⚪ naiveté

   ⚪ gloss

10. During their famous clash, Jung was ambivalent about Freud so he attacked the father of modern psychoanalysis even as he _____ him.

    ⚪ enlightened

    ⚪ chastened

    ⚪ revered

    ⚪ despised

    ⚪ understood

11. Hers was not a quick but rather a thorough intelligence; however _____, she came to _____ all things touching her life.

    ⚪ unmindfully . . . embrace

    ⚪ desperately . . . appreciate

    ⚪ slowly . . . jettison

    ⚪ methodically . . . discern

    ⚪ ploddingly . . . understand

12. Considering the _____ era in which the novel was written, its tone and theme are remarkably _____.

    ◯ enlightened . . . disenchanted

    ◯ scholarly . . . undramatic

    ◯ superstitious . . . medieval

    ◯ permissive . . . puritanical

    ◯ undistinguished . . . commonplace

13. Feuds tend to arise in societies that _____ centralized government; when public justice is difficult to enforce, private recourse is more _____.

    ◯ espouse . . . acceptable

    ◯ affirm . . . objectionable

    ◯ dislike . . . satisfying

    ◯ reject . . . brutal

    ◯ lack . . . effective

14. He must always be the center of attention; he would rather be criticized than _____.

    ◯ ignored

    ◯ selfish

    ◯ remembered

    ◯ praised

    ◯ different

15. Greek philosophers tried to _____ contemporary notions of change and stability by postulating the existence of the atom, _____ particle from which all varieties of matter are formed.

    ◯ personify . . . a mutating

    ◯ reconcile . . . an indivisible

    ◯ simplify . . . a specific

    ◯ eliminate . . . an infinitesimal

    ◯ confirm . . . an interesting

16. Many believe that jazz improvisation is a creation of the twentieth century, but it is _____ improvisation has its _____ in the figured-bass techniques of the seventeenth and eighteenth centuries.

    ◯ unlikely . . . roots

    ◯ possible . . . past

    ◯ arguable . . . origin

    ◯ proven . . . future

    ◯ interesting . . . unity

17. Whales hurt nothing and no one in their peaceful migrations through the earth's seas, yet are savagely hunted by man, who _____ superior need.

    ◯ assumes

    ◯ perpetuates

    ◯ retains

    ◯ assimilates

    ◯ manifests

18. His unbridled curiosity led him to explore every field of _____, yet his _____ stances kept him at odds with the devout society he so wanted to be acknowledged by.

    ○ science . . . interesting

    ○ interest . . . common

    ○ thought . . . unorthodox

    ○ hope . . . heretical

    ○ study . . . optimistic

19. Because of his inherent _____, Harry steered clear of any job that he suspected could turn out to be a travail.

    ○ impudence

    ○ insolence

    ○ eminence

    ○ indolence

    ○ integrity

20. First published in 1649, Pacheco's _____ treatise contains not only chapters outlining iconography and technique, but also commentary on contemporary painters that now _____ our most comprehensive information on these artists, as well as the most thorough discussion available on Baroque aesthetics.

    ○ inconsequential . . . comprises

    ○ invaluable . . . constitutes

    ○ historical . . . lacks

    ○ superficial . . . supports

    ○ important . . . excludes

21. Very little is know of the writer Theophilus; however, from his eclectic writings, we can _____ that he was well _____.

    ○ assume . . . educated

    ○ understand . . . disciplined

    ○ appreciate . . . respected

    ○ expect . . . exposed

    ○ acknowledge . . . received

22. Her systematic approach to scientific research was often rewarded in her _____ life, but it proved disastrous when her _____ mind examined every flaw in her friends and family, preventing her from truly appreciating others.

    ○ career . . . disorganized

    ○ private . . . analytical

    ○ public . . . fragile

    ○ professional . . . methodical

    ○ family . . . orderly

23. Personal correspondence is often a marvelous reflection of the spirit of an age; the subtle _____ of Swift's epistles mirrored the eighteenth-century delight in elegant _____.

    ○ profundity . . . ditties

    ○ poignancy . . . pejoratives

    ○ contempt . . . anachronisms

    ○ provinciality . . . pomposity

    ○ vitriol . . . disparagement

24. Our spokesperson seems to be uncertain of our eventual victory but _____ facing the alternative, as if merely admitting the possibility of defeat would lead to the dread thing itself.

   ◯ unsure of

   ◯ complacent when

   ◯ fearful of

   ◯ certain of

   ◯ helped by

25. Victorien Sardou's play *La Tosca* was originally written as a _____ for Sarah Bernhardt and later _____ into the famous Puccini opera.

   ◯ role . . . reincarnated

   ◯ biography . . . changed

   ◯ metaphor . . . edited

   ◯ present . . . fictionalized

   ◯ vehicle . . . adapted

26. Because the law and custom require that a definite determination be made, the judge is forced to behave as if the verdict is _____, when in fact the evidence may not be _____.

   ◯ negotiable . . . persuasive

   ◯ justified . . . accessible

   ◯ unassailable . . . insubstantial

   ◯ incontrovertible . . . admissible

   ◯ self-evident . . . conclusive

27. The author presumably believes that all businessmen are _____, for her main characters, whatever qualities they may lack, are virtual paragons of _____.

   ◯ clever . . . ingenuity

   ◯ covetous . . . greed

   ◯ virtuous . . . deceit

   ◯ successful . . . ambition

   ◯ cautious . . . achievement

28. Filmed on a ludicrously _____ budget and edited at breakneck speed, Melotti's documentary nonetheless _____ the Cannes critics with its ingenuity and verve.

   ◯ low. . .disappointed

   ◯ inflated . . . distracted

   ◯ uneven . . . amused

   ◯ disproportionate . . . appalled

   ◯ inadequate . . . surprised

29. Ginnie expects her every submission to be published or selected for performance, and this time her _____ is likely to be _____.

   ◯ candor . . . dispelled

   ◯ anticipation . . . piqued

   ◯ enthusiasm . . . dampened

   ◯ optimism . . . vindicated

   ◯ awareness . . . clouded

30. His opponent found it extremely frustrating that the governor's solid support from the voting public was not eroded by his _____ of significant issues.

    ◯ exaggeration

    ◯ misapprehension

    ◯ discussion

    ◯ selection

    ◯ acknowledgment

Directions: In each of the following questions, a related pair of words or phrases is followed by five pairs of words or phrases. Select the pair that best expresses a relationship similar to that expressed in the original pair.

31. ELECTRICITY : WIRE ::

    ◯ fluid : pipe

    ◯ car : highway

    ◯ river : bank

    ◯ light : bulb

    ◯ music : instrument

32. SCOLD : BERATE ::

    ◯ predict : foresee

    ◯ threaten : impend

    ◯ counsel : advise

    ◯ retreat : retire

    ◯ respect : venerate

33. PLUMMET : DESCEND ::

    ◯ kick : boot

    ◯ whirl : turn

    ◯ indicate : show

    ◯ decorate : nullify

    ◯ begin : conclude

34. RIG : TEAM ::

    ◯ train : locomotive

    ◯ steamer : piston

    ◯ sled : rail

    ◯ car : truck

    ◯ windjammer : crew

35. INTEREST : ENTHRALL ::

    ◯ corrupt : tempt

    ◯ squeeze : crush

    ◯ buoy : undergird

    ◯ abstain : surrender

    ◯ reproach : offend

36. RECANT : BELIEF ::

    ◯ repeat : catechism

    ◯ reincarnate : soul

    ◯ perjure : axiom

    ◯ vacillate : vow

    ◯ repeal : law

37. ENLISTMENT : CONSCRIPTION ::

    ◯ rapprochement : arbitration

    ◯ surrender : bombardment

    ◯ resignation : dismissal

    ◯ contemplation : instruction

    ◯ acceptance : rejection

38. CEPHALIC : SKULL ::

    ◯ notable : achievement

    ◯ cylindrical : vertebrae

    ◯ neural : nerves

    ◯ angular : scapula

    ◯ audible : apparition

39. COBBLER : LEATHER ::

    ◯ chandler : wax

    ◯ executrix : paper

    ◯ actor : words

    ◯ cartwright : wheels

    ◯ prosthetist : limbs

40. INFLAMMABLE : IGNITED ::

    ◯ fragile : shattered

    ◯ flexible : broken

    ◯ somber : mourned

    ◯ famous : plagiarized

    ◯ small : magnified

41. TRUSS : SUPPORT ::

    ◯ calcium : bone

    ◯ fence : barrier

    ◯ tile : patio

    ◯ wood : burn

    ◯ bridge : water

42. REEL : TAPE ::

    ◯ ball : string

    ◯ turntable : record

    ◯ tire : wheel

    ◯ skein : yarn

    ◯ spool : thread

43. SHINGLE : ROOF ::

    ◯ rind : melon

    ◯ armor : knight

    ◯ feather : wing

    ◯ patch : cloth

    ◯ blanket : bed

44. LEGERDEMAIN : MAGICIAN ::

    ◯ rhetoric : orator

    ◯ baggage : immigrant

    ◯ justice : lawyer

    ◯ map : cartographer

    ◯ tractor : farmer

45. INDISPUTABLE : QUESTION ::
    - ○ unlikely : know
    - ○ amoral : perform
    - ○ incredible : prove
    - ○ immutable : change
    - ○ insoluble : submerge

46. UNSCATHED : DAMAGE ::
    - ○ ameliorated : improvement
    - ○ obliterated : invisibility
    - ○ rolled : smoothness
    - ○ shaken : homogeneity
    - ○ arid : dampness

47. PROTRACTION : DURATION::
    - ○ extension : length
    - ○ retraction : instant
    - ○ corruption : truth
    - ○ taxation : wealth
    - ○ altercation : shape

48. CHARACTERIZATION : PARODY ::
    - ○ serialization : novel
    - ○ drama : musical
    - ○ theater : vaudeville
    - ○ saga : epic
    - ○ portrait : caricature

49. EARTH : KNOLL ::
    - ○ cells : prison
    - ○ sand : dune
    - ○ nuclei : atom
    - ○ eggs : nest
    - ○ hair : head

50. ATROPHY : INACTIVITY ::
    - ○ resistance : timidity
    - ○ frown : anger
    - ○ growth : youth
    - ○ rot : refrigeration
    - ○ debt : overspending

51. NOD : ASSENT ::
    - ○ glance : beneficence
    - ○ shudder : rudeness
    - ○ wink : mystification
    - ○ shrug : indifference
    - ○ frown : capriciousness

52. IRK : SOOTHING ::
    - ○ inspire : elevating
    - ○ support : undermining
    - ○ provoke : irritating
    - ○ denounce : vilifying
    - ○ laud : conciliating

53. VEGETATE : ACTIVE ::

    ○ resist : beaten

    ○ mope : gloomy

    ○ grow : small

    ○ hassle : obnoxious

    ○ accept : questioning

54. PROPONENT : THEORY ::

    ○ nonbeliever : sin

    ○ traitor : country

    ○ adherent : belief

    ○ attorney : law

    ○ scientist : hypothesis

55. species : organism ::

    ○ specialty : physician

    ○ origin : idea

    ○ language : foreigner

    ○ genre : literature

    ○ family : ancestry

56. DISCHARGED : SOLDIER ::

    ○ fired : cannon

    ○ graduated : student

    ○ appointed : judge

    ○ transferred : employee

    ○ docked : salary

57. CUT : LACERATION ::

    ○ park : place

    ○ slit : gap

    ○ knife : separation

    ○ hole : puncture

    ○ boil : blister

58. OUTFOX : STRATEGY ::

    ○ outdo : trickery

    ○ defeat : stamina

    ○ outlast : force

    ○ victimize : terror

    ○ outrun : speed

59. COAX : BLANDISHMENTS ::

    ○ amuse : platitudes

    ○ compel : threats

    ○ deter : tidings

    ○ batter : insults

    ○ exercise : antics

60. TITLED : NOBLE ::

    ○ elected : candidate

    ○ acclaimed : artist

    ○ commissioned : officer

    ○ deposed : ruler

    ○ initiated : argument

Directions: Each passage in this group is followed by questions based on its content. After reading a passage, choose the best answer to each question. Answer all questions following a passage on the basis of what is stated or implied in that passage.

Declassification of government documents has shed new light on the events comprising the Cuban Missile Crisis of October 1962. Prior to the accessibility of these records, the only sources

(5) of account of the Crisis for scholars and historians were the personal memoirs and narratives of the officials who served under Kennedy and Khrushchev during this period.

Many of the declassified documents are

(10) transcriptions and notes of meetings between members of the CIA and President Kennedy's Cabinet, as well the President himself. The revelations in these documents have demonstrated the inadvertent inaccuracies and intended obscurities

(15) inherent in the first-person narratives of the Crisis, and have aided historians from all three countries involved in the crisis to get a more authentic representation of what truly transpired, and for what reasons. Of perhaps the most interest to historians

(20) are declassified correspondences between John F. Kennedy and Nikita Khruschev that challenge the idea that the height of the crisis extended only over the course of thirteen days. Indeed, these letters indicate that the crisis was far from resolved by

(25) Khruschev's October 28 decision to withdraw the Soviet missiles from Cuba; instead it endured far into the following month, while America slept fitfully under the illusion of peace.

61. The author is mainly concerned with

○ petitioning the government to make all classified documents of historic interest accessible to the general public.

○ discounting the sense of danger many Americans felt during the Cuban Missile Crisis.

○ revealing a calculated deception perpetrated by members of Kennedy's Cabinet.

○ illustrating how previously accepted ideas based on hearsay are being refuted by concrete evidence.

○ portraying in detail the events that transpired during the Cuban Missile Crisis.

62. According to the passage, which of the following statements is/are true of the Cuban Missile Crisis?

I. The Crisis is still shrouded in mystery.

II. The memoirs of those closely involved in the Crisis were not entirely factual.

III. The Crisis spanned thirteen tense days.

○ I only

○ II only

○ III only

○ I and II only

○ II and III only

63. The author's use of the phrase "inadvertent inaccuracies and intended obscurities" suggests all of the following EXCEPT

○ historical record is often skewed by human perception.

○ the revision of the Missile Crisis history is not an anomaly.

○ every politician deals in deception and prevarication.

○ details of the Crisis were purposely omitted or vague.

○ memory is incapable of recapturing the full details of an event.

Two of the most revered poets in American history, Walt Whitman and Emily Dickinson, are seemingly a study in contrast. But the nature in which both nineteenth-century poets chose to lead (5) their lives, which has deceivingly set them apart in the eyes of many historians, is actually their greatest similarity. Whitman's energetic wanderings around the United States and his informal, inquisitive disposition was directly reflected in his (10) style of verse and subject matter. He was a self-proclaimed man of the people, larger than life, interested in breaking down social preconceptions and boundaries, using his explorations of reality and the world at large in an attempt to translate (15) the language of the universal soul. As he was open to the world, so was his style of poetry; rambling and unconstrained, yet accessible. While Whitman's style was a mirror of his external forays, Emily Dickinson's travels into the dark (20) inner realms echoed throughout her writings. Where Whitman blazed an ample path for the masses, the introspective Dickinson beckoned them to get lost in her spare verse. Deftly picking and choosing her words, her vivid, aphoristic style (25) was the distillation of a life spent in solitary contemplation and experimentation with form.

The common bond shared between Whitman and Dickinson was each poet's obsessive drive for self-discovery. Though both poets' explorations (30) into meaning took them on two very different journeys, the courage required for those personal voyages was tantamount, and the resulting work was an unconventional brilliance that still exerts its influence upon American poetry to this day.

64. Which of the following best describes the author's attitude toward Dickinson and Whitman?

○ Unwarranted esteem

○ Justified admiration

○ Feigned interest

○ Undisguised contempt

○ Undue criticism

65. The "greatest similarity" the author refers to in line 7 is the poets'

○ introverted natures.

○ fondness for travel.

○ ceaseless explorations.

○ disdain for other art.

○ lack of formal education.

66. It can be inferred from the passage that

○ Whitman's poetry has more relevance today than Dickinson's.

○ Walt Whitman and Emily Dickinson did not get along.

○ Emily Dickinson's subject matter is more profound than Whitman's.

○ Emily Dickinson was a reclusive figure.

○ Walt Whitman enjoyed more success in his life than Dickinson.

A main component of NASA's search for evidence of life on Mars is the identification of biosignatures. The most common of these indicative markers of extant or extinct life are carbonate

(5) minerals, which are formed when carbon dioxide in the atmosphere reacts with other minerals and liquid water. A widely held belief among astrobiologists is that proof of running or standing liquid water can be construed as diagnostic evidence of

(10) the existence of life. It has been established that a large portion of the red planet's surface contains areas of frozen water, leading some scientists to theorize that the climate of ancient Mars was hotter and wetter than today, with a greenhouse-

(15) like atmosphere heavy with carbon dioxide. In this type of atmosphere, the existence of vast oceans similar to that of Earth would have been a very real possibility. Images of the landscape of Mars have lent support to these theories. Massive

(20) surface erosions resembling the Grand Canyon and land features that appear to be dried-up sea floor suggest that liquid water was indeed present on Mars at one point in the planet's history. But recent findings on the planet paint a different

(25) picture. If this model of ancient Mars were true, there should be a significant carbonate presence on the planet, but this is not the case. Though trace carbonates have been identified, the amounts are not commensurate with the prolonged exis-

(30) tence of large bodies of flowing liquid water. These curious findings support other scientific theories that purport that Mars was never warm and wet, and that except for a few very brief cataclysmic instances in its history, Mars has always

(35) been a frozen planet, at least on the surface. However, if this proves to be true, it does not necessarily preclude the existence of life on the red planet. Indeed, a critical flaw in the extraterrestrial search for biosignatures like carbonates is that we

(40) are applying traditional criteria for diagnostic markers of life on Earth to another planet, and as new discoveries are teaching us, our understanding of life on our own planet is limited, and accordingly, so is our index of biosignatures. For

(45) example, microscopic life forms have recently been found in some of the most extreme temperatures and environments on our planet that scientists previously believed were completely inhospitable to the support of life. Evidence of

(50) rock-eating microbes has been discovered almost a mile beneath the ocean floor, and living in the seemingly dead deep-freeze of Antarctic ice. Elsewhere, other microbes have been found thriving in caustic environments of toxic gas, and

(55) swimming in scorching sulfur pools. Such findings contradict the traditional idea that a specified, delicate set of circumstances is necessary for the development and sustenance of life. Ironically enough, this leads us to the conclusion that before

(60) we can embark upon a truly effective search for life on other planets, we must start with an exhaustive one right here on Earth.

67. The primary purpose of the passage is to

○ describe different astrobiological theories about the history of Mars.

○ dispute the possibility of the existence of any life form on Mars.

○ detail the extraterrestrial implications of new life-form discoveries for Earth.

○ offer an alternate strategy for effectively identifying signs of extraterrestrial life.

○ illustrate the uses and limitations of biosignatures as a means of inferring extraterrestrial life.

68. The author indicates that the discovery of very few carbonates on the surface of Mars mainly served to

   ○ support the idea that the climate of Mars was once warm and wet.

   ○ prove incontrovertibly that life has never existed on Mars.

   ○ prompt astrobiologists to turn their attention to Earth for answers.

   ○ cast doubt on a popular theory about the climate of ancient Mars.

   ○ spawn an entirely new theory about the history of Mars.

69. In the context of the passage, which of the following best describes the author's opinion on the astrobiologists' "extraterrestrial search for biosignatures" (lines 38–39)?

   ○ The search is an investigation of an exigent nature.

   ○ The search is an interesting endeavor somewhat circumscribed in scope.

   ○ The search is a nonsensical waste of money and effort.

   ○ The search is critical to better understanding our own planet's history.

   ○ The search is a quest fueled by suspicious motives.

70. According to the passage, which of the following statements is/are true of Mars?

   I.   There are carbonate minerals present on its surface.

   II. It once had a greenhouse-like atmosphere.

   III. It shares geological similarities with Earth.

   ○ I only

   ○ II only

   ○ I and II only

   ○ I and III only

   ○ I, II, and III

71. All of the following statements can be inferred from the examples of the "new discoveries" on Earth (line 42) EXCEPT

   ○ the ice on Mars is possibly a biosignature.

   ○ scientific knowledge is constantly being revised.

   ○ it is possible that life may be found deep beneath the surface of Mars.

   ○ bacterial life is much heartier and persistent than previously realized.

   ○ carbonates are not applicable as a biosignature on other planets

72. Which of the following details, if added to the passage, would best support the theory that Mars was never wet or warm?

    ○ The erosion on the surface of Mars may have been forged by flash floods created from the fiery impact of huge asteroids covered in ice.

    ○ The apparent canyons and sea floors were formed by years of superheated flowing lava.

    ○ A huge asteroid impact caused the carbon dioxide gas in the Martian atmosphere to dissipate into space.

    ○ Carbonate levels similar to that on the surface of Mars have been discovered in a riverbed in Spain.

    ○ Fossilized evidence of Earth-like flora has been uncovered near Mars's north pole.

73. The function of the passage's final sentence is to

    ○ summarize the main points made about biosignatures in the passage.

    ○ propose a radical idea concerning the search for signs of extraterrestrial life.

    ○ draw a conclusion from the examples given in the two preceding sentences that applies to the entire passage.

    ○ disparage the conventional thinking of many of those who work in the field of astrobiology.

    ○ reiterate the idea that searching for biosignatures on Mars is a pointless task.

74. It can be inferred from the passage that which of the following would be considered an extraterrestrial biosignature?

    I.   A sedimentary fossil

    II. Amino acids associated with life on Earth

    III. Apparent surface erosion caused by a liquid

    ○ I only

    ○ II only

    ○ I and II only

    ○ I and III only

    ○ I, II, and III

Light has been used as a beacon to mariners for thousands of years, for as long as man has taken to the sea. From the first primitive light beacons evolved the modern lighthouse, found on almost
(5) every waterway and coast in the world. To the uneducated eye each of these lighthouses, despite their distinct locations, seem to be irrelevant variations on a *homogeneous* design. However, nothing could be further from the truth; from
(10) height to lenses, each lighthouse is as unique as the landscape that surrounds it.

There is not one feature of a lighthouse that is arbitrary. By day, the varying color patterns painted on lighthouses help sailors
(15) distinguish their location along the coastline. These patterns, known as "daymarks," are usually a combination of white, black, or red, can be painted in broad bands or spirals, and none is alike.
(20) The earliest modern lighthouses employed a catoptric light system that used parabolic silver mirrors to reflect lamplight into a concentrated beam. Often, this bowl- or cone-shaped reflector would be made to spin around the lamp, rotating

(25) the beam in the "searchlight" manner typical of many lighthouses. An everyday example of a catoptric light system can be found in a common household flashlight. In 1822, a revolutionary, multiprismatic lens designed by Jean Augustin

(30) Fresnel ushered in the dioptric optical system for lighthouses, able to produce a five-times more powerful beam using the same light source as the catoptric system. Instead of reflecting the light, the Fresnel lens, which is actually a series of

(35) concentric rings of segmental lenses, refracted it. By 1860, every existing lighthouse in the United States had been converted to a Fresnel lens, and to fully take advantage of this more powerful light beam, lighthouses built after the lens's introduc-

(40) tion stood much taller than their predecessors. Later, an even more effective optical system known as the catadioptric system was developed, which was a hybrid of the two earlier systems. By 1900, most lighthouses began to convert to electricity and use

(45) incandescent bulbs; prior to that, lanterns fueled by wood, coal, or oil served as a lighthouse's source light for the optical system.

The patterns of light beams emitted from these three different systems are as varied and individual

(50) as daymarker patterns. Each lighthouse has its own characteristic intervals of light and eclipse. These intervals, known as nightmarks or signatures, are set in specific patterns defined with such names as *flashing, occulting, group flashing,* or

(55) *group occulting.* Beacons that are characterized as "flashing" have intervals of darkness that are longer in duration than the intervals of light; "occulting" lights display the opposite of this pattern. "Group flashing" or "group occulting"

(60) light patterns are simple groups of small flashes or eclipses. Obviously, there is no flash-eclipse pattern to a steady, uninterrupted "fixed" light, but rare patterns known as *fixed flashing* do exist; in such patterns, the beacon's light fluctuates

(65) between a higher and lower beam intensity.

What distinguishes each lighthouse is the rate of repetition for the intervals of flash and eclipse or fixed flashing. This unique repetition rate is called a *period*, and each lighthouse's period is charted in

(70) United States Coast Guard publications known as *light lists*. In addition to a lighthouse's nightmarks, its daymarks are included in these charts as well. Smart sailors still value these charts because they know that long after their fragile radios and radar

(75) rust into uselessness, the stalwart lighthouses will still be standing tall.

75. The author's primary purpose is to

○ relate a charming tale.

○ detail the specific functions of a lighthouse.

○ illustrate a point made by the author.

○ offer an unbiased opinion.

○ enumerate lighthouse facts.

76. Based on the passage, which of the following is probably NOT true of lighthouses?

○ The earliest lighthouses were bonfires built on the shore to guide fishermen back to the beach.

○ Up until very recently, the capturing and defending of lighthouses was often of strategic naval importance during a war.

○ The invention of the incandescent bulb lessened the duties of a lighthouse keeper.

○ A lighthouse's "period" is randomly assigned from a list.

○ The tallest standing lighthouse has a catadioptric light system.

77. Based on information from the passage, a pattern defined as "group fixed occulting" would consist of

    ◯ a group of small fluctuations in light intensity.

    ◯ a group of small intervals of darkness that last longer than the intervals of light.

    ◯ a group of small intervals of light that last longer than the intervals of darkness.

    ◯ a group of small intervals of light and darkness that are equal in duration.

    ◯ This pattern is not possible.

78. In line 8, *homogenous* most closely means

    ◯ different.

    ◯ uniform.

    ◯ sturdy.

    ◯ colorful.

    ◯ antiquated.

79. According to the passage, which of the following statements is/are true of catoptric light systems?

    I.   They were installed in lighthouses built prior to the 1820s.
    II. They use refraction to create a concentrated light beam.
    III. Only a few remain in American lighthouses today.

    ◯ I only

    ◯ III only

    ◯ I and II only

    ◯ I and III only

    ◯ I, II, and III

80. Based on the passage, it can be inferred that all of the following employ either a catoptric or dioptric light system EXCEPT a

    ◯ headlight.

    ◯ flashlight.

    ◯ film projector.

    ◯ lantern.

    ◯ laser.

81. According to the passage, an operational lighthouse must

    ◯ be manned by lighthouse keepers.

    ◯ have a generic period.

    ◯ be of at least a certain height.

    ◯ possess distinct daymarks and nightmarks.

    ◯ use a catadioptric optical system.

82. Based on the final sentence of the passage, it can be inferred that the author would describe a sailor who relies solely on technology as a means of navigation as

    ◯ a typical example of the contemporary mariner.

    ◯ better equipped for adversity than his predecessors.

    ◯ overconfident in his own skills.

    ◯ an incompetent novice.

    ◯ ill-prepared for an equipment failure.

It is very hard to prove or disprove the existence of the Loch Ness Monster because of the characteristics of the very loch that it supposedly inhabits. Loch Ness has cold, murky waters that

(5) yield almost zero visibility, a surface area of almost 22 square miles, and depths approaching 1,000 feet. Though the oldest reference to the monster can be traced back as far as A.D. 565, the present incarnation of "Nessie" first caught the modern

(10) public's eye in April of 1933, shortly after local hotel owners Mr. and Mrs. John Mackay reportedly spotted, in their own words, "an enormous animal rolling and plunging." They detailed their incident to the *Inverness Courier,* and suddenly the

(15) Loch Ness monster was plucked from historical obscurity to be reborn in the pages of the world news. Since then there have been innumerable hoaxes, unexplained sightings, and serious scientific investigations which have turned up some

(20) interesting, yet inconclusive evidence. Recently, after the most technologically advanced search to date, a group of researchers working for the BBC concluded that the creature simply does not exist. But the daunting evidence of the researchers has

(25) seemingly not deterred the legions of tourists and part-time Nessie hunters. Apparently, as long as there exists the slightest possibility of Nessie being real, the hotels around the Loch, as they have been since 1933, will be full of intrigued souls hoping

(30) to catch just a glimpse of a real-life monster.

83. Which of the following best describes the author's attitude toward the existence of the Loch Ness Monster?

   ◯ Enthusiastic belief

   ◯ Detached skepticism

   ◯ Tepid neutrality

   ◯ Fanatical incredulousness

   ◯ Interested detachment

84. It can be inferred from the passage that the only way the mystery of the Loch Ness Monster will be solved is if

   ◯ Loch Ness is completely drained.

   ◯ it is somehow proven that 99 percent of the unexplained sightings were complete fabrications.

   ◯ an intensive investigation is performed using the most cutting edge technology.

   ◯ it is revealed that the creature originally spotted in A.D. 565 was actually a large otter.

   ◯ a small whale washes up on the shores of the Loch.

85. The author includes the detail that the Mackays were local hotel owners to primarily suggest that they

   ◯ were familiar with the area.

   ◯ had seen the monster before but never reported it.

   ◯ fabricated the story to drum up business.

   ◯ knew of the original Loch Ness monster stories.

   ◯ were regular, everyday people.

The Recording Industry Association of America (RIAA) estimates music piracy is the source of over four billion dollars each year in lost profits. Though *music piracy* is a general term that

(5) encompasses a broad array of illegal practices involving the duplication and distribution of recorded music (such as counterfeiting and bootlegging for personal monetary profit), the one area of piracy that occupies the majority of

(10) the nation's attention is the contentious practice of music file sharing on peer-to-peer (P2P) websites.

Despite the RIAA's recent crackdown on illegal file-sharing by levying heavy fines against offenders, P2P websites are still thriving. Though (15) there is a small minority of the file-sharing population who truly believe they should not have to pay to listen to their favorite music, this percentage hardly occupies the lion's share of illegal downloaders. So why are so many people (20) breaking the law? The RIAA equates the illegal downloading of an album of music to the act of shoplifting that same album from a record store, and they have a logically sound argument. However, the devious act of physically pilfering (25) something from a record store, and all the tangible consequences it entails, is hardly present in the action of pressing a keyboard button from the *repose* of one's home.

86. The author's primary purpose is to

    ◯ describe a contrasting viewpoint.

    ◯ explain a popular practice.

    ◯ offer an extraordinary insight.

    ◯ cite relevant facts.

    ◯ challenge a popular opinion.

87. The author states that all of the following are true of file-sharing EXCEPT

    ◯ it is conducted on peer-to-peer websites.

    ◯ it is an illegal practice that is subject to fines.

    ◯ it is the sole source of over four billion dollars in lost revenues.

    ◯ the RIAA considers the act on par with shoplifting.

    ◯ it is the most notorious of all forms of music piracy.

88. *Repose*, as used in the passage, most nearly means

    ◯ tranquility.

    ◯ stress.

    ◯ anonymity.

    ◯ obviousness.

    ◯ kitchen.

The four Galilean satellites of Jupiter probably experienced early, intense bombardment. Thus, the very ancient surface of Callisto remains scarred by impact craters. The younger, more (5) varied surface of Ganymede reveals distinct light and dark areas, the light areas featuring networks of intersecting grooves and ridges, probably resulting from later iceflows. The impact sites of Europa have been almost completely erased, (10) apparently by water outflowing from the interior and instantly forming vast, low, frozen seas. Satellite photographs of Io, the closest of the four to Jupiter, were revelatory. They showed a landscape dominated by volcanos, many erupting, (15) making Io the most tectonically active object in the solar system. Since a body as small as Io cannot supply the energy for such activity, the accepted explanation has been that, forced into a highly eccentric orbit, Io is engulfed by tides stem- (20) ming from a titanic contest between the other three Galilean moons and Jupiter.

89. According to the passage, which of the following is probably NOT true of the surface of Io?

    ○ It is characterized by intense tectonic activity.

    ○ Its volcanos have resulted from powerful tides.

    ○ It is younger than the surface of Callisto.

    ○ It is distinguished by many impact craters.

    ○ It has apparently not been shaped by internal force.

90. It can be inferred that the geologic features found in the light areas of Ganymede were probably formed

    ○ subsequent to the features found in the dark areas.

    ○ in an earlier period than those in the dark areas.

    ○ at roughly the same time as the features found in the dark areas.

    ○ primarily by early bombardment.

    ○ by the satellite's volcanic activity.

91. It can be inferred that the author regards current knowledge about the satellites of Jupiter as

    ○ insignificant and disappointing.

    ○ grossly outdated.

    ○ complete and satisfactory.

    ○ ambiguous and contradictory.

    ○ persuasive though incomplete.

A pioneering figure in modern sociology, French social theorist Emile Durkheim examined the role of societal cohesion on emotional well-being. Believing that scientific methods should be applied
(5) to the study of society, Durkheim studied the level of integration of various social formations and the impact that such cohesion had on individuals within the group. He postulated that social groups with high levels of integration serve to buffer their
(10) members from frustrations and tragedies that could otherwise lead to desperation and self-destruction. Integration, in Durkheim's view, generally arises through shared activities and values.

Durkheim distinguished between *mechanical*
(15) *solidarity* and *organic solidarity* in classifying integrated groups. *Mechanical solidarity* dominates in groups in which individual differences are minimized and group devotion to a common aim is high. Durkheim identified *mechanical solidarity*
(20) among groups with little division of labor and high rates of cultural similarity, such as among more traditional and geographically isolated groups. *Organic solidarity*, in contrast, prevails in groups with high levels of individual differences,
(25) such as those with a highly specialized division of labor. In such groups, individual differences are a powerful source of connection, rather than of division. Because people engage in highly differentiated ways of life, they are by necessity
(30) interdependent. In these societies, there is greater freedom from some external controls, but such freedom occurs in concert with the interdependence of individuals, not in conflict with it.

Durkheim realized that societies may take
(35) many forms and consequently that group allegiance can manifest itself in a variety of ways. In both types of societies outlined above, however, Durkheim stressed that adherence to a common set of assumptions about the world was
(40) a necessary prerequisite for maintaining group integrity and avoiding social decay.

92. The author is primarily concerned with

   ○ supporting a specific approach to the study of the integration of social groups.

   ○ comparing different ways that group dynamics maintain allegiance among group members.

   ○ illustrating how a highly specialized division of labor can protect individuals from depression.

   ○ determining what type of society will best suit an individual's emotional needs.

   ○ contrasting a traditional view of a social phenomenon with a more recent one.

93. The passage contrasts *mechanical solidarity* with *organic solidarity* along which of the following parameters?

   ○ The degree to which each relies on objective measures of group coherence

   ○ The manner and degree to which members are linked to the central group

   ○ The means by which each allows members to rebel against the group norm

   ○ The length of time that each has been used to describe the structure of societies

   ○ The effectiveness of each in serving the interests of its members

94. It can be inferred from the passage that

   ○ as societies develop, they progress from *organic solidarity* to *mechanical solidarity*.

   ○ group integration enables societies to mask internal differences to the external world.

   ○ Durkheim preferred *organic solidarity* to *mechanical solidarity*.

   ○ individuals from societies with high degrees of *organic solidarity* would be unable to communicate effectively with individuals from societies that rest on *mechanical solidarity*.

   ○ the presence of some type of group integration is more important for group perpetuation than the specific form in which it is manifest.

95. The passage states that *organic solidarity* predominates in societies with relatively high levels of intragroup dissimilarity because

   ○ it enables individual differences to be minimized.

   ○ it causes societies to become more highly specialized, thus aiding industrialization.

   ○ individuals who engage in highly specialized activities must rely on others to ensure that their basic needs are met.

   ○ these societies are at greater risk of being affected by social stressors.

   ○ these societies are more likely to engage in shared activities and values.

Directions: Each question below consists of a word printed in capital letters, followed by five words or phrases. Choose the word or phrase that is most nearly opposite in meaning to the word in capital letters.

Because some of the questions require you to distinguish fine shades of meaning, be sure to consider all the choices before deciding which one is best.

96. DIFFIDENT :

   ◯ indolent

   ◯ exigent

   ◯ apocryphal

   ◯ confident

   ◯ endemic

97. PHLEGMATIC :

   ◯ apathetic

   ◯ rustic

   ◯ excitable

   ◯ banal

   ◯ erudite

98. ENERVATE :

   ◯ energize

   ◯ engender

   ◯ dither

   ◯ inundate

   ◯ inure

99. IMPRECATION :

   ◯ arbitration

   ◯ benediction

   ◯ alleviation

   ◯ rejoinder

   ◯ proclivity

100. OPPROBRIUM :

   ◯ honor

   ◯ prudence

   ◯ scintilla

   ◯ umbrage

   ◯ ostentation

101. NOISOME :

   ◯ fragrant

   ◯ multifarious

   ◯ maudlin

   ◯ candid

   ◯ garrulous

102. CUPIDITY :

   ◯ hegemony

   ◯ intrepidity

   ◯ largess

   ◯ antipathy

   ◯ penury

103. COSSET :

- ⬯ lampoon
- ⬯ ossify
- ⬯ husband
- ⬯ advocate
- ⬯ challenge

104. LOQUACIOUS :

- ⬯ taciturn
- ⬯ obdurate
- ⬯ quiescent
- ⬯ sardonic
- ⬯ specious

105. PATHOGENIC :

- ⬯ diaphanous
- ⬯ trenchant
- ⬯ venerable
- ⬯ salubrious
- ⬯ sanguine

106. SATIATE :

- ⬯ prevaricate
- ⬯ kindle
- ⬯ disabuse
- ⬯ burnish
- ⬯ slake

107. PRODIGAL :

- ⬯ furtive
- ⬯ disparate
- ⬯ banal
- ⬯ irascible
- ⬯ frugal

108. FOMENT :

- ⬯ quash
- ⬯ mitigate
- ⬯ bolster
- ⬯ assuage
- ⬯ aggrandize

109. HETEROGENEOUS :

- ⬯ hoary
- ⬯ tangential
- ⬯ homogenous
- ⬯ unconscionable
- ⬯ monastic

110. VOLUBLE :

- ⬯ reticent
- ⬯ turgid
- ⬯ audacious
- ⬯ latent
- ⬯ tawdry

111. LUCID :

  ◯ endemic

  ◯ florid

  ◯ intrepid

  ◯ inchoate

  ◯ fanatical

112. LACHRYMOSE :

  ◯ perspicacious

  ◯ sanguine

  ◯ inimical

  ◯ surly

  ◯ glib

113. STOLID :

  ◯ erudite

  ◯ volatile

  ◯ ignoble

  ◯ wily

  ◯ judicious

114. ENGENDER :

  ◯ deface

  ◯ lionize

  ◯ palliate

  ◯ vex

  ◯ extinguish

115. TORPOR :

  ◯ polemic

  ◯ antipathy

  ◯ vim

  ◯ guile

  ◯ invective

116. EUPHONY :

  ◯ cacophony

  ◯ monotony

  ◯ chicanery

  ◯ cartography

  ◯ hyperbole

117. ZEAL :

  ◯ dissatisfaction

  ◯ coarseness

  ◯ apathy

  ◯ wrath

  ◯ impudence

118. ERRONEOUS :

  ◯ careful

  ◯ vigorous

  ◯ accurate

  ◯ convincing

  ◯ thoughtful

119. COGNIZANT :

  ◯ obsequious

  ◯ oblivious

  ◯ vigilant

  ◯ intangible

  ◯ unwise

120. TENTATIVE :

  ◯ permanent

  ◯ finite

  ◯ definite

  ◯ adjacent

  ◯ amiable

121. BAWDY :

  ◯ prudish

  ◯ superfluous

  ◯ gaunt

  ◯ ethereal

  ◯ legitimate

122. ABET :

  ◯ exaggerate

  ◯ arrange

  ◯ refuse

  ◯ deter

  ◯ confuse

123. DISPASSIONATE :

  ◯ sentient

  ◯ conspicuous

  ◯ compassionate

  ◯ partisan

  ◯ heedless

124. PANEGYRIC :

  ◯ defamatory essay

  ◯ formal monologue

  ◯ binding contract

  ◯ witty aside

  ◯ closing remark

125. PROLIX :

  ◯ recalcitrant

  ◯ unimportant

  ◯ obstinate

  ◯ diverse

  ◯ pithy

直角三角形

勾股定理 $a^2 + b^2 = c^2$

2次函数公式 ① $x^2 - y^2 = (x+y)(x-y)$ $\Rightarrow$ $x^2 - xy + xy - y^2$

$x^2 - y^2$

相互抵消

② $x^2 + 2xy + y^2 = (x+y)(x+y)$ $\Rightarrow$ $x^2 + xy + xy + y^2$

$\underline{2xy}$ $\Rightarrow x^2 + 2xy + y^2$

③ $x^2 - 2xy + y^2 = (x-y)(x-y)$ $\Rightarrow$ $x^2 - xy - xy - y^2$

$\underline{-2xy}$ $x^2 - 2xy + y^2$

圆

d: 直径 r: 半径

直径 = 两条半径之和.

周长: 2π乘以半径 或者 π乘以直径 $\Rightarrow 2\pi r / \pi d$

面积: π × 半径的平方 $\Rightarrow \pi r^2$

角度: 圆的内角和是 360°

O是圆心: 圆的中心点

n° 是圆的一个内角

B是A, C的中点.

$\dfrac{n°}{360} = \dfrac{ABC周长}{圆的周长} = \dfrac{OABC的面积}{圆的面积}$

①

a、b、c 就是三个内角

A、B、C 就是三个外角

#1 三角形 ✓

内角和 等于三个内角之和 (180度)
外角和 等于三个外角相加 (360度)

公式：$a+b+c=180°$ $A+B+C=360°$

► 一个外角等于两个与它不相邻的内角之和！

例如：$B=a+c$ $C=a+b$ $A=b+c$

◄ 面积公式 (S)：$S = \frac{1}{2}$ 底 × 高

锐角   直角   钝角 (作辅助线)

高 底   高   高

底   底   底

总结：任意两边之和 一定 大于第三条边 (如图)
$a+b>c$ $a+c>b$ $b+c>a$

a   b

c

#2 角度 ✓

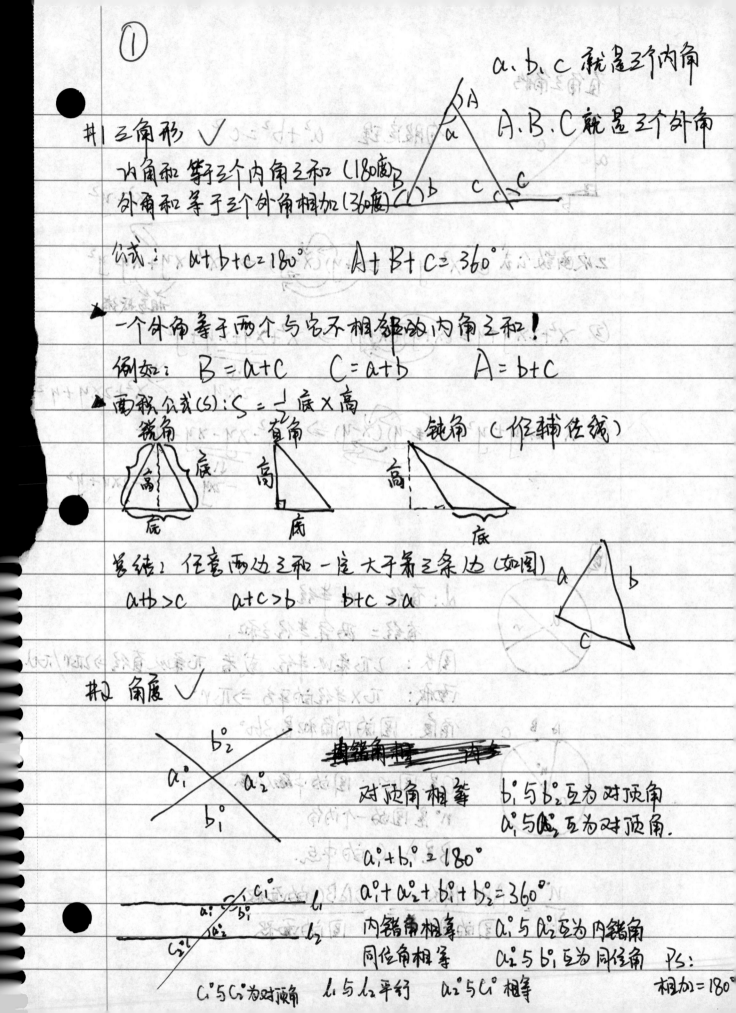

b_2
a_1 a_2
b_1

~~同错角相等~~   ~~内角~~

对顶角相等 b_1 与 b_2 互为对顶角
            a_1 与 a_2 互为对顶角.

$a_1+b_1=180°$

$a_1+a_2+b_1+b_2=360°$

c_1
a_1 c_1
a_2 b_1 l_1
b_2 l_2
c_2

内错角相等 a_1 与 b_2 互为内错角
同位角相等 a_2 与 b_1 互为同位角   PS：

c_1 与 c_2 为对顶角 l_1 与 l_2 平行 a_2 与 b_1 相等   相加 $=180°$

$$速度 = \frac{路程}{时间} \qquad 平均速度 = \frac{总路程}{总时间} \qquad 速率 =$$

$$(Ratio)速率 = \frac{A的速度}{B的速度} \qquad / \qquad 比率 = \frac{A的量}{B的量}$$

$$增加量/率 = \frac{现在的数量 - 之前的数量}{之前的数量} \times 100\%$$

$$~~下降率~~ = \frac{~~原来的~~ 过去的 - 现在的}{过去的}$$

$$下降率 = \frac{原先的 - 现在的}{原先的} \times 100\%$$

必背※ $\quad x \cdot x = x^2 \qquad$ 两个 x 相乘

$x^{-a} = \dfrac{1}{x^a} \qquad$ 把负号去掉 "x" 变成 "$\frac{1}{x}$" "a"是根 $\Rightarrow \dfrac{1}{x^a}$

$x^0 = 1 \qquad$ 所有数字的零次方都等于1（虚零除外）

因为不存在！！

$x^a x^b = x^{a+b} \quad \underline{(死记)}$

负数的奇数根都是负数 如：$(-1)^1 = -1 \quad (-2)^3 = -8$

$\underline{\underline{-2 \times (-2) \times (-2) = -}}$

负数的偶数根都是正数 如$(-2)^2 = 4 \quad (-3)^2 = 9$

$\underline{\underline{-3 \times (-3) = 9}}$

正方形面积公式(S): 边长的平方

$$S = a^2$$

长方形的面积公式(S): 长乘以宽

$$S = ab$$

平行四边形面积公式(S) 底乘以高

$$S = l \times h$$

梯形面积公式(S) $\frac{1}{2}$(上底+下底)乘以高

$$S = \frac{1}{2}(a+b) \times h$$

圆柱

体积 = π乘以半径的平方再乘以高 $\Rightarrow \pi r^2 h$

总面积 = 两倍的π乘以半径的平方 加上 两倍的π乘以半径再乘以高

$$2\pi r^2 + 2\pi r h$$

柱体 体积 = 长乘以宽再乘以高

$$= a \cdot b \cdot c$$

总面积 = 两倍的 (长乘宽加长乘高加宽乘高)

$$= 2(ab + ac + bc)$$

"私记!!!"

① $\sqrt{a} \times \sqrt{b} = \sqrt{ab}$

② $\dfrac{\sqrt{a}}{\sqrt{b}} = \sqrt{\dfrac{a}{b}}$

③ $a\sqrt{c} + b\sqrt{c} = (a+b)\sqrt{c}$

④ $\sqrt{a} + \sqrt{b} \neq \sqrt{a+b}$ （注意!!! $\sqrt{a}$ 加 $\sqrt{b}$ 不等于 $\sqrt{a+b}$）

⑤ $(\sqrt{a})^2 = a$

$a(b+c) = ab + ac$　　　　$|-x| = |x|$　　"$|x|$" 撤绝对值 = 正数

$nCk = \dfrac{n!}{k!(n-k)!}$　如：$2C6 = \dfrac{2}{6(2-6)} = -\dfrac{1}{12}$

$\dfrac{a+b}{c} = \dfrac{a}{c} + \dfrac{b}{c}$　　　　　斜率 "k"

组合值：$\dfrac{A \times B}{A+B}$

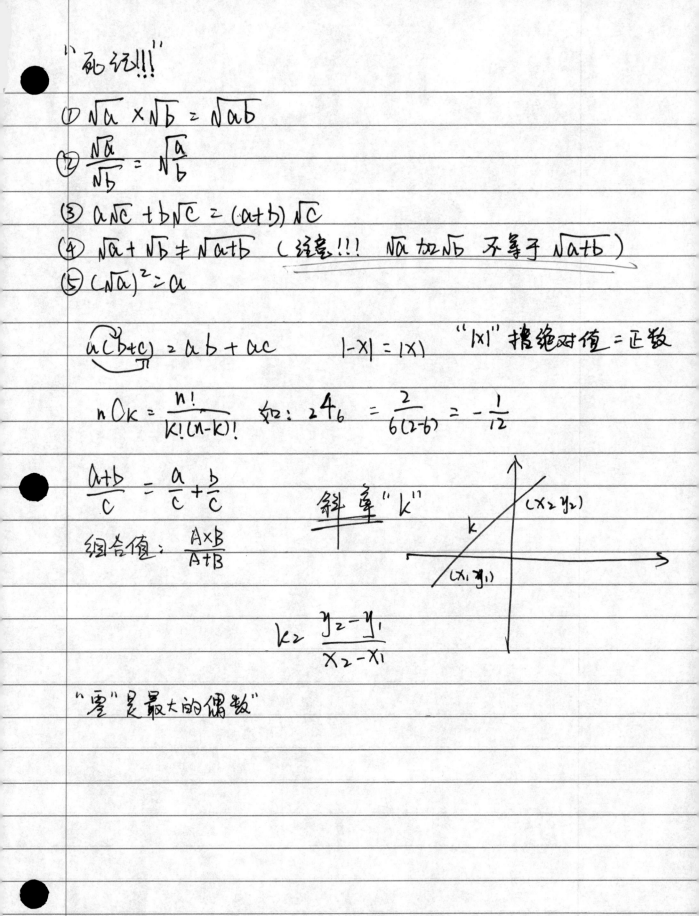

$k = \dfrac{y_2 - y_1}{x_2 - x_1}$

"零" 是最大的偶数

Use this sheet to help you remember your math content, and also be sure to make use of the Kaplan methods on the reverse side.

GRE*
KAPLAN
TEST PREP AND ADMISSIONS
*GRE is a registered trademark of Educational Testing Service.

TRIANGLES:

$x + y + z = 180$ (Interior angles)

$a + b + c = 360$ (Exterior angles)

$a = y + z;\ b = x + z;\ c = x + y$

$\text{Area} = \dfrac{1}{2}\text{ base} \times \text{height}$

Sum of any 2 sides > 3rd side

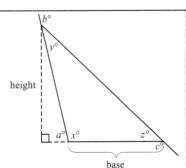

ANGLES:

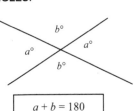

l_1 and l_2 are parallel

$a + b = 180$

COMMON FRACTION PERCENT EQUIVALENTS:

$\dfrac{1}{8} = 12\dfrac{1}{2}\%$ $\dfrac{1}{6} = 16\dfrac{2}{3}\%$

$\dfrac{3}{8} = 37\dfrac{1}{2}\%$ $\dfrac{1}{3} = 33\dfrac{1}{3}\%$

$\dfrac{5}{8} = 62\dfrac{1}{2}\%$ $\dfrac{2}{3} = 66\dfrac{2}{3}\%$

$\dfrac{7}{8} = 87\dfrac{1}{2}\%$ $\dfrac{5}{6} = 83\dfrac{1}{3}\%$

RIGHT TRIANGLES:

Side Ratios
(Pythagorean Triples)
3:4:5
5:12:13

$a^2 + b^2 = c^2$

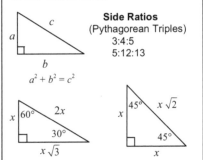

CIRCLES:

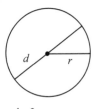 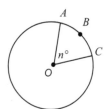

$d = 2r$
$C = 2\pi r$ or πd
$A = \pi r^2$
360° around

$\dfrac{n}{360} = \dfrac{\text{Arc } ABC}{\text{Circum.}} = \dfrac{\text{Area of sector } OABC}{\text{Area of circle } O}$

CLASSIC QUADRATICS:
$x^2 - y^2 = (x + y)(x - y)$
$x^2 + 2xy + y^2 = (x + y)(x + y)$
$x^2 - 2xy + y^2 = (x - y)(x - y)$

ORDER OF OPERATIONS:
PEMDAS—Parentheses, Exponents, Multiplication and Division, Addition and Subtraction

FOIL:
First, Outer, Inner, Last

QUADRILATERALS: Sum of interior angles = 360°

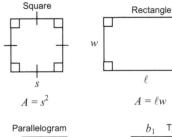

Square
$A = s^2$

Rectangle
$A = \ell w$

Parallelogram
$A = bh$

Trapezoid
$A = \dfrac{1}{2}(b_1 + b_2)h$

OTHER FORMULAS AND THINGS TO KNOW:

$\text{Speed} = \dfrac{\text{Distance}}{\text{Time}}$ $\text{Average} = \dfrac{\text{Sum of the terms}}{\text{Number of terms}}$ $\text{Average Speed} = \dfrac{\text{Total Distance}}{\text{Total Time}}$ $\text{Rate} = \dfrac{\text{Quantity of } A}{\text{Quantity of } B}$

$\%\text{ Increase} = \dfrac{\text{New Amount} - \text{Original Amount}}{\text{Original Amount}} \times 100\%$ $\%\text{ Decrease} = \dfrac{\text{Original Amount} - \text{New Amount}}{\text{Original Amount}} \times 100\%$

EXPONENT RULES:

$x \cdot x = x^2$ $(x^a)^b = x^{ab}$

$x^{-a} = \dfrac{1}{x^a}$ $\dfrac{x^a}{x^b} = x^{a-b}$

$x^0 = 1$ (negative)^{odd} = negative

$x^a x^b = x^{a+b}$ (negative)^{even} = positive

RADICAL RULES:

$\sqrt{a}\sqrt{b} = \sqrt{ab}$

$\dfrac{\sqrt{a}}{\sqrt{b}} = \sqrt{\dfrac{a}{b}}$

$a\sqrt{c} + b\sqrt{c} = (a+b)\sqrt{c}$

$\sqrt{a} + \sqrt{b} \neq \sqrt{a+b}$

$(\sqrt{a})^2 = a$

NUMBERS:

0 is an even integer.

1 is *not* prime.

2 is the lowest prime number.

Primes: 2, 3, 5, 7, 11, 13, etc.

Mode: the most common number(s) in a set

Median: the middle term in a set of ascending or descending numbers; when the set has an even number of numbers, the average of the two middle terms

Only (odd) × (odd) and (odd) + (even) yield odd numbers.

MISCELLANEOUS:

$a(b + c) = ab + ac$ $|-x| = |x|$ $x\% \text{ of } y = y\% \text{ of } x$

$_nC_k = \dfrac{n!}{k!(n-k)!}$ $\dfrac{a+b}{c} = \dfrac{a}{c} + \dfrac{b}{c}$ $\text{Combined Time} = \dfrac{A \times B}{A + B}$

UNIFORM SOLIDS:

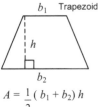

$V = \pi r^2 h$
$SA = 2\pi r^2 + 2\pi rh$

$V = \ell wh$
$SA = 2(\ell w + \ell h + wh)$

COORDINATE PLANE: In the *xy*-plane, the *y*-axis is vertical. and the *x*-axis is horizontal.

$\text{Slope} = \dfrac{y_2 - y_1}{x_2 - x_1}$

GG4061C

The Kaplan Method for GRE Issue Essays

1) Take the issue apart.
- Consider both sides of the issue in your own words.
2) Select the points you will make.
- Decide whether to agree or disagree, naming two to four reasons.
3) Organize, using Kaplan's Issue Essay template.
- In paragraph 1, restate the issue; agree or disagree.
- In paragraph 2, introduce a point of agreement or disagreement, with relevant detailed support.
- In paragraph 3, add a second point of agreement or disagreement, with relevant detailed support.
- In additional paragraphs, continue to bring in points of agreement or disagreement as time permits. (Time valve #1: skip if need be.)
- In the second-to-last paragraph, address an opposition to the argument and refute it with relevant detailed support. (Time valve #2: combine with conclusion if need be.)
- In the last paragraph, conclude with a final statement about your stance on the issue.
4) Type your essay.
5) Proofread.

The Kaplan Method for GRE Argument Essays

1) Take the argument apart.
- Determine the conclusion, evidence, and assumptions.
- Consider the circumstances under which the assumptions would be valid/invalid.
- Consider what would strengthen the argument.
2) Select the points you will make.
- Decide which of the argument's weaknesses are critical, and for which of those you can marshal evidence.
3) Organize, using Kaplan's Argument Essay template.
- In paragraph 1, put the argument in your own words.
- In paragraph 2, point out a flaw in the author's argument and explain why it is questionable.
- In paragraph 3, identify another point of fault; explain.
- In additional paragraphs, describe other points of fault, as time permits. (Time valve #1: skip if need be.)
- In the second-to-last paragraph, describe a piece of evidence that would strengthen the argument, if this evidence were true. (Time valve #2: combine with conclusion if need be.)
- In the final paragraph, conclude by stating that without such evidence the argument does not convince you.
4) Type your essay.
5) Proofread.

The Kaplan Method for GRE Problem Solving

1) Study the question stem and make sure you know what is being asked.
2) Study the answer choices for hints on how to approach the question.
3) Choose an approach or combine approaches:
   a) Use a strategy.
   b) Do the straightforward math.
   c) Guess strategically.
4) Read the question again, making sure your answer makes sense.

The Kaplan Method for GRE Quantitative Comparisons

1) Study the centered information and the columns.
2) Choose an approach or combine approaches.
   a) Use a strategy.
   b) Do the straightforward math.
   c) Guess strategically.

The Kaplan Method for GRE Reading Comprehension

1) Read the passage, write a Passage Map, and note Topic, Scope, and Purpose.
2) Read the question stem and determine which type of question it is.
3) Answer the question, following the Kaplan strategies for that question type.
   a) On Global questions, use your Passage Map, Topic, Scope, and Purpose/Main Idea to prephrase an answer.
   b) On Detail questions, use your Passage Map to locate the relevant text in the passage. If necessary, read that portion of the passage again. Then prephrase a response.
   c) On Inference questions, search for the answer choice that follows from the passage.
   d) On Logic questions, determine the author's intentions in a particular part of the passage, and prephrase an answer.

The Kaplan Method for Analogies

1) Build a bridge between the stem words.
2) Plug the bridge into the answer choices.
3) Adjust the bridge if necessary.

The Kaplan Method for One-Blank Sentence Completions

1) Read the sentence, looking for clues.
2) Predict an answer.
3) Select the answer choice that most closely matches your prediction.
4) See whether the sentence makes sense with your choice inserted.

The Kaplan Method for Two-Blank Sentence Completions

1) Read the sentence, looking for clues.
2) Decide which blank is easier to predict, and make a prediction for that blank.
3) Eliminate choices that don't match your prediction.
4) Read the remaining choices into your sentence and decide which choice works for both blanks.

The Kaplan Method for Antonyms (when you can define the stem word)

1) Define the stem word.
2) Predict it's opposite.
3) Select the choice that most closely matches your prediction.

The Kaplan Method for Antonyms (when you cannot define the stem word)

1) Find opposites of each answer choice.
2) Eliminate choices with no clear opposite.
3) Select the answer choice whose opposite is most likely to be the meaning of the stem word.

ANSWERS AND EXPLANATIONS

1. B	26. E	51. D	76. D	101. A
2. C	27. A	52. B	77. E	102. C
3. D	28. E	53. E	78. B	103. E
4. C	29. D	54. C	79. A	104. A
5. E	30. B	55. D	80. D	105. D
6. A	31. A	56. B	81. D	106. B
7. D	32. E	57. B	82. E	107. E
8. C	33. B	58. E	83. B	108. A
9. D	34. A	59. B	84. A	109. C
10. C	35. B	60. C	85. C	110. A
11. E	36. E	61. D	86. B	111. D
12. D	37. C	62. B	87. C	112. B
13. E	38. C	63. C	88. A	113. B
14. A	39. A	64. B	89. D	114. E
15. B	40. A	65. C	90. A	115. C
16. C	41. B	66. D	91. E	116. A
17. A	42. E	67. E	92. B	117. C
18. C	43. B	68. D	93. B	118. C
19. D	44. A	69. B	94. E	119. B
20. B	45. D	70. D	95. C	120. C
21. A	46. E	71. E	96. D	121. A
22. D	47. A	72. A	97. C	122. D
23. E	48. E	73. C	98. A	123. D
24. C	49. B	74. C	99. B	124. A
25. E	50. E	75. C	100. A	125. E

DIAGNOSTIC TOOL

Tally up your score and write down your results below.

Total

Total Correct: _____ out of 125 correct

Percentage Correct: # you got right × 100 ÷ 125: _____

By Question Type

Sentence Completions: _____ out of 30 correct

Analogies: _____ out of 29 correct

Antonyms: _____ out of 34 correct

Reading Comprehension: _____ out of 30 correct

DIAGNOSE YOUR RESULTS

Look back at the questions you got wrong and think back on your experience answering them.

Step 1: Find the Road Blocks

Some questions you struggled to answer. To improve your score, you need to pinpoint exactly what element of these "road blocks" tripped you up. To do that, ask yourself these two questions:

Am I weak in the skills being tested?

Sentence Completions test your ability to recognize the point of the sentence and find the best word(s) to fit this meaning. That means you have to understand the sentence, and know what all the answer choices mean. Did you find the sentence to be too dense or complex? You may need to work on your critical reading skills. If you need extra help in this department, TRY the *Kaplan GRE Exam Verbal Workbook*, which contains focused review of the fundamental rules for Sentence Corrections, as well as exercises to build speed and accuracy.

You also need a good vocabulary for Sentence Corrections, and for **Antonyms** and **Analogies**, too. If your vocabulary needs a boost, TRY the *Kaplan GRE Exam Vocabulary in a Box*.

Reading Comprehension questions test critical reading skills, such as whether you can summarize the main idea of a passage, differentiate between ideas explicitly stated and those implied, make inferences based on information in a text, or deduce the author's attitude about a topic. If you need extra help in this department, TRY the *Kaplan GRE Exam Verbal Workbook*, which contains strategies to help you develop the specific reading skills you need for better efficiency and comprehension on Test Day.

Was it the question types that threw me off?

Then you need to become more comfortable with them! Go back to the beginning of this chapter and review the Kaplan principles and methods for the question types you struggled with. Make sure you understand them, and know how to apply them. These strategies help to improve your speed and efficiency on Test Day.

Also get as much practice as you can, so you grow more at ease with the question type format. For even more practice, TRY the *Kaplan GRE Exam Verbal Workbook*, which includes practice sets for each question type, and a full-length Verbal practice section.

Step 2: Find the Blind Spots

Some questions you answered quickly and confidently, but got them wrong anyway!

When you come across wrong answers like these, you need to figure out what you thought you were doing right, what it turns out you were doing wrong, and why that happened! The best way to do that is to read the answer explanations!

They give you a detailed breakdown of why the correct answer is correct, and why all the other answer choices are wrong. This helps to reinforce the Kaplan principles and methods for each question type, and helps you figure out what blindsided you so it doesn't happen again. Also, just like with your "road blocks," try to get in as much practice as you can.

Step 3: Reinforce Your Strengths

Now read through all the answer explanations for the ones you got right. Again, this helps to reinforce the Kaplan principles and methods for each question type, which in turn helps you work more efficiently so you can get the score you want. Keep your skills sharp with more practice. Look for words you didn't know the meanings of, and learn them!

As soon as you are comfortable with all the GRE question types and Kaplan methods, complete a full-length practice test under timed conditions. In this way, practice tests serve as milestones; they help you to chart your progress! So don't save them all for the final weeks.

For even more practice, you can also TRY the GRE Quiz Bank! You get more than 1,000 questions that you can access 24/7 from any Internet browser, each with comprehensive explanations. You can even customize your quizzes based on question type, content, and difficulty level. Take quizzes in Timed Mode to test your stamina or in Tutor Mode to see explanations as you work. Best of all, you also get detailed reports to track your progress.

Visit Kaptest.com/GRE for more details on our Quiz Bank and for more on our other online and classroom-based options.

1. B

For the first blank, look for a word that describes a desert and explains why the mummies are still intact. After the comma, there is an important context clue. The word *whereas* signifies contrast. It indicates that the Egyptian conditions are different from those described in the second half of the sentence, which is where the conditions found in tropical rain forests are explained. So, the context clue *whereas* indicates that the first blank will be the opposite of humid. Likewise, the second blank tells about Aztec mummies, which you know will be the opposite of what is true of Egyptian mummies. If the Egyptian mummies are still intact, then Aztec mummies must not have survived.

A good prediction for this sentence is: "The dryness of the desert explains why Egyptian mummies are still around, whereas the humidity in tropical rain forests explains why so few Aztec mummies have survived."

Predictions for both blanks are pretty precise, so start with either one. Looking for a word that means "dryness" for the first blank directs you to **(B)** and **(C)**. Both *aridity* and *dehydration* mean "lacking in moisture," but the second word in **(C)**, *decay*, is the opposite of what you're looking for. You need a word that means "survived." **(B)**, *endured,* is perfect. Hold onto **(B)** and check the others. The first word in **(A)**, **(D)**, and **(E)** eliminates these answers. All of these words may be true of the desert, but none of them means "dry."

2. C

In this sentence, you learn that they did something until only one option remained open to them—a desperate, last-minute solution. They must have waited or put off their work until they had no recourse.

A good prediction for this sentence is: "They delayed until there was no choice but a last-minute solution to solve the problem."

Starting with the first blank because the prediction is pretty definite, **(B)** and **(C)** look good. Eliminate **(B)** because the second word, *envision,* that is, "predict or foresee," does not convey the meaning of a solution. The second word in **(C)**, *implement*, means "execute or achieve," so **(C)** works well for both blanks. Based on the first word, **(A)**, **(D)**, and **(E)** can be eliminated. Of these three only **(E)**, *filibustered,* suggests delaying, but even it has a more specific meaning that is not applicable here. To filibuster is to interrupt or delay something from occurring by engaging in activities such as long speeches and discourse.

3. D

This is a fairly long sentence whose blanks occur toward the end. Take the sentence apart, paraphrasing what each phrase means, and pay close attention to the first few lines, which will tell you how to fill in the blanks. The context clue *but because* after the first comma is critical in directing you to the right answer. *But* indicates that a contrast is coming, and the word *because* tells you that an explanation will be given. The second part of the sentence will contrast with the first and will tell you why it is so. In the first part, you learn that the engine was a *marvel* that reduced pollution. However, it was not *fuel-efficient.* The word *because* tells you that the lack of fuel efficiency led to something, unlike the fact that the engine was so marvelous. The fact that it reduced pollution must not have been important anymore, since there was a *panic over fuel shortages.*

A good prediction for this sentence is: "The engine was rejected or modified in the 1970s, when concerns about pollution gave way to panic over fuel shortages."

Working with the first blank, **(C)**, **(D)**, and **(E)** look good. While *modified* in the first blank of **(C)** makes sense, the second phrase, *opinion on,* is too broad. You're not told if it was a positive or negative opinion that gave way or what direction it gave way to. This answer, then, is not precise enough and would not warrant modifying the engine. In **(D)**, if a *preoccupation with* pollution gave way to panic over fuel shortages, that would explain why the engine was no longer valued. This is a much stronger phrase than *opinion on.* This looks like the best answer, but check the others to be sure. The second word in **(E)** does not fit the context. A mere loss of *interest in* pollution would not explain abandoning a marvelous engine. Eliminate **(A)** and **(B)** based on the first word in each, since neither of them suggests that the engine was rejected or changed in anyway.

4. C

The semicolon between these two clauses is a context clue. It tells you that the second thought will be a continuation of, or will support, the first thought. The basic meaning of the first half of the sentence is that friendship has its limits no matter what. The first blank must be filled with something that reinforces the notion of having limits in all cases. The second half of the sentence says that advice that is thrust upon someone cannot be considered an act of friendship. The second blank will be filled with a word that describes advice that is *thrust insistently* on someone—advice that is not asked for.

A prediction for this sentence is: "All friendship, no matter how close, has boundaries; unwanted advice, when thrust upon someone, is rarely a sign of friendship."

Choice **(C)** looks good right away because the first word, *intimate,* matches your prediction of *close,* and the second word, *unsolicited,* is perfect, too. Choice **(A)** and **(D)** can be eliminated because the first word in each is the opposite of *close.* The first word in **(B)** and **(E)** might be all right if nothing else were better, but both can be eliminated on the basis of the second word in each. *Obverse* means "inside out or upside down," which doesn't make sense in this context, and *desired* is the opposite of your prediction.

5. E

The word *despite* is a context clue that tells you that there is a change or contrast later in the sentence. Despite something from the critics, the poet's work sold steadily. The critics must not have favored the poetry, which would explain why it would be surprising that the work still sold well. For the first blank, look for a word that suggests the critics' disapproval. The second blank is harder to figure out. You know the word will describe the critics, but many words, both positive and negative, could work here. Evaluate the meaning of each of the choices to narrow it down.

A good prediction, for the first blank at least is: "Despite negative responses from (some type) of critics, the poetry sold well."

Starting with the first blank since it is more precise, **(E)** seems to be just right. *Vitriol* means severe criticism, which would work in the first blank, and *influential* in the second blank explains why it's surprising that these type of critics' responses did not negatively impact the sales of the book. Run through the other answers quickly. From the first word, you can eliminate **(A)** because *zeal* is positive, and you need a negative word. Choice **(C)** does not fit well in the first blank either, because *tedium* may be defined as boredom. Receiving boring responses from the critics does not mean that the responses were negative. **(B)** and **(D)** can be eliminated because of the second word in each. It is not logical that the response of *obscure* or *ineffectual* critics would explain the contrast suggested by the word *despite*. If the critics have no influence, it would not be surprising that the books sold well. Look for a word that would justify the context clue *despite*.

6. A

The commas after the first blank are important clues that tell you what type of word you are looking for. Because it is set off with commas, the phrase *from production to projection* simply renames the word in the preceding blank. This phrase describes every aspect of the film industry, so the correct word will, too. Since all of these components were *held by one company,* it makes sense that a monopoly would eventually arise. In the second blank, you're looking for something that expresses the fact that monopolies were bound to arise.

A good prediction for this answer is: "Because the different components were arranged so that all aspects of the business were held by one company, monopolistic practices were bound to arise."

Predictions for both of these blanks are pretty definite, but the second is a little more precise, so start there. Choice **(A)** looks good right away because *inevitable* means that it was bound to happen, which was your prediction for the second blank. *Opportunities for control* works well in the first blank, too. This one looks good. Hold onto it and check the others. Choices **(C)** and **(E)** can be eliminated because the second word in each does not convey the meaning that something would have to happen. Choices **(B)** and **(D)** can be eliminated because the words for the first blank, *burdens of business* and *means of solicitation,* are not logical in context. Having control of all of the components of the film industry would certainly not be burdens, nor would all of them act as a means of soliciting.

7. D

The first blank describes something that the peasants tried to conceal as they knelt before the body of the dictator's son. This doesn't sound like a very positive situation. They are kneeling and we know that they live under a dictatorship, so it is likely that the peasants are being required to do this. The second part of the sentence supports this theory. You learn that *far from affection,* something else motivates them. Consequently, you're looking for a negative word in both blanks.

Many words would work in these blanks, so evaluate each choice carefully looking for two negative words that fit in this context.

Starting with the second blank since you have a little more information to work with there, **(D)** looks like the best answer. It makes sense that *fear* would bring them to the wake of the dictator's son. The first word, *trepidation,* also fits the sentence, since it means "apprehension." Choice **(A)** can be eliminated because there is no indication in the sentence that the peasants are concealing *sarcasm,* and they would not show this if they felt something as extreme as *hatred.* Likewise, the second word in **(B)**, *violence,* is not suggested from the clues. **(C)**, *adulation,* and **(E)**, *patriotism,* are positive.

8. C

The context clue *despite* at the beginning of this sentence helps you figure this one out. Because *despite* indicates that the two parts of the sentence are contrasting with each other, you know that *despite the increased attention* on this issue, something has happened. You would expect that with increased attention, there would be fewer crimes committed by this group. However, the word *despite* indicates that what you might expect does not prove to be true. You're looking for the opposite of what you would normally expect given these circumstances.

A good prediction for this one is: "Despite increased attention on juvenile delinquency, there's been an increase in crimes."

Working with the second blank since it is more specific, **(B)**, **(C)**, and **(E)** look good. After considering the first blank, though, only **(C)** makes sense. The first word in **(B)**, *offered,* is not strong enough. Simply offering attention to this issue does not tell you whether or not attention was actually given. You need something more definitive in the first blank to indicate that the expected cause and effect was not realized. **(E)** can be eliminated since the first word, *withdrawn,* is the opposite of what you're looking for. Hold onto **(C)** and check the remaining two. **(A)** and **(D)** are inappropriate, since the second word in each doesn't have a contrasting meaning to the first clause. You must have a contrast because of the word *despite* in the first clause.

9. D

The context clue *contradicted* tells you that the blank will be opposite in meaning to *cynicism*—something like innocence.

A good prediction: "The Beatles' music was characterized by a superficial innocence subtly contradicted by an inherent, deeper cynicism."

Choice **(D)** looks good right away because *naiveté* means "innocence." None of the other choices comes close to being opposite in meaning to *cynicism.*

10. C

The keyword in this sentence is *ambivalent.* An ambivalent attitude is one that contains both positive and negative feelings. You know that the negative side of Jung's attitude is that he attacked Freud. However, even as he attacked Freud, Jung did something that must have been positive in order to have shown ambivalence.

Many positive words would work here, so it would be hard to predict an answer. Instead, go directly to the choices and evaluate each one carefully in the context of the sentence.

Choice (C) looks good since *revered* is a very positive word. Choices (B) and (D) can be eliminated because they are negative. Choice (A) is out because it doesn't make sense in the context of the sentence. If Jung *enlightened* Freud, it might have a positive effect on Freud, but it is impossible to say whether this would have a positive or negative impact on Jung. Choice (E) is not a good answer because *understood* doesn't provide a contrast with *attacked.*

11. E

The context clue *but* in the first clause indicates that her intelligence has two contrasting qualities: it is not *quick,* yet it is *thorough.* Since the two clauses are joined by a semicolon, you know that the second will support or elaborate upon the first. There is more information available on the second blank. Of the two qualities, the latter one, her thoroughness, is what is being described. The first blank must reflect the other quality, slowness.

The first blank can be predicted, but the second is not as precise. A working prediction is: "Her intelligence was not quick, but it was thorough; however slowly, she would come to understand all things eventually."

Since the prediction for the first blank is more precise, start there. Choices (C) and (E) look good because the first word in each matches your prediction. Looking at the second blank, (C) can be eliminated. It would not make sense that she would *jettison,* or get rid of, all things in her life. Choice (E) looks good for both blanks. Eliminate (A) and (B), because the first word in each does not relate to how slowly she thinks. Similarly, eliminate (D), because *methodically* does not indicate how slowly the thinking is done, just the manner in which it is done.

12. D

The most helpful approach to figuring out what should go in each of these blanks is to pay attention to the overall context. Two words are especially important here—*considering* at the beginning of the sentence and *remarkably* before the second blank. Think about how these words are typically used, and determine that the two words will be opposites of each other. "Considering that the era is a certain way, it's remarkable or surprising that the theme and tone are something different." You're looking for opposites.

Since many different options are available for these blanks, it would be hard to predict an answer. Just be sure that the answer contains two opposite or contrasting words.

Considering the permissive era in which the novel was written, its tone and theme are remarkably puritanical.

13. E

The semicolon between these clauses indicates a close connection between the two. The first clause tells you that *feuds tend to arise* in societies that feel a certain way about *centralized government.* In the second clause, you learn more about these societies— *public justice is difficult to enforce* in them. These societies must not have strong, centralized governments. This helps you with the first blank. The *private recourse* mentioned at the end of the second clause is referring to *feuds,* since a feud is a fight or dispute between factions or families that tends to be a private matter. So, feuds, or private recourse, tend to occur in these societies.

A prediction: "Feuds tend to arise in societies that do not have centralized governments; when public justice is unavailable, private recourse is more common."

Choice (**E**) looks like a good answer right away because *lack* is very close to your prediction, and *effective* would make sense in this context, too. Choices (**A**) and (**B**) can be eliminated, because the first word in each would mean that these societies are in favor of centralized government. Choice (**C**) can be eliminated since a *dislike of* centralized government would not in itself make public justice *difficult to enforce.* You need a stronger word in the first blank that would explain why public justice is not an option for these societies. Moreover, you don't know whether or not private recourse is more *satisfying* when public justice is hard to enforce. Choice (**D**) can be eliminated because even though the first word, *reject,* is a good selection, the second word, *brutal,* is unsupported by the sentence. You do not know that the recourse is "more brutal" in these societies than in others. You only know that the recourse tends to be private rather than public.

14. A

The semicolon between these clauses is a context clue; these two ideas are closely related or elaborate upon each other. Since the blank is in the second clause, you'll look to the first for direction. There you discover that this person requires lots of attention. The second clause will be consistent with this notion; it explains just how much he needs this attention. He would rather be criticized than have what happen? Not get any attention.

A prediction: "He'd rather be criticized than ignored."

Choice (**A**) matches the prediction, but look at the others just to be sure. Scanning the other choices quickly you see that all of the remaining options do not support the first part of the sentence. None of these other choices reinforces the idea that he always has to be the center of attention.

15. B

Greek philosophers were trying to do something with the *notions of change and stability*. The first thing you notice is that *change* and *stability* are starkly opposing ideas. Therefore, they must have been doing more than just trying to understand change and stability, which really wouldn't be that difficult anyway. They must have been trying to rationalize something about both of them. The first blank, then, will be filled with a word that expresses what they were trying to resolve about change and stability. The way they tried to do this was to hypothesize about the existence of a *particle* that could explain both change and stability. This particle is the atom from which all varieties of matter are formed, and would include both changing and stable things. The second blank will describe the atom in some way.

The first blank is easier to predict : "Greek philosophers tried to resolve notions of change and stability." Carefully evaluate the choices for the second blank.

Choice **(B)** is the only one in which the first word reflects the context of the sentence. *Reconcile* (which means "settle a dispute") is the perfect description of trying to rationalize the simultaneous existence of opposing forces. The second word looks good, too. Choices **(A)**, **(C)**, **(D)**, and **(E)** can be eliminated on the basis of the first word in each. There is no suggestion in the sentence that any of these things is what the philosophers wanted to do.

16. C

The context clue *but* after the comma indicates that a contrast is coming. At the beginning of the sentence, you're told that *many* think jazz improvisation first occurred in the twentieth century. The second part of this sentence will no doubt dispute this belief.

A good prediction is: "But it is believed that improvisation has its beginnings in the seventeenth and eighteenth centuries."

Beginning with the choices for the second blank, **(A)** and **(C)** are the closest matches. **(A)** can be eliminated because the first word, *unlikely,* is the opposite of what you're looking for. **(C)** seems to fit both blanks well. Hold onto it, and check the others. **(B)** is out because it is idiomatically incorrect to say that improvisation had its *past* in the seventeenth or eighteenth centuries. **(D)** doesn't work because the second word, *future,* is illogical. **(E)** also doesn't make sense because the second word, *unity,* is unsupported in the sentence.

17. A

From key phrases in this sentence you know that the whales are *peaceful,* yet are *savagely* hunted. From the tone, you can assume that the author disapproves of the situation. The blank, then, will be filled with something that suggests man's *superior need* is not a real one.

A prediction for this sentence: "Whales are savagely hunted by man, who argues for superior need, or believes he has superior need."

Choice (**A**) looks good because *assumes* matches the tone and content of this sentence. Choice (**B**) does not work because there is nothing in the sentence that tells you how long this has been going on. Choices (**C**) and (**E**) can be ruled out because they are not consistent with the author's tone. The author thinks it is bad that the whales are hunted. The author would not agree that man *retains* or *manifests* superior need. Both of these answers imply that man has a right to hunt the whales. Choice (**D**), *assimilates,* is not logical in this context. What would the phrase *man assimilates superior need* mean?

18. C

The context clue *yet* between the clauses indicates that there will be a contrast in this sentence. You are told that his *unbridled curiosity* resulted in his exploration of every field, which is a positive thing. The contrast comes when, after the word *yet,* you find out something negative. He wanted to be acknowledged by a society, that was *devout*. The second blank, describing his stances, must be filled with a word that would not be acceptable to a devout society. Since *devout* means "devoted to religion," the word will have to mean "antireligious." For the first blank, any word that conveys the idea that he explored many different subjects would work.

You can make a pretty definite prediction for the second blank in this sentence, but the first blank could be filled with various words. A partial prediction is "yet his sacrilegious stances kept him at odds with a devout society."

Checking the second word, you are immediately drawn to (**C**) and (**D**), both of which have the meaning of "against accepted religious beliefs." Choice (**C**) looks good for both blanks because *every field of thought* conveys the idea of a wide array of subjects. Choice (**D**) doesn't work for the second blank because *field of hope* doesn't relate to the breadth of his explorations but more to expectations; besides, it's not really clear what the phrase *every field of hope* is meant to signify. Choice (**C**) seems correct, but review the others. There is no reason in (**A**) that his *interesting* stances would be objectionable to a devout society, and *field of science* is too limited. He may have explored much more than just *science*. In (**B**) and (**E**), *interest* and *study* work for the first blank, but *common* and *optimistic* don't make sense for the second. A *devout society* would not necessarily reject a *common* or *optimistic* stance.

19. D

The blank in this sentence needs a word that describes Harry's personality. He doesn't want a job that will be a *travail*. Since *travail* means hard work, something that is extremely difficult, the missing word will reflect that disposition. Harry doesn't like to work hard.

A good prediction is: "Due to his laziness, Harry avoided jobs that might be a travail."

Choice (**D**), *indolence,* is perfect because it means "laziness," but look at the others to double check this answer. Choices (**A**) and (**B**), *impudence* and *insolence,* are incorrect because they both describe someone who is disrespectful. Harry just doesn't like to work. Choice (**C**), *eminence,* means "high rank" or "high repute," neither of which work here. It doesn't make sense that Harry's *eminence* would make him want to avoid work. Choice (**E**), *integrity,* can be eliminated. It means honesty and has nothing to do with the desire or lack of desire to work.

20. B

The first blank in this sentence will describe Pacheco's *treatise.* (A treatise is a detailed, formal writing.) Later in the sentence you find out that this treatise contains information on iconography, technique, and contemporary painters. Already this sounds like a broad and significant treatise. This is confirmed after the second blank, when you're told that the treatise is *our most comprehensive information* on these subjects. The word in the first blank will definitely be a positive one.

You can't predict specific words, but you know you're looking for a positive word in the first blank, and that the second has to describe how the information is used now.

Looking for a positive word in the first blank leads to (**B**), (**E**), and possibly (**C**). Choice (**C**) does not look very promising because *historical* is neither positive nor negative, and the second word, *lacks,* definitely rules this answer out. It's not logical that a treatise filled with so much information would now *lack* our most comprehensive information on these topics. Choice (**B**) looks good for both blanks. Even though *important* is a good selection for the first blank in (**E**), the second word, *excludes,* does not make sense. An important treatise, filled with so much information, would not *exclude* our most comprehensive information. Choices (**A**) and (**D**) can be eliminated—the first word in both is negative.

21. A

Two important context clues help in this sentence—the semicolon between the clauses and the word *however.* The semicolon indicates that the two clauses will contain similar thoughts; the second half of the sentence goes on to explain or elaborate upon the first. The word *however* indicates that even though the second clause will discuss the same topic as the first, something new or different has been brought in. In the first clause, you're told that not much is known about this writer. The second clause tells you that even though you don't know much about him, his something about him. Since the word *eclectic* means "drawn from various sources," you can get a sense of what should go in the second blank. Some way or another, Theophilus was exposed to a lot of different information.

A prediction: "From his writings, we can presume him to be well traveled, well educated, or well versed."

Choice **(A)** looks like a good match right away, although **(D)** seems to work as well. Both words in **(A)** are logical and sound correct in the sentence. In **(D)**, *expect* is fine for the first blank, but *exposed* doesn't work in the second. It is idiomatically incorrect to say that he was *well exposed*. Since we can eliminate **(D)**, **(A)** looks like your answer. Choices **(B)**, **(C)**, and **(E)** can be rejected because the second word in each is not consistent with the meaning of *eclectic*. It is from his *eclectic writings* that you can make an assumption about him. So, the second blank must be filled with a word that underscores the meaning of *eclectic*.

22. D

The first blank describes the aspect of life that was rewarded by *her systematic approach*. From the key phrase, it is likely that this aspect will be found in her work life as opposed to her home life, but confirm that with the other information in the sentence. The word *but* after the comma is a context clue, indicating that there will be a contrast between the two clauses. So, her approach is helpful in one aspect of her life, but is detrimental in her personal life. The first blank will describe her life at work. The second blank will be filled with a word that describes her mind. You already know from the beginning of the sentence that she has a systematic approach to her research. The second missing word must be a descriptive word that is consistent with this systematic approach.

A prediction: "Her systematic approach was rewarded in her work life, but was disastrous when her analytical mind examined every flaw in her friends and family."

Starting with the first blank, two choices fit perfectly, **(A)** and **(D)**. Choice **(C)** might seem okay at first, but a *public* life does not necessarily mean "work." Since there are other selections that are more precise, you don't need one that is not a strong match. Choice **(A)** can be eliminated because the second word, *disorganized,* is contradictory to the sentence. Choice **(D)** is perfect for both blanks. **(B)** and **(E)** can be eliminated because the first word in each is the opposite of what you're looking for. The first blank describes her work life, not her "private" or "family" life.

23. E

The semicolon is a context clue that this is a sentence with continuity. The second half must agree with the first. If *personal correspondence* reflects *the spirit of the age,* then Swift's epistles, or letters, must reflect the spirit of this. That is, whatever quality that is represented by the first blank must also agree with the quality represented in the second blank.

(E) works best: *vitriol* is abuse, so this would mirror his society's love of *elegant disparagement.* Choice **(A)** can be eliminated because there is no link between *profundities* and *ditties* (songs). Choices **(B)**, **(C)**, and **(D)** can also be eliminated because the words in each are not necessarily linked.

24. C

The context clue *but* before the blank indicates that a contrast is coming. The spokesperson seems unsure of a victory, but feels something about facing the alternative. After the comma, you get an idea of what that something is. Apparently, the spokesperson doesn't want to admit it, due to a superstition that just saying it would make it happen.

A good prediction is: "The spokesperson is afraid to face the alternative, as if admitting the possibility would make it happen."

Choice (C) is a perfect match. For (A) to work, the context clue before the blank would have to be *and,* indicating that the two things are closely linked. The spokesperson is unsure of the victory and unsure of facing the alternative. Even that doesn't make great sense, but *unsure of* will definitely not work with the contrast context clue *but* before the blank. Choice (B) is unacceptable, since *complacent* means *unconcerned.* Choices (D) and (E) are contradicted in the sentence. If the spokesperson is *uncertain of* the victory, he couldn't be *certain of* facing the future. And if the spokesperson is fearful of something, as we're told at the end of the sentence, then it's unlikely that he'd feel *helped by* it.

25. E

Taking a creative work like a play and moving it into another medium is an act of adaptation, so having seen *adapted* among the choices you might have been drawn right away to correct choice (E). And *vehicle* should not have been problematic for you—the sentence refers to *vehicle* not as a means of conveyance but as a means of display or expression. We can infer that *La Tosca* was Bernhardt's vehicle in the sense that it was created for her, to display her particular talents. (The purpose of any "star vehicle" is to showcase that star.)

It is incorrect to say that a play is written as a *role* (A)—written "to provide a role" would be more acceptable grammatically—and a work is not *reincarnated* from one medium into another, that verb being best reserved for the reembodiment or rebirth of living entities. The idea of *La Tosca*'s being a *biography* (B) for Bernhardt doesn't make sense (if the play were about her life, *biography of* would work), so this choice is out even though *changed* isn't bad in the second blank. A *metaphor* (C) is a poetic or figurative representation of something, and though we might call a play a metaphor for some event or idea we would not be likely to do so for a human being; *edited* provides a further complication, in that the process of editing requires pruning and revision, whereas changing a play into a musical drama requires a great deal more firsthand creativity. And while M. Sardou might well have offered *La Tosca* as a *present* to Mme. Bernhardt (D), *fictionalized* won't do; a real-life event can be fictionalized—into a play or an opera—but that verb cannot apply to something that is already fiction.

26. E

If the requirement is that the verdict be a "definite determination," then a judge is pressured to consider a verdict to be definitely determined even when there is some room for doubt. (This analysis is supported by the author's use of the phrases *as if,* meaning something hypothetical, and *when in fact,* meaning that which is actually true.) Thus, if the evidence in a case is not *conclusive* **(E)**, if there is room for doubt as to the guilt of the accused, a verdict based upon it probably will not be *self-evident* but will have to be treated as such by a judge (in the face of law and custom, that is).

Certainly if the evidence in a case is not *persuasive* **(A)**, if the conclusion stemming from the evidence is debatable, it surely does suggest there's room for doubt. But pressure for a definite determination would hardly force a judge to view a verdict as *negotiable*, that is, open for debate among the interested parties and possibly subject to revision. On the contrary, the more *negotiable* the verdict, the less "definitely determined" it's likely to be. *Justified* **(B)** works well—the judge might have to consider this verdict warranted even if the evidence didn't support it—but *accessible* in none of its meanings (easily approached; obtainable; open to influence) fits the context. Similarly the first words of **(C)** and **(D)**, *unassailable* and *incontrovertible* respectively, give us what we need—a verdict that must be seen as a "definite determination"—but their respective second words shoot the choices down. Evidence that's not *insubstantial* is substantial, and there's no contradiction between an *unassailable* verdict and one based on substantial evidence. *Admissible* plays on your associations with real-life law, but the issue of whether or not something may properly be brought into evidence is far removed from the author's central point.

27. A

The author mentioned in this sentence believes that businessmen are models of some quality; *whatever qualities they may lack* implies that whatever bad points they possess, there's this one particular good thing about them. All of this should lead you to **(A)**— if an author's main characters are businessmen, and if they're all paragons of *ingenuity* (meaning inventively talented), one could easily be led to the presumption that the author thinks all businessmen are *clever*.

Several of the wrong answers play off your possible biases about people in the business world, **(B)** being the most blatant in that regard. That choice is tempting only because an author's use of many *greedy* businessman characters might suggest that that author thinks all businessmen are *covetous*. But labeling businessmen as greedy contradicts the sense of "whatever qualities they may lack"—as we noted, we need a positive quality. (Also, *paragons of greed* is awkward.) One who is morally upright or *virtuous* **(C)** would hardly be a paragon of *deceit* (lying, falseness). Characters possessing great *ambition* **(D)** wouldn't necessarily make one presume that the author believes all such people are *successful*, since ambition and success in a field don't always go hand in hand; and there's even less connection between businessman characters who demonstrate great *achievement* (**E**) and a conclusion that, in the creator's opinion, all businessmen are *cautious*.

28. E

The first blank describes what type of budget the film had. The context clue *and* after the word *budget* tells you that the budget and the rate at which it was edited are either both positive or both negative. Consequently, since the editing was done at a hectic pace, the budget must have been restricted in some way. The context clue *nonetheless* indicates contrast, suggesting that what you would expect after reading the first part of the sentence does not prove to be true. Instead of the negative reaction you would expect from the first part of the sentence, a positive word must describe the critics' responses. The critics must have liked the film even though the budget and editing were done under severe constraints.

A good prediction for this is: "Filmed on a low budget and edited quickly, the film nonetheless was well received by the critics."

Starting with the first blank because it is more precise, you are immediately drawn to (**A**) and (**E**). Although in (**A**) *low* works perfectly for the first blank, *disappointed* in the second blank is contrary to the sense of the sentence. Choice (**E**) looks good for both blanks. Choices (**B**) and (**D**) can be eliminated because the second word in each is negative. The second word in (**C**), *pleased,* looks good, but the first word doesn't make sense in describing the budget. How could a budget be *ludicrously uneven*?

29. D

The "submissions" described must be manuscripts: apparently Ginnie is an author who believes she'll strike gold every time she sends in a story or play. The structural signal *and* suggests that her expectations are going to be taken a step further. Now her *optimism* will be *vindicated* (**D**) and she'll be published. That structural signal, by the way, is what keeps (**C**) from being correct: If the signal were *but,* then we'd need a contrast, and Ginnie's "dampened enthusiasm" would contrast strongly with her typical expectations of success. Since Ginnie always figures that her stuff will be accepted, there's no reason for the sentence to point to her *anticipation* being *piqued* (**B**) on this particular occasion: her anticipation is always piqued (aroused, excited). Nothing in the sentence refers to or even hints at Ginnie's habit of speaking frankly, so it would be improper to conclude with a reference to her *candor* (**A**), *dispelled* or not. Similarly, Ginnie's perennial optimism about her chances at publication really has nothing to do with her *awareness* (**E**), but even if you justify it as a reference to "awareness of her chances to be published," a *clouded* awareness would suggest she's going to get shot down this time, and would require a contrast signal like *but* rather than *and.*

30. B

No candidate would be pleased at his or her opponent's "solid support from the voting public," but any candidate would become mighty frustrated if such support continued despite overwhelming reasons why it should cease. In this instance, we can infer that the popular governor remains popular despite the fact that he either doesn't understand "significant issues" or has made foolish choices as to what the "significant issues" are. In line with that analysis only **(B)** works: if the governor *misapprehended*, or misunderstood, the issues, how frustrating it would be to his opponent when the public seemed not to care!

You might have been tempted by **(C)** or **(D)**, and both are wrong for pretty much the same reason—each is too neutral in tone. The other choices are a good deal worse. It's not clear how a candidate would *exaggerate* **(A)** significant issues, nor why public support would be expected to erode as result of such overstatement; and a candidate's *acknowledgment* **(E)** of the key issues—recognition of their existence, perhaps even of their significance—would probably have an effect opposite to the erosion of voter support.

31. A

A bridge for this stem might be: *electricity* flows through a *wire*. When you check the answer choices, the word pair with the same bridge is **(A)**, *fluid* flows through a *pipe*. Does a *car* flow through a *highway* **(B)**? No; eliminate. A *river* flows between *banks*, not through them. Eliminate **(C)**. *Light* flows through a *bulb*. Eliminate. **(E)** *Music* flows through an *instrument*.

32. E

It is easier to work from right to left with this Analogy. You might make the following bridge: to *berate* is to *scold* to a great degree. *Foresee* and *predict* **(A)** are synonyms, as are *impend* and *threaten* **(B)**, and *advise* and *counsel* **(C)**, so eliminate all three choices. To *retire* is not to *retreat* to a great degree; eliminate **(D)**. Choice **(E)** is your answer: to *venerate* is to *respect* to a great degree.

33. B

To *plummet* is to *descend* rapidly. Let's try the answer choices. To *kick* is to *boot* rapidly. No; eliminate **(A)**. To *whirl* is to *turn* rapidly. Yes; keep **(B)**. To *indicate* is to *show* rapidly. No; eliminate **(C)**. To *decorate* is to *nullify* rapidly. No; eliminate **(D)**. To *begin* is to *conclude* rapidly. No; eliminate **(E)**.

34. A

A *rig* is pulled by a *team*. Let's try the answer choices. A *train* is pulled by a *locomotive*. Yes; keep **(A)**. A *steamer* is pulled by a *piston*. No; eliminate **(B)**. A *sled* is pulled by a *rail*. No; eliminate **(C)**. A *car* is pulled by a *truck*. No; eliminate **(D)**. A *windjammer* is pulled by a *crew*. No; eliminate **(E)**.

35. B

It is easier to work from right to left with this Analogy. To *enthrall* is to *interest* to a great degree. Let's try the answer choices. To *tempt* is to *corrupt* to a great degree. No; eliminate (**A**). To *crush* is to *squeeze* to a great degree. Yes; keep (**B**). To *undergird* is to *buoy* to a great degree. No; eliminate (**C**). To *surrender* is to *abstain* to a great degree. No; eliminate (**D**). To *offend* is to *reproach* to a great degree. No; eliminate (**E**).

36. E

To *recant* is to reverse a statement of *belief*. Let's try the answer choices. To *repeat* is to reverse a statement of *cathechism*. No; eliminate (**A**). To *reincarnate* is to reverse a statement of *soul*. No; eliminate (**B**). To *perjure* is to reverse a statement of *axiom*. No; eliminate (**C**). To *vacillate* is to reverse a statement of *vow*. No; eliminate (**D**). To *repeal* is to reverse a statement of *law*. Yes; (**E**) is the correct choice.

37. C

Enlistment is voluntary; *conscription* is forced. Let's try the answer choices. *Rapprochement* (the reestablishment of cordial relations between two countries) is voluntary; *arbitration* is forced. No; eliminate (**A**). *Surrender* is voluntary; *bombardment* is forced. No; eliminate (**B**). *Resignation* is voluntary; *dismissal* is forced. Yes; keep (**C**). *Contemplation* is voluntary; *instruction* is forced. No; eliminate (**D**). *Acceptance* is voluntary; *rejection* is forced. No; eliminate (**E**).

38. C

Cephalic means related to the *skull*. Let's try the answer choices. *Notable* means related to *achievement*. Not necessarily; eliminate (**A**). *Cylindrical* means related to *vertebrae*. No; eliminate (**B**). *Neural* means related to *nerves*. Yes; keep (**C**). *Angular* means related to *scapula* (shoulder blade). No; eliminate (**D**). *Audible* means related to *apparition*. No; eliminate (**E**).

39. A

A *cobbler* (shoe-maker) uses *leather* as a raw material. Let's try the answer choices. A *chandler* (candle-maker) uses *wax* as a raw material. Yes; keep (**A**). An *executrix* (a woman appointed to execute a will) uses *paper* as a raw material. No; eliminate (**B**). An *actor* uses *words* as a raw material. No; eliminate (**C**). (**D**) A *cartwright* (cart-maker) uses *wheels* as a raw material. No; eliminate (**D**). A *prosthetist* uses *limbs* as a raw material. No; eliminate (**E**).

40. A

Something *inflammable* is easily *ignited*. Let's try the answer choices. Something *fragile* is easily *shattered*. Yes; keep (**A**). Something *flexible* is easily *broken*. No; eliminate (**B**). Something *somber* (dark, gloomy) is easily *mourned*. No; eliminate (**C**). Something *famous* is easily *plagiarized*. No; eliminate (**D**). Something *small* is easily *magnified*. No; eliminate (**E**).

41. B

A *truss* provides *support.* Let's try the answer choices. A *calcium* provides *bone.* No; eliminate **(A)**. A *fence* provides a *barrier.* Yes; keep **(B)**. A *tile* provides *patio.* No; eliminate **(A)**. A *wood* provides *burn.* No; eliminate **(D)**. A *bridge* provides *water.* No; eliminate **(E)**.

42. E

It is easier to work from right to left with this Analogy. *Tape* is wound around a *reel.* Let's try the answer choices. *String* is wound around a *ball.* No; eliminate **(A)**. *Record* is wound around a *turntable.* No; eliminate **(B)**. *Wheel* is wound around a *tire.* No; eliminate **(C)**. *Yarn* is wound around a *skein (*a length of thread or yarn wound in a loose long coil). No; eliminate **(D)**. *Thread* is wound around a *spool.* Yes; **(E)** is the correct answer.

43. B

A *shingle* protects a *roof.* Let's try the answer choices. A *rind* protects a *melon.* No; eliminate **(A)**. *Armor* protects a *knight.* Yes; keep **(B)**. A *feather* protects a *wing.* No; eliminate **(C)**. A *patch* protects a *cloth.* No; eliminate **(D)**. A *blanket* protects a *bed.* No; eliminate **(E)**.

44. A

Legerdemain is a skill used by a *magician.* Let's try the answer choices. *Rhetoric* is a skill used by an *orator.* Yes; keep **(A)**. *Baggage* is a skill used by an *immigrant.* No; eliminate **(B)**. *Justice* is a skill used by a *lawyer.* No; eliminate **(C)**. *Map* is a skill used by a *cartographer.* No; eliminate **(D)**. *Tractor* is a skill used by a *farmer.* No; eliminate **(E)**.

45. D

It is easier to work from right to left with this Analogy. You can't *question* something that is *indisputable.* Let's try the answer choices. You can't *know* something that is *unlikely.* No; eliminate **(A)**. You can't *perform* something that is *amoral.* No; eliminate **(B)**. You can't *prove* something that is *incredible.* No; eliminate **(C)**. You can't *change* something that is *immutable.* Yes; keep **(D)**. You can't *submerge* something that is *insoluble.* No; eliminate **(E)**.

46. E

Something *unscathed* lacks *damage.* Let's try the answer choices. Something *ameliorated* lacks *improvement.* No; eliminate **(A)**. Something *obliterated* lacks *invisibility.* No; eliminate **(B)**. Something *rolled* lacks *smoothness.* No; eliminate **(C)**. Something *shaken* lacks *homogeneity* (similarity). No; eliminate **(D)**. Something *arid* lacks *dampness.* Yes; keep **(E)**.

47. A

A *protraction* is an increase in *duration.* Let's try the answer choices. An *extension* is an increase in *length.* Yes; keep **(A)**. A *retraction* is an increase in *instant.* No; eliminate

(B). A *corruption* is an increase in *truth*. No; eliminate **(C)**. A *taxation* is an increase in *wealth*. No; eliminate **(D)**. An *altercation* (argument) is an increase in *shape*. No; eliminate **(E)**.

48. E

A *characterization* altered for comic effect is called a *parody*. Let's try the answer choices. A *serialization* altered for comic effect is called a *novel*. No; eliminate **(A)**. A *drama* altered for comic effect is called a *musical*. No; eliminate **(B)**. A *theater* altered for comic effect is called *vaudeville*. No; eliminate **(C)**. A *saga* altered for comic effect is called an *epic*. No; eliminate **(D)**. A *portrait* altered for comic effect is called a *caricature*. Yes; the correct answer is **(E)**.

49. B

A *knoll* is a mound of *earth*. Let's try the answer choices. Is a *prison* a mound of *cells*? No. Eliminate **(A)**. Is a *dune* a mound of *sand*? Yes. Keep **(B)**. Is an *atom* a mound of *nuclei*? No. Eliminate **(C)**. Is a *nest* a mound of *eggs*? No. Eliminate **(D)**. Is a *head* a mound of *hair*? No. Eliminate **(E)**.

50. E

Atrophy is caused by *inactivity*. Let's try the answer choices. *Resistance* is not caused by *timidity,* but rather by boldness. Eliminate **(A)**. A *frown* may be caused by *anger,* but it may also be caused by other emotions. Eliminate **(B)**. *Growth* and *youth* have no strong bridge. Eliminate **(C)**. *Rot* is usually caused by a lack of *refrigeration*. No; eliminate **(D)**. *Debt* is caused by *overspending*. Since this is the only choice that works, **(E)** is the answer.

51. D

A *nod* is a gesture of *assent*. Let's try the answer choices. A *glance* is simply a look, not necessarily a gesture of *beneficence*. Eliminate **(A)**. A *shudder* is usually a gesture of fear, not of *rudeness*. Eliminate **(B)**. A *wink* is not a gesture of *mystification*. Eliminate **(C)**. A *shrug* is a gesture of *indifference*. Keep **(D)**. A *frown* is not a gesture of *capriciousness* (whimsy). Eliminate **(E)**.

52. B

Something that *irks* is not *soothing*. Let's try the answer choices. Something that *inspires* is *elevating*. No; eliminate **(A)**. Something that *supports* is not *undermining*. Yes; keep **(B)**. Something that *provokes* can be *irritating,* although it doesn't have to be. Eliminate **(C)**.

Something that *denounces* can *vilify.* No; eliminate **(D)**. Something that *lauds* (praises) may well be *conciliating* (pleasing). No; eliminate **(E)**.

53. E

One who *vegetates* is inert or not *active*. If this gave you trouble, think of vegetables, which are markedly inactive living things, or perhaps the expression "veg out" meaning to stagnate, not think or do anything. Similarly, one who *accepts* (**E**) takes things as they are without doubting, doesn't call things into question; he or she is therefore not *questioning*.

Notice that the stimulus conveys a sense of definition—a vegetator by definition is not active; such a sense is missing from (**A**), since one who *resists* may or may not be *beaten*, now or at some future time. When one *mopes* (**B**), it's usually because one feels *gloomy*—a gloomy person is characterized by moping, not a lack thereof. If a plant *grows* (**C**) from a height of 2 feet and 9 inches to a whopping 3 feet, it has indeed grown but remains *small*. As for (**D**), someone who *hassles* you is probably *obnoxious,* or at least can't be said to show a lack of obnoxiousness.

54. C

A *proponent* is someone who argues in favor of or supports some idea or practice. Someone who supports the civil-rights movement can be said to be a proponent of that cause. So we could say that one who supports a particular *theory* is a *proponent* of that *theory,* just as one who support or argues in favor of a particular *belief* (**C**) can be called an *adherent* of that *belief.* If *adherent* gave you trouble, think of *adhere* (to sick to) or *adhesive* (something that makes things stick together).

While a *nonbeliever* (**A**) might be likely to commit a sin in the eyes of others, the term *nonbeliever* is rarely applied to a person who supports a particular *sin*. A *traitor* (**B**) doesn't support his particular *country,* he betrays it; in betraying one country he may be supporting another, but in that sense he becomes a patriot, not a traitor, so this still doesn't work out. Now an *attorney* (**D**) does deal with the *law,* and must (or should, anyway) support the law. But we really can't say that an attorney is someone who supports a particular law—attorneys deal with all sorts of laws, and are honor-bound to respect them all, whereas adherents or proponents are so-called because of their devotion to one particular idea. And a *scientist* (**E**) is just as likely to condemn a given *hypothesis* as support it—and at any rate, his position on hypotheses is not what defines him as a scientist.

55. D

Species is a category of living things, and living things are known as *organisms. Species* refers to the particular type of organism in question, just as *genre* (**D**) is a term used to classify or categorize types of *literature.* Human beings are the species known as *Homo sapiens,* so that's how we're classified among all organisms. The novels of Agatha Christie are classified as mysteries: *mystery* is the classification of them among books.

Physicians (**A**) are, to an extent, categorized by their *specialty*—the obstetricians are different from the pediatricians, etcetera. But *species* and *genre* are both formal means of classification of their respective worlds, and they specifically break down the various groups for purposes of study. The specialty of a physician, on the other hand, isn't so definitive—it's just the branch of medicine the doctor happens to be most involved with. And no one breaks down the group *physicists* into specialties for the purposes of study. The *origin* (**B**) of an *idea* is not the idea's category—it's where the idea comes from. And the *language* (**C**) of a *foreigner* is not a category. Finally, *family* (**E**) is used in several figurative senses to classify things (for example, the tiger is a member of the cat family), but as it relates to *ancestry* it really carries no meaning other than that of a synonym (your ancestry, or the line of your ancestors, is your family).

56. B

Discharged is what a *soldier* is said to be when his or her tour of duty is up and he or she is released from commitment to the armed forces, just as *graduated* (**B**) is what a *student* is said to be when he or she has completed a particular stage of schooling, and is released. *Fired* (**A**) can be applied to a *cannon* that has made a shot, but it's the cannonball in this case that's released, not the cannon. In states in which *judges* (**C**) are not elected, they are *appointed* to the bench—that is, an important official such as the governor or the president appoints the judge to a job. But that begins his or her commitment rather than ends it. An *employee* (**D**) who has been *transferred* has not been released, but had his responsibilities shifted or been relocated. And *docked* (**E**), as it pertains to *salary*, refers to money withheld from an employee, usually as punishment for poor work. *Docked* does not refer to a salary that has finished its responsibility.

57. B

A *laceration* is a large *cut*, especially as it pertains to a wound. Or you could say a cut is an especially small or minor laceration. (A laceration might require stitches—a cut generally requires a Band-Aid.) Similarly, a *slit* (**B**) is a tiny crack, cut, or separation in something, and can be called a small *gap*.

The precise relationship between *park* (**A**) and *place* isn't entirely clear—perhaps "the park is a place" or "I can't find a place to park"? (And in Monopoly, there's always Park Place.) At any rate, this isn't what we're after. By cutting, a *knife* (**C**) can separate, but a knife isn't a small *separation* itself. A *hole* (**D**) and a *puncture* are really the same thing, and you can't say that the former is a smaller version of the latter. And as for (**E**), not only are *boils* and *blisters* very different from each other, medically speaking, but even if they were more alike, blisters are often smaller sores than boils.

58. E

To *outfox* someone is to defeat or win out over him by means of superior *strategy*, just as to *outrun* (**E**) someone is to beat him by means of superior *speed*. This is one of those items in which the vocabulary is simple, and you may therefore be prone to overconfidence and careless mistakes. The choices have to be examined carefully here. The most tempting wrong answer was perhaps (**A**), since it is true that one can *outdo* another by means of *trickery*. But *outfoxing*, *outrunning*, and *outlasting* are all specific kinds of outdoing that have to do with specific method, whereas *outdoing* is very general, and could apply to strategy and speed just as easily as it applies to trickery—there are unlimited ways to outdo someone. The same is true of *defeat* (**B**)—it's simply too general, and there are many means of defeating someone other than having greater *stamina*. To *outlast* someone (**C**) is, of course, to defeat him by means of superior endurance, or superior patience, not specifically by means of superior *force*. And *victimizing* someone (**D**) may indeed require *terror*, but victimizing has nothing to do with winning, and there are means other than terror by which people are victimized.

59. B

The stimulus and correct answer are really flip sides of each other, but the actions they describe share a common purpose—to get someone to do what you want him to do. In fact, if the stimulus failed—if you couldn't *coax* (or persuade) someone through a series of flattering and cajoling actions and speeches known as *blandishments,* you might take the next step and attempt to *compel* (**B**) him by making *threats*.

Platitudes (**A**) are trite, dull remarks, usually trotted out as if they were fresh and new but not usually trotted out for the purpose of *amusing* someone. If your aim was to *deter* (**C**) someone from a particular course, there are many more effective tools than *tidings*, which are news, information, or data. You might *batter* someone (**D**) with *insults*—in a figurative sense, at least—but you would not use them to batter someone into doing something. And to *exercise* (**E**) often amounts to engaging in *antics,* but you don't use antics to exercise someone into doing something—not even in the alternative meaning of the verb *exercise,* that is, to annoy or make uneasy.

60. C

Here's one that's easier to work with if we phrase the relationship from right to left. A person is called a *noble* (noun) because he or she is *titled*—that is, he or she has been bestowed with a title, such as Sir, Lord, or Squire. Similarly, an *officer* (**C**), especially one of the military, is an officer because he or she's been *commissioned*.

A *candidate* (**A**) may or may not be *elected*—the first word describes an ambition rather than an existing status. An especially good *artist* may be *acclaimed* (**B**), or highly praised, but that doesn't make him or her an artist. A *deposed* (**D**) *ruler* is one who has been kicked out. What initiates an argument cannot be made analogous to the stimulus.

61. D

To answer this global question, it is important to not confuse the subject of the passage—the events of the Cuban Missile Crisis—with the author's intended purpose for writing the passage. Rather than recount in detail what transpired during the Crisis (**E**), the author offers examples of how unbiased facts revealed in declassified documents challenged and revised previously accepted accounts of the events, which were all based on the personal narratives and memoirs of those closely involved. This is best summarized in (**D**). The author offers nothing in the passage to support (**A**), and though in line 14 he does suggest that members of Kennedy's Cabinet were deceptive (**C**), this is just a supporting detail. Rather than discount *the sense of danger* felt during the Crisis (**E**), the author states in the last sentence that most Americans were oblivious to the true danger involved.

62. B

To answer this question you must look to details in the passage to verify the truth of each given statement. In the second paragraph the author states that the "revelations" in the declassified documents have allowed historians to get a much more accurate idea of the events encompassing the crisis. This statement seems to refute Statement I, so you can discard (**A**) and (**D**). The author's mention of "inadvertent inaccuracies and intended obscurities" (line 14) in the memoirs backs up Statement II, and without going any further, you can deduce that the only possible answer is (**B**). Remember, there can only be one correct answer, and if Statement II is true, Statement III must be false because (**C**) states that only III could be true, which you have just proven impossible. You can then eliminate (**E**). The last two sentences of the passage, which relate how the crisis extended much longer than previously believed, prove your deduction to be correct.

63. C

Looking at the answer choices, the word *every* in (**C**) should immediately catch your attention. Test-makers will often include a choice that presents an extreme example of a legitimate answer as a distracter to lure the test-taker in answering incorrectly. While the phrase in question certainly suggests that there was a certain amount of deception and lying in the memoirs and narratives of the politicians involved in the Crisis, it in no way makes the extreme inference that *every* politician engages in such practices. Choice (**C**) is probably your answer, but it's best to check all the other choices to make sure. "Inadvertent inaccuracies" suggests an error in memory recall or perception, so (**A**) and (**E**) are not possible answers. An "intended obscurity" suggests a detail *purposely omitted or vague,* so you can also eliminate (**D**). You can assume that the Cuban Missile Crisis was not the only historic account taken directly from personal narratives and memoirs, so it can be inferred that the revisions to the inaccuracies and obscurities present in this case are not an *anomaly*; therefore (**B**) is incorrect. That leaves your original choice, (**C**), as the answer.

64. B

The best approach to a question like this is to think of it in positive and negative terms. The author's attitude towards both poets, which he established in the very first sentence of the passage, was definitely positive. Knowing this, you can eliminate all the "negative" choices: (**C**), (**D**), and (**E**). *Esteem* (**A**) and *admiration* (**B**) are synonymous, so you must look to their modifiers for the answer. Was the author's attitude of esteem towards both poets *unwarranted* (**A**)? Certainly not; according to the author, Whitman and Dickinson are *Two of the most revered poets in American history* whose work *still* *exerts its influence upon American poetry to this day.* This information justifies the author's attitude of admiration for the poets, so (**B**) is correct.

65. C

The author states that the *greatest similarity* between the two poets was the *nature in which both poets chose to lead their lives.* So what you are looking for is what that "nature" was. In the passage, Dickinson is described as *introspective* (line 22) and *solitary* (line 25), which suggests an introverted nature, however, Whitman is described as having a somewhat gregarious nature; therefore, (**A**) can be eliminated. Don't confuse the author's references to Emily Dickinson's *travels* (line 19), *journeys* (line 30), and *voyages* as an implied "fondness for travel," (**B**) these are all metaphors for her deep introspection. However, the author uses these metaphors to compare Walt Whitman's energetic *wanderings* around the country to Dickinson's introspection. Though Whitman's explorations were physical, and Dickinson's were inward, they were both components of each poet's *obsessive drive for self-discovery* (lines 28–29), so (**C**) is your answer. The two remaining choices, (**D**) and (**E**), are not suggested anywhere in the passage.

66. D

To answer this inference question, you need to match clues from the text to the correct choice. Start with (**A**): is it suggested anywhere in the passage that one poet's work has more relevance today? The answer is no; in fact, the final line states that both poets' remain influential to this day. As for (**B**), other than stating the fact that Whitman and Dickinson were contemporaries, there is no suggestion that they were even acquainted with each other. The author does imply in line 17 that Whitman's poetry is more accessible than Dickinson's, but that does not necessarily mean that his poetry was any less profound, so (**C**) is incorrect. It also doesn't suggest that he enjoyed more success, either (**E**). That leaves you with choice (**D**). There are numerous clues in the passage to infer this choice is correct. The author refers to Emily Dickinson as *introspective* and state that she spent her life in *solitary contemplation.* Also in contrasting the two poets, the author refers to Whitman as *open to the world.* It can be assumed from that statement that Dickinson was the opposite. Choice (**D**) is your answer.

67. E

It was no mistake that the test maker set the choice concerning different theories about Mars at the top (**A**)—It's a very attractive choice because the passage does describe two specific Mars theories in some detail. But in the context of the passage as a whole, these theories are support for what the passage is really about: biosignatures. The first half of the passage describes the uses of biosignatures as a means of inferring extraterrestial life, and the second half of the passage is concerned with its limitations. Looking through the choices, these two items best match (**E**), which is the correct answer.

Nowhere in the passage is the possibility of life on Mars disputed **(B)**, or does the author offer an alternative to searching for biosignatures **(D)**, so both are incorrect. At the end of the passage the author does infer that there are extraterrestrial implications for discoveries on Earth **(C)**, but there are no details offered regarding implications, and either way, it is not the passage's primary purpose.

68. D

The author indicates that the discovery of very few carbonates suggests that there probably were never large bodies of water on Mars similar to that on Earth. This directly contradicts a theory offered in the passage proposing that the climate on Mars was once warm and wet. Consequently, **(A)** is eliminated, and **(D)** is the correct answer. As for **(B)**, though carbonates are a biosignature, to make the extreme statement that their general absence on Mars proves beyond a doubt that life never existed there would be a mistake; in fact the author specifically states in lines 37–38 that a lack of carbonates *does not necessarily preclude the existence of life.* Choice **(C)** is a distortion of details from the passage; the author suggests that scientists should *turn their attention to Earth for answers,* but it is never indicated that they do. Finally, while **(E)** is probably true, it is not stated anywhere in the passage.

69. B

A good strategy for answering these kind of questions is to refer back to the text for each answer to see which choices are supported by the passage and which are not. Does the author imply anywhere in the passage that the search for life on Mars is an urgent matter? No, so **(A)** is incorrect. As for **(B)**, the author's knowledge on the subject certainly suggest that she finds it *interesting,* and it can also be inferred that the she believes the search is *circumscribed in scope* from her statement in lines 43–44 about the limited index of biosignatures. Choice **(B)** looks like the answer, but it's always best to look at all answer choices before definitively choosing an answer. Looking at **(C)**, the conclusion that the author draws in the final sentence of the passage could infer that she believes that the extraterrestrial search for biosignatures is a waste of *efforts,* but money is never mentioned or suggested. Also, the final sentence directly contradicts **(D)**; the author believes that the further investigation of Earth is important to understanding Mars, not vice-versa. Finally, suspicious motives are not hinted at anywhere in the passage, so **(E)** is off your list. Choice **(B)** is the answer.

70. D

For this question, you must look to the passage for specific details about Mars. Don't be fooled into thinking that Statement I is untrue, there are carbonates present on the surface of Mars, they are just *not commensurate with the prolonged existence of large bodies of flowing liquid water.* Knowing this option is true, you can exclude **(B)**. Statement II is mentioned early in the passage as part of a theory that is subsequently discounted. Thus, you can eliminate choices **(C)** and **(E)**. Features of Mars that resemble the Grand Canyon and dried-up sea floor support Statement III, so this is true as well. If Statements I and III are true **(D)**, then **(A)** must be excluded. Choice **(D)** is the correct answer.

71. E

This question asks for the choice that cannot be inferred by the examples of the new discoveries the author gives in the passage. Do any of the examples from Earth share something in common with Mars? Yes, the fact life has been found in the "seemingly dead deep-freeze of Antarctic ice" may suggest the possibility of life in the "areas of frozen water" (line 12) on Mars, so **(A)** is excluded. In line 24, the author statement that the new discoveries contradict traditional scientific ideas infers that *scientific knowledge is constantly being revised* **(B)**. The specific traditional scientific idea contradicted is that "a specified, delicate set of circumstances is necessary for the development and sustenance of life;" **(D)** may be excluded. From the examples, it stands to reason that if microbes can be found a mile beneath the ocean floor, it is possible that they may also be *found deep beneath the surface of Mars* **(C)**. You are left with only one possible answer, and it's the correct one: **(E)**. These new discoveries do not devalue carbonates as a biosignature, they simply illustrate the author's point that there are numerous, alternative possibilities.

72. A

Look for the choice that best fits with the details already supplied in the passage about the theory of Mars as a frozen planet, as well as serves to strengthen theory as a whole. Choice **(A)** immediately fits those criteria. The flashfloods would explain the formation of canyons and apparent sea floor on Mars without the "the prolonged existence of large bodies of flowing liquid water" (line 30). It also could also describe one of the "very brief cataclysmic instances" mentioned when discussing the theory (lines 33–34). Choice **(A)** looks like it could be the answer. Years of superheated flowing lava **(B)** could explain the erosion on Mars, but doesn't match well with the idea of a frozen planet. Choice **(C)** implies that the greenhouse-like Mars did exist at one point, so this choice can be excluded. Along those lines, **(E)** can be excluded as well; *evidence of Earth-like flora* suggests that the climate at one time was similar to Earth, and therefore temperate. As for **(D)**, this choice would be very good support for the "wet and warm" theory as well because implies that liquid water could have existed on Mars even with evidence to the contrary. The first choice was the best, **(A)**.

73. C

The author uses the final sentence to wrap up the entire passage as well as state his opinion on the astrobiological search for biosignatures. In **(A)**, the word *summarize* is all you really need to read to know that the choice is incorrect; the final sentence is not a summary of any point from the passage. Choice **(B)** is intriguing because in a way the conclusion the author draws in the final sentence is a *proposal,* but to call it a *radical idea* is too extreme of a description for **(B)** to be correct; the author bases the conclusion on solid examples that make it seem like common sense. Based on what we've just established, **(C)** seems like the correct answer. The author's conclusion in the final sentence regarding "a truly effective search" for extraterrestrial life is drawn from the examples in the two preceding sentences, and it wraps up the passage nicely. Choice **(C)** is your answer. Choice **(D)** is incorrect because though the final sentence offers a revised course of action for astrobiology, it is not disparaging in tone or vocabulary. Choice **(E)** cannot be correct because it would be impossible to *reiterate* a point from the passage that was never made in the first place.

74. C

In the passage, the author defines biosignatures as *indicative markers of extant or extinct life* (lines 3–4), or, to be more exact, anything that *can be construed as diagnostic evidence of the existence of life* (lines 9–10). Applying these definitions to the three statements given in the question, it is obvious that a fossil would be considered a biosignature, so Statement I is true. You can therefore eliminate **(B)**. A key word in the definitions from the passage is *construed,* which in this context can be defined as *interpreted as.* Looking at Statement II, could *amino acids associated with life on Earth* possibly be interpreted as a sign of life on Mars? It's fair to say that your answer would be *yes*; Statement II is true as well. Choices **(A)** and **(D)** can be excluded. Statement III is a bit tricky; if it said that the surface erosion was caused by liquid *water,* **(E)** would be your answer. However, the option does not specify what type of liquid caused the surface erosion, and therefore it cannot be considered true. Choice **(C)** is the correct answer.

75. C

In the first paragraph the author states that each "lighthouse is as unique as the landscape that surrounds it," and uses the rest of the passage to prove that point with specific examples. Clearly, the correct answer here is **(C)**. Choice **(A)** can be quickly eliminated because it this an informative essay, not a *tale*, with a tone much too formal to be considered *charming*. **(B)** is incorrect because the only functions of a lighthouse mentioned are the fact that it acts a beacon at night and a landmark by day, both terms too general to be described as *specific*. The only real opinion offered in the passage is found in the last sentence, so **(D)** is incorrect. The passage does enumerate many lighthouse facts, but these function as support of the primary purpose, not the purpose itself; **(E)** is incorrect.

76. D

This is a tough question that asks you to choose the one answer that could not possibly be inferred from details in the passage. Here, that one answer is **(D)**. The first sentence of the second paragraph states that there is not *one* arbitrary feature about a lighthouse, which directly contradicts the statement that a *"period" is randomly assigned by from a list.* It is easy to infer from the passage's opening sentence that **(A)** is probably true, so it can be excluded. It is also not a stretch to assume that a structure that serves as a navigational beacon and landmark for mariners would be considered strategically important to a navy during a war, so **(B)** can be excluded as well. As for **(C)**, the use of wood, coal, and oil to fuel the lanterns would require work on the part of a keeper that would not be necessary with the introduction of the bulb—exclude this one, too. Line 40 of the passage states that lighthouses built after the introduction of the Fresnel lens were *much taller than their predecessors,* so it can be inferred that **(E)** is true, too. Again, **(D)** is the correct answer.

77. E

This question asks you to reason from information provided in the passage what a light pattern called "group fixed occulting" would consist of. Since the term "group" basically defines itself, forget about it for now and concentrate on the other two adjectives. The passage states that "occulting" represents a pattern opposite that of "flashing," where the dark interval or "eclipse" dominates the pattern, rather than the light interval. *Fixed flashing* is defined in lines 64–65 as a pattern that fluctuates "between a higher and lower beam intensity." It can be reasoned then, that *fixed occulting* is the opposite—a pattern that fluctuates between a higher and lower intensity of darkness. This makes no sense in terms of light beacons, and is therefore impossible; **(E)** is your answer. Choice **(A)** would be *group fixed flashing*; and **(B)** and **(C)** were defined in the passage as *group occulting* and *group flashing,* respectively. Choice **(D)** cannot be reasoned from the passage because a name for a pattern with equal intervals of light and darkness was not offered.

78. B

If you don't know the meaning of *homogeneous,* you can easily figure it out in context. The author states that the design of lighthouses *seems* homogeneous to the uneducated eye, but in reality *each lighthouse is as unique as the landscape that surrounds it.* This contrasts *homogeneous* with the word *unique.* Of the choices, the only word that would retain that contrast if it replaced *homogeneous* in the passage is *uniform,* so **(B)** is your answer. *Different* **(A)** is an antonym of homogenous; and **(C)**, **(D)**, and **(E)**, while all applicable as adjectives to describe the design of lighthouses, do not make sense in context.

79. A

According to the passage the *earliest modern lighthouses employed a catoptric light system,* and the Fresnel lens, associated with the dioptric system, was not invented until 1822, so Statement I is true. Eliminate **(B)**. The passage also states that by 1860 *every existing lighthouse in the United States* had a Fresnel lens, so Statement III is false. You can then exclude **(D)** and **(E)**. Finally, line 35 states that it was the dioptric system that used *refraction,* not the catoptric system, which was based on reflection, so Statement II is false, as well. You can eliminate **(C)**, which leaves **(A)** as your answer.

80. D

It's very easy to get hung up worrying about the differences in the two optical systems and make this question much harder than it actually is. The important thing to recognize is that although one system reflects light and the other refracts it, they both accomplish the same thing: they concentrate a light into a powerful beam. The only choice that does not project a *concentrated* beam of light is **(D)**, a lantern, and that's your answer. As stated in lines 45–47, a lantern can be used in an optical system, but it does not utilize one. Choices **(A)** and **(E)** use dioptric optical systems, and **(B)** and **(C)** use catoptric systems.

81. D

The only choice supported by details from the passage is **(D)**. Line 19 states that no two daymarks are alike; and line 68 states that each lighthouse's "period" (*i.e.* a nightmark) is unique. This last statement proves **(B)** to be incorrect. Choice **(A)** is incorrect because there are no details offered about lighthouse keepers in the passage. Choice **(C)** can be excluded on those same grounds; though its mentioned that lighthouses were built taller after the introduction of the Fresnel lens, no specific height requirement is detailed. Choice **(E)** is the trickiest of the choices because lines 36–37 does state that all lighthouses were converted to Fresnel lenses, and therefore dioptric systems; but there it is not specifically stated that *every* lighthouse was later changed to a catadioptric system.

82. E

In the final sentence the author refers to sailors who still understand the value of lighthouses as "smart," and then contrasts the modern navigational devices *radios and radar* to lighthouses with the adjectives *fragile* and *stalwart*. In other words, the author believes that technology is not infallible, and if one were to solely rely upon it for navigating, one would be *ill prepared* if that technology failed. Therefore, **(E)** is your answer. Choices **(A)** and **(C)** are incorrect because the author offers nothing in the passage to suggest he would describe that sailor as "typical" or "overconfident," and **(B)** can be eliminated on the very grounds that made **(E)** correct. Choice **(D)**— though the closest of the choices to being to correct—is too extreme of a statement to completely fit the bill.

83. B

Though the author does not state outright if he believes or disbelieves in Nessie, the fact that he does not bother to offer anything in support of the monster's existence (other than that it can't be completely disproved), is enough to exclude the choices that are positive or neutral in nature: **(A)**, **(C)**, and **(E)**. Choices **(B)** and **(D)** remain. In this type of question, an adjective like *fanatical* usually indicates a choice too extreme to be correct; **(D)** can be eliminated. That leaves **(B)** as the correct answer.

84. A

The last sentence of the passage holds the key to answering this question. In that sentence the author states that *Apparently, as long as there exists the slightest possibility of Nessie being real* people will remain intrigued. Therefore you must look for the choice that contains the solution to the mystery that leaves no room for doubt. The only choice that meets that criterion, though obviously impossible, is **(A)**. This immediately disqualifies **(B)**, **(D)**, and **(E)**; and the example in the passage of the BBC team's investigation proves that **(C)** is incorrect. Again, **(A)** is your answer.

85. C

The author's reference in the final sentence to the hotels around Loch Ness being full since 1933 is more than evidence to suggest that he believes that the Mackays lied to *drum up business* **(C)**. Though **(A)** is certainly suggested by the given detail, the implication serves no significant purpose in terms of the overall passage, and so is wrong. Unlike **(A)**, choices **(B)** and **(D)**, though very possible, cannot be inferred from the information in the passage, and thus are incorrect. Finally, **(E)** is wrong because the idea that the author offered the detail that the Mackays were local hotel owners to suggest that they *were regular, everyday people* is unrelated to the purpose of the passage, and therefore irrelevant.

86. B

The choice that best answers this primary purpose question is **(B)**. In the beginning of the passage, the author introduces the subject of file-sharing and enumerates this popular practice's consequences on the recording industry. By offering a solid opinion in the latter half of the passage, the author is able to feasibly explain why so many people would engage in a known illegal practice. This description of the passage best fits with **(B)**. The author's mention in line 16 of those who believe they should not have to pay for music is certainly a description of a contrasting viewpoint **(A)**; and he does indeed cite facts relevant to the passage **(D)**, but these are just supporting details, not the primary purpose, and therefore incorrect. In the final sentence of the passage the author does offer an insight, but it's hardly *extraordinary,* so you can cross off **(C)**. Nowhere in the passage does the author challenge a popular opinion, so **(E)** can be eliminated as well.

87. C

At first glance, it may seem that every one of the choices in this explicit detail question is supported by the passage. In a situation like this, you should then look for a choice that contains a distortion of a passage detail. Here, that choice is **(C)**. True, it is stated in the passage that the RIAA claims music piracy is the source of over four billion dollars lost in revenues annually, but as the passage also states, *music piracy* is a blanket term for a number of illegal practices, of which illegal file-sharing is only a part, not the *sole source*. Choice **(C)** is your answer. All the other choices are explicit details easily found in the passage.

88. A

GRE vocabulary questions can often be answered by recognizing a contrast in the surrounding context of the word in question. In this question, the contrast established is between *repose* and the *devious act of physically pilfering something from a record store . . .* From this you can see that **(E)** should be eliminated because it makes no sense in context. Neither do **(C)** or **(D)**, so you can scratch those, too. You are now left with two antonyms—**(A)** tranquility and **(B)** stress—and there's your contrast. Choice **(B)** describes the shoplifting situation, so **(A)** is your answer. Plug it into the sentence for *repose,* and you'll see that it fits into the context of the statement.

89. D

GRE science passages often focus on one big contrast—and the questions will focus on the same contrast, again and again. Thus even detail questions like this one are really "main idea" questions in disguise. In this passage, the big contrast is between moons that have remained unchanged since their "early, intense bombardment" (line 2), and those whose surfaces have been altered in more recent epochs. Io is mentioned in the last three sentences. These sentences stress recent, indeed ongoing, changes in the satellite's surface. By inference, most impact craters from the long-ago bombardments have probably been obliterated **(D)**. Continuing tectonic activity **(A)** is mentioned explicitly; tides **(B)** are mentioned in the final sentence as the probable cause of the tectonic activity, and hence the active volcanos. Inferably Io's surface is younger than the "very ancient" surface of Callisto, **(C)**. Choice **(E)** is the only tricky choice. The phrase *tectonically active* may automatically conjure up the idea of internal forces, since these cause tectonic activity on the earth. But it's explicitly stated (lines 16–17) that Io is too small to supply its own energy for such activity, so **(E)** is true.

90. A

Again, keep your eye on the big contrast. The bombardments, and the craters that record them, were laid down long ago; thus a surface marked by impact craters (the dark areas of Ganymede) is older than one not so marked (the lighter areas). In addition, it's mentioned that some features of the light areas probably result from later iceflows. Thus, **(A)** is correct, ruling out **(B)** and **(C)**. The light areas feature grooves and ridges probably resulting from these iceflows, not from early bombardment **(D)**. Volcanic activity, **(E)**, is not mentioned in relation to Ganymede.

91. E

The passage conveys a great deal of information, which the author implicitly accepts, ruling out **(A)**. (The word used for the photographs of Io—*revelatory*—is enough by itself to eliminate this choice.) The fact that information about Io comes from satellite photographs rules out **(B)**. No contradictions are mentioned, and though areas of uncertainty remain, **(D)**'s *ambiguous and contradictory* will not work as a general characterization. On the other hand, **(C)** is out because of the cautious language used throughout: *probably* (twice), *apparently,* and *the accepted explanation.* Hence the knowledge is persuasive though incomplete, as specified in **(E)**.

92. B

The topic of this passage is Emile Durkheim's study of social cohesion in society and the author's purpose might be summed up as describing two different ways that societies can maintain social integration among their members. A roadmap of the paragraph structure might look like this: paragraph 1 introduces Durkheim and his study of social groups; paragraph 2 discusses two ways societies can maintain social integration; paragraph 3 offers a broader context for interpreting the evidence in paragraph 2.

The final paragraph gives you the key to answering this global question. The author is describing different ways that societies can function without choosing a side or advocating a specific position. You can rule out **(A)** immediately for its strong stand. Choice **(C)** distorts a detail beyond its acceptable scope. While the passage does discuss how social cohesion can function in societies with high degrees of labor specialization, this is not the author's main goal. Choice **(D)** takes a prescriptive stance, and the author never tells us how to live our lives. Finally, **(E)** makes a comparison that is not there. Both of the mechanisms for maintaining social solidarity were developed by Durkheim at the same time and are part of the same worldview, namely, his. The comparison between a traditional and a recent view is inapplicable here.

93. B

What is the crucial difference between *mechanical solidarity* and *organic solidarity*? The level of homogeneity in the group in which each functions. Neither one relies on any measure, objective or otherwise, of group coherence. Rather, they describe the way societies function naturally, ruling out **(A)**. Choice **(C)** introduces the notion of rebellion, a concept that is not mentioned in the passage and hence, cannot be correct. Choice **(D)** is wrong because the two types of solidarity were developed by Durkheim at the same time; we do not have a traditional view and a more recent view of the same phenomenon, but rather two different ways that societies can function within the same worldview. Choice **(E)** brings into question the effectiveness of each, and the last paragraph makes it clear that either one can serve its members needs equally well.

94. E

In this inference question, you will need to think about the author's opinion as you approach the answer choices. Choice **(A)** is wrong because the author never discusses the two forms of *solidarity* as being related to each other, nor does he discuss the transformation of societies over time. Choice **(B)** is outside the scope, as the relationship of individual societies to the world-at-large is not an issue that concerns the author. Choice **(C)** makes a subjective statement about Durkheim that is never suggested by the passage. Choice **(D)** makes a comparison between the two types of social groups that is not supported by the passage. Choice **(E)**, however, is basically a close paraphrase of the final paragraph of the passage. The particular type of integration that exists within a given society is less important than that it is present in some form.

95. C

In this detail question, you should research the second paragraph, where *organic solidarity* is discussed. There you'll find Durkheim's reasoning for why it exists in societies with high levels of heterogeneity. *Organic solidarity* prevails in societies with fewer similarities among members because when a society is highly specialized its members rely on each other out of necessity—as a way to ensure that everyone's needs are met. Reading through the answers, **(C)** should jump out at you as conveying this sentiment.

Choice **(A)** is the opposite of what we want. In societies in which *organic solidarity* dominates, individual differences are relatively high. Choice **(B)** implies a causal relationship between *organic solidarity* and the way a society is organized, but *organic solidarity* is simply a term to describe the way a society *is* functioning; it is not an active agent of anything. Choice **(D)** uses information that was never mentioned in the passage—namely, that some societies are more likely to be affected by social stressors. Finally, **(E)** misappropriates information from the section on societies in which *mechanical solidarity* dominates. Societies that operate by *organic solidarity*, by contrast, tend not to be comprised of members who lead highly similar lives.

96. D

To be *diffident* is to be shy, retiring, or timid. In other words, it is to lack self-confidence. The opposite of being *diffident* is being *confident* **(D)**. Choice **(A)**, *indolent*, means habitually lazy. *Exigent* **(B)** means urgent. Choice **(C)** *apocryphal* means of doubtful authenticity. Choice **(E)** *endemic* means inherent or belonging to a particular area.

97. C

Phlegmatic is from the root *phlegm*. One of the meanings of *phlegm* is sluggishness of temperament, from the middle English use of the word as one of the four temperaments, or humors, of man. You may have heard the phrase "a phlegmatic temperament." If so, you would look for an antonym that could describe a type of temperament. Perhaps you normally think of *phlegm* as the stringy mucus associated with respiratory ailments, and that is also a useful place to start. Think of the qualities of *phlegm,* such as thick, sluggish, immovable, and you are halfway to the correct answer, *excitable* **(C)**. Defining *phlegmatic* will also help you eliminate **(A)** *apathetic,* which means uncaring, and is closer to a synonym than an antonym. Choice **(B)**, *rustic*, means rural, and can also be eliminated. *Banal* **(D)** means predictable or boring, and thus is also closer to a synonym than an antonym. Choice **(E)**, *erudite,* means learned or scholarly.

98. A

Enervate is related to *nerve,* and therefore to *nervous.* Those words have a connotation of strength or energy. The suffix *ate* provides the action necessary to make the word a verb, and the prefix *en* takes away the energizing action. The opposite of take away strength is the correct choice, (**A**), *energize.* You may also recall a phrase such as "felt enervated." If so, you would look for an antonym that could be adapted (by the addition of *ed*) to be used with the word "felt." To *engender* (**B**) is to cause or bring about. To *dither* (**C**) is to act without clear purpose. Choice (**D**), *inundate,* means to overwhelm, and *inure* (**E**) means to accustom or become used to.

99. B

Imprecation is the noun form of *imprecate,* to curse. An *imprecation* is, therefore, a curse. It is often used in conjunction with the word "hurled," as in "he hurled imprecations at his enemy." If a similar phrase comes to mind, you will know an imprecation is not a positive thing! Once you have defined the word, it becomes easier to choose (**B**) *benediction,* which means blessing, as the correct answer. *Arbitration* (**A**) is the process of judging a dispute. Choice (**C**) *alleviation* is the provision of relief by making something onerous more bearable. A *rejoinder* (**D**) is a response, and a *proclivity* (**E**) is a natural inclination or predisposition.

100. A

Opprobrium is public disgrace. It is often paired with the word *suffer,* as in to "suffer opprobrium." If that phrase came to mind, you could pick the antonym among these choices, *honor* (**A**). *Prudence* (**B**) means wisdom. Choice (**C**) *scintilla* is a trace amount. Choice (**D**) *umbrage* is offense, as in the phrase "take umbrage." *Ostentation* (**E**) is excessive showiness. Its adjective form, *ostentatious,* is more frequently used.

101. A

The word *noisome* means stinking, as in a *noisome* odor. The antonym is *fragrant* (**A**). Choice (**B**) *multifarious* means diverse or multifold. Choice (**C**) *maudlin* means overly sentimental. *Candid* (**D**) means honest in speech, as in a *candid* opinion. *Garrulous* (**E**) means tending to talk a lot and is a distracter meant to play on an association with the word "noisy."

102. C

Cupidity is greed or irresistible desire for material goods. Its antonym, therefore, is *largess* (**C**), a generous giving or benevolence, which carries a connotation of giving to the less fortunate or inferior. *Hegemony* (**A**) is the domination of one state or group over another state or group; it is, therefore, similar to *cupidity,* but on the state level, rather than on the individual level. *Intrepidity* (**B**) is a fearless, even reckless, courage. Choice (**D**) *antipathy* is an extreme dislike (the root *path* rarely signaling anything good). *Penury* (**E**) is extreme poverty or lack of resources. *Penury* is not an antonym of *cupidity* because the former addresses a material fact while the latter speaks of a psychological state.

103. E

The verb *cosset* means to pamper or treat with great care. Its opposite is to *challenge* (**E**), in the sense of requiring great effort or even daring. To *lampoon* (**A**) is to ridicule with satire. To *ossify* (**B**) is to harden or set in a rigidly conventional pattern, or to change into bone. As a verb, *husband* (**C**) means to manage economically, as in the phrase "husband resources." Choice (**D**) *advocate* means to speak in favor of.

104. A

Loquacious means talkative. Its antonym, *taciturn,* (**A**) means silent. *Obdurate* (**B**) means hardened in feeling or resistant to persuasion. Choice (**C**) *quiescent* means motionless or dormant. *Sardonic* (**D**) means cynical or scornfully mocking. The word *specious* (**E**) means deceptively attractive or seemingly plausible but fallacious, as in a "specious argument."

105. D

Pathogenic means causing disease, from the Greek *pathos,* meaning suffering. Its antonym is answer (**D**) *salubrious,* which means healthful or therapeutic. Choice (**A**) *diaphanous* means delicate or gauzy and is often used to describe fabric, as in "diaphanous curtains." *Trenchant* (**B**) means incisive, sharp, even caustic or cutting, as in a "trenchant observation." Choice (**C**) *venerable* means respected due to age, and can be associated with the better-known word *venerate,* a verb meaning to respect deeply. *Sanguine* (**E**) means cheerfully optimistic; a *sanguine* person might be said to wear rose-colored glasses.

106. B

Satiate is a verb that means to satisfy fully, even to the point of overindulgence. The antonym is *kindle* (**B**), which means to ignite or inspire. It is often used in the context of fire, but can also be used in an abstract context, as when speaking of "kindling interest." Choice (**A**) *prevaricate* is to lie or deviate from the truth. *Disabuse* (**C**) means to set right or free from error, as in to "disabuse him of a misunderstanding." To *burnish* (**D**) is to polish, and to *slake* (**E**) is to calm down or moderate, more nearly a synonym of *satiate* than an antonym.

107. E

Prodigal means extravagant or wasteful, with the classic phrase being "prodigal son." An antonym of *prodigal* is *frugal,* (**E**). *Frugal* means thrifty, even to the point of being cheap. Choice (**A**) *furtive* means secret or stealthy, even underhanded. *Disparate* (**B**) means fundamentally or entirely different, as in "disparate cultures." Choice (**C**) *banal* means predictable or boring. *Irascible* (**D**) means ornery or easily made angry.

108. A

To *foment* is to arouse or incite. An antonym for *foment* is *quash* (**A**), meaning to suppress or put down, as in to "quash a rebellion." Both *foment* and *quash* are often used in speaking of a rebellion. Choice **(B)** *mitigate* means to soften or lessen the effects of something. *Bolster* **(C)** is to support or prop up, either literally or, more often, figuratively, as in to "bolster an argument." Choice **(D)** *assuage* means to make something unpleasant less severe, as in the phrase "to assuage her guilt." To *aggrandize* **(E)** is to increase in power, influence, or reputation and is often coupled with *self*, as in "self-aggrandizement."

109. C

Heterogeneous means composed of unlike parts. The prefix *hetero-* means different or diverse. Its opposite is *homo-*, which means same. The antonym of *heterogeneous*, then, is *homogenous* **(C)**, which means of a similar kind. *Hoary* **(A)** means very old, often with the connotation of white or gray from age. *Tangential* **(B)** means digressing or extraneous to the matter at hand. Choice **(D)** *unconscionable* means unfair or unjust, even indefensibly so. *Monastic* **(E)** is from the same root as *monk*. It means extremely plain, even austere, as in a monastery.

110. A

Voluble means talkative or speaking easily. Its opposite is **(A)** *reticent*. *Reticent* means reserved, but with a connotation of silent. Choice **(B)** *turgid* means bloated or swollen, as from a fluid. *Audacious* **(C)** means fearless or daring, as in "an audacious feat." Choice **(D)** *latent* refers to potential that is not readily apparent, that is dormant. *Tawdry* **(E)** means gaudy, cheap, and showy.

111. D

Lucid means clear and easy to understand. Its opposite here is *inchoate* **(D)**, which means disorganized and incoherent, usually with the sense of not yet fully formed, as in an "inchoate thought." Choice **(A)** *endemic* means inherent or belonging to a particular area. Choice **(B)** *florid* is used to describe something that is excessively decorated or embellished, usually in an ostentatious manner. *Intrepid* **(C)** means fearless and resolutely courageous, often paired with *adventurer*. Choice **(E)** *fanatical* is often shortened to the word *fan*. In its full form it refers to excessive enthusiasm and unquestioning devotion and has a negative connotation.

112. B

Lachrymose means tearful or weepy, either literally or temperamentally. Its antonym here is **(B)** *sanguine*, which means cheerfully optimistic, with a rose-tinged connotation. Choice **(A)** *perspicacious* means keen-witted, astute, or shrewd. *Inimical* **(C)** means hostile or unfriendly. It is used with the preposition *to*, as in "the adversaries are inimical to each other." Choice **(D)** *surly* means rude and bad-tempered. *Glib* **(E)** means easily and casually fluent, with overtones of insincerity. It usually refers to speaking but can also be used to describe an attitude.

113. B

The adjective *stolid* means unemotional, perhaps lacking concern or sensitivity. Its opposite is answer (**B**) *volatile. Volatile* means easily aroused or changeable, even explosive, either in material fact or, as here, in temperament. Choice (**A**) *erudite* means scholarly, learned, or bookish. Choice (**C**) *ignoble* uses the prefix *ig-* to reverse the meaning of *noble*. To be *ignoble* is to have low moral standards. *Wily* (**D**) means clever, with a connotation of deception. *Judicious* (**E**) means sensible or showing good judgment. It shares a root with *judgment* and *judge*.

114. E

To *engender* is to cause or bring about, from the same root as *generate*. Its antonym is *extinguish* (**E**), which means to put out or put an end to. The prefix *ex-* almost always signals a meaning that includes the word *out,* as in *exit*. Choice (**A**) *deface* means to vandalize by marring the appearance of. To *lionize* (**B**) is to treat as a celebrity or to honor. Choice (**C**) *palliate* means to mitigate or ease something onerous. To *vex* (**D**) is to annoy or irritate, especially by confusing, as in a "vexing question."

115. C

Torpor is extreme mental and physical sluggishness. The opposite of *torpor* is *vim* (**C**), meaning vitality and energy. *Vim* is often paired with *vigor* to increase its power. Choice (**A**) *polemic* is a verbal attack or argument. *Antipathy* (**B**) means extreme dislike. *Guile* (**D**) is deceit or trickery. Choice (**E**) *invective* refers to abusive language.

116. A

Euphony is pleasant or harmonious sound. Its antonym is (**A**) *cacophony,* a harsh, jarring noise or discordant sound. *Monotony* (**B**) refers to something without variation, tediously the same, as a droning sound. Choice (**C**) *chicanery* is deception by craft or guile. *Cartography* (**D**) refers to the science and art of making maps. Choice (**E**) *hyperbole* refers to a purposeful exaggeration for effect, as in a tall tale.

117. C

Zeal means enthusiasm or fanaticism, so if you predict its opposite you should come up with something like *indifference,* or the actual correct response, (**C**) *apathy*.

118. C

Erroneous means incorrect, so a good prediction for its opposite would be *correct*. Of the answer choices, the closest match is (**C**), *accurate*.

119. B

To be *cognizant* is to be aware. Look for a word that means *unaware*. Choice (**B**), *oblivious,* is a nice match. Choice (**A**), *obsequious,* means overly flattering or servile. If you get stuck, try making opposites of the answer choices and comparing the opposites with the stem word. This should help you eliminate close seconds such as (**E**), *unwise*.

120. C

Tentative means provisional or unsettled, as in "a tentative plan"—one that may or may not be carried out. So its best opposite would be **(C)**, *definite.* If you were familiar with the phrase "a tentative plan" you could have also used this phrase to eliminate answer choices. If you can describe a plan as *tentative,* you should also be able to use the opposite of *tentative* to describe a plan. But a *permanent* plan, a *finite* plan, an *adjacent* plan, and an *amiable* plan all sound a bit funny. Only a *definite* plan makes sense.

121. A

Bawdy means racy or lewd. A good opposite would be *straitlaced* or *proper.* Choice **(A)**, *prudish,* fits perfectly. Of the wrong answers, *superfluous* means unnecessary, *gaunt* means thin, *ethereal* means heavenly or immaterial, and *legitimate* means legal or authentic.

122. D

To *abet* means to aid or assist. The phrase "aiding and abetting" is actually a redundancy, much like the phrase "to cease and desist." A good opposite for abet, therefore, would be *hinder.* Choice **(D)**, *deter,* is a good match.

123. D

Someone who's *dispassionate* is unbiased or objective. A good prediction for its opposite would be *biased* or *unfair.* Choice **(D)**, *partisan,* meaning biased in favor of one side, matches beautifully. Of the wrong answer choices, *sentient* means conscious or aware; *stoic* means expressionless or impassive.

124. A

A *panegyric* is a tough GRE-friendly word meaning formal or elaborate praise in writing or oration. Therefore the best opposite would be **(A)**, *defamatory essay.* On tough Antonyms, particularly ones with phrases in the answer choices, you can always go to answer choices and try to make opposites of them; not all words or phrases have good opposites, and these can be eliminated. For instance, what's a good opposite for **(D)**, *witty aside*? Likewise, **(B)**, *formal monologue,* and **(C)**, *binding contract,* don't lead to clear-cut opposites. The best rule of thumb when you're dealing with unfamiliar Antonym stems is to make opposites of the answer choices, eliminating any choice that takes you more than five seconds to come up with an opposite, make your best guess, and when stuck between two good guesses, go for the one that's more extreme.

125. E

Once again you're given a tough GRE-friendly stem word, *prolix,* so if you knew that *prolix* means wordy you could come up with the correct answer, **(E)**, *pithy,* meaning to the point. Otherwise, once again you'd have to work with the answer choices. For instance, if you had a sense that *prolix* has a somewhat negative word charge, you eliminate choices that have negative word charges, **(A)**, **(B)**, and **(C)**. You could also make opposites of the answer choices; for instance, the opposite of **(D)**, *diverse,* would be similar. If you don't think that *prolix* means similar, you can eliminate that answer choice. A final word about Antonyms: Sometimes you simply won't know the stem word—staring at it for a couple of minutes is not going to get you closer to the correct answer. Using word charge, word roots, and word associations, and making opposites of the answer choices can all help you, but at some point, you just have to make your best guess and move on.

CHAPTER 4: QUANTITATIVE SECTION

- Learn the basic principles for success on the Quantitative section
- Get to know Kaplan's techniques for classic GRE math problems
- Complete the 60-Question Quantitative Practice Set

INTRODUCTION

You'll have 45 minutes to complete 28 questions in the Quantitative section. The GRE tests the same sort of mathematical concepts that the SAT does: arithmetic, algebra, and geometry. There is no trigonometry or calculus tested on the GRE. However, if you are doing really well on the GRE Quantitative section you may see a few topics you didn't see on the SAT, such as probability, combinations and permutations, and data analysis concepts such as standard deviation, range, mean, median, and mode. Every math concept that you may possibly see on the test can be found in the Math Reference resources at the end of this book.

While we're reminiscing about the SAT, it's worth mentioning that there are three other big differences between SAT math and GRE math. First, you are not allowed to use a calculator on the GRE. This is not as bad as it sounds. You may have to brush up a little on your computing skills, but the truth is that GRE math questions don't involve a lot of calculation. In fact, if a question seems to involve a lot of calculation, you should look at it again—there's bound to be a shortcut that will allow you to avoid crunching the numbers. In this chapter we'll give you some examples of this and show you how to use shortcuts.

A second difference between GRE math and SAT math relates specifically to geometry problems that contain diagrams. On the SAT, such diagrams are always drawn to scale, unless a note beneath the diagram informs you that the diagram is NOT drawn to scale. On the GRE, such diagrams are not necessarily drawn to scale, except when a note beneath the diagram informs you that the diagram IS drawn to scale. This means that on the GRE, unlike on the SAT, you generally cannot use the diagram to eyeball angle measures and lengths. It also means that just because a figure looks like a square or an equilateral triangle, you cannot assume this to be the case. Instead you have to rely on the information in the problem, and in some cases you may want to redraw the diagram to get a better sense of what's going on.

The third difference should come as good news. You are given more time to answer math questions on the GRE than is the case on the SAT. As noted, you'll have 45 minutes to answer 28 questions, which consist of three question types: Quantitative Comparisons, Problem Solving, and Data Interpretation. The chart below shows how many questions you can expect of each question type, as well as the amount of time you should spend per question on each question type, very roughly speaking.

	Quantitative Comparison	Word Problems	Data Interpretation
Number of Questions	approx. 14	approx. 10	approx. 4
Time per Question	45 to 60 seconds	1.5 to 2 minutes	2 to 3 minutes

NEW QUANTITATIVE QUESTION TYPE—NUMERIC ENTRY

Essentially, the Numeric Entry question type does not provide any answer choices at all. None. Zip. Zero! You have to do the math, work out your answer, and type it in the box provided.

The most important thing to keep in mind here is to read through the question very carefully; make sure you know exactly what's being asked of you. Then check your work just as carefully. Here's a sample Numeric Entry question and answer explanation.

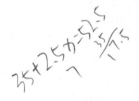

The health club charges $35 per month plus $2.50 for each aerobic class attended. How many aerobic classes were attended for the month, if the total monthly charge was $52.50?

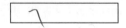

Click on the answer box, and then type in a number. Use backspace to erase.

Answer: 7

Translate the situation into an algebraic equation, and then solve for the unknown variable. You are asked to find the number of classes attended; assign the variable x to represent the number of aerobics classes attended. The monthly fee is $35, plus $2.50 for every class attended, or 2.5 times x (the number of classes).

The equation is therefore $35 + 2.5x = 52.50$.

Subtract 35 from both sides of the equation: $2.5x = 17.5$

Divide both sides by 2.5. The answer, therefore, is 7.

QUANTITATIVE COMPARISONS

On Quantitative Comparisons, or QCs, as we like to call them, instead of solving for a particular value, your job is to compare two quantities. At first, these questions tend to throw test takers because of their weird format. But once you become used to them, they should actually take less time to solve than other math question types. Doing well on QCs begins with understanding what makes them different from other math questions.

The difficulty of the QCs will depend on how well you are doing in the section. In each question, you'll see two mathematical expressions. One is in Column A, the other in Column B. Your job is to compare them. Some questions include additional information about one or both quantities. This information is centered, and is essential to making the comparison.

QCs are the only questions type on the GRE with four instead of five answer choices. The answer choices to QCs never change. Here's what they look like:

- ⬭ The quantity in Column A is greater.
- ⬭ The quantity in Column B is greater.
- ⬭ The two quantities are equal.
- ⬭ The relationship cannot be determined from the information given.

Because the answer choices to QCs never change, from here on in we will omit the answer choices from the QC examples in this book. To score high on QCs, learn what the answer choices stand for, and know these cold. The directions to QCs look something like this:

This question consists of two quantities, one in Column A and one in Column B. You are to compare the two quantities and choose

- ⬭ if the quantity in Column A is greater;
- ⬭ if the quantity in Column B is greater;
- ⬭ if the two quantities are equal;
- ⬭ if the relationship cannot be determined from the information given.

> Common information: In a question, information concerning
> one or both of the quantities to be compared is centered above
> the two columns. A symbol that appears in both columns
> represents the same thing in Column A as it does in Column B.

Now that you are familiar with the answer choices and directions, let's look at QCs and strategies to make quick comparisons.

THE 2 BASIC PRINCIPLES OF QUANTITATIVE COMPARISONS

Answer choices (**A**), (**B**), and (**C**) all represent definite relationships between the quantities in Column A and Column B. But (**D**) represents a relationship that cannot be determined. Here are two things to remember about (**D**) that will help you decide when to pick it:

Principle 1. Choice (D) Is Never Correct If Both Columns Contain Only Numbers.

The relationship between numbers is unchanging, but choice (**D**) means more than one relationship is possible.

Principle 2. Choice (D) Is Always Correct If You can Demonstrate Two Different Relationships Between the Columns.

Here's what we mean by this. Suppose you ran across the following QC:

Column A	Column B
$2x$	$3x$

If x is a positive number, Column B is greater than Column A. If $x = 0$, the columns are equal. If x equals any negative number, Column B is less than Column A. Because more than one relationship is possible, the answer is (**D**). In fact, as soon as you find a second possibility, stop working and choose (**D**).

On this question we *picked numbers* to compare the two quantities. This is just one strategy that can be used to quickly find the correct answer to a QC.

KAPLAN'S 6-STEP METHOD FOR QUANTITATIVE COMPARISONS

Here are six Kaplan strategies that will enable you to make quick comparisons. In the rest of this chapter you'll learn how they work and you'll try them on practice problems.

Step 1. Compare, don't calculate.

This strategy is especially effective when you can estimate the quantities in a QC.

Step 2. Compare piece by piece.

This works on QCs that compare two sums or two products.

Step 3. Make one column look like the other.

This is a great approach when the columns look so different that you can't compare them directly.

Step 4. Do the same thing to both columns.

Change both columns by adding, subtracting, multiplying, or dividing by the same amount on both sides in order to make the comparison more apparent.

Step 5. Pick numbers.

Use this to get a handle on abstract algebra QCs.

Step 6. Redraw the diagram.

Redrawing a diagram can clarify the relationships between measurements.

Step 1. Compare, Don't Calculate.

This strategy is especially effective when you can estimate the quantities in a QC. Let's have a look at the following problem:

Column A	Column B
$\frac{1}{4}+\frac{1}{5}+\frac{1}{6}+\frac{1}{7}$	$\dfrac{1}{\frac{1}{4}+\frac{1}{5}+\frac{1}{6}+\frac{1}{7}}$

$$\frac{1}{\frac{1}{6}}=6$$

This problem would be a nightmare to calculate under timed conditions. But the only thing you need to figure out is if one quantity is greater than the other (remember, choice (**D**) is not included here since both quantities contain only numbers).

While you may not know the sum of the four fractions in Quantity A, you do know two things:

$\frac{1}{4}+\frac{1}{4}+\frac{1}{4}+\frac{1}{4}=1$ and $\frac{1}{5}, \frac{1}{6}$, and $\frac{1}{7}$ are each smaller then $\frac{1}{4}$. These two facts tell you that Quantity A is less than 1 and Quantity B, its reciprocal, must be greater than 1. So choice (**B**) is correct. QCs rarely, if ever, ask for exact values, so don't waste time finding them unless you have to.

Step 2. Compare Piece by Piece.

Column A	Column B
$w > x > 0 > y > z$	
$w + y$	$x + z$

In this problem, there are four variables—w, x, y, and z. Compare the value of each "piece" in each column. If every "piece" in one column is greater than a corresponding "piece" in the other column and the only operation involved is addition, the column with the greater individual values will have the greater total value.

From the given information, we know that $w > x$ and $y > z$. Therefore, the first term in Column A, w, is greater than the first term in Column B, x. Similarly, the second term in Column A, y, is greater than the second term in Column B, z. Because each piece in Column A is greater than the corresponding piece in Column B, Column A must be greater; the answer is **(A)**.

Step 3. Make One Column Look Like the Other.

When the quantities in Columns A and B are expressed differently, you can often make the comparison easier by changing one column to look like the other. For example, if one column is a percent, and the other a fraction, try converting the percent to a fraction.

Column A	Column B
$x^2 - x = x(x - 1)$	$x^2 - x$

Here Column A has parentheses, and Column B doesn't. So make Column A look more like Column B—get rid of those parentheses. You then end up with $x^2 - x$ in both columns, which means they are equal and the answer is **(C)**.

Try another example, this time involving geometry.

Column A	Column B

The diameter of circle O is d and the area is a.

$$\frac{\pi d^2}{2} \qquad\qquad a$$

Make Column B look more like Column A by rewriting a, the area of the circle, in terms of the diameter, d. The area of any circle equals πr^2, where r is the radius. Since the radius is half the diameter, we can plug in $\dfrac{d}{2}$ for r in the area formula to get $\pi\left(\dfrac{d}{2}\right)^2$ in Column B. Simplifying, we get $\dfrac{\pi d^2}{4}$. Since both columns contain π, we can simply compare $\dfrac{d^2}{2}$ with $\dfrac{d^2}{4}$. $\dfrac{d^2}{4}$ is half as much as $\dfrac{d^2}{2}$, and since d^2 must be positive because it is a distance, Column A is greater and **(A)** is correct.

Step 4. Do the Same Thing to Both Columns.

Some QC questions become much clearer if you change not just the appearances but also the values of both columns. Treat them like two sides of an inequality, with the sign temporarily hidden.

You can add or subtract the same amount from both columns, and multiply or divide by the same positive amount without altering the relationship. You can also square both columns if you're sure they're both positive. But watch out: multiplying or dividing an inequality by a negative number reverses the direction of the inequality sign. Since it alters the relationship between the columns, avoid multiplying or dividing by a negative number.

In the QC below, what could you do to both columns?

$$4a + 2 = 7b$$

Column A	Column B

$$4a + 3 = 7b$$

$$\frac{20a + 10}{5} = 4a + 2 \qquad = \qquad \frac{35b - 5}{5} = 7b - 1$$

All the terms in the two columns are multiples of 5, so divide both columns by 5 to simplify. You're left with $4a + 2$ in Column A and $7b - 1$ in Column B. This resembles the equation given in the centered information. In fact, if you add 1 to both columns, you have $4a + 3$ in Column A and $7b$ in Column B. The centered equation tells you they are equal. Thus (**C**) is correct.

In the next QC, what could you do to both columns?

Column A	Column B

$$y > 0$$

$$1 + \frac{y}{1 + y} \qquad \qquad 1 + \frac{1}{1 + y}$$

First subtract 1 from both sides. That gives you $\dfrac{y}{1 + y}$ in Column A, and $\dfrac{1}{1 + y}$ in Column B. Then multiply both sides by $1 + y$, which must be positive since y is positive. You're left comparing y with 1.

You know y is greater than 0, but it could be a fraction less than 1, so it could be greater or less than 1. Since you can't say for sure which column is greater, the answer is (**D**).

Step 5. Pick Numbers.

If a QC involves variables, try picking numbers to make the relationship clearer. Here's what you do:

- Pick numbers that are easy to work with.
- Plug in the numbers and calculate the values. Note the relationship between the columns.
- Pick another number for each variable and calculate the values again.

Column A	Column B
	$r > s > t > w > 0$
$\dfrac{r}{t}$	$\dfrac{s}{w}$

Try $r = 4$, $s = 3$, $t = 2$, and $w = 1$. Then Column A $= \dfrac{r}{t} = \dfrac{4}{2} = 2$. And Column B $= \dfrac{s}{w} = \dfrac{3}{1} = 3$. So in this case, Column B is greater than Column A.

Always pick more than one number and calculate again. In the previous example, we first found Column B was bigger. But that doesn't mean Column B is always bigger and that the answer is (**B**). It does mean the answer is not (**A**) or (**C**). But the answer could still be (**D**)—not enough information to decide. If time is short, guess between (**B**) and (**D**). But whenever you can, pick another set of numbers and calculate again.

As best you can, make a special effort to find a second set of numbers that will alter the relationship. Here for example, try making r a lot larger. Pick $r = 30$ and keep the other variables as they were. Now Column A $= \dfrac{30}{2} = 15$. This time, Column A is greater than Column B, so (**D**) is correct.

Pick different kinds of numbers. Don't assume all variables represent positive integers. Unless you're told otherwise, variables can represent 0, negative numbers, or fractions. Since different kinds of numbers behave differently, always pick a different kind of number the second time around. In the previous example, we plugged in a small positive number the first time and a larger number the second.

In the next three examples, we pick different numbers and get different results. Since we can't find constant relationships between Columns A and B, in all cases the answer is (**D**).

Column A		Column B
3^n	$n > 2$	n^3

If $n = 3$, Column A and Column B both equal 3^3 or 27.
If $n = 4$, Column A $= 3^4 = 81$ and Column B $= 4^3 = 64$, so Column A is greater.

Column A		Column B
	$x \neq 0$	
x		$\dfrac{1}{x}$

If $x = 3$, Column A $= 3$ and Column B $= \dfrac{1}{3}$, so Column A is greater.

If $x = \dfrac{1}{3}$, Column A $= \dfrac{1}{3}$ and Column B $= \dfrac{1}{\frac{1}{3}} = 3$, so Column B is greater.

<u>Column A</u>	<u>Column B</u>
x	x^2

If $x = \dfrac{1}{2}$, Column A = $\dfrac{1}{2}$ and Column B = $\dfrac{1}{4}$, so Column A is greater.

If $x = 2$, Column A = 2 and Column B = 4, so Column B is greater.

Step 6. Redraw the Diagram.

- Redraw a diagram if the one that's given confuses you.
- Redraw scale diagrams to exaggerate crucial differences.

As we noted earlier, geometry diagrams on the GRE may be misleading. Two angles or lengths may look equal as drawn in the diagram, but the given information tells you that there is a slight difference in their measures. The best strategy in this case is to redraw the diagram, exaggerating the difference so that their relationship can be clearly seen.

<u>Column A</u>	<u>Column B</u>

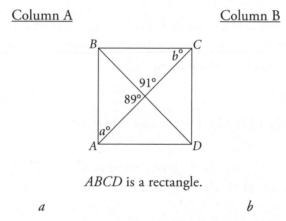

ABCD is a rectangle.

a	b

Redraw this diagram to exaggerate the difference between the 89° degree angle and the 91° angle. In other words, make the larger angle much larger, and the smaller angle much smaller. The new rectangle that results is much wider than it is tall.

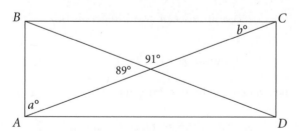

In the new diagram where the crucial difference jumps out, *a* is clearly greater than *b*.

AVOID QC TRAPS

To avoid QC traps, always be alert. Don't assume anything. Be especially cautious near the end of the question set.

DON'T BE TRICKED BY MISLEADING INFORMATION

Watch out for this in the following QC.

<u>Column A</u>   <u>Column B</u>

Joaquin is taller than Bob.

Joaquin's weight in pounds   Bob's weight in pounds

The test makers hope you think, "If Joaquin is taller, he must weigh more." But there's no guaranteed relationship between height and weight, so you don't have enough information. The answer is (**D**). Fortunately, problems like this are easy to spot if you stay alert.

DON'T ASSUME

A common QC mistake is to assume that variables represent positive integers. As we saw in using the picking numbers strategy, fractions or negative numbers often show another relationship between the columns.

<u>Column A</u>   <u>Column B</u>

When 1 is added to the square of x the result is 37.

x 6

It is easy to assume that x must be 6, since the square of x is 36. That would make (**C**) correct. However, it is possible that $x = -6$. Since x could be either 6 or −6, the answer is (**D**).

DON'T FORGET TO CONSIDER OTHER POSSIBILITIES

If an answer looks obvious, it may very well be a trap. Consider the QC below.

The product of two integers is 6.

<u>Column A</u>   <u>Column B</u>

The average of the two integers   2

The factors of 6 are 1, 2, 3, and 6. The average of 1 and 6 is 3.5 (1 + 6, divided by 2), and the average of 2 and 3 is 2.5 (2 + 3 divided by 2). Since both of these result in an average that's greater than 2, the unsuspecting test taker will quickly choose (**A**) and move on. But there's another way to arrive at a product of 6—by multiplying two negative integers. The average of −1 and −6 is −3.5 and the average of −2 and −3 is −2.5, making (**D**) the correct answer.

DON'T FALL FOR LOOK-ALIKES

Just because two expressions look similar, they may be mathematically different.

Column A	Column B
$\sqrt{5} + \sqrt{5}$	$\sqrt{10}$

At first glance, forgetting the rules of radicals, you might think these quantities are equal and that the answer is (**C**). But compare each piece to a benchmark number to see this isn't the case. Each $\sqrt{5}$ in Column A is bigger than $\sqrt{4}$, so Column A is more than 4. The $\sqrt{10}$ in Column B is less than another familiar number, $\sqrt{16}$, so Column B is less than 4. The answer is (**A**).

 KAPLAN STRATEGY

Kaplan's basic principles for success on Quantitative Comparisons are:

- Memorize the answer choices cold.

- Compare the two expressions piece by piece.

- Make one column look like the other by converting or rewriting one of the expressions to match the other.

- Do the same thing to both columns.

- Pick numbers to make the relationship clearer.

- Redraw scale diagrams to clarify and/or to exaggerate crucial differences.

- Don't be misled by QC traps!

QUANTITATIVE COMPARISON PRACTICE SET

	Column A	Column B
1.	$x^2 + 2x - 2$	$x^2 + 2x - 1$

$x = 2y$ y is a positive integer.

	Column A	Column B
2.	4^{2y}	2^x

$$\frac{x}{y} = \frac{z}{4}$$

x, y, and z are positive.

	Column A	Column B
3.	$6x$	$2yz$

	q, r, and s are positive integers. $qrs > 12$	
4.	$\dfrac{qr}{5}$	$\dfrac{3}{s}$

	$x > 1 \quad y > 0$	
5.	y^x	$y^{(x+1)}$

	$7p + 3 = r$	
	$3p + 7 = s$	
6.	r	s

In triangle XYZ, the measure of angle X equals the measure of angle Y.

7.	The degree measure of angle Z	The degree measure of angle X plus the degree measure of angle Y

	$h > 1$	
8.	The number of minutes in h hours	$\dfrac{60}{h}$

Square A Square B

9.	$\dfrac{\text{Perimeter of square } A}{\text{Perimeter of square } B}$	$\dfrac{\text{Length of } WY}{\text{Length of } PR}$

QUANTITATIVE COMPARISON PRACTICE SET ANSWERS AND EXPLANATIONS

1. B

Comparing the respective pieces of the two columns, the only difference is the third piece: −2 in Column A and −1 in Column B. We don't know the value of x, but whatever it is, x^2 in Column A must have the same value as x^2 in Column B, and $2x$ in Column A must have the same value as $2x$ in Column B. Since any quantity minus 2 must be less than that quantity minus 1, Column B is greater than Column A.

2. A

Replacing the exponent x in Column B with the equivalent value given in the problem, we're comparing 4^{2y} with 2^{2y}. Since y is a positive integer, raising 4 to the exponent $2y$ will result in a greater value than raising 2 to the exponent $2y$.

3. B

Do the same thing to both columns until they resemble the centered information. When we divide both columns by $6y$ we get $\dfrac{6x}{6y}$ or $\dfrac{x}{y}$ in Column A, and $\dfrac{2yz}{6y}$, or $\dfrac{z}{3}$ in Column B. Since $\dfrac{x}{y} = \dfrac{z}{4}$, and $\dfrac{z}{3} > \dfrac{z}{4}$ (because z is positive), $\dfrac{z}{3} > \dfrac{x}{y}$.

4. D

Do the same thing to both columns to make them look like the centered information. When we multiply both columns by $5s$ we get qrs in Column A and 15 in Column B. Since qrs could be any integer greater than 12, it could be greater than, equal to, or less than 15.

5. D

Try $x = y = 2$. Then Column A $= y^x = 2^2 = 4$. Column B $= y^{x+1} = 2^3 = 8$, making Column B greater. But if $x = 2$ and $y = \dfrac{1}{2}$, Column A $= \left(\dfrac{1}{2}\right)^2 = \dfrac{1}{4}$ and Column B $= \left(\dfrac{1}{2}\right)^3 = \dfrac{1}{8}$. In this case, Column A is greater than Column B, so the answer is **(D)**.

6. D

Pick a value for p, and see what effect it has on r and s. If $p = 1$, $r = (7 \times 1) + 3 = 10$, and $s = (3 \times 1) + 7 = 10$, and the two columns are equal. But if $p = 0$, $r = (7 \times 0) + 3 = 3$, and $s = (3 \times 0) + 7 = 7$, and Column A is smaller than Column B. Since there are at least two different possible relationships, the answer is **(D)**.

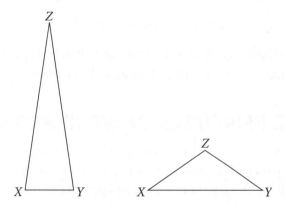

7. D

Since angle X = angle Y, it is an isosceles triangle. We can draw two diagrams with X and Y as the base angles of an isosceles triangle. In one diagram, make the triangle tall and narrow, so that angle X and angle Y are very large, and angle Z is very small.

In this case, Column B is greater. In the second diagram, make the triangle short and wide, so that angle Z is much larger than angle X and angle Y. In this case, Column A is greater. Since more than one relationship between the columns is possible, the correct answer is **(D)**.

8. A

The "obvious" answer here is **(C)**, because there are 60 minutes in an hour, and 60 appears in Column B. But the number of minutes in h hours would equal 60 times h, not 60 divided by h. Since h is greater than 1, the number in Column B will be less than the actual number of minutes in h hours, so Column A is greater. Choice **(A)** is correct.

9. C

We don't know the exact relationship between square A and square B, but it doesn't matter. The problem is actually just comparing the ratios of corresponding parts of two squares. Whatever the relationship between them is for one specific length in both squares, the same relationship will exist between them for any other corresponding length. If a side of one square is twice the length of a side of the second square, the diagonal will also be twice as long. The ratio of the perimeters of the two squares is the same as the ratio of the diagonals. Therefore, the columns are equal. Choice **(C)** is correct.

WORD PROBLEMS

In the Quantitative section on the GRE, you will have to solve problems that test a variety of mathematical concepts. Word Problems typically deal with percentages, simultaneous equations, symbolism, special triangles, multiple and oddball figures, mean, median, mode, range, and probability. You can expect about 10 Word Problems. As with other question types, the more questions you get right, the harder the questions you will see.

The directions that you'll see will look something like this:

> Each of Questions 16–20 has five answer choices. For each of these questions, select the best answer choice given.

THE 2 BASIC PRINCIPLES OF WORD PROBLEMS

To truly do well on GRE math, you need to develop an approach that keeps you from getting bogged down on hard questions or from making careless errors. The GRE math section has two defining characteristics, which we've translated into two basic principles.

Principle 1. The GRE is not a math test...

Traditional math tests require that you show all your work before you get credit—they test the process as well as the answer. But the GRE tests only the answer—how you get there isn't important. Since time is usually your biggest concern on the GRE, the best way to each solution is the quickest way, and that is often not by "doing the math."

Principle 2. ...It's a critical-reasoning test.

GRE math questions are created to measure critical reasoning, your ability to recognize the core math concept in a problem and come up with the right answer. As a result, while the questions aren't necessarily mathematically difficult, they are tricky. That means that hard word problems will have traps in the answer choices. We'll show you how to avoid them. And we'll show you how to take advantage of question formats to give you more of what you need on Test Day—time.

KAPLAN'S 3-STEP METHOD FOR PROBLEM WORD PROBLEMS

Step 1. Read through the question carefully.

Step 2. Decide which approach you will use to answer the question. Be on the lookout for shortcuts. Depending on the question and the answer choices, you may choose to

- use straightforward math to solve;
- apply a backdoor strategy to solve; or
- eliminate unlikely answer choices and make your best guess.

Step 3. Double-check the question again to make sure that you have answered the question that was asked, and then confirm your answer.

Now let's look at how these strategies work.

Step 1. Read Through the Question Carefully.

Okay, this may sound a bit obvious. Of course you're going to read through the question. How else can you solve the problem? In reality, this is not quite as obvious as it seems. The point here is that you need to read the entire question carefully *before* you start to solve the problem. If you don't, it's incredibly easy to make a careless mistake. Take a look at the following problem.

> At Blinky Burgers restaurant, two hamburgers and five orders of French fries cost the same as four hamburgers and two orders of French fries. If the restaurant charges $1.50 for a single order of French fries, how much does it charge for two hamburgers?
>
> ⬭ $2.25
>
> ⬭ $3.00
>
> ⬭ $4.50
>
> ⬭ $5.00
>
> ⬭ $6.00

This question contains a classic trap that's very easy to fall into if you didn't read the question carefully. Can you spot the trap? Notice that you are being asked to find the cost of two hamburgers, not one. Many test takers will get this question wrong by finding the price for one hamburger, and then forgetting to double it. It's a careless mistake to make, but it's easy to be careless when you're taking a high-stakes standardized test like the GRE. That's why you always want to make sure to read the question carefully before you attempt to answer the question

Step 2. Decide Which Approach You Will Use to Answer the Question.

Once you understand what the question is asking, it's time to decide on the best approach to solve the question. Sometimes the "textbook" way to solve the problem is the long way. For instance, in this problem, the textbook way to solve the problem would be to translate the English into algebra equations: $2H + 5F = 4H + 2F$ and $F = 1.50$. From there you could substitute 1.50 for F into the first equation, solve for H, and then multiply your answer by 2.

But if you think carefully, there's often an easier approach. Here, for instance, if two hamburgers and five orders of fries cost the same as four hamburgers and two orders of fries, take away all the items that are the same in the two orders and you're left with three orders of fries costing the same as two hamburgers. Since one order of fries costs $1.50, three orders of fries cost $4.50, so $4.50 must also be the cost of two hamburgers. The correct answer is (C), and you didn't even have to set up any algebra equations.

Step 3. Double-Check the Question Again to Make Sure That You Have Answered the Question That Was Asked.

This step may seem redundant, but it takes very little time and it's better to be safe than sorry. You don't have to reread the entire problem, just the sentence that contains the question. Here we see that once again that we were indeed looking for the cost of two hamburgers, so we can confirm choice (C) and move on.

BACKDOOR APPROACHES TO WORD PROBLEMS

Sometimes the textbook approach will be the best way to find the answer to a Word Problem. Other times, however, as we've just seen, applying common sense or backdoor strategies will get you to the correct answer more quickly and easily. The key is to be open to creative approaches to problem solving. Often this involves taking advantage of the multiple-choice format of a Word Problem.

Three methods in particular are extremely useful when you don't see—or would rather not use—the textbook approach to solving a question. These strategies aren't always quicker than more traditional methods, but they're a great way to make confusing problems more concrete. And if you know how to apply these strategies, you're guaranteed to nail that correct answer every time you use them.

These strategies are:

- Picking numbers
- Backsolving
- Elimination

Let's examine these strategies now.

PICKING NUMBERS

As we saw with QCs, picking numbers is a handy strategy for "abstract" problems—ones using variables, either expressed or implied, rather than numbers. An expressed variable appears in the question ("Jane had x apples and 3 oranges..."). Questions with implied variables describe a problem using just numbers, but the only way to solve the problem is by setting up an equation that uses variables. Problems that lend themselves to the picking numbers strategy involve simple enough math, but the variables make the problem complex. They include those where:

- both the question and the answer choices have variables, expressed or implied;
- the problem tests a number property you don't recall;
- the problem and the answer choices deal with percents or fractions; and/or
- the problem and the answer choices deal with percents or fractions.

Step 1. Pick simple numbers to stand in for the variables.

Step 2. Answer the question using the numbers you picked.

Step 3. Try all the answer choices using the numbers you picked, eliminating those that gave you a different result.

Step 4. Try different values if more than one answer choice works.

Don't worry. Step 4 is rarely necessary. Let's try this strategy on the following problem.

> If a sausage-making machine produces 3,000 sausages in h hours, how many sausages can it produce in m minutes?
>
> ○ $\dfrac{m}{50h}$
>
> ○ $\dfrac{50h}{m}$
>
> ○ $\dfrac{mh}{50}$
>
> ○ $\dfrac{50m}{h}$
>
> ○ $50mh$

You may feel like solving this problem algebraically, but picking numbers here is just as quick and a whole lot safer. The key is to pick numbers that do the unit converting for you. For instance, here the rate is given as 3,000 sausages in h hours, but the question asks you how many sausages can be made in m minutes. So let's begin by picking 60 for m, thus converting our minutes into one hour. And now make h an easy number, such as $h = 2$. Now the question asks: If 3,000 sausages can be made in 2 hours, how many sausages can be made in 60 minutes? The answer is quite obviously 1,500. Now go to the answer choices to find 1,500.

(A) $\dfrac{m}{50h} = \dfrac{60}{50 \times 2}$, which is way too small.

(B) $\dfrac{50h}{m} = \dfrac{50 \times 2}{60}$, which is still too small.

(C) $\dfrac{mh}{50} = \dfrac{60 \times 2}{50}$, which is also too small.

(D) $\dfrac{50m}{h} = \dfrac{50 \times 60}{2} = 1,500$. That's the ticket!

(E) $50mh = 50 \times 60 \times 20$. Too big.

So **(D)** is the answer.

PICKING NUMBERS PRACTICE SET

1. If $a > 1$, what is the value of $\dfrac{2a + 6}{a^2 + 2a - 3}$?

   ○ a

   ○ $a + 3$

   ○ $\dfrac{2}{a - 1}$

   ○ $\dfrac{2a}{a - 3}$

   ○ $\dfrac{a - 1}{a}$

2. When n is divided by 14 the remainder is 10. What is the remainder when n is divided by 7?

   ◯ 2

   ◯ 3

   ◯ 4

   ◯ 5

   ◯ 6

3. If $r = 3s$, $s = 5t$, t $= 2u$, and $u \neq 0$, what is the value of $\dfrac{rst}{u^3}$?

   ◯ 30

   ◯ 60

   ◯ 150

   ◯ 300

   ◯ 600

4. An antique dealer usually charges 20 percent more than his purchase price for any vase sold in his store. During a clearance sale, all items are marked 10 percent off. If the dealer sells a vase during the clearance sale, his profit on the vase (sale price minus purchase price) is what percent of the purchase price of the vase?

   ◯ 8%

   ◯ 9%

   ◯ 10%

   ◯ 11%

   ◯ 12%

5. In a certain orchestra, each musician plays exactly one instrument. If $\frac{1}{5}$ of the musicians play brass instruments, and the number of musicians playing wind instruments is $\frac{2}{3}$ greater than the number of musicians playing brass instruments, what fraction of the musicians in the orchestra play neither brass nor wind instruments?

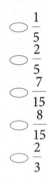

○ $\frac{1}{5}$

○ $\frac{2}{5}$

○ $\frac{7}{15}$

○ $\frac{8}{15}$

○ $\frac{2}{3}$

PICKING NUMBERS PRACTICE SET ANSWERS AND EXPLANATIONS

1. C

You could solve this problem using algebra, but we'll pick numbers here. The question tells you that $a > 1$, so you could begin by picking 2 for a here.

Thus, $\dfrac{2a+6}{a^2+2a-3} - \dfrac{2(2)+6}{2^2+2(2)-3} = \dfrac{10}{5} = 2$.

So you are looking for an answer choice that equals 2 when $a = 2$.

(A) $a = 2$, so keep it.

(B) $a + 3 = 2 + 3 = 5$. Eliminate.

(C) $\dfrac{2}{a-1} = \dfrac{2}{2-1} = 2$, so keep it.

(D) $\dfrac{2a}{a-3} = \dfrac{2 \times 2}{2-3} = -4$. Eliminate.

(E) $\dfrac{a-1}{2} = \dfrac{2-1}{2} = \dfrac{1}{2}$. Eliminate.

All right, we confess. We did this deliberately, just to make you go through step 4. Now pick a different number for a, say $a = 3$. If we run that through the expression in the question stem we get:

$$\frac{2a+6}{a^2+2a-3} - \frac{2(3)+6}{3^2+2(3)-3} = \frac{12}{12} = 1$$

So 1 is our new target number. Now if we put $a = 3$ into the remaining answer choices, there's only one choice that works:

(A) $a = 3$. No good.

(C) $\dfrac{2}{a-1} = \dfrac{2}{3-1} = 1$, so **(C)** is the answer. Okay, it took some effort, but it wasn't so bad.

2. B

Note that just because the answer choices don't contain variables, that doesn't mean you can't pick numbers to make an abstract problem more concrete. The key here is to pick a number for n that leaves a remainder of 10 when divided by 14. The easiest strategy is to pick $n = 24$ (because $14 + 10 = 24$). Now try out your number: $24 \div 7 = 3$, with a remainder of 3 left over. Thus, the answer is **(B)**.

3. E

The other variables all build upon u, so pick a small number for u and figure out values for r, s, and t.

For instance, if $u = 1$, then $t = 2u$, so $t = 2$; $s = 5t$, so $s = 10$; and $r = 3s$, so $r = 30$. So $\dfrac{rst}{u^3} - \dfrac{30 \times 10 \times 2}{1 \times 1 \times 1} = 600$, and **(E)** is the answer.

You'll notice that picking numbers worked in questions 2 and 3, even though there were numbers, rather than variables, in the answer choices. We often employ a different strategy when there are numbers in the answer choices, which we will look at soon. But there are two other times when there won't be variables in the answer choices, or even explicitly in the questions, but the questions will be perfect candidates for picking numbers.

We refer to those funky Word Problems that contain percents or fractions in the answer choices, and unknown values in the questions. By picking numbers for the unknown values in these questions, they become much easier to answer. The key is to know what numbers to pick.

Here, take a look. Try answering the following questions on your own by picking numbers, and then we'll see how your method squares with ours.

4. A

Let's begin by picking $100 for the original cost of the vase. So the dealer pays $100 for the vase, but he usually charges 20 percent more, or $120 for it. During the sale the vase's price is reduced 10 percent. Ten percent of $120 is $12, so the final sale price of the vase is $108, meaning the dealer made a profit of $\dfrac{8}{100}$ or 8 percent of his original purchase price. So the correct answer is **(A)**.

5. C

Since 15 is the largest denominator in the answer choices, let's assume there are 15 musicians in the orchestra. Since $\dfrac{1}{5}$ of these were brass musicians, that means there are 3 brass musicians in the orchestra. The number of wind musicians is $\dfrac{2}{3}$ greater than this, that is $\frac{2}{3}$ greater than 3, so there are 2 more wind musicians than brass musicians, or 5 wind musicians altogether. So, of the 15 musicians, $3 + 5 = 8$ play either wind or brass instruments. That leaves 7 people who play neither instrument. So the fraction of musicians who play neither instrument is $\frac{7}{15}$. Choice **(C)** is the correct answer.

Now let's look at our second backdoor strategy for dealing with ugly math questions.

BACKSOLVING

Some math problems don't have variables that let you substitute picked numbers, or they require an unusually complex equation to find the answer. In cases like these, you're best off trying to backsolve the problem. Simply plug the given answer choices back into the question until you find the one that works. Unfortunately, there are no hard-and-fast rules that identify a picking numbers question from a backsolving problem. You have to rely on two things: The experience you gain from answering practice questions, and your instinct. Combining these two skills will point you to the fastest solution for answering a problem. If you do this using the system outlined below, it shouldn't take long.

Step 1. Estimate Whether the Answer Will Be Small or Large.

Eyeball the question and predict whether the answer will be small or large. Your estimate needn't (and shouldn't) be precise; it just has to reflect your "feel" for the relative size of the answer.

Step 2. Start With (B) or (D).

For small-quantity answers, start backsolving with answer choice **(B)**; for large-quantity answers, start with **(D)**. By starting with **(B)** or **(D)**, you increase your chances of getting the right answer on the first try by taking advantage of the format of GRE answers: they're listed in ascending order. You have a 40 percent chance of getting the correct answer in a single try.

For example, if you start with **(B)**, you have these three possibilities: **(B)** is right, **(A)** is right (because **(B)** is too big), or **(B)** is too small. If you start with **(D)**, the possibilities are: **(D)** is right, **(E)** is right (because **(D)** is too small), or **(D)** is too big. And if you apply your estimate first (Is the answer small or large?), you can greatly improve your chances of hitting the correct answer in one shot.

Step 3. Test the Choice That You Did Not Start With.

If **(B)** is too small or **(D)** is too large, you'll have three choices left. In either case, testing the middle remaining choice immediately reveals the correct answer. For example, if you started with **(B)** and it was too small, you'd be left with **(C)**, **(D)**, and **(E)**. If **(D)** turns out to be too large, you'd be left with **(A)**, **(B)** or **(C)**.

BACKSOLVING PRACTICE SET

1. At Central Park Zoo, the ratio of sea lions to penguins is 4:11. If there are 84 more penguins than sea lions, how many sea lions are there?

    ○ 24

    ○ 36

    ○ 48

    ○ 72

    ○ 121

2. If $\dfrac{3x}{4} + 10 = \dfrac{x}{8} + 15$, then $x =$

    ○ 4

    ○ 8

    ○ 10

    ○ 12

    ○ 16

3. What is the value of x if $\dfrac{x+1}{x-3} = \dfrac{x+2}{x-4} = 0$?

    ○ −2

    ○ −1

    ○ 0

    ○ 1

    ○ 2

BACKSOLVING PRACTICE SET ANSWERS AND EXPLANATIONS

1. C

Since there are more penguins than sea lions, let's start small with answer choice (**B**), 36. If there are 36 sea lions, there are 36 + 84 = 120 penguins, so the ratio of sea lions to penguins is $\dfrac{36}{120} = \dfrac{3}{10}$. Too small.

That means that correct answer must be (**C**), (**D**), or (**E**). Let's try the middle remaining choice, which is (**D**), 72. Since 72 + 84 = 156, the ratio of sea lions to penguins is $\dfrac{72}{156} = \dfrac{6}{13}$. Too big. Therefore, the correct answer is (**C**), 48. If you do the math, it checks out. Since $48 + 84 = 132$, the ratio of sea lions to penguins is $\dfrac{48}{132} = \dfrac{4}{11}$.

2. B

Answer choice **(D)**, 12, seems a bit too big to be the right answer, so let's start again with choice **(B)**, 8. That means $x = 8$. If we plug that in to the equation, we get:

$$\frac{3 \times 8}{4} + 10 = \frac{8}{8} + 15$$

$$\frac{24}{4} + 10 = 1 + 15$$

$$6 + 10 = 16$$

3. D

In this instance, answer choice **(B)** could be too small, so let's start at the other end, with answer choice (D):

$$\frac{x+1}{x-3} - \frac{x+2}{x-4} = \frac{1+1}{1-3} - \frac{1+2}{1-4} = -1 + 1 = 0$$

Since the equation is true for **(D)**, it must be the answer.

ELIMINATION

How quickly can you solve this problem?

> Jenny has 228 more marbles than Jack. If Bob gave each of them 133 marbles, she will have twice as many marbles as Jack. How many marbles does Jenny have?
>
> ◯ 95
>
> ◯ 190
>
> ◯ 228
>
> ◯ 323
>
> ◯ 456

If you backsolved or did the algebra, it might take you a minute or so to find the answer. If you know a bit about number properties, however, you can solve it in far less time without doing any calculations.

If Jenny and Jack each had 133 more marbles (an odd number), Jenny would have twice as many (an even number) as Jack. Since an even number minus an odd number is an odd number, Jenny must currently have an odd number of marbles. That allows us to eliminate **(B)**, **(C)**, and **(E)**, all without doing any math. It gets better: Jenny has

228 more marbles than Jack, so she can't possibly have 95 marbles, which allows you to eliminate **(A)** as well. Therefore, the correct answer has to be **(D)** and you didn't have to do any textbook math to get it!

The answer is that elimination works on fewer problems than either picking numbers or backsolving. Where you can apply it, it's very fast. When you can't, the other two methods and even the straightforward math are good fallback strategies. You should use elimination if:

- the gap between the answer choices is wide and the problem is easy to estimate, or
- you recognize the number property the test-maker is really testing.

Numbers can have inherent relationships with each other, called number properties. Odd and even numbers, for example, behave in predictable ways. These number properties—the inherent relationships between numbers (odd/even, percent/whole, prime/composite)—are what allow you to eliminate incorrect answers in number-property problems without doing the math.

The marbles problem also illustrates how the GRE is testing your critical reasoning skills. You could do the straight math, but if you apply critical thinking to the problem, it's actually saying, "I'm asking if you know the properties of odd and even numbers."

ELIMINATION PRACTICE SET

1. If 3,000 is 15 percent of *e*, what is 35 percent of *e*?

○ 4,000

○ 4.500

○ 5,200

○ 5,800

○ 7,000

2. A helium pump releases 1,184 units of helium every 37 seconds. At this rate, how many units of helium will it release in a minute?

○ 736

○ 1,327

○ 1,920

○ 2,564

○ 3,122

READ MORE

For more math review and practice, try Kaplan's *GRE Exams Math Workbook*.

3. For every 3,256 widgets produced, exactly 16 are defective. At this rate, how many widgets were produced during a period in which exactly 36 widgets were defective?

- ⬭ 3,256
- ⬭ 4,884
- ⬭ 7,326
- ⬭ 9,768
- ⬭ 14,652

ELIMINATION PRACTICE SET ANSWERS AND EXPLANATIONS

1. E

We know what 15% of *e* is (3,000), and we're looking for 35%. Now, 15% is a little less than half of 35%. In other words, 15% $\times$ 2 = 30%, which is just slightly less than 35%.

Therefore, the correct answer must be slightly more than 3,000 × 2, which equals 6,000. You don't even have to do any math to figure out that **(E)** is the only possible answer.

Using math, e = $\dfrac{3,000}{15}$ = 20,000 and 35% of 20,000 is 20,000 $\times$ 0.35 = 7,000.

2. C

The numbers in this problem aren't very clean but the choices are fairly wide apart, so we'll eliminate rather than doing the math. Thirty-seven seconds is a little more than half a minute, so the correct answer needs to be a little less than twice 1,184. **(A)** and **(B)** are way too small, so we'll eliminate those. Round up 1,184 to 1,200 and it becomes easier to see that **(D)** and **(E)** are too large. That leaves **(C)**, the correct answer. Here's the math: the pump puts out 1,184 units in 37 seconds, so it must be outputting 1,184/37 = 32 = 32 units per second. There are 60 seconds in a minute, so the pump is pumping 60 $\times$ 32 = 1,920 units of helium in a minute.

3. C

The choices look ugly but they are spaced apart, so this is another good problem for elimination. Thirty-six is a bit more than twice 16, so the total number of widgets when 36 are defective should be a bit more than twice 3,256. Only **(C)** and **(D)** come close, but **(D)** is roughly three times 3,256, which is too much. Therefore, **(C)** is correct. Here's the math: call *w* the number of widgets produced when 36 are defective. We'll set up the proportion and solve for *w*.

$$\frac{16}{3,256} = \frac{36}{w}$$

$$\frac{2}{407} = \frac{36}{w}$$

$$2w = 14,652$$

$$w = 7,326$$

 KAPLAN STRATEGY ————————————————————————

Kaplan's basic priciples for success on Word Problems are:

- Read the question stem carefully for clues.

- Decide which method you will use for choosing an answer: straightforward math, picking numbers, backsolving, elimination, or guessing.

- Check the question stem again before choosing your answer to be 100 percent sure that you are answering correctly.

CLASSIC GRE MATH TECHNIQUES

The following strategies will help you conquer specific math questions, Kaplan-style. We will review percentages, simultaneous equations, symbolism, special triangles, multiple and oddball figures, mean, median, mode, and range, and probability. The practice sets for each section contain both QCs and Word Problems.

KAPLAN'S APPROACH TO PERCENTAGES

Last year Julie's annual salary was $20,000. This year's raise brings her to an annual salary of $25,000. If she gets the same percent raise every year, what will her salary be next year?

- ◯ $27,500

- ◯ $30,000

- ◯ $31,250

- ◯ $32,500

- ◯ $35,000

In percent problems, you're usually given two pieces of information and asked to find the third. When you see a percent problem, remember:

If you are solving for a percent:

$$\text{Percent} = \frac{\text{Part}}{\text{Whole}}$$

If you need to solve for a part:

$$\text{Percent} \times \text{Whole} = \text{Part}$$

This problem asks for Julie's projected salary for next year—that is, her current salary plus her next raise.

You know last year's salary ($20,000), and you know this year's salary ($25,000), so you can find the difference between the two salaries:

$$\$25,000 - \$20,000 = \$5,000 = \text{her raise}$$

Now find the percent of her raise, by using the formula

$$\text{Percent} = \frac{\text{Part}}{\text{Whole}}$$

Since Julie's raise was calculated on last year's salary, divide by $20,000.

$$\text{Percent raise} = \frac{\$5,000}{\$20,000} = \frac{1}{4} = 25$$

You know she will get the same percent raise next year, so solve for the part. Use the formula: Percent $\times$ Whole = Part. Her raise next year will be 25% $\times$ \$25,000 = $\frac{1}{4}$ $\times$ 25,000 = \$6,250. Add that amount to this year's salary and you have her projected salary:

$$\$25,000 + \$6,250 = \$31,250, \text{ or } (\textbf{C}).$$

Make sure that you change the percent to either a fraction or a decimal before beginning calculations. You will save time on Test Day if you can translate common percents into their fraction and decimal equivalents.

$$\frac{1}{5} = 20\% = 0.2 \qquad \frac{1}{4} = 25\% = 0.25$$

$$\frac{1}{3} = 33\frac{1}{3}\% = 0.\overline{3} \qquad \frac{1}{2} = 50\% = 0.5$$

$$\frac{2}{3} = 66\frac{2}{3}\% = 0.\overline{6} \qquad \frac{3}{4} = 75\% = 0.75$$

PERCENTAGES PRACTICE SET

	Column A	Column B
1.	5% of 3% of 45	6.75

2. If a sweater sells for $48 after a 25 percent markdown, what was its original price?

- ○ $56
- ○ $60
- ○ $64
- ○ $68
- ○ $72

PERCENTAGES PRACTICE SET ANSWERS AND EXPLANATIONS

1. B

Percent $\times$ Whole = Part. Five percent of (3% of 45) = $0.05 \times (0.03 \times 45) = 0.05 \times 1.35 = 0.0675$, which is less than 6.75 in Column B.

2. C

We want to solve for the original price, the Whole. The percent markdown is 25%, so $48 is 75% of the whole: Percent $\times$ Whole = Part.

$$75\% \times \text{Original Price} = \$48$$
$$\text{Original Price} = \frac{\$48}{0.75} \ \$64$$

KAPLAN'S APPROACH TO SIMULTANEOUS EQUATIONS

If $p + 2q = 14$ and $3p + q = 12$, then $p =$

- ○ −2
- ○ −1
- ○ 1
- ○ 2
- ○ 3

According to the rules of algebra, in order to get a numerical value for each variable, you need as many different equations as there are variables to solve for. So, if you have two variables, you need two independent equations.

You could tackle this problem by solving for one variable in terms of the other, and then plugging this expression into the other equation. But the simultaneous equations that appear on the GRE can usually be handled in an easier way.

But as in the previous example, usually, you will be able to combine the equations—by adding or subtracting them—to cancel out all but one of the variables. You can't eliminate p or q by adding or subtracting the equations in their present form. But look what happens if you multiply both sides of the second equation by 2:

$$2(3p + q) = 2(12)$$
$$6p + 2q = 24$$

Now when you subtract the first equation from the second, the qs will cancel out so you can solve for p:

$$\begin{array}{r} 6p + 2q = 24 \\ -[p = 2q = 14] \\ \hline 5p + 0 = 10 \end{array}$$

If $5p = 10$, $p = 2$.

SIMULTANEOUS EQUATIONS PRACTICE SET

1. If $x + y = 8$ and $y - x = -2$, then $y =$

   ○ -2

   ○ 3

   ○ 5

   ○ 8

   ○ 10

2. If $m - n = 5$ and $2m + 3n = 15$, then $m + n =$

   ○ 1

   ○ 6

   ○ 7

   ○ 10

   ○ 15

SIMULTANEOUS EQUATIONS PRACTICE SET ANSWERS AND EXPLANATIONS

1. B
When you add the two equations, the xs cancel out and you find that $2y = 6$, so $y = 3$.

2. C
Multiply the first equation by 2, then subtract the first equation from the second to eliminate the ms and find that $5n = 5$, or $n = 1$. Plugging this value for n into the first equation shows that $m = 6$, so $m + n = 7$, **(C)**.

$$2m + 3n = 15 \qquad\qquad n = 1 \qquad\qquad m = 6$$
$$-2m + 2n = -10 \qquad m - n = 5 \qquad m + n = 6 + 1 = 7$$
$$5n = 5 \qquad\qquad m = 6$$

KAPLAN'S APPROACH TO SYMBOLISM

You should be quite familiar with the arithmetic symbols $+$, $-$, $\times$, $\div$, and %. Finding the value of $10 + 2$, $18 - 4$, 4×9, or $96 \div 16$ is easy. However, on the GRE, you may come across bizarre symbols. You may even be asked to find the value of $10 \star 2$, $5 \ast 7$, $10 \ast 6$, or $65 \heartsuit 2$.

The GRE test makers put strange symbols in questions to confuse or unnerve you. Don't let them. The question stem always tells you what the strange symbol means. Although this type of question may look difficult, it is really an exercise in plugging in. Take a look.

> If $a \star b = \sqrt{a + b}$ for all nonnegative numbers, what is the value of $10 \star 6$?
>
> ○ 0
>
> ○ 2
>
> ○ 4
>
> ○ 8
>
> ○ 16

To solve, just plug in 10 for a and 6 for b into the expression $\sqrt{a + b}$. That equals $\sqrt{10 + 6}$ or $\sqrt{16}$ or 4. Choice (**C**) is correct.

When a symbolism problem includes parentheses, do the operations inside the parentheses first. Now let's look at a more involved symbolism question.

> If $a \blacktriangle$ means to multiply a by 3 and $a \ast$ means to divide a by -2, what is the value of $((8 \ast)\blacktriangle)\ast$?
>
> ○ -6
>
> ○ 0
>
> ○ 2
>
> ○ 3
>
> ○ 6

First find $8\ast$. This means to divide 8 by -2, which is -4. Working out to the next set of parentheses, we have $(-4)\blacktriangle$, which means to multiply -4 by 3, which is -12.

Lastly, we find (-12)✹, which means to divide -12 by -2, which is 6. Choice **(E)** is correct.

SYMBOLISM PRACTICE SET

<u>Column A</u>   <u>Column B</u>

If $x \neq 0$, let ♠ x be defined by ♠ $x = x - \dfrac{1}{x}$

1. -3 ♠ (-3)

2. If r ❤ $s = r(r - s)$ for all integers r and s, then 4 ❤ $(3$ ❤ $5)$ equals

   ○ -8

   ○ -2

   ○ 2

   ○ 20

   ○ 40

QUESTIONS 3–4 REFER TO THE FOLLOWING DEFINITION:

$$c \star d = \frac{c - d}{c}, \text{ where } c \neq 0$$

3. $12 \star 3 =$

   ○ -3

   ○ $\dfrac{1}{4}$

   ○ $\dfrac{2}{3}$

   ○ $\dfrac{3}{4}$

   ○ 3

4. If $9 \star 4 = 15 \star k$, then $k =$

   ○ 3

   ○ 6

   ○ $\dfrac{20}{3}$

   ○ $\dfrac{25}{3}$

   ○ 9

SYMBOLISM PRACTICE SET ANSWERS AND EXPLANATIONS

1. B

Plug in −3 for x: $\spadesuit \, x = -3 - \dfrac{1}{-3} = -3 + \dfrac{1}{3} = -2\dfrac{2}{3}$, which is greater than −3 in Column A.

2. E

Start in the parentheses and work out:

$$(3 \heartsuit 5) = 3(3 - 5) = 3(-2) = -6; \quad 4 \heartsuit (-6) = 4[4 - (-6)] = 4(10) = 40.$$

3. D

Plug in 12 for c and 3 for d: $12 \star 3 = \dfrac{12 - 3}{12} = \dfrac{9}{12} = \dfrac{3}{4}$.

4. C

Plug in on both sides of the equation:

$$\frac{9 - 4}{9} = \frac{15 - k}{15}$$

$$\frac{5}{9} = \frac{15 - k}{15}$$

Cross-multiply and solve for k:

$$75 = 135 - 9k$$

$$-60 = -9k$$

$$\frac{-60}{-9} = k$$

$$\frac{20}{3} = k$$

KAPLAN'S APPROACH TO SPECIAL TRIANGLES

Special triangles contain a lot of information. For instance, if you know the length of one side of a 30-60-90 triangle, you can easily work out the lengths of the others. Special triangles allow you to transfer one piece of information around the whole figure.

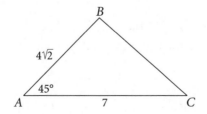

In the triangle above, what is the length of side *BC*?

○ 4

○ 5

○ $4\sqrt{2}$

○ 6

○ $5\sqrt{2}$

The triangle in the previous question may *look* like a right isosceles triangle, but you can't trust diagrams on the GRE! Don't make assumptions on GRE geometry questions. Use the information provided in the question instead.

The following are the special triangles you should look for on the GRE.

Equilateral Triangle

All interior angles are 60° and all sides are of the same length.

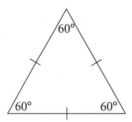

Isosceles Triangle

Two sides are of the same length and the angles facing these sides are equal.

Right Triangle

Right triangles contain a 90° angle. The sides are related by the Pythagorean theorem. $a^2 + b^2 = c^2$ where *a* and *b* are the legs and *c* is the hypotenuse.

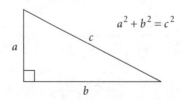

The "Special" Right Triangle

Many triangle problems contain "special" right triangles, whose side lengths always come in predictable ratios. If you recognize them, you won't have to use the Pythagorean theorem to find the value of a missing side length.

The 3-4-5 Right Triangle

Be on the lookout for multiples of 3-4-5 as well.

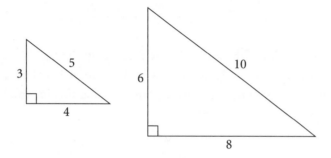

The Isosceles Right Triangle

Note the side ratio: 1 to 1 to $\sqrt{2}$.

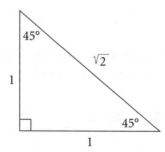

The 30-60-90 Right Triangle

Note the side ratio: 1 to $\sqrt{3}$ to 2, and which side is opposite which angle.

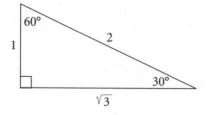

Getting back to our example, you can drop a vertical line from *B* to line *AC*. This divides the triangle into two right triangles.

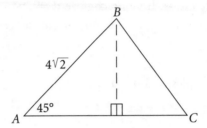

That means you know two of the angles in the triangle on the left: 90° and 45°. So this is an isosceles right triangle, with sides in the ratio of 1 to 1 to $\sqrt{2}$. The hypotenuse here is $4\sqrt{2}$, so both legs have length 4. Filling this in, you have:

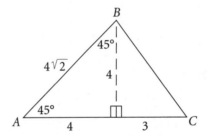

Now you can see that the legs of the smaller triangle on the right must be 4 and 3, making this a 3-4-5 right triangle, and the length of hypotenuse *BC* is 5.

SPECIAL TRIANGLES PRACTICE SET

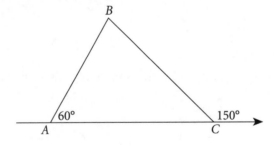

1. In triangle *ABC*, if *AB* = 4, then *AC* =

    ⬭ 10

    ⬭ 9

    ⬭ 8

    ⬭ 7

    ⬭ 6

<u>Column A</u>   <u>Column B</u>

In the coordinate plane, point R has coordinates $(0, 0)$ and point S has coordinates $(9, 12)$.

2.   The distance from R to S 16

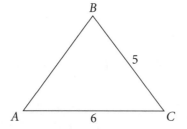

3. If the perimeter of triangle ABC above is 16, what is its area?

- ◯   8
- ◯   9
- ◯   10
- ◯   12
- ◯   15

SPECIAL TRIANGLES PRACTICE SET ANSWERS AND EXPLANATIONS

1. C

Angle BCA is supplementary to the angle marked 150°, so angle $BCA = 180° − 150° = 30°$. Since the interior angles of a triangle sum to 180°, angle A + angle B + angle $BCA = 180°$, so angle $B = 180° − 60° − 30° = 90°$. So triangle ABC is a 30-60-90 right triangle, and its sides are in the ratio $1:\sqrt{3}:2$. The side opposite the 30°, AB, which we know has a length of 4, must be half the length of the hypotenuse, AC. Therefore $AC = 8$, and that's **(C)**.

2. B

Draw a diagram. Since RS isn't parallel to either axis, the way to compute its length is to create a right triangle with legs that are parallel to the axes, so their lengths are easy to find. We can then use the Pythagorean theorem to find the length of RS.

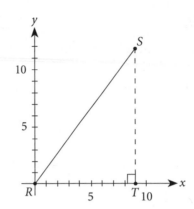

Since *S* has a *y*-coordinate of 12, it's 12 units above the *x*-axis, so the length of *ST* must be 12. And since *T* is the same number of units to the right of the *y*-axis as *S*, given by the *x*-coordinate of 9, the distance from the origin to *T* must be 9. So we have a right triangle with legs of 9 and 12. You should recognize this as a multiple of the 3-4-5 triangle. $9 = 3 \times 3$; $12 = 3 \times 4$; so the hypotenuse *RS* must be 3×5, or 15. That's the value of Column A, so Column B is greater.

3. D

To find the area you need to know the base and height. If the perimeter is 16, then $AB + BC + AC = 16$; that is, $AB = 16 - 5 - 6 = 5$. Since $AB = BC$, this is an isosceles triangle. If you drop a line from vertex *B* perpendicular to *AC,* it will divide the base in half. This divides the triangle up into two smaller right triangles:

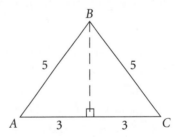

These right triangles each have one leg of 3 and a hypotenuse of 5; therefore they are 3-4-5 right triangles. So the missing leg (which is also the height of triangle *ABC*) must have length 4. We now know that the base of *ABC* is 6 and the height is 4, so the area is $\frac{1}{2} \times 6 \times 4$, or 12. Choice (**D**).

KAPLAN'S APPROACH TO MULTIPLE AND ODDBALL FIGURES

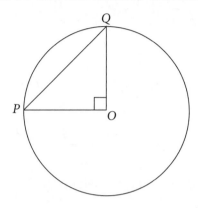

In the figure above, if the area of the circle with center O is 9π, what is the area of triangle POQ ?

○ 4.5

○ 6

○ 3.5π

○ 4.5π

○ 9

In a problem that combines figures, you have to look for the relationship between the figures. For instance, if two figures share a side, information about that side will probably be the key.

In this case the figures don't share a side, but the triangle's legs are important features of the circle—they are radii. You can see that $OP = OQ$ = the radius of circle O.

The area of the circle is 9π. The area of a circle is πr^2, where r is the radius. So $9\pi = \pi r^2$, $9 = r^2$, and the radius r is 3. The area of a triangle is $\frac{1}{2}$ base × height. Therefore, the area of $\triangle POQ$ is $\frac{1}{2}(\text{leg}_1 \times \text{leg}_2) = \frac{1}{2}(3 \times 3) = \frac{9}{2} = 4.5$. Choice (**A**) is correct.

But what if, instead of a number of familiar shapes, you are given something like this?

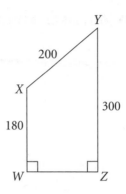

What is the perimeter of quadrilateral *WXYZ* ?

○ 680

○ 760

○ 840

○ 920

○ 1,000

Try breaking the unfamiliar shape into familiar ones. Once this is done, you can use the same techniques that you would for multiple figures. Perimeter is the sum of the lengths of the sides of a figure, so you need to find the length of *WZ*. Drawing a perpendicular line from point *X* to side *YZ* will divide the figure into a right triangle and a rectangle. Call the point of intersection *A*.

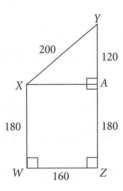

Opposite sides of a rectangle have equal length, so *WZ* = *XA* and *WX* = *ZA*. *WX* is labeled as 180, so *ZA* = 180. Since *YZ* measures 300, *AY* is 300 − 180 = 120. In right triangle *XYA*, hypotenuse *XY* = 200 and leg *AY* = 120; you should recognize this as a multiple of a 3-4-5 right triangle. The hypotenuse is 5 × 40, and one leg is 3 × 40, so *XA* must be 4 × 40 or 160. (If you didn't recognize this special right triangle you could have used the Pythagorean theorem to find the length of *XA*.) Since *WZ* = *XA* = 160, the perimeter of the figure is 180 + 200 + 300 + 160 = 840. Choice (**C**) is correct.

MULTIPLE AND ODDBALL FIGURES PRACTICE SET

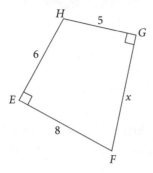

1. What is the value of *x* in the figure above?

   ◯ 4

   ◯ $3\sqrt{3}$

   ◯ $3\sqrt{5}$

   ◯ $5\sqrt{3}$

   ◯ 9

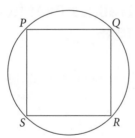

2. In the figure above, square *PQRS* is inscribed in a circle. If the area of square *PQRS* is 4, what is the radius of the circle?

   ◯ 1

   ◯ $\sqrt{2}$

   ◯ 2

   ◯ $2\sqrt{2}$

   ◯ $4\sqrt{2}$

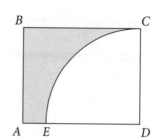

3. In the figure above, the quarter circle with center *D* has a radius of 4 and rectangle *ABCD* has a perimeter of 20. What is the perimeter of the shaded region?

○ $20 - 8\pi$

○ $10 + 2\pi$

○ $12 + 2\pi$

○ $12 + 4\pi$

○ $4 + 8\pi$

MULTIPLE AND ODDBALL FIGURES PRACTICE SET ANSWERS AND EXPLANATIONS

1. D

Draw a straight line from point *H* to point *F*, to divide the figure into two right triangles.

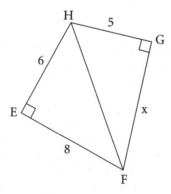

ΔEFH is a 3-4-5 right triangle with a hypotenuse of length 10. Use the Pythagorean theorem in ΔFGH to find *x*:

$$x^2 + 5^2 = 10^2$$

$$x^2 + 5^2 = 100$$

$$x^2 = 75$$

$$x = \sqrt{75}$$

$$x = \sqrt{25}\sqrt{3}$$

$$x = 5\sqrt{3}$$

2 B

Draw in diagonal *QS* and you will notice that it is also a diameter of the circle. Since the area of the square is 4 its sides must each be 2. The diagonal of a square is always the length of a side times $\sqrt{2}$, because the diagonal becomes the hypotenuse of a special, right $2:2:2\sqrt{2}$ triangle.

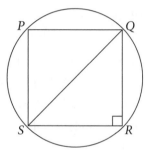

Think of the diagonal as dividing the square into two isosceles right triangles. Therefore, the diagonal $= 2\sqrt{2} =$ the diameter; the radius is half this amount or $\sqrt{2}$.

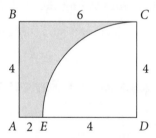

3. C

The perimeter of the shaded region is $BC + AB + AE +$ arc *EC*. The quarter circle has its center at *D*, and point *C* lies on the circle, so side *DC* is a radius of the circle and equals 4. Opposite sides of a rectangle are equal so *AB* is also 4. The perimeter of the rectangle is 20, and since the two short sides account for 8, the two longer sides must account for 12, making *BC* and *AD* each 6. To find *AE*, subtract the length of *ED*, another radius of length 4, from the length of *AD*, which is 6; *AE* = 2. Since arc *EC* is a quarter circle, the length of the arc *EC* is $\frac{1}{4}$ of the circumference of a whole circle with radius 4: $\frac{1}{4} \times 2\pi r = \frac{1}{4} \times 8\pi = 2\pi$. So the perimeter of the shaded region is $6 + 4 + 2 + 2\pi = 12 + 2\pi$.

KAPLAN'S APPROACH TO MEAN, MEDIAN, MODE, AND RANGE

The GRE has always tested the concept of a mean, which is also called the arithmetic mean, for no good reason. The mean of several numbers is simply their average. Whenever you see *arithmetic mean* on the GRE, it's not a trick—it just means *average*.

The median of several terms is the number that evenly divides the terms into two groups; half of the terms are larger than the median and half of the terms are smaller than the median. If there is an odd number of terms, the median will be the same as the middle number (not necessarily the average or the mode). If there are an even number of terms, the median will be halfway between the two terms closest to the middle.

For the set {4, 5, 7, 23, 5, 67, 10}, the median is 7, since this divides the set into two smaller sets of three terms each, {4, 5, 5} and {10, 23, 67}.

The mode is even simpler. It's just the term that occurs most frequently in a set of numbers. If two or more numbers are tied for the most occurrences, then each is considered a mode.

For the set {4, 5, 7, 23, 5, 67, 10}, the mode is 5, because it occurs the greatest number of times of any of the terms.

The range is just the difference between the largest term and the smallest term in a set of numbers. Just subtract the smallest from the biggest and you will have the range. If you've written them in ascending order to find the median, you can find this quickly.

For the set {4, 5, 7, 23, 5, 67, 10}, the range is 63, because the greatest number, 67, minus the smallest, 4, equals 63.

MEAN, MEDIAN, MODE, AND RANGE PRACTICE SET

	Column A	Column B
1.	The median of the integers from 1 through 31, inclusive.	16
2.	2^6	The range of the series {8, 9, 9, 15, 71}

3. The only test scores for the students in a certain class are 44, 30, 42, 30, x, 44, and 30. If x equals one of the other scores and is a multiple of 5, what is the mode for the class?

- ◯ 5
- ◯ 6
- ◯ 15
- ◯ 30
- ◯ 44

4. If half the range of the increasing series {11, *A* , 23, *B* , *C* , 68, 73} is equal to its median, what is the median of the series?

  ○ 23

  ○ 31

  ○ 33

  ○ 41

  ○ 62

MEAN, MEDIAN, MODE, AND RANGE PRACTICE SET
ANSWERS AND EXPLANATIONS

1. C

Inclusive just means you should include the numbers on the ends—in this case, 1 and 31. The number right in the middle of this series is 16. One way to find the number in the middle of an arithmetic series, such as a sequence of consecutive numbers, is to add the highest and lowest numbers together and divide this sum by 2: 1 + 31 = 32 and $\frac{32}{2}$ = 16.

2. A

The product of 2^6 is 64. The range of the series in Column B equals 71 − 8, which equals 63.

3. D

Since *x* equals one of the other scores, it must equal either 30, 42, or 44. And since it must also be a multiple of 5, we can conclude that *x* equals 30. That means that four of the students—more than earned any other score—earned a score of 30, which makes 30 the mode.

4. B

Don't get confused by all the variables; just concentrate on what you know. The range must be the difference of the smallest term and the largest term. Since this is an increasing series, the smallest term must be 11 and the largest must be 73. The difference between them is 62, so that's the range. Half of the range, then, is 31, so 31 must equal the median of the series.

KAPLAN'S APPROACH TO PROBABILITY

A probability is the fractional likelihood of an event occurring. It can be represented by a fraction ("the probability of it raining today is $\frac{1}{2}$"), a ratio ("the odds of it raining today are 50:50"), or a percent ("the probability of rain today is 50 percent"). You can translate probabilities easily into everyday language: $\frac{1}{100}$ = "one chance in a hundred" or "the odds are one in a hundred."

To find probabilities, count the number of desired outcomes and divide by the number of possible outcomes.

$$\text{Probability} = \frac{\text{Number of Desired Outcomes}}{\text{Number of Possible Outcomes}}$$

For example, what is the probability of throwing a 5 on a six-sided die? There is one desired outcome—throwing a 5. There are six possible outcomes—one for each side of the die. So the probability = $\frac{1}{6}$

All probabilities are between 0 and 1 inclusive. A "0 probability" means there is zero chance of an event occurring (*i.e.*, it can't happen). A "1 probability" means that an event has a 100 percent chance of occurring (*i.e.*, it must occur). The higher the probability, the greater chance that an event will occur. You can often eliminate answer choices by having some idea where the probability of an event occurring falls within this range.

The odds of throwing a 5 on a die are $\frac{1}{6}$ so the odds of not throwing a 5 are $\frac{5}{6}$. Therefore, you have a much greater probability of not throwing a 5 on a die than of throwing a 5.

PROBABILITY PRACTICE SET

Column A	Column B

The probability of rain on Thursday is 50 percent. The probability that it will not rain on Friday is $\frac{1}{4}$.

1. The probability of rain on Thursday | The probability of rain on Friday

A hat contains an equal number of red, blue, and green marbles.

2. The probability of picking a red marble out of the hat | The probability of picking a green marble out of the hat

3. If there are 14 women and 10 men employed in a certain office, what is the probability that one employee picked at random will be a woman?

- ○ $\frac{1}{6}$
- ○ $\frac{1}{14}$
- ○ $\frac{7}{12}$
- ○ 1
- ○ $\frac{7}{5}$

4. If Tom flips a fair coin twice, what is the probability that at least one head will be thrown?

$\bigcirc \dfrac{1}{4}$

$\bigcirc \dfrac{1}{3}$

$\bigcirc \dfrac{1}{2}$

$\bigcirc \dfrac{2}{3}$

$\bigcirc \dfrac{3}{4}$

PROBABILITY PRACTICE SET ANSWERS AND EXPLANATIONS

1. B

The probability of rain on Thursday is $\dfrac{1}{2}$ and the probability of rain on Friday is $\dfrac{3}{4}$.

2. C

The number of desired outcomes is the same in each case, since there are an equal number of red and green marbles. The number of possible outcomes in each case is also the same, since the marbles are all being pulled from the same hat. Therefore the probabilities are the same.

3. C

$$\text{Probability} = \left(\frac{\text{Number of Desired Outcomes}}{\text{Number of Possible Outcomes}} \right) = \left(\frac{\text{Number of Women}}{\text{Number of People}} \right) = \frac{14}{24} = \frac{7}{12}.$$

4. E

Desired outcomes = HH or HT or TH. Possible outcomes = HH or HT or TH or TT.
Probability = $\dfrac{3}{4}$.

DATA INTERPRETATION

Data Interpretation questions are often statistics-oriented. Each set of charts is followed up by three to five questions. You'll see Data Interpretation questions frequently on the GRE.

THE 2 BASIC PRINCIPLES OF DATA INTERPRETATION QUESTIONS

Principle 1. Slow Down.

There's always a lot going on in Data Interpretation problems—both in the charts and in the questions themselves. Rushing through this information can necessitate a re-read or result in careless mistakes. Two quicker reads usually take longer and result in retaining less information than one unhurried read, so use your time efficiently—spend enough time to understand the information you're given.

Principle 2. A Question Is a Question Is a Question.

Although Data Interpretation questions tend to be more time-consuming than problem-solving questions, they aren't necessarily more difficult. Tables, bar graphs, and line graphs generally ask for values such as median and mode. Pie charts tend to focus on percentages and converting percentages to numbers. Let's take a look at how to handle them effectively.

KAPLAN'S 3-STEP METHOD FOR DATA INTERPRETATION QUESTIONS

Step 1. Familiarize Yourself With the Tables and Graphs.

Tables, graphs, and charts often come in complementary pairs (a manufacturer's total revenue and his revenue by product line, for example). Familiarize yourself with the information and with their complementary nature before you try to tackle the questions. Pay particular attention to these components:

- **Title.** This may sound obvious, but it's important. Read the chart title to ensure you get your information from the right source.
- **Scale.** Check the scales to see how the information is measured. A common mistake is giving the right quantity but the wrong units (*e.g.,* minutes instead of seconds).
- **Notes.** Read any accompanying notes—they're often the key to answering the questions.
- **Key.** If there are multiple bars or lines on a graph, make sure to refer to and understand the key—another common trap is giving the correct quantity for the wrong item.

Step 2. Answer the Questions that Follow.

Data Interpretation questions require a strong understanding of fractions and percents, and good attention to detail. Questions later in a set tend to be trickier than earlier ones. For instance, if a question set contains two graphs, the first question likely refers to just one graph, and a later question may ask you to combine data from both graphs. If you didn't use both graphs for this later question, the chances are good you'd get it wrong.

Step 3. Approximate Wherever Possible.

No matter how hard graph questions appear at first glance, you can usually simplify them by taking advantage of their answer-choice format: by approximating the answer rather than calculating it wherever possible, you can quickly identify the right one.

As we saw with Word Problems, estimation is one of the fastest ways to solve math problems. Data Interpretation questions benefit from this strategy, as they tend to be the most time-consuming questions to answer.

DATA INTERPRETATION PRACTICE SET

Questions 1–5 are based on the following graphs.

MEGACORP, INC. REVENUE AND PROFIT DISTRIBUTION FOR FOOD- AND NONFOOD-RELATED OPERATIONS, 1984–1989

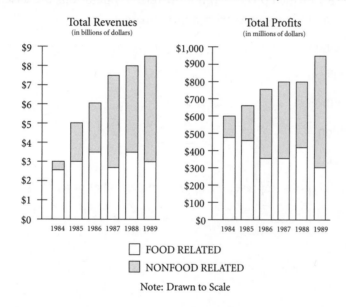

Note: Drawn to Scale

PERCENT OF REVENUES FROM FOOD-RELATED OPERATIONS IN 1989 BY CATEGORY

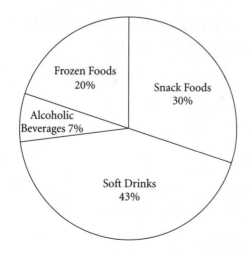

1. Approximately how much did total revenues increase from 1984 to 1987?

   ○ $0.5 billion

   ○ $1.5 billion

   ○ $4 billion

   ○ $4.5 billion

   ○ $5 billion

2. For the year in which profits from food-related operations increased over the previous year, *total revenues* were approximately

   ○ $3.5 billion.

   ○ $4.5 billion.

   ○ $5.7 billion.

   ○ $6 billion.

   ○ $8 billion.

3. In 1988, total profits represented approximately what percent of Megacorp's total revenues?

   ○ 50%

   ○ 20%

   ○ 10%

   ○ 5%

   ○ 1%

4. For the first year in which revenues from nonfood-related operations surpassed $4.5 billion, total profits were approximately

   ○ $250 million.

   ○ $450 million.

   ○ $550 million.

   ○ $650 million.

   ○ $800 million.

5. In 1989, approximately how many millions of dollars were revenues from frozen food operations?

    ◯ 1,700

    ◯ 1,100

    ◯ 900

    ◯ 600

    ◯ 450

DATA INTERPRETATION PRACTICE SET ANSWERS AND EXPLANATIONS

1. D

This question asks about total revenues, so you should refer to the left bar graph. The trickiest part is making sure you correctly extract information from the appropriate bars, in this case for 1984 and 1987. Total revenues for 1984 appear to be $3 million and for 1987 they appear to be about $7.5 million (if you're ever having trouble getting a fix on a quantity on a bar graph, place the edge of a piece of paper along the top of the bar to read the scale better). So the increase is roughly $7.5 billion – $3 million = $4.5 billion.

2. E

The wording is somewhat tricky here, and you have to refer to both bar graphs. First you have to refer to the right bar graph to find the lone year in which food-related profits increased over the previous year—the only year in which the unshaded portion of the bar goes up is 1988. Now that you've zeroed in on the year, you must refer to the left bar graph to determine the total *revenues* for that year, which appear to be about $8 billion.

3. C

This is percent question, so first you have to extract the information from the bar graphs. From the right bar graph, the total profits for 1988 appear to be $800 million; from the left bar graph, total revenues for that year appear to be $8 billion (*i.e.,* $8,000 million). Now you just have to convert the part/whole into a percent:

$$\frac{800 \text{ milion}}{8,000 \text{ milion}} = \frac{1}{10} = 10\%.$$

4. E

First you have to find the year for which revenues from nonfood-related operations surpassed $4.5 billion, so refer to the left bar graph. Finding the correct bar is made more difficult by the fact that you have to deal with the shaded portion, which is not grounded at $0. So you may want to make a ruler from a sheet of paper, using the scale to mark off the length represented by $4.5 billion, and using this to locate the appropriate bar. You should then be able to see that 1987 is the year in question. The question asks for total *profits*, so once again refer to the right bar graph and you'll see the profits for that year are around $800 million.

5. D

Finally you have a question that refers to the pie chart. You are asked about revenues from frozen food operations, and the pie chart informs you that frozen foods represent 20 percent of all food-related revenues for 1989. To convert this into an amount you need to locate the amount of food-related revenues for 1989, so once again refer to the left bar graph where you'll find the food-related revenues in 1989 were about $3 billion, or $3,000 million. 20 percent of $3,000 million is $600 million.

If you are scoring above 700 on GRE Math, you may get some hard questions involving concepts that we haven't reviewed in this chapter, including:

- Standard deviation
- Multiple-event probability
- Permutations
- Combinations
- Sequences
- Graphs of functions

These and other tricky math concepts are explained in the Math Reference at the end of this book. Now use what you have learned in this chapter to tackle some Quantitative practice questions.

SUMMARY

Kaplan's 6-Step Method for Quantitative Comparisons is:

Step 1. Compare piece by piece.

Step 2. Make one column look like the other.

Step 3. Do the same thing to both columns.

Step 4. Pick numbers.

Step 5. Redraw the diagram.

Step 6. Avoid QC traps.

Kaplan's 3-Step Method for Word Problems is:

Step 1. Read through the question carefully.

Step 2. Decide which approach you will use to answer the question. Be on the lookout for shortcuts. Depending on the question and the answer choices, you may choose to

- use straightforward math to solve;
- apply a backdoor strategy to solve; or
- eliminate unlikely answer choices and make your best guess.

Step 3. Double-check the question again to make sure that you have answered the question that was asked, and then confirm your answer.

Kaplan's 3-Step Method for Data Interpretation questions is:

Step 1. Familiarize yourself with the graph(s).

Step 2. Answer the questions that follow.

Step 3. Approximate wherever possible.

QUANTITATIVE PRACTICE SET

Numbers

All numbers are real numbers.

Figures

The position of points, lines, angles, etcetera, may be assumed to be in the order shown; all lengths and angle measures may be assumed to be positive.

Lines shown as straight may be assumed to be straight.

Figures lie in the plane of the paper unless otherwise stated.

Figures that accompany questions are intended to provide useful information. However, unless a note states that a figure has been drawn to scale, you should solve the problems by using your knowledge of mathematics, and not by estimation or measurement.

Directions

Each of the following Questions 1–30 consists of two quantities, one in Column A and one in Column B. You are to compare the two quantities and choose

◯ if the quantity in Column A is greater;

◯ if the quantity in Column B is greater;

◯ if the two quantities are equal; or

◯ if the relationship cannot be determined from the information given.

Common Information

In a question, information concerning one or both of the quantities to be compared is centered above the two columns. A symbol that appears in both columns represents the same thing in Column A as it does in Column B.

Column A	Column B
1. (50)(10)(8)	(10)(5)(90)

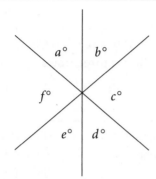

Column A	Column B
2. $a + c + e$	$b + d + f$
3. The number of hours it takes a train to travel 700 miles	The number of hours it takes a car to travel 700 miles
4. $\dfrac{0.009}{0.0003}$	30

There are x dictionaries in a bookstore. After $\dfrac{1}{8}$ of them were purchased, 10 more dictionaries were shipped in bringing the total number of dictionaries to 52.

Column A	Column B
5. x	50
6. $(41)^2 - (21)^2$	$(41 - 21)^2$

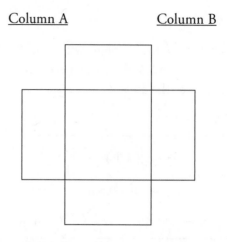

Two rectangles with dimensions 2 meters by 4 meters overlap to form the figure above. All the angles shown have measure 90°.

Column A	Column B
7. The perimeter of the figure, in meters	16
8. $(\sqrt{5} + \sqrt{5})^2$	$5 + 5\sqrt{5}$
9. The average (arithmetic mean) of 100, 101, and 103	The median of 100, 101, and 103

A and B (not shown) are points of the circumference of the circle with center O. The length of chord AB is 15.

Column A	Column B
10. Circumference of circle O	12π

$$x = \frac{4}{3}r^2h^2$$

$$x = 1$$

r and h are positive.

Column A	Column B
11. h	$\dfrac{\sqrt{3}}{2r}$

Column A	Column B

ΔABC lies in the xy-plane with C at $(0, 0)$, B at $(6, 0)$, and A at (x, y), where x and y are positive. The area of ΔABC is 18.

12. y	6

For $x \neq y$, $x \, \Phi \, y = \dfrac{x + y}{x - y}$

$p > 0 > q$

13. $p \, \Phi \, q$	$q \, \Phi \, p$

14. $\dfrac{1}{3} + \dfrac{1}{3}$	$\dfrac{1}{3} \times \dfrac{1}{3}$

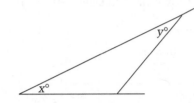

15. $x + y$	180

16. 16 percent of 30	15 percent of 31

$x^5 = -32$

17. x^3	$2x^2$

$x < y < z$

$0 < z$

18. x	0

Column A	Column B

$6(10)^n > 60{,}006$

19. n	6

In a three-digit positive integer y, the hundreds' digit is three times the units' digit.

20. The units' digit of y	4

21. The perimeter of a square with side 4	The circumference of a circle with diameter 5

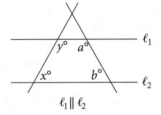

$\ell_1 \parallel \ell_2$

22. $2(x + y)$	$x + a + y + b$

$\dfrac{2x}{3} = \dfrac{2y}{5} = \dfrac{2z}{7}$

z is positive.

23. $x + y$	z

The product of two integers is 10.

24. The average (arithmetic mean) of the two integers	3

$n > 0$

The remainder when n is divided by 3 is 1, and the remainder when $n + 1$ is divided by 2 is 1.

25. The remainder when $n - 1$ is divided by 6	3

Column A	Column B

The average (arithmetic mean) bowling score of n bowlers is 160. The average of these n scores together with a score of 170 is 161.

26. n 10

27. $7^5 + 7^6$ 8×7^5

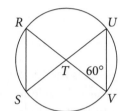

The circle has center T. The measure of angle TVU is 60°.

28. RT RS

After five adults leave a party, there are three times as many children as adults. After a further 25 children leave the party, there are twice as many adults as children.

29.   The original   14
      number of adults

There are at least 200 apples in a grocery store. The ratio of the number of oranges to the number of apples is 9 to 10.

30.   The number of   200
      oranges in the
      store

31.   What is the probability of rolling a 7 with a single roll of two fair dice?

   ○ $\frac{1}{12}$

   ○ $\frac{1}{6}$

   ○ $\frac{2}{7}$

   ○ $\frac{1}{3}$

   ○ $\frac{7}{12}$

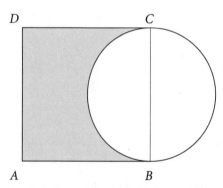

32.   In the above square $ABCD$, the side AB is has a length of 4. It is overlaid with a circle, with a diameter BC. What is the area of the shaded region?

   ○ $16 - 2\pi$

   ○ $16 - 4\pi$

   ○ $16 - 16\pi$

   ○ $4 - \pi$

   ○ $4 - 2\pi$

33. If A and B and C are positive, and $A \blacklozenge B = \dfrac{A+B}{B}$, and $C \clubsuit = C + 3$, what is the value of $(9\clubsuit) \blacklozenge 3$?

   ◯ 3

   ◯ 5

   ◯ 9

   ◯ 15

   ◯ 16

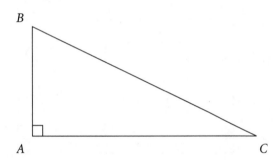

34. In right triangle ABC above, side AB has a length of 5, while side BC has a length of 13. What is the area of ABC ?

   ◯ 65

   ◯ 60

   ◯ 38

   ◯ 30

   ◯ 20

35. If the average test score of 4 students is 85, what will the fifth student need to score in order to have the new average be 86?

   ◯ 90

   ◯ 88

   ◯ 87

   ◯ 86

   ◯ 85

36. If it takes three days for 10 workers to finish building one house, how long will it take 15 workers to finish four houses?

   ◯ 15

   ◯ 10

   ◯ 8

   ◯ 6

   ◯ 4

37. Meg is twice as old as Rolf, but three years ago, she was two years older than Rolf is now. How old is Rolf now?

   ◯ 11

   ◯ 10

   ◯ 8

   ◯ 7

   ◯ 5

38. Rectangle *A* has a length of 12 inches and a width of 5 inches. Rectangle *B* has a length of 9 inches and a width of 10 inches. By what number must the area of rectangle *A* be multiplied in order to get the area of rectangle *B*?

   ○ $\frac{2}{3}$

   ○ $1\frac{1}{4}$

   ○ $1\frac{1}{2}$

   ○ $2\frac{1}{2}$

   ○ $3\frac{1}{2}$

39. The cost, in cents, of manufacturing *x* crayons is $570 + 0.5x$. The crayons sell for 10 cents each. What is the minimum number of crayons that would need to be sold that so that the revenue received is at least equal to the manufacturing cost?

   ○ 50

   ○ 57

   ○ 60

   ○ 61

   ○ 1,140

40. If $xy \neq 0$, $\frac{1-x}{xy} =$

   ○ $\frac{1}{xy} - \frac{1}{y}$

   ○ $\frac{x}{y} - \frac{1}{x}$

   ○ $\frac{1}{xy} - 1$

   ○ $\frac{1}{xy} - \frac{x^2}{y}$

   ○ $\frac{1}{x} - \frac{1}{y}$

Questions 41–45 are based on the following graphs.

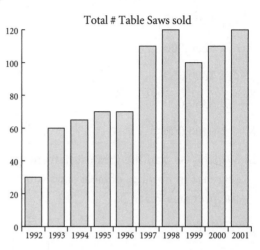

Total # Table Saws sold

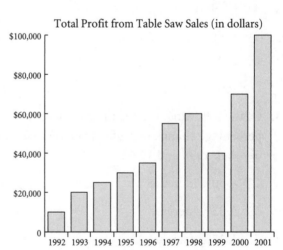

Total Profit from Table Saw Sales (in dollars)

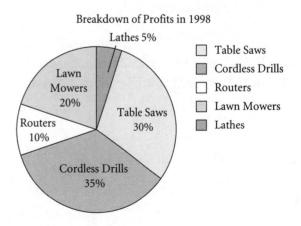

Breakdown of Profits in 1998

41. In 1998, what were the total profits from sales of all the hardware tools?

    ○ $200,000

    ○ $250,000

    ○ $300,000

    ○ $350,000

    ○ $400,000

42. Which year had the greatest percentage increase in number of table saws sold from the previous year?

    ○ 1993

    ○ 1995

    ○ 1997

    ○ 2000

    ○ 2001

43. Of the following, what is the closest to the percentage change in profits from table saws between 1998 and 1999?

    ○ A 50% increase

    ○ A 33% increase

    ○ A 17% decrease

    ○ A 33% decrease

    ○ A 50% decrease

44. If the fixed cost of manufacturing table saws in 1993 was $22,000, how much did each table saw sell for?

    ○ $300

    ○ $450

    ○ $500

    ○ $600

    ○ $700

45. In 1998, what were the approximate profits from the sales of cordless drills?

    ○ $50,000

    ○ $70,000

    ○ $80,000

    ○ $90,000

    ○ $100,000

46. A pizza recipe gives the quantities of each ingredient used to make a round pizza 12 inches in diameter. If Kristy wants to use the recipe to make a pizza 24 inches in diameter that has the same thickness as the pizza that is 12 inches in diameter, by what factor should she multiply the amounts of each ingredient?

    ○ 2

    ○ 3

    ○ 3.5

    ○ 4

    ○ 5

47. Corporation X splits up into five separate, smaller companies: Company A, Company B, Company C, Company D, and Company E. Company A gets $\frac{3}{5}$ of Corporation X's offices, and the rest of the companies divide the remaining offices equally among themselves. If Company A and Company B together have 70 offices between them, how many offices did Corporation X originally have?

    ○ 49

    ○ 50

    ○ 90

    ○ 100

    ○ 140

48. $\left(\dfrac{1}{4}-1\right)\left(\dfrac{1}{5}-1\right)=$

- $\dfrac{3}{5}$
- $\dfrac{1}{20}$
- $\dfrac{1}{20}$
- $-\dfrac{3}{5}$
- -1

49. If a printing press can print 11 complete pages in 30 seconds, how many complete pages can it print in 155 seconds?

- 37
- 46
- 54
- 56
- 65

50. How many odd integers are between $\dfrac{10}{3}$ and $\dfrac{62}{3}$?

- 19
- 18
- 10
- 9
- 8

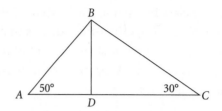

51. In the figure above, if BD bisects $\angle ABC$, then the measure of $\angle BDC$ is

- 50°.
- 90°.
- 100°.
- 110°.
- 120°.

52. If $d = \dfrac{c-b}{a-b}$, then $b =$

- $\dfrac{c-d}{a-d}$.
- $\dfrac{c+d}{a+d}$.
- $\dfrac{ca-d}{ca+d}$.
- $\dfrac{c-ad}{1-d}$.
- $\dfrac{c+ad}{d-1}$.

53. If $x > 0$, then $(4^x)(8^x) =$

- 2^{9x}.
- 2^{8x}.
- 2^{6x}.
- 2^{5x}.
- 2^{4x}.

54. In one class in a school, 30 percent of the students are boys. In a second class that is half the size of the first, 40 percent of the students are boys. What percent of both classes are boys?

○ 20%

○ 25%

○ 28%

○ 30%

○ $33\frac{1}{3}$%

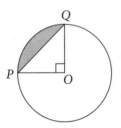

55. In a circle O above, if ΔPOQ is a right triangle and radius OP is 2, what is the area of the shaded region?

○ $4\pi - 2$

○ $4\pi - 4$

○ $2\pi - 2$

○ $2\pi - 4$

○ $\pi - 2$

56. If $n = 14 \times 22 \times 39$, which of the following is NOT an integer?

○ $\dfrac{n}{21}$

○ $\dfrac{n}{24}$

○ $\dfrac{n}{26}$

○ $\dfrac{n}{42}$

○ $\dfrac{n}{77}$

Question 57–60 refer to the following graphs:

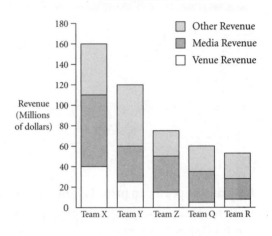

57. For the team with the median amount of venue revenue for 1997, media revenue represented approximately what percent of that team's total revenue for that year?

○ 25%

○ 30%

○ 40%

○ 55%

○ 60%

58. Of the following, which is the closest to the amount of revenues, in millions of dollars, earned by Team X through food sales in 1997?

    ○ 7

    ○ 10

    ○ 14

    ○ 18

    ○ 22

59. Ticket sales represented approximately what percent of total revenue for Team X in 1997?

    ○ 2.5%

    ○ 4%

    ○ 10%

    ○ 25%

    ○ 40%

60. If Team Y earned a total revenue of $150 million in 1998, Team Y's total revenue increased by approximately what percent from 1997 to 1998?

    ○ 20%

    ○ 25%

    ○ 30%

    ○ 35%

    ○ 40%

ANSWERS AND EXPLANATIONS

1. B	13. D	25. C	37. E	49. D
2. C	14. A	26. B	38. C	50. E
3. D	15. B	27. C	39. C	51. C
4. A	16. A	28. C	40. A	52. D
5. B	17. B	29. A	41. A	53. D
6. A	18. D	30. D	42. A	54. E
7. C	19. D	31. B	43. D	55. E
8. A	20. B	32. A	44. E	56. B
9. A	21. A	33. B	45. B	57. C
10. A	22. C	34. D	46. D	58. C
11. C	23. A	35. A	47. D	59. A
12. C	24. D	36. C	48. A	60. B

DIAGNOSTIC TOOL

Tally up your score and write down your results below.

Total

Total Correct: _____ out of 60 correct
Percentage Correct: # you got right × 100 ÷ 60: _____

By Question Type

Quantitative Comparisons (questions 1–30)_____ out of 30 correct
Word Problems (questions 31–40, 46–56) _____ out of 21 correct
Data Interpretations (questions 41–45, 57–60)_____ out of 9 correct

DIAGNOSE YOUR RESULTS

Look back at the questions you got wrong and think back on your experience answering them.

STEP 1: FIND THE ROAD BLOCKS

Some questions you struggled to answer. To improve your score, you need to pinpoint exactly what element of these "road blocks" tripped you up. To do that, ask yourself these two questions:

Am I weak in the skills being tested?

This will be very easy for you to judge. Maybe you've forgotten how to figure out the area of a triangle, or what PEMDAS stands for. Or maybe math just isn't your thing.

If you know you need to brush up on your math skills, TRY the *Kaplan GRE Exam Math Workbook*, which contains focused review of all the fundamental math concepts tested on the GRE, as well as practice exercises to build speed and accuracy.

Was it the question types that threw me off?

Then you need to become more comfortable with them! Quantitative Comparisons have a very unique format, and Data Interpretation questions can be daunting with their charts, graphs, and tables. If this was a problem for you, go back to the beginning of this chapter and review the Kaplan principles and methods for the question types you struggled with. Make sure you understand the principles, and how to apply the methods. These strategies help to improve your speed and efficiency on Test Day. Remember, it's not a math test; it's a critical-reasoning test.

Also, get as much practice as you can so that you grow more at ease with the question type formats. For even more practice, TRY the *Kaplan GRE Exam Math Workbook*, which includes practice sets for each question type.

STEP 2: FIND THE BLIND SPOTS

Some questions you answered quickly and confidently, but got them wrong anyway!

When you come across wrong answers like these, you need to figure out what you thought you were doing right, what it turns out you were doing wrong, and why that happened! The best way to do that is to **read the answer explanations!**

They give you a detailed breakdown of why the correct answer is correct, and why all the other answer choices are wrong. This helps to reinforce the Kaplan principles and methods for each question type, and helps you figure out what blindsided you so it doesn't happen again. Also, just like with your "road blocks," try to get in as much practice as you can.

STEP 3: REINFORCE YOUR STRENGTHS

Now read through all the answer explanations for the ones you got right. Again, this helps to reinforce the Kaplan principles and methods for each question type, which in turn helps you work more efficiently so you can get the score you want. Keep your skills sharp with more practice.

As soon as you are comfortable with all the GRE question types and Kaplan methods, complete a full-length practice test under timed conditions. In this way, practice tests serve as milestones; they help you to chart your progress! So don't save them all for the final weeks.

For even more practice, you can also TRY the GRE Quiz Bank! You get more than 1,000 questions that you can access 24/7 from any Internet browser, each with comprehensive explanations. You can even customize your quizzes based on question type, content, and difficulty level. Take quizzes in Timed Mode to test your stamina or in Tutor Mode to see explanations as you work. Best of all, you also get detailed reports to track your progress.

Visit Kaptest.com/GRE for more details on our Quiz Bank and for more on our other online and classroom-based options.

1. B

Divide both columns by 10 to get (50)(8) in Column A and (5)(90) in Column B. Divide both columns again by 10 to get (5)(8) in Column A and (5)(9) in Column B. Divide once more by 5, and you're left with 8 in Column A and 9 in Column B.

2. C

There are three sets of vertical angles in this diagram: (a, d), (b, e), and (c, f). In Column A you can substitute b for e since they are vertical angles, and therefore equal: this leaves the sum $a + b + c$ in Column A. Since these are the three angles on one side of a straight line, they sum to 180. Similarly, substituting e for b in Column B, $b + d + f$ is the same thing as $d + e + f$, or also 180. The two columns are equal.

3. D

You may have read this and thought to yourself, "Well, a train moves much faster than a car. Therefore Column B must be bigger." Well, trains may move faster than cars in the real world, but not on the GRE. That falls into the category of foolish assumptions. For all you know, the car is some new model that travels 350 miles per hour, while the train could be some broken down old locomotive that can't handle more than 15 miles per hour. You need more information.

4. A

Change the decimal fraction in Column A to something more manageable. Multiply both the numerator and denominator by 10,000—the same as moving each decimal point four digits to the right.

$$\frac{0.09}{0.0003} \times \frac{10,000}{10,000} = \frac{0.09 \times 10,000}{0.0003 \times 10,000} = \frac{900}{3} = 300$$

5. B

Try to set the columns equal. If x is 50, then the bookstore started out with 50 dictionaries. Then $\frac{1}{8}$ of them were purchased. You can see already that the columns can't be equal, since $\frac{1}{8}$ of 50 won't yield an integer. But go ahead and see whether the answer is **(A)** or **(B)**. Since $\frac{1}{8}$ of 50 is close to 6, after these dictionaries were purchased, the store would have been left with about 50 − 6 or 44 dictionaries. Then they received 10 more, giving a total of about 54 dictionaries. But this is more than the store actually ended up with; they only had 52. Therefore, they must have started with *fewer* than 50 dictionaries, and Column B is bigger. (As always, the last thing you care about is how many dictionaries they really had.)

6. A

You should have decided immediately there must be a shortcut here; multiplying out the values of the columns would take too long. (It may also have occurred to you that the answer cannot be **(D)**—since all you are dealing with here are numbers, there must be some way to compare the columns, even if you do have to calculate the values.) So you might have asked yourself whether the columns look like anything familiar. In fact, Column A looks a lot like a difference of squares. It can be factored, then, into

$$(41)2 - (21)2 = (41 - 21)(41 + 21) = (20)(62)$$

Now how does this compare to $(41 - 21)^2$ or $(20)^2$ in Column B? Column A is larger: 20×62 is larger than 20×20.

7. C

You may have thought this was a choice **(D)**; after all, you don't know exactly where the boards overlap, whether it is in the middle of each board, as pictured, or whether it is near the end of one of the boards. But that doesn't matter; all you need to know is that they overlap, and that all the angles are right angles. If the boards did not overlap it would be easy to find the perimeter: 2 + 2 + 4 + 4 or 12 for each board, or 24 for both boards. Now, since the boards do overlap, the perimeter of the figure will be smaller than that, but how much smaller? It will be smaller by the amount of that "lost perimeter" in the middle; the perimeter of the square where the boards overlap. (You know it's a square, since all the angles are right angles.) The length of a side of that square is the shorter dimension of each of the boards: 2. Therefore, the perimeter of the square is 4×2 or 8. The perimeter of the figure, then, is 24 − 8 or 16. The two columns are equal.

8. A

Start by simplifying the quantity in Column A: $(\sqrt{5} + \sqrt{5})^2$ is the same as $(2\sqrt{5})^2$ which is $2^2 \times (\sqrt{5})^2$ or 4×5 or 20. Subtract 5 from both columns, and you're left with 15 in Column A and $5\sqrt{5}$ in Column B. Now divide both sides by 5, and you're left with 3 in Column A and $\sqrt{5}$ in Column B. If you did not know that $3 > \sqrt{5}$, you could square both quantities—but you really should know that $\sqrt{5}$ is less than 3; after all, 3^2 is 9. Column A is larger.

9. A

This question requires no computation but only a general understanding of how averages work, and what the word "median" means. The median of a group of numbers is the "middle number"; it is the value above which half of the numbers in the group fall, and below which the other half fall. If you have an even number of values, the median is the average of the two "middle" numbers; if you have an odd number of values, the median is one of the values. Here, in Column B, the median is 101. In Column A, if the numbers were 100, 101, and 102, then the average would also be 101, but since the third number, 103, is larger than 102, then the average must be larger than 101. Column A is greater than 101, and Column B equals 101; Column A is larger.

10. A

Start with the information you are given. You know that the length of the chord is 15. What does that mean? Well, since you don't know exactly where A or B is, that doesn't mean too much, but it does tell you that the distance between two points on the circumference is 15. That tells you nothing much about the radius or diameter of the circle *except* that the diameter must be at least 15. If the diameter were less than 15, then you couldn't have a chord that was equal to 15. The diameter is always the longest chord in a circle. The diameter of the circle is 15 or greater, so the circumference must be at least 15π That means that Column A must be larger than Column B.

11. C

This is a complex equation. Since Column A has only h in it, solve the equation for h, leaving h on one side of the equal sign and r on the other side. First substitute the value for x into the equation, then solve for h in terms of r.

$x = \dfrac{4}{3}r^2h^2$	Substitute 1 for x.
$1 = \dfrac{4}{3}r^2h^2$	Divide both sides by $\dfrac{4}{3}$.
$\dfrac{3}{4} = r^2h^2$	Take the positive square root of both sides, using the information that r and h are positive.
$\dfrac{\sqrt{3}}{2} = rh$	Divide both sides by r to get h alone.
$h = \dfrac{\sqrt{3}}{2r}$	The two columns are equal.

12. C

A diagram can be very helpful for solving this problem. You know where points B and C are; they're on the x-axis. You don't know where A is however, which may have made you think that the answer is choice (**D**). But you're given more information; you know that the triangle has an area of 18. The area of any triangle is one-half the product of the base and the height. Make side *BC* the base of the triangle; you know the coordinates of both points, so you can find their distance, and the length of that side. *C* is at the origin, the point (0,0); *B* is at the point (6,0). The distance between them is the distance from 0 to 6 along the *x*-axis, or just 6. So that's the base; what about the altitude? Well, since you know that the area is 18, you can plug what you know into the area formula.

$$\text{Area} = \frac{1}{2}\text{ base} \times \text{height}$$
$$18 = \frac{1}{2} \times 6 \times \text{height}$$
$$\text{Height} = \frac{18}{3}$$
$$\text{Height} = 6$$

That's the other dimension of the triangle. The height is the distance between the *x*-axis and the point *A*. Now you know that *A* must be somewhere in the first quadrant, since both the *x*- and *y*-coordinates are positive. Don't worry about the *x*-coordinate of the point, since that's not what's being compared; you care only about the value of *y*. You know that the distance from the *x*-axis to the point is 6, since that's the height of the triangle; and that *y* must be positive. Therefore, the *y*-coordinate of the point must be 6; that's what the *y*-coordinate *is*: a measure of the point's vertical distance from the *x*-axis. (Note that if you hadn't been told that *y* was positive, there would be two possible values for *y*: 6 and −6. A point that's 6 units below the *x*-axis would also give a triangle with height 6.) You still don't know the *x*-coordinate of the point, and in fact you can't figure that out, but you don't care. You know that *y* is 6; therefore, the two columns are equal.

13. D

Picking numbers will help you solve this problem. With symbolism problems like this, it sometimes helps to put the definition of the symbol into words. For this symbol, you can say something like "*x* Φ *y* means take the sum of the two numbers, and divide that by the difference of the two numbers." One good way to do this problem is to pick some values. You know that *p* is positive and *q* is negative. So suppose *p* is 1 and *q* is −1. Figure out what *p* Φ *q* is first. You start by taking the sum of the numbers, or 1 + (−1) = 0. That's the numerator of the fraction, and you don't really need to go any further than that. Whatever their difference is, since the numerator is 0, the whole fraction must equal 0. (The difference can't be 0 also, since *p* ≠ *q*.) So that's *p* Φ *q*; now what about *q* Φ *p*? Well, that's going to have the same numerator as *p* Φ *q*: 0. The only thing that changes when you reverse the order of the numbers is the denominator of the fraction. So *q* Φ *p* has a numerator of 0, and that fraction must equal 0 as well.

So you've found a case where the columns are equal. Try another set of values, and see whether the columns are always equal. If *p* = 1 and *q* = −2, then the sum of the numbers is 1 + (−2) or −1. So that's the numerator of the fraction in each column.

Now for the denominator of $p \Phi q$ you need $p - q$ or $1 - (-2) = 1 + 2 = 3$. Then the value of $p \Phi q$ is $\frac{-1}{3}$. The denominator of $q \Phi p$ is $q - p$ or $-2 - 1 = -3$. In that case, the value of $q \Phi p$ is $\frac{-1}{-3}$ or $\frac{1}{3}$. In this case, the columns are different; therefore, the answer is **(D)**.

14. A

$\frac{1}{3} + \frac{1}{3}$ is $\frac{2}{3}$. $\frac{1}{3} \times \frac{1}{3} = \frac{1}{9}$. Since $\frac{2}{3} > \frac{1}{9}$. Column A is larger.

15. B

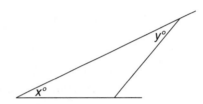

The sum of the three interior angles of a triangle is 180°. Since x and y are only two of the angles, their sum must be less than 180 degrees. Column B is greater.

16. A

Sixteen percent of 30 is $\frac{16}{100}(30)$ or $\frac{(16)(30)}{100}$. Similarly, 15 percent of 31 is $\frac{15}{100}(31)$ or $\frac{(15)(31)}{100}$. We can ignore the denominator of 100 in both columns, and just compare $(16)(30)$ in Column A to $(15)(31)$ in Column B. Divide both columns by 15; we're left with 31 in Column B and $(16)(2)$ or 32 in Column A. Since $32 > 31$, Column A is larger.

17. B

Start by working with the sign of x, and hope that you won't have to go any further than that. If x^5 is negative, then what is the sign of x? It must be negative—if x were positive, then any power of x would also be positive. Since x is negative, Column A, x^3, which is a negative number raised to an odd exponent, must also be negative. But what about Column B? Whatever x is, x^2 must be positive (or zero, but we know that x can't be zero); therefore, the quantity in Column B must be positive. We have a positive number in Column B and a negative number is Column A; Column B must be greater.

18. D

We could pick numbers here, or else just use logic. We know that z is positive, and that x and y are less than z. But does that mean that x or y must be negative? Not at all—they could be, but they could also be positive. For instance, suppose $x = 1$, $y = 2$, and $z = 3$. Then Column A would be larger. However, if $x = -1$, $y = 0$, and $z = 1$, then Column B would be larger. We need more information to determine the relationship between the columns.

19. D

Divide both sides of the inequality by 6. We're left with $(10)^n > 10{,}001$, which $10{,}001$ can also be written at $10^4 + 1$, so we know that $(10)^n > 10^4 + 1$. Therefore, the quantity in Column A, n, must be 5 or greater. Column B is 6; since n could be less than, equal to, or greater than 6, we need more information.

20. B

Try to set the columns equal. Could the units' digit of y be 4? If it is, and the hundreds' digit is three times the units' digit, then the hundreds' digit must be . . . 12? That can't be right. A digit must be one of the integers 0 through 9; 12 isn't a digit. Therefore, 4 is too big to be the units' digit of y. We don't know what the units' digit of y is (and we don't care either), but we know that it must be less than 4. Column B is greater than Column A.

21. A

The perimeter of a square with side 4 is 4(4) or 16. The circumference of a circle is the product of π and the diameter, so the circumference in Column B is 5π. Since π is approximately 3.14, $5(\pi)$ is approximately 5(3.14) or 15.70, which is less than 16. Column A is greater.

22. C

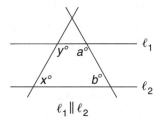

Column B is the sum of all the angles in the quadrilateral. The sum of the angles in any quadrilateral is 360 degrees. Column B is 360. In Column A, angle x and angle y are angles made when a transversal cuts a pair of parallel lines, in this case, ℓ_1 and ℓ_2. Such angles are either equal or supplementary. Angles x and y obviously aren't equal, so they must be supplementary, and their sum is 180. Then Column A is $2(x + y) = 2 \times 180$ or 360. The columns are equal.

23. A

One way to work here is to pick numbers. Just make sure that anything you pick satisfies the requirements of the problem. How about picking $x = 3$, $y = 5$, and $z = 7$, since in the equation these numbers would cancel with their denominators, thus leaving us with the equation $2 = 2 = 2$. Therefore, we know that these values satisfy the equation. In addition, if $z = 7$, then z is positive, so we have satisfied the other requirement as well. Then the sum of x and y, in Column A, is $3 + 5$ or 8. This is larger than z, so in this case, Column A is larger. That's just one example though; we should really try another one. In fact, any other example we pick that fits the initial information will have Column A larger. To see why, we have to do a little messy work with the initial equations; on the test, you should just pick a couple of sample values, then go on to the next questions.

Start by dividing all of the equations through by 2, and multiply all of the terms through by $3 \times 5 \times 7$, to eliminate all the fractions. This leaves us with:

$$35x = 21y = 15z$$

Now let's put everything in terms of x.

$$x = x \qquad y = \frac{35}{21}x = \frac{5}{3}x \qquad z = \frac{35}{15}x = \frac{7}{3}x$$

Then in Column A, the sum of x and y is $x + \frac{5}{3}x = \frac{8}{3}x$. In Column B, the value of z is $\frac{7}{3}x$. Now since z is positive, x and y must also be positive. (If one of them is negative, that would make all of them negative.) Since x is positive, $\frac{8}{3}x > \frac{7}{3}x$. Column A is greater.

The moral here is that proving that one column must be bigger can involve an awful lot of time on some GRE QC questions—more time than you can afford on the test. Try to come up with a good answer, but don't spend a lot of time proving it. Even if you end up showing that your original suspicion was wrong, it's not worth it if it took five minutes away from the rest of the problems.

24. D

The best place to start here is with pairs of integers that have a product of 10. The numbers 5 and 2 have a product of 10, as do 10 and 1, and the average of each of these pairs is greater than 3, so you may have thought that **(A)** was the correct answer. If so, you should have stopped yourself, saying, "That seems a little too easy for such a late QC question. They're usually trickier than that." In fact, this one was. There's nothing in the problem that limits the integers to positive numbers: they can just as easily be negative. The numbers −10 and −1 also have a product of 10, but their average is a negative number—in other words, less than Column B. We need more information here; the answer is **(D)**.

25. C

The best way to do this question is to pick numbers. First we have to figure out what kind of number we want. Since $n + 1$ leaves a remainder of 1 when it's divided by 2, we know that $n + 1$ must be an odd number. Then n itself is an even number. We're told that n leaves a remainder of 1 when it's divided by 3. Therefore, n must be 1 more than a multiple of 3, or $n - 1$ is a multiple of 3. So what are we looking for? We've figured out that n should be an even number, that's one more than a multiple of 3. So let's pick a number now. How about 10? That's even, and it's one more than a multiple of 3. Then what's the remainder when we divide $n - 1$, or $10 - 1 = 9$, by 6? We're left with a remainder of 3: 6 divides into 9 one time, with 3 left over. In this case, the columns are equal.

Now since this a QC and there's always a possibility that we'll get a different result if we pick a different number, we should either pick another case, or else use logic to convince ourselves that the columns will always be equal. Let's do the latter here. Since n is even, $n - 1$ must be odd. We saw before that $n - 1$ is a multiple of 3, so we now know that it is an odd multiple of 3. Does this tell us anything about $n - 1$'s relation to 6? Yes, it does: $n - 1$ is 3 multiplied by an odd number m, which can be written as $2p + 1$ where p is an integer. So $n - 1 = 3(2p + 1) = 6p + 3$. $6p$ is a multiple of 6, so the remainder when $n - 1$ is divided by 6 must be 3. The answer is **(C)**.

26. B

A quick way to analyze a problem such as this one is to realize that the additional bowler with a score of 170 is raising everyone else's average by one point from 160 to 161. Her score is $161 + 9$, so she has 9 extra points that she can distribute to the remaining bowlers by which to raise their scores. Therefore, she can raise the average score of exactly 9 other bowlers from 160 to 161, so $n = 9$ and Column B is greater.

27. C

Remember, compare, don't calculate! But in order to compare, you need to put both columns into a similar form. Factoring 7^5 out of both terms in Column A will help you to do just that: $7^5 + 7^6 = 7^5(1 + 7) = 7^5 \times 8 = 8 \times 7^5$. So the two quantities are equal.

28. C

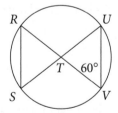

There are many steps involved with this problem, but none of them is too complicated. The circle has its center at point T. To start with the triangle at the right, its vertices are at T and two points on the circumference of the circle. This makes two of its sides radii of the circle. Since all radii must have equal length, this makes the triangle an isosceles triangle. In addition, we're told one of the base angles of this triangle has measure 60°. Then the other base angle must also have measure 60° (since the base angles in an isosceles triangle have equal measure). Then the sum of the two base angles is 120°, leaving $180 - 120$ or 60° for the other angle, the one at point T.

Now, ∠*RTS* is opposite this 60° angle; therefore, its measure must also be 60°. Δ*RST* is another isosceles triangle; since ∠*RTS* has measure 60°, the other two angles in the triangle must also measure 60°. So what we have in the diagram is two equilateral triangles. *RT* and *RS* are two sides in one of these triangles; therefore, they must be of equal length, and the two columns are equal.

29. A

Start by setting the columns equal. Suppose there were originally 14 adults at the party. Then after 5 of them leave, there are 14 − 5 or 9 adults left. There are 3 times as many children as adults, so there are 3 × 9 or 27 children. Then 25 children leave the party, so there are 27 − 25 or 2 children left. So 9 adults and 2 children remain at this party. Is that twice as many adults as children? No, it is more than 4 times as many, So this clearly indicates that the columns can't be equal—but does it mean that Column A is bigger or Column B is bigger? Probably the simplest way to decide is to pick another number for the original number of adults, and see whether the ratio gets better or worse. Suppose we start with 13 adults. After 5 adults leave, there are 13 − 5 or 8 adults. Multiplying 3 times 8 gives 24 children. Now if 25 children leave, we're left with 24 − 25 or −1 children. But that's no good; how can you have a negative number of children? This means we've gone the wrong way; our ratio has gotten worse instead of better. So 14 isn't right for the number of adults, and 13 is even worse, so the correct number must be something more than 14, and Column A is bigger.

30. D

We know that the ratio of oranges to apples is 9 to 10, and that there are "at least" 200 apples. The ratio tells us that there are more apples than oranges. How does that help us? Good question. It helps us because it tells us that there could be fewer than 200 oranges in the store. Could there be more than 200? Sure. If there were a lot more than 200 apples, say 600 apples, then there would be a lot more than 200 oranges. So we have one situation in which Column A is larger, and another case in which Column B is larger. We need more information to decide.

31. B

The probability formula is:

$$\text{Probability} = \frac{\text{Number of desired outcomes}}{\text{Number of possible outcomes}}$$

When a die is rolled, there are six possible outcomes. When two dice are rolled, the number of possible outcomes is 6 × 6, or 36. Getting a total value of 7 can be achieved in the following ways: (1, 6), (2, 5), (3, 4), (4, 3), (5, 2), and (6, 1). There are six possible ways. So the probability of rolling a total of 7 is $\frac{6}{36}$, which can be reduced to $\frac{1}{6}$.

32. A

The area of the shaded region is the area of the square minus the area of the portion of the circle that is inside the square. The area of a square is its side squared. The area of square $ABCD$ is $4^2 = 4 \times 4$, which is 16. Now let's find the area of the portion of the circle that is inside the square. Since the diameter of the circle is a side of the square, we know that exactly one-half of the circle's area is inside the square. Since the diameter of the circle is twice the radius, the radius of the circle is $\frac{4}{2}$, or 2. The area of a circle with a radius r is πr^2. The area of the complete circle in this question is $\pi(2^2)$, which is 4π. So half the area of this circle is 2π. Thus, the area of the shaded region is $16 - 2\pi$.

33. B

Let's first find the value of 9♣. Then we will find the value of (9♣) ♦ 3.

Since $C♣ = C + 3$, $9♣ = 9 + 3 = 12$.
So $9♣ = 12$.
Then $(9♣) ♦ 3 = 12 ♦ 3$.
Since $A ♦ B = \dfrac{A + B}{B}$, $12 ♦ 3 = \dfrac{12 + 3}{3} = \dfrac{15}{3} = 5$.
Thus, $(9♣) ♦ 3 = 5$.

34. D

Since one leg of the right triangle is 5 and the hypotenuse is 13, we have a special right triangle, the 5-12-13 right triangle. So the length of AC is 12. We can also use the Pythagorean theorem to find the length of AC. We have:

$$(AC)^2 + 5^2 = 13^2$$
$$(AC)^2 + 25 = 169$$
$$(AC)^2 = 144$$
$$AC = 12$$

The area of a triangle is $\frac{1}{2}$ times base times height. The area of a right triangle is $\frac{1}{2} \times (\text{leg})_1 \times (\text{leg})_2$ because one leg can be considered to be the base and the other leg can be considered to be the height. So the area of triangle ABC is $\frac{1}{2} \times (AC) \times (AB) = \frac{1}{2} \times 12 \times 5 = 6 \times 5 = 30$. Choice (**D**) is your answer.

35. A

The average formula is

$$\text{Average} = \frac{\text{Sum of the terms}}{\text{Number of terms}}. \text{ Therefore,}$$

Sum of the terms = Average × Number of terms.

The sum of the scores of the four students whose average was 85 is $85(4) = 340$. Let's call the fifth student's score x_5. If the new average is to be 86, then the sum of the scores of all five students is $340 + x_5$. Then $\dfrac{340 + x_5}{5} = 86$, $340 + x_5 = 430$, and $x_5 = 90$, making (**A**) the correct choice.

36. C

In the first scenario, each day, $\dfrac{1\ house}{3\ days} = \dfrac{1}{3}$ of the house will be built. Since there are 10 workers, each person can build $\dfrac{1}{30}$ of a house each day. In the second scenario, there are 15 workers, so that means $15 \times \dfrac{1}{30} = \dfrac{1}{2}$ a house can be built each day. Four houses could, therefore, be built in 8 days: $\dfrac{4\ houses}{\dfrac{1}{2}\ house/day} = 4 \times 2 = 8$ days.

37. E

This question can be broken into two functions, with two unknowns, Meg's age now (M) and Rolf's age now (R):

> i. $M = 2 \times R$
> ii. $M - 3 = R + 2$

$$M = 2R$$
$$\underline{-(M - 3 = R + 2)}$$
$$3 = R - 2$$

Subtracting ii. from i., the result is $3 = R - 2$, which can be rewritten as $R = 5$. Rolf is 5 years old now.

38. C

The area of a rectangle is length times width.

The area of rectangle A is $12 \times 5 = 60$.

The area of rectangle B is $9 \times 10 = 90$.

So the area 60 of rectangle A must be multiplied by a number which we will call x to obtain the area 90 of rectangle B.

Then $60x = 90$. So $x = \dfrac{90}{60} = \dfrac{3}{2} = 1\dfrac{1}{2}$.

39. C

The cost of manufacturing x crayons is $(570 + 0.5x)$ cents. Since each crayon sells for 10 cents, x crayons will sell for $10x$ cents. We want the smallest value of x such that $10x$ cents is at least $570 + 0.5x$ cents. So we must solve the inequality $10x \geq 570 + 0.5x$ for the range of values that x can have.

We have:

$$10x \geq 570 + 0.5x$$
$$9.5x \geq 570$$
$$x \geq \frac{570}{9.5}$$
$$x \geq 60$$

The minimum number of crayons is 60.

40. A

We can write that $\dfrac{1-x}{xy} = \dfrac{1}{xy} - \dfrac{x}{xy}$. Canceling a factor of x from the numerator and denominator of $\dfrac{x}{xy}$, we have $\dfrac{x}{xy} = \dfrac{1}{y}$.

So $\dfrac{1-x}{xy} = \dfrac{1}{xy} - \dfrac{x}{xy} = \dfrac{1}{xy} - \dfrac{1}{y}$.

Thus, $\dfrac{1-x}{xy} = \dfrac{1}{xy} - \dfrac{1}{y}$.

41. A

From the second bar graph, the profits from table saws in 1998 were about $60,000. From the pie chart, table saws were 30% of the total profits. Let's call the total profits T dollars. Then 30% of T dollars is $60,000. So $0.3T = 60,000$, and

$$T = \frac{60,000}{0.3} = 60,000 \times \frac{10}{10} \times \frac{1}{0.3} \times 10 = \frac{600,000}{3} = 200,000.$$

42. A

The year with the biggest percent increase over the previous year will be the year where the increase is the biggest fraction of the amount in the previous year. We see that in 1993, the increase from 1992 was approximately $60 - 30$, or 30. This is approximately a 100 percent increase, and the greatest percent increase over the previous year among all the years from 1993 through 2001. There was a greater increase from 1996 to 1997 than from 1992 to 1993. The increase from 1996 to 1997 was about $110 - 70 = 40$. However, the percent increase from 1996 to 1997 is approximately $\dfrac{40}{70} \times 100\%$, which is less than 100%.

43. D

In 1998, the profits from table saws were approximately $60,000. In 1999, the profits from table saws were approximately $40,000. From 1998 to 1999 there was a decrease in the profits from table saws. In general,

$$\text{Percent decrease} = \frac{\text{Original value} - \text{New value}}{\text{Original value}} \times 100\%.$$

Here, the percent decrease is approximately

$$\frac{\$60,000 - \$40,000}{\$60,000} \times 100\%$$

$$= \frac{\$20,000}{\$60,000} \times 100\% = \frac{1}{3} \times 100\% = 33\frac{1}{2}.$$

A percent decrease of $33\frac{1}{3}\%$ is closest to **(D)**.

44. E

In 1993, the profits were $20,000. Using the formula Profit = Revenue − Cost, we have that Revenue = Cost + Profit. The cost was $22,000. So the revenue was $22,000 + $20,000 = $42,000. Since in 1993, 60 table saws were sold, each table saw was sold for $\dfrac{\$42,000}{60}$, which is $700.

45. B

In 1998, the profits from table saws were about $60,000 and this profit is 30% of the total profits. Let's call the total call the total profits T dollars. Then 30% of T dollars is $60,000. So $0.3T = 60,000$, and $T = \dfrac{60,000}{0.3} = 60,000 \times \dfrac{10}{0.3} \times 10 = \dfrac{600,000}{3} = 200,000.$

The total profits in 1998 were approximately $200,000. The profits from cordless drills were 35% of the total. So the profits from cordless drills were approximately $0.35(\$200,00)$, which is $70,000.

46. D

Since the thickness of the pizza will be the same, we only need to be concerned with the area of the pizza. The factor by which Kristy needs to multiply the amounts of the ingredients is the same factor by which the area of the pizza will be multiplied when the diameter increases from 12 inches to 24 inches.

A pizza with a 12-inch diameter has a radius of 6 inches and an area of $\pi r^2 = \pi(6)^2 = 36\pi$ square inches. The 24-inch pizza has a radius of 12 inches and an area of $\pi r^2 = \pi(12)^2 = 144\pi$ square inches. Since $144 = 36 \times 4$, Kristy should multiply the amounts of the ingredients by 4, which is **(D)**.

47. D

Company A gets $\dfrac{3}{5}$ of the offices, so the remaining 4 companies get $1 - \dfrac{3}{5} = \dfrac{2}{5}$ of the offices. Thus, each of the 4 other companies gets one-fourth of $\dfrac{2}{5}$ of the offices, or $\left(\dfrac{1}{4}\right)\left(\dfrac{2}{5}\right) = \dfrac{2}{20} = \dfrac{1}{10}$ of the offices. Therefore, Companies A and B together got $\dfrac{3}{5} + \dfrac{1}{10} = \dfrac{6}{10} + \dfrac{1}{10} = \dfrac{7}{10}$ of the offices. Thus, their 70 offices equal $\dfrac{7}{10}$ of the total offices.

So, if n is the original number of offices, then $\dfrac{7}{10}n = 70$, $7n = 700$, an $n = 100$.

Choice **(D)** is correct.

48. A

Although we could multiply everything out using FOIL, it is much easier to use PEMDAS. First we will combine the numbers inside the parentheses and then multiply the results together:

Find common denominators:
$$\left(\frac{1}{4}-1\right)\left(\frac{1}{5}-1\right)=\left(\frac{1}{4}-\frac{4}{4}\right)\left(\frac{1}{5}-\frac{5}{5}\right)$$

Subtract the fractions:
$$\left(\frac{1}{4}-\frac{4}{4}\right)\left(\frac{1}{5}-\frac{5}{5}\right)=\left(-\frac{3}{4}\right)\left(-\frac{4}{5}\right)$$

Multiply the results:
$$\left(-\frac{3}{4}\right)\left(-\frac{4}{5}\right)=\frac{12}{20}$$

Simplify:
$$\frac{12}{20}=\frac{3}{5}.$$

Choice (**A**) is correct.

49. D

This is a rate problem; we are given the rate at which the press prints pages and asked to find the number of pages printed in 155 seconds. First, let's calculate the rate, or number of pages per second. We just divide 11 pages by 30 seconds:

$$\text{rate} = \frac{11 \text{ copies}}{30 \text{ seconds}} = \frac{11}{30} \text{ pages per second.}$$

Now we just need to multiply the rate by the time, 155 seconds. This will give us $\left(\frac{11}{30} \text{pages per second}\right)(155 \text{ seconds}) = \frac{(11)(155)}{30}$ pages printed in 155 seconds. To

simplify $\frac{(11)(155)}{30}$, don't try to multiply 11 by 155. Instead, notice that 155 = 150 + 5 and 150 can easily be divided by 30. If we replace 155 with 150 + 5, the arithmetic will become a lot simpler:

$$\frac{(11)(155)}{30} = 11\left(\frac{150+5}{30}\right)$$

$$= 11\left(\frac{150}{30}+\frac{5}{30}\right) = 11\left(\frac{5+1}{6}\right) = 55+\frac{11}{6}$$

So it looks as if we have fractional pages, which doesn't make sense. But remember that the question asked how many *complete* pages could be printed in 155 seconds. So we can actually just drop the fraction; that will give us the number of complete pages. Since $\frac{11}{6}=1\frac{5}{6}$, it represents just 1 complete page. So, the total number of complete pages in 155 seconds is 55 + 1 = 56. Choice (**D**) is correct.

We could also have approached $\dfrac{(11)(155)}{30}$ another way. We know that $150 = 30 \times 5$, so we know that $\dfrac{155}{30}$ is slightly greater than 5 and therefore $11\left(\dfrac{155}{30}\right)$ must be slightly greater than $11(5)$, or 55. Only **(D)** is slightly greater than 55. Choice **(C)** will not work because we know that we will have at least 55 complete pages, since $\dfrac{(11)(155)}{30}$ is greater than 55.

50. E

Here we're asked for the odd integers between $\dfrac{10}{3}$ and $\dfrac{62}{3}$. First let's be clearer about this range. $\dfrac{10}{3}$ is the same as $3\dfrac{1}{3}$, and $\dfrac{62}{3}$ is the same as $20\dfrac{2}{3}$. So we need to count the odd integers between $3\dfrac{1}{3}$ and $20\dfrac{2}{3}$. We can't include 3, since 3 is less than $3\dfrac{1}{3}$. Similarly, we can't include 21, since it's larger than $20\dfrac{2}{3}$. So the odd integers in the appropriate range are 5, 7, 9, 11, 13, 15, 17, and 19. That's a total of 8.

51. C

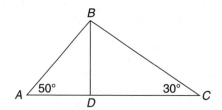

Notice that we're given the measures of two interior angles in $\triangle ABC$: $\angle BAC$ measures 50° and $\angle BCA$ measures 30°. Therefore, $\angle ABC$, the third interior angle in $\triangle ABC$, measures $180 - (50 + 30)$, or $180 - 80$, or 100°. Since BD bisects $\angle ABC$, BD splits up $\angle ABC$ into two smaller angles equal in measure, $\angle ABD$ and $\angle DBC$. Therefore, the measure of $\angle DBC$ is half the measure of $\angle ABC$, so $\angle DBC$ measures $\dfrac{1}{2}(100)$, or 50°. Now we can use this information along with the fact that $\angle BCD$ measures 30° to find $\angle BDC$. Since these three angles are interior angles of $\triangle BDC$, their measures sum to 180°. So $\angle BDC$ measures $180 - (50 + 30)$, or 100°.

52. D

Solve for b in terms of a, c, and d.

$$d = \frac{c-b}{a-b}$$

Clear the denominator by
multiplying both sides by $a - b$. $d(a - b) = c - b$

Multiply out parentheses. $da - db = c - b$

Gather all bs on one side. $b - db = c - da$

Factor out the bs on the
left hand side.

$$b(1 - d) = c - da$$

Divide both sides by $1 - d$
to isolate b.

$$b = \frac{c - ad}{1 - d}$$

53. D

Remember the rules for operations with exponents. First you have to get both powers
in terms of the same base so you can combine the exponents. Note that the answer
choices all have base 2. Start by expressing 4 and 8 as powers of 2.

$$(4^x)(8^x) = (2^2)^x \times (2^3)^x$$

To raise a power to an exponent, multiply the exponents:

$$(2^2)^x = 2^{2x}$$

$$(2^3)^x = 2^{3x}$$

To multiply powers with the same base, add the exponents:

$$2^{2x} \times 2^{3x} = 2^{(2x + 3x)}$$

$$= 2^{5x}$$

54. E

Pick a sample value for the size of one of the classes. The first class might have 100
students. That means there are 30 percent of 100 or 30 boys in the class. The second
class is half the size of the first, so it has 50 students, of which 40 percent of 50 = 20
are boys. This gives us 100 + 50 = 150 students total, of whom 30 + 20 = 50 are boys.
So $\frac{50}{150} = \frac{1}{3}$ of both classes are boys. Now convert $\frac{1}{3}$ to a percent.

$$\frac{1}{3} = \frac{1}{3} \times 100\% = 33\frac{1}{3}\%.$$

55. E

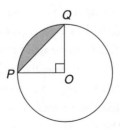

The area of the shaded region is the area of the quarter-circle (sector OPQ) minus the
area of right triangle OPQ. The radius of circle O is 2, so the area of the quarter-circle is

$$\frac{1}{4}\pi r^2 = \frac{1}{4} \times \pi(2)^2 = \frac{1}{4} \times 4\pi = \pi$$

Each leg of the triangle is a radius of circle O, so the area of the triangle is

$$\frac{1}{2}bh = \frac{1}{2} \times 2 \times 2 = 2$$

Therefore, the area of the shaded region is $\pi - 2$.

56. B

The easiest way to handle this type of question is to break n even further down into prime factors. Thus $n = 2 \times 7 \times 2 \times 11 \times 3 \times 13$. Now check out the answer choices:

(A) $\quad \dfrac{n}{21} = \dfrac{2 \times 7 \times 2 \times 11 \times 3 \times 13}{3 \times 7} = 2 \times 2 \times 11 \times 13$

(B) $\quad \dfrac{n}{24} = \dfrac{2 \times 7 \times 2 \times 11 \times 3 \times 13}{2 \times 2 \times 2 \times 3} = \dfrac{7 \times 11 \times 13}{2}$

(C) $\quad \dfrac{n}{26} = \dfrac{2 \times 7 \times 2 \times 11 \times 3 \times 13}{2 \times 13} = 7 \times 2 \times 11 \times 3$

(D) $\quad \dfrac{n}{42} = \dfrac{2 \times 7 \times 2 \times 11 \times 3 \times 13}{7 \times 3 \times 2} = 2 \times 11 \times 13$

(E) $\quad \dfrac{n}{77} = \dfrac{2 \times 7 \times 2 \times 11 \times 3 \times 13}{7 \times 11} = 2 \times 2 \times 3 \times 13$

Only **(B)** is not an integer.

57. C

Before you get started answering any graph question, begin by examining the graphs. Here you have two graphs, a segmented bar graph representing team revenue breakdowns for five teams, and a pie chart showing the distribution of venue revenues for Team X. You're now ready to attack the question, which asks you to find the team with the median revenue for 1997 and to determine what percent of that team's revenues are media revenue. This question must refer to the first graph, and the first part of question—finding the team with the "median" revenue—is a simple matter. "Median" refers to the number in the middle, and since here the bar graphs are arranged in ascending order, the question clearly refers to Team Z, the bar in the middle of the graph. The fastest approach to the answer here (and throughout graph questions generally) is to approximate. The downside to bar graphs is that it's often very hard to get a read on the values. The upside is that if you approximate, often you don't have to read the values. Here we need to determine what percent of the bar is represented by media revenue (the segment in the middle—always be especially careful to isolate the correct piece of data). By approximating, you should be able to see that the middle segment is more than a third and less than a half of the entire bar. Thus the correct answer has to be between 33% and 50%. The only answer that works is **(C)**, 40%.

58. C

The trick to this question is that it involves *both* graphs. The question asks for the amount Team X earned through food sales, which takes us first to the pie chart, where we see that food sales accounted for 35% of the venue revenues for Team X. But to convert that to a dollar amount, we need a figure for the amount earned in venue revenues by Team X. According to the bar graph, this is somewhere around $40 million. Now we just have to take 35% of $40 million: $0.35 \times 40 = 14$, so the answer is **(C)**, 14.

59. A

This question also involves both graphs, since you have to determine the percent of *total* team revenues represented by ticket sales. Beginning at the pie chart, you see that ticket sales represent 10% of the venue revenue for Team X. But venue revenue represents only one portion of the total team revenue, so **(C)**, 10%, is out, as well as **(D)** and **(E)**, since the answer must be less than 10%. Next, examine the bar graph. We've already seen that venue revenue is approximately $40 million. It looks like total team revenue is approximately $160 million, so venue revenue represents about one quarter of the total team revenue. The easiest approach is to approximate by dividing 10% by 4, since ticket sales represent around 10% of one-quarter of the total team revenue. One-fourth of 10% is 2.5%, so the correct choice is **(A)**, 2.5%.

60. B

Percent change problems are extremely popular graph questions, and as long as you know how to set them up they're generally no problem. This question asks for the approximate percent increase in Team Y's total revenue from 1997 to 1998, so we need to figure out (roughly) the amount of increase, place that over the original (or smaller) amount, and then convert the fraction into a percent. We are given the total revenue for 1998 as $150 million, so we just need to locate the total revenue for 1997 from the bar graph. It looks to be approximately $120 million, so the amount of increase is $30 million, and the original (or smaller) amount is $120 million. Now let's apply our formula:

$$\text{Percent increase} = \frac{\$30 \text{ milliion}}{\$120 \text{ million}} \times 100\%$$

$$= \frac{1}{4} \times 100\% = 25\%$$

So **(B)** is the answer.

CHAPTER 5: ANALYTICAL WRITING SECTION

- Learn the four basic principles of success on the Analytical Writing Section
- Learn and practice Kaplan's 22 Principles for Effective Writing
- Practice writing and evaluating Issue and Argument essays

The ability to write clearly about complex subjects is an important part of graduate school. In October 2002, ETS incorporated a standardized way for schools to evaluate a student's academic writing ability to the GRE General Test: a section called the Analytical Writing Assessment (AWA). This section tests a test taker's critical thinking and analytical writing skills.

WHAT TO EXPECT

The Analytical Writing section consists of two timed essay sections. The first is what ETS calls *Present Your Perspective on an Issue* (we'll just call it *the Issue essay*): you'll be shown two essay topics—each a sentence or paragraph that expresses an opinion on an issue of general interest. You must choose one of the two topics. You'll then have 45 minutes to plan and write an essay that communicates your own view on the issue. Whether your agree or disagree with the opinion on the screen is irrelevant; what matters is that you support your view with relevant examples and statements.

The second of the two writing tasks is *Analyze an Argument* (or *the Argument essay*). This time, you'll be shown a paragraph that argues a certain point. You will then be given 30 minutes to assess that argument's logic. As with the Issue essay, it won't matter whether you agree with what you see on the screen. The test makers want you to critique the reasoning behind the argument, and not the argument itself.

For a pool of potential topics for both the Issue and the Argument essays, view ETS's extensive list at **gre.org/stuwrit.html**. You will also see some sample prompts in this chapter and in the Practice Test.

ESSAYS AND THE CAT

For the Analytical Writing section of the GRE, the essay directions and prompts will be delivered on the computer and you'll have to type your essays. At the start of the section, you will be given a brief tutorial on how to use the CAT. Don't worry: using the word processor for the Analytical Writing section is very simple; the only functions you'll use are: *insert text*, *delete text*, *cut and paste*, and *undo*. You'll be well acquainted with these commands by the time you start writing.

HOLISTIC SCORING

The Analytical Writing section is scored first by a human grader, and then by a computerized program developed by ETS to check the human grader. If the grader and the program's scores do not agree by an amount determined by ETS, a second human grader scores the essay, and the final score is the average of the two graders' scores. You'll receive your Analytical Writing score by mail within 10–15 days of your test date.

Another difference: the Analytical Writing section is scored holistically. Holistic scoring uses a single letter or a number—on the GRE it's a number from 0 to 6—to provide an overall evaluation of an essay as a whole. A holistic score emphasizes the interrelation of various thinking and writing qualities in an essay (such as content, organization, or syntax) and tries to denote the unified effect that all of these elements combine to produce. Although the Analytical Writing section consists of two separate essays, a single score is reported, representing the average of your scores for the two essays.

While each of the two essay tasks requires a different type of response and so has a slightly different set of grading criteria, the following list will give you a general idea of the guidelines a GRE grader will have in mind when reading your essays.

6 AND 5.5: "OUTSTANDING" ESSAY

- Insightfully presents and convincingly supports an opinion on the issue or a critique of the argument
- Communicates ideas clearly and is generally well organized; connections are logical
- Demonstrates superior control of language: grammar, stylistic variety, and accepted conventions of writing; minor flaws may occur

5 AND 4.5: "STRONG" ESSAY

- Presents well-chosen examples and strongly supports an opinion on the issue or a critique of the argument
- Communicates ideas clearly and is generally well organized; connections are logical
- Demonstrates solid control of language: grammar, stylistic variety, and accepted conventions of writing; minor flaws may occur

4 AND 3.5: "ADEQUATE" ESSAY

- Presents and adequately supports an opinion on the issue or a critique of the argument
- Communicates ideas fairly clearly and is adequately organized; logical connections are satisfactory
- Demonstrates satisfactory control of language: grammar, stylistic variety, and accepted conventions of writing; some flaws may occur

3 AND 2.5: "LIMITED" ESSAY

- Succeeds only partially in presenting and supporting an opinion on the issue or a critique of the argument
- Communicates ideas unclearly and is poorly organized
- Demonstrates less than satisfactory control of language: contains significant mistakes in grammar, usage, and sentence structure

2 AND 1.5: "WEAK" ESSAY

- Shows little success in presenting and supporting an opinion on the issue or a critique of the argument
- Struggles to communicate ideas; essay shows a lack of clarity and organization
- Meaning is impeded by many serious mistakes in grammar, usage, and sentence structure

1 AND 0.5: "FUNDAMENTALLY DEFICIENT" ESSAY

- Fails to present a coherent opinion and/or evidence on the issue or a critique of the argument
- Fails to communicate ideas; essay is seriously unclear and disorganized
- Lacks meaning due to widespread and severe mistakes in grammar, usage, and sentence structure

0: "UNSCORABLE" ESSAY

- Completely ignores topic
- Attempts to copy the assignments
- Is written in a foreign language or contains undecipherable text

THE 6 BASIC PRINCIPLES OF GRE WRITING

GRE writing is a simple, two-stage process: first you decide what you want to say about a topic, and then you figure out how to say it. If your writing style isn't clear, your ideas won't come across, no matter how brilliant they are. Good GRE English is not only grammatical but also clear and concise, and by using some basic principles, you'll be able to express your ideas clearly and effectively in both of your essays.

PRINCIPLE 1. YOUR CONTROL OF LANGUAGE IS IMPORTANT.

Writing that is grammatical, concise, direct, and persuasive displays the "superior control of language" (as the test makers call it) that earns top GRE scores. To achieve effective GRE style in your essays, you should pay attention to the following points.

Grammar

Your writing must follow the rules of standard written English. If you're not confident of your mastery of grammar, brush up before the test.

Diction

Diction means word choice. For example, do you use the words *affect* and *effect* correctly? Be careful with such commonly confused words as *precede/proceed, principal/principle, whose/who's,* and *stationary/stationery.*

Syntax

Syntax refers to sentence structure. Always construct your sentences so that your ideas are clear and understandable. Vary your sentence structure, sometimes using simple sentences and other times using sentences with clauses and phrases.

PRINCIPLE 2. IT'S BETTER TO KEEP THINGS SIMPLE.

Perhaps the single most important thing to bear in mind when writing GRE essays is to keep it simple. This rule applies to word choice, sentence structure, and organization. If you obsess about how to spell an unusual word, you can lose your flow of thought. The more complicated your sentences are, the more likely it is that they will be plagued by errors. The more complex your organization gets, the more likely it is that your argument will get bogged down in convoluted sentences that obscure your point. But keep in mind that simple does not mean simplistic. A clear, straightforward approach can still be sophisticated and convey perceptive insights.

PRINCIPLE 3. MINOR GRAMMATICAL FLAWS WON'T TORPEDO YOUR SCORE.

Many test takers mistakenly believe that they'll lose points because of a few mechanical errors such as misplaced commas, misspellings, or other minor glitches. Occasional mistakes of this type will not dramatically affect your GRE essay score. In fact, the test makers' description of a top-scoring essay acknowledges that there may be minor grammatical flaws. The essay graders understand that you are writing first-draft essays. They will not be looking to take points off for minor errors, provided you don't make them consistently. However, if your essays are littered with misspellings and grammar mistakes, then the graders may conclude that you have a serious communication problem.

READ MORE

For targeted writing techniques and practice, check out Kaplan's *GRE Exam Writing Workbook.*

To write an effective essay, you must be concise, forceful, and correct. An effective essay wastes no words, makes its point in a clear, direct way, and conforms to the generally accepted rules of grammar and form.

PRINCIPLE 4. KEEP SIGHT OF YOUR GOAL.

Remember, your goal isn't to become a prize-winning stylist; it's to write two solid essays that will convince admissions officers you can analyze and construct an argument and communicate your ideas to a reader. GRE essay graders don't expect rhetorical flourishes, but they do expect effective expression.

PRINCIPLE 5. SUPPORT YOUR ESSAY WITH EVIDENCE.

There have been studies that show that writing a longer essay can lead to increased points. However, there is a smart way to increase the length and power or your essay without weighing it down with wordy and awkward phrases (more on that in a moment). Support your points with a variety of evidence, including: anecdotes; statistics; examples from literature, history, or current events; and expert opinions. Don't worry if you don't have specific examples from all of these areas, these are just some examples of types of evidence you could use to bolster your points. Your main points for the Issue essay will be reasons supporting or opposing the issue presented. Your main points for the Argument essay will be types of evidence given in the argument itself that strengthen or weaken the argument. For both essays, you can use examples from the list above to support your main points.

PRINCIPLE 6. INCLUDE A STRONG INTRODUCTION AND CONCLUSION.

A strong introduction and conclusion will maximize the effectiveness of your essays. Introduce each essay by restating the issue or argument clearly and stating your position. Conclude each essay by summarizing your points, restating your position, and placing the essay in a larger context with a brief general statement about why the ideas in your essay are important or relevant.

 KAPLAN STRATEGY ———————————————————

Kaplan's basic principles for success in GRE writing are:

- Control your use of language to produce grammatical, concise, direct, and persuasive essays.

- Keep things simple in word choice, sentence structure, and organization.

- Don't stress about minor grammatical flaws; they won't sink your score.

- Stick to your point.

- Expand your writing with strong evidence.

- Include an introduction and a conclusion.

KAPLAN'S 5-STEP METHOD FOR GRE WRITING

Here's the deal: you have a limited amount of time to show the GRE essay scorers that you can think logically and express yourself in clearly written English. They don't care how many syllables you can cram into a sentence or how fancy your phrases are. They care that you're making sense. Whatever you do, don't try to hide beneath a lot of hefty words and abstractions. Just make sure that everything you say is clearly written and relevant to the topic. Get in there, state your main points, back them up, and get out.

Let's look at some strategies to help you ace this section of the test.

STEP 1. TAKE THE ISSUE/ARGUMENT APART.
- Identify the topic (the broad subject).
- Identify the scope (the specific aspect of the topic you'll be dealing with).
- Identify the conclusion (the main idea the author wanted to establish in the prompt).
- Locate the evidence used to support the conclusion.
- Look for assumptions (pieces of evidence that are not explicitly stated, but that must be true in order for the argument to hold water).
- Note any terms that are ambiguous and need defining.

STEP 2. SELECT THE POINTS YOU WILL MAKE.
- In the Issue essay, think of the arguments for both sides and make a decision as to which side you will support or the exact extent to which you agree with the stated position.
- In the Argument essay, identify all the important gaps between the evidence and the conclusion. Think of remedies for the problems you discover.

STEP 3. ORGANIZE YOUR THOUGHTS.
- Outline what you want to say in the introduction, in the middle paragraphs (one point per paragraph), and in your final paragraph.
- Determine what evidence you will use to support each point.
- Lead with your best arguments.
- Think about how the essay as a whole will flow.

STEP 4. TYPE YOUR ESSAY.
- Start out and conclude with strong statements.
- Be forceful.
- Make transitions, link related ideas; it will help your writing flow.

STEP 5. PROOFREAD.

- Save enough time to read through the entire essay.
- Have a sense of the errors you are liable to make.

Now let's see how these steps work with an Issue assignment.

THE ISSUE ESSAY

The Issue essay requires you to construct your own argument by making claims and providing evidence to support your position on a given issue.

The screen directions will ask you to take a position on the issue and instruct you to explain your position convincingly, using reasons or examples to back up your assertions.

The directions for the Issue essay will be similar to this:

> You will have 45 minutes to plan and write an essay that communicates your perspective on a given topic. Choose one of the two topics provided. No other topics are admissible for this essay.
>
> The topic is a short quotation that expresses an issue of general interest. Write an essay that agrees with, refutes, or qualifies the quotation, and support your opinion with relevant information drawn from your academic studies, reading, observation, or other experiences.
>
> Feel free to consider the issue for a few minutes before you begin your writing. Be certain that your ideas are fully developed and organized logically and make sure you have enough time left to review and revise what you've written.

THE ISSUE PROMPT

Expect a sentence or two that discuss a broad, general issue, sometimes presenting two competing points of view, sometimes only one. Either way, it will state an argument for which one or more counterarguments could be constructed. While the issue will be one upon which reasonable people could disagree, it will not bring up an emotionally charged religious or social issue.

In short, the topic will present a point of view. Your job is to form an opinion on the topic and make a case for that opinion.

The Issue topics you see may be similar to these:

The invention of gunpowder was the single most destructive achievement in history.

The main purpose of a college education should be to prepare oneself for a specific career.

—

The drawbacks to the use of nuclear power mean that it is not a long-term solution to the problem of meeting ever-increasing energy needs.

APPLYING KAPLAN'S 5-STEP METHOD TO THE ISSUE ESSAY

Let's use Kaplan's 5-Step Method on this sample Issue prompt:

The drawbacks to the use of nuclear power mean that it is not a long-term solution to the problem of meeting ever-increasing energy needs.

Step 1. Take the Issue Apart.

Topic: Energy sources

Scope: Whether or not nuclear power is a suitable replacement for other forms of energy

Conclusion: Nuclear power is not a solution to the problem of meeting ever-increasing energy needs

Evidence: Unnamed drawbacks

Assumptions:

- Nuclear power has the potential to meet long-term energy needs.
- Nuclear power is not our only energy option.

Step 2. Select the Points You Will Make

Your job, as stated in the directions, is to decide whether or not you agree and explain your decision. Some would argue that the use of nuclear power is too dangerous, while others would say that we can't afford not to use it. So which side do you take? Remember, this isn't about showing the admissions people what your deep-seated beliefs about the environment are—it's about showing that you can formulate an argument and write it down. Quickly think through the pros and cons of each side, and choose the side for which you have the most relevant things to say. For this topic, that process might go something like this:

Arguments for the use of nuclear power:

- Inexpensive compared to other forms of energy
- Fossil fuels will eventually be depleted
- Solar power still too problematic and expensive

Kaplan $5,000 Brighter Future Sweepstakes 2009 Complete and Official Rules

1. NO PURCHASE IS NECESSARY TO ENTER OR WIN. A PURCHASE WILL NOT INCREASE YOUR CHANCES OF WINNING.

2. PROMOTION PERIOD. The "Kaplan $5,000 Brighter Future Sweepstakes" ("Sweepstakes") commences at 6:59 A.M. EST on April 1, 2009 and ends at 11:59 P.M. EST on March 31, 2010. Entry forms can be found online at kaptest.com/brighterfuturesweeps. All online entries must be received by March 31, 2010 at 11:59 P.M. EST.

3. ELIGIBILITY. This Sweepstakes is open to legal residents of the 50 United States and the District of Columbia and Canada (excluding the Province of Quebec) who are sixteen (16) years of age or older as of April 1, 2009. Officers, directors, representatives and employees of Kaplan (from here on called "Sponsor"), its parent, affiliates or subsidiaries, or their respective advertising, promotion, publicity, production, and judging agencies and their immediate families and household members are not eligible to enter.

4. TO ENTER. To enter simply go to kaptest.com/brighterfuturesweeps and fill-out the online entry form between April 1, 2009 and March 31, 2010.

As part of your entry, you will be asked to provide your first and last name, email address, permanent address and phone number, parent or legal guardian name if under eighteen (18), and the name of your undergraduate school.

LIMIT ONE ENTRY PER PERSON AND EMAIL ADDRESS. Multiple entries will be disqualified. Entries are void if they contain typographical, printing or other errors. Entries generated by a script, macro or other automated means are void. Entries that are mutilated, altered, incomplete, mechanically reproduced, tampered with, illegible, inaccurate, forged, irregular in any way, or otherwise not in compliance with these Official Rules are also void. All entries become the property of the Sponsor and will not be returned to the entrant. Sponsor and those working on its behalf will not be responsible for lost, late, misdirected or damaged mail or email or for Internet, network, computer hardware and software, phone or other technical errors, malfunctions and delays that may occur. Entries will be deemed to have been submitted by the authorized account holder of the email account from which the entry is made. The authorized account holder is the natural person to whom an email address is assigned by an Internet access provider, online service provider or other organization (e.g. business, educational institution, etc.) responsible for assigning email addresses for the domain associated with the submitted email address. By entering or accepting a prize in this Sweepstakes, entrants agree to be bound by the decisions of the judges, the Sponsor and these Official Rules and to comply with all applicable federal, state and local laws and regulations. Odds of winning depend on the number of eligible entries received.

5. WINNER SELECTION. Two (2) winners will be selected for the First Prize; two (2) winners for the Second Prize, five (5) winners for the Third Prize, five (5) winners for Fourth Prize, five (5) winners for the Fifth Prize, and 25 winners for the Sixth Prize from all eligible entries received in a random drawing to be held on or about May 11, 2010. The drawing will be conducted by an independent judge whose decisions shall be final and binding in all regards. Participants need not be present to win. Please note that if the entrant selected as the winner resides in Canada, he/she will have to correctly answer a timed, test-prep question in order to be confirmed as the winner and claim the prize.

6. WINNER NOTIFICATION AND VALIDATION. Winners of the drawing will be notified by mail within 10 days after the drawing. An Affidavit of Eligibility and Compliance with these Official Rules and a Liability and (unless prohibited) Publicity Release must be executed and returned by the potential winner within twenty-one (21) days after prize notification is sent. If the winner is under eighteen (18) years of age, the prize will be awarded to the winner's parent or legal guardian who will be required to execute an affidavit. Failure of the potential winner to complete, sign and return any requested documents within such period or the return of any prize notification or prize as undeliverable may result in disqualification and selection of an alternate winner in Sponsor's sole discretion. You are not a winner unless your submissions are validated.

In the event that a winner chooses not to accept his or her prize, does not respond to winner notification within the time period noted on the notification or does not return a completed Affidavit of Eligibility and Compliance with these Official Rules and a Liability and (unless prohibited) Publicity Release within twenty-one (21) days after prize notification is sent, the prize may be forfeited and an alternate winner selected in Sponsor's sole discretion.

7. PRIZES.
• First Prize: Two (2) winners will be selected to win $5,000.00 USD.
• Second Prize: Two (2) winners will be selected to win $1,000.00 USD.
• Third Prize: Five (5) winners will be selected to win their choice of a Free Kaplan SAT, ACT, GMAT, GRE, LSAT, MCAT, DAT, OAT, or PCAT Classroom Course (retail value up to $1,899).
• Fourth Prize: Five (5) winners will be selected to win their choice of Ten (10) Free Hours of GMAT, GRE, LSAT, MCAT, DAT, OAT, PCAT Private Tutoring (retail value of $1,500), or Ten (10) Free Hours of SAT, ACT, PSAT Premier Tutoring (retail value of $2,000).
• Fifth Prize: Five (5) winners will be selected to win their choice of Three (3) Free Hours of Admissions Consulting for Precollege (retail value of $450) or three (3) Free Hours of Business School, Law School, Grad School or Med School Admissions Consulting (retail value of $729).
• Sixth Prize: Twenty-five (25) winners will be selected to win $100.00 USD.
For winners of the Third and Fourth Prizes, the winner must redeem the course at Kaplan locations in the US offering them and have completed the program before December 31, 2012.

Prizes are not transferable. No substitution of prizes for cash or other goods and services is permitted, except Sponsor reserves the right in its sole discretion to substitute any prize with a prize of comparable value. Any applicable taxes or fees are the winner's sole responsibility. All prizes must be redeemed within 21 days of notice of award and course prizes used by December 31, 2012.

8. GENERAL CONDITIONS. By entering the Sweepstakes or accepting the Sweepstakes prize, winner accepts all the conditions, restrictions, requirements and/or regulations required by the Sponsor in connection with the Sweepstakes. Unless otherwise prohibited by law, acceptance of a prize constitutes permission to use winner's name, picture, likeness, address (city and state) and biographical information for advertising and publicity purposes for this and/or similar promotions, without prior approval or compensation. Acceptance of a prize constitutes a waiver of any claim to royalties, rights or remuneration for said use. Winner agrees to release and hold harmless the Sponsor, its parent, affiliates and subsidiaries, and each of their respective directors, officers, employees, agents, and successors from any and all claims, damages, injury, death, loss or other liability that may arise from winner's participation in the Sweepstakes or the awarding, acceptance, possession, use or misuse of the prize. Sponsor reserves the right in its sole discretion to modify or cancel all or any portions of the Sweepstakes because of technical errors or malfunctions, viruses, hackers, or for other reasons beyond Sponsor's control that impair or corrupt the Sweepstakes in any manner. In such event, Sponsor shall award prizes at random from among the eligible entries received up to the time of the impairment or corruption. Sponsor also reserves the right in its sole discretion to disqualify any entrant who fails to comply with these Official Rules, who attempts to enter the Sweepstakes in any manner or through any means other than as described in these Official Rules, or who attempts to disrupt the Sweepstakes or the kaptest.com website or to circumvent any of these Official Rules.

9. WINNERS' LIST. Starting August 15, 2010, a winners' list may be obtained by sending a self-addressed, stamped envelope to: "$5,000 Kaplan Brighter Future Sweepstakes" Winners' List, Kaplan Test Prep and Admissions Marketing Department, 1440 Broadway, 8th Floor New York, NY 10018. All winners' list requests must be received by December 1, 2010.

10. USE OF ENTRANT AND WINNER INFORMATION. The information that you provide in connection with the Sweepstakes may be used for Sponsor's and select Corporate Partners' purposes to send you information about Sponsor's and its Corporate Partners' products and services. If you would like your name removed from Sponsor's mailing list or if you do not wish to receive information from Sponsor or its Corporate Partners, write to:

Direct Marketing Department
Attn: Kaplan Brighter Future Sweepstakes Opt Out
1440 Broadway
8th Floor
New York NY 10018

11. SPONSOR. The Sponsor of this Sweepstakes is: Kaplan Test Prep and Admissions and Kaplan Publishing, 1440 Broadway, 8th Floor New York, NY 10018.

12. THIS SWEEPSTAKES IS VOID WHERE PROHIBITED, TAXED OR OTHERWISE RESTRICTED BY LAW.

All trademarks are the property of their respective owner.

Arguments against the use of nuclear power:

- Harmful to the environment
- Dangerous to mankind
- Safer alternatives already exist
- Better alternatives may lie undiscovered

Again, it doesn't matter which side you take. Let's say that in this case you decide to argue against nuclear power. Remember, the question is asking you to argue why the cons of nuclear power outweigh the pros—the inadequacy of this power source is the end you're arguing toward, so don't list it as a supporting argument.

Step 3. Organize Your Argument.

You've already begun to think out your arguments and the evidence you will use to support each argument—that's why you picked the side you did in the first place. Now's the time to write them all out, including ones that weaken the opposing side.

Nuclear power is not a viable alternative to other sources of energy because

- radioactive, spent fuel has leaked from storage sites (too dangerous).
- reactor accidents can be catastrophic—Three Mile Island, Chernobyl (too dangerous).
- more research into solar power will bring down its cost (weakens opposing argument).
- solar-powered homes and cars already exist (alternatives proven viable).
- renewable resources require money only for the materials needed to harvest them (alternatives are cheaper in the long run).
- energy companies don't spend money on alternatives; no vested interest (better alternatives lie undiscovered).

Step 4. Write Your Essay.

Remember, open up with a general statement and then assert your position. From there, get down your main points.

Your essay for this assignment might look like one of the following sample essays. As a basis for comparison, we've included one outstanding essay that deserves a score of "6," and one adequate essay that deserves a score of "4." Think about the differences you find in these two essays, then read our own assessments.

Sample Issue Essay 1

Proponents of nuclear energy as "the power source for the future," have long touted its relative economy, "clean burning" technology, and virtually inexhaustible fuel supply. However, a close examination of the issue reveals that nuclear energy proves more problematic and dangerous than other forms of energy production and thus is not an acceptable solution to the problem of meeting ever-increasing energy needs.

First and foremost, nuclear power production presents the problem of radioactive waste storage. Fuel by-products from nuclear fission remain toxic for thousands of years, and the spills and leaks from existing storage sites have been hazardous and costly to clean up. This remains true despite careful regulation and even under the best of circumstances. Even more appalling is the looming threat of accidents at the reactor itself: Incidents at the Three Mile Island and Chernobyl power plants and at other production sites have warned us that the consequences of a nuclear meltdown can be catastrophic and felt worldwide.

But beyond the enormous long-term environmental problems and short-term health risks, the bottom line issue for the production of energy is one of economics. Power production in our society is a business just like any other, and the large companies that produce this country's electricity and gas claim they are unable to make alternatives such as solar power affordable. Yet—largely due to incentives from the federal government—there already exist homes heated by solar power, and cars fueled by the sun. If the limited resources devoted to date to such energy alternatives have already produced working models, a more intensive, broadly based, and supported effort is likely to make those alternatives less expensive and problematic.

Besides the benefits in terms of both of cost and safety, renewable resources such as solar and hydroelectric power represent far better options in the long run for development: They require money only for the materials needed to harvest them. While sunlight and water are free, the innovative technologies and industrial strategies devised to harness them have created a geometric progression of spin-offs affecting fields as diverse as agriculture, real estate, space exploration, and social policy. They have also repeatedly produced secondary economic and social benefits, such as the large recreational and irrigation reservoirs created in the American Southwest behind large hydroelectric dams like the Hoover and Grand Coullee.

While it may now be clear that the drawbacks to the use of nuclear power are too great, it should also be apparent that the long-term benefits of renewable resources would reward investment. If these alternatives are explored more seriously than they have been in the past, safer and less expensive sources of power will undoubtedly live up to their promise. With limited resources at our disposal and a burgeoning global population to consider, further investment in nuclear power would mark an unconscionable and unnecessary waste of time and money.

Sample Issue Essay 2

That there may be drawbacks in the production of nuclear power is undeniable but I believe that one cannot underestimate the need for and importance of this form of energy in addressing our long-term energy needs. The ever-increasing demand for energy is a good example of a problem that requires the development of many sources. If there were no nuclear energy there would be no reliable and readily available alternatives to imported oil for the majority of our energy needs.

There are some problems that must get solved in the long term for nuclear energy, but there are other problems that will certainly follow if we depend only on the alternatives. Fossil fuels will eventually be depleted, while solar power remains problematic and expensive. It will take years to be able to develop, never mind whether it will ever make sense in economical or even technological terms. Nuclear power is already inexpensive compared to these other forms, in a technology that exists today. And in the meantime long-term problems such as nuclear fuel sources and waste storage might be solved by technological means such as the development of nuclear fusion.

I am currently working in the financial field where the need for cheap energy becomes obvious. Such recent crises as the California power crisis, OPEC quotas, the fight over ANWR and the collapse of Enron have contributed to a faltering economy. It would be unrealistic, not to mention unfair to the general public, to expect them to continue to endure these crises and threats and perhaps go to war when a viable virtually inexhaustible supply of energy lies at hand. The key is to not give up on this source while it holds long-term promise. My personal experience as a trader tells me that a long-term commitment to nuclear power would help stabilize the energy sector, while not doing so means that the uncertainty of the status quo will remain. Whether it be an OPEC decision, a war or a coup, a nationalization of resources or any other crisis, the current energy supply is under constant threat. The list of scenarios can go on longer than one would think and it's just impossible for us to predict where the next shock will come from.

Although the need for safety and continuing research is apparant, it would be hard to survive in the present circumstances without the nuclear power option also. When our nation depends on others, we open ourselves up to potential blackmail. Nuclear power, a technology that we developed and at which we excel, is there to help add the long-term stability that may be lacking. The most important thing to remember with nuclear power is both its

strengths and weaknesses and capitalize on the strengths to achieve the
energy goal that is desired.

Step 5. Proofread Your Work.

Take that last couple of minutes to catch any glaring errors.

Assessment of Sample Issue Essay 1: Outstanding, Score of "6"

This essay is carefully constructed throughout, enabling the reader to move effortlessly from point to point as the writer examines the multifaceted implications of the issue. The writer begins by acknowledging arguments for the opposing side, and then uses his thesis statement ("a close examination of the issue reveals that nuclear energy proves more problematic and dangerous than other forms of energy production") to explain his own position on the issue. He proceeds to provide compelling reasons and examples to support the premise, and then takes the argument to an effective conclusion. The writing is clean, concise, and error-free. Sentence structure is varied, and diction and vocabulary are strong and expressive.

Assessment of Sample Issue Essay 2: Adequate, Score of "4"

This essay presents a generally competent argument on one side of the topic at hand. The writer points out the need for a "reliable and readily available" alternative to fossil fuel energy supplies and argues that both will be needed in the short run. But by the time we reach the third paragraph, the discussion wanders. The final paragraph adds little, and the last sentence in particular is ineffective. The writer displays only adequate control of syntax and usage throughout the essay, and the vocabulary, while up to the task, lacks precision.

THE ARGUMENT ESSAY

The Argument essay requires you to critique the construction of someone else's argument by assessing its claims and evaluating the evidence provided. You are not being asked to agree or disagree with the author's *position* or *conclusion*; instead, you must analyze the *line of reasoning* used in the argument.

The screen directions will instruct you to decide how convincing you find the argument. To make your case, first analyze the argument itself and evaluate its use of evidence; second, explain how a different approach or more information would make the argument itself better (or possibly worse).

The directions for the Argument essay will look something like this:

> You will have 30 minutes to plan and write a critique of an
> argument presented in the form of a short passage. You will be

asked to consider the logical soundness of the argument. No other topics are admissible for this essay.

Your essay will be evaluated in terms of the following:

- identifying and analyzing the argument's important points;

- organizing, developing, and expressing your ideas;

- supporting your ideas with relevant reasons and/or examples; and

- demonstrating a knowledge of standard written English.

Feel free to consider the issue for a few minutes before planning your response and beginning your writing. Be certain that your ideas are fully developed and organized logically, and make sure you have enough time left to review and revise what you've written.

THE ARGUMENT PROMPT

This time you're given an expressed point of view—an "argument"—that contains a conclusion and supporting evidence. Here the writer tries to persuade you of something (her conclusion) by citing some evidence. You should read the "arguments" in the prompts with a critical eye. Be on the lookout for *assumptions* in the way the writer moves from evidence to conclusion.

The topic you see in the Argument section may be similar to these:

The problem of poorly trained teachers that has plagued the state public school system is bound to become a good deal less serious in the future. The state has initiated comprehensive guidelines that oblige state teachers to complete a number of required credits in education and educational psychology at the graduate level before being certified.

The commercial airline industry in the country of Freedonia has experienced impressive growth in the past three years. This trend will surely continue in the years to come, since the airline industry will benefit from recent changes in Freedonian society: Incomes are rising, most employees now receive more vacation time, and interest in travel is rising, as shown by an increase in media attention devoted to foreign cultures and tourist attractions.

The Kiddie Candy Company has instituted a new policy of paying factory employees for the number of candies each employee produces, rather than for the time they spend producing the candy. This policy will increase the number and raise the quality of the candies produced, allow the company to reduce their staff size, and enable their factories to operate for fewer hours. Ultimately, both the factory employees and the company will benefit from these changes, as the best workers will keep their jobs and the company will earn a profit in the coming year.

APPLYING KAPLAN'S 5-STEP METHOD TO AN ARGUMENT ESSAY

Let's use Kaplan's 5-Step Method on this sample Argument prompt:

The following appeared in a memo from the secretary of the state's new teacher development committee:

The problem of poorly performing teachers that has plagued the state public school system is bound to become a good deal less serious in the future. The state has initiated comprehensive guidelines that oblige state teachers to complete a number of required credits in education and educational psychology at the graduate level before being certified.

Explain how logically persuasive you find this argument. In discussing your viewpoint, analyze the argument's line of reasoning and its use of evidence. Also explain what, if anything, would make the argument more valid and convincing or help you to better evaluate its conclusion.

Step 1. Take the Argument Apart.

Topic: The state public school system

Scope: How to solve the problem of poorly performing teachers

Conclusion: The problem of poorly performing teachers that has plagued the state public school system is bound to become a good deal less serious in the future.

Evidence: The state has initiated comprehensive guidelines that oblige state teachers to complete a number of required credits in education and educational psychology at the graduate level before being certified.

Assumptions:

- Credits in education will improve teachers' classroom performance.
- Current bad teachers haven't already met this standard of training.
- Current bad teachers will not still be teaching in the future, or will have to be trained, too.

Step 2. Select the Points You Will Make.

Analyze the use of evidence in the argument. Determine whether there's anything relevant that's not discussed.

- Whether the training will actually address the cause of the problems
- What "poorly performing" means
- How to either improve or remove the bad teachers now teaching

Also determine what types of evidence would make the argument stronger or more logically sound. In this case, we need some new evidence supporting the assumptions.

- Evidence verifying that this training will make better teachers
- Evidence making it clear that current bad teachers haven't already had this training
- Evidence suggesting why all or many bad teachers won't still be teaching in the future (or why they'll be better trained)

Step 3. Organize Your Essay.

For an essay on this topic, your opening sentence might look like this:

> The argument that improved academic training, ensured by requiring credits in education and psychology, will substantially alleviate the current problem of poorly trained teachers may seem logical at first glance.

Then use your notes as a working outline. You will primarily be addressing the ways in which the assumptions seem unsupported. You might also recommend new evidence you'd like to see and explain why. Remember to lead with your best arguments.

Step 4. Write Your Essay.

Begin writing your essay now. Your essay for this assignment might look like one of the following sample essays. As a basis for comparison, we've included one outstanding essay that deserves a score of "6," and one adequate essay that deserves a score of "4."

Sample Argument Essay 1

The argument that improved academic training, ensured by requiring credits in education and psychology, will substantially alleviate the current problem of poorly performing teachers may seem logical at first glance. However, the conclusion relies upon assumptions for which there is no clear evidence and upon terms which lack definition.

First, the writer assumes that the required courses will produce better teachers. In fact, the courses might be entirely irrelevant to the teachers' failings. Suppose, for example, the main problem lies in cultural and linguistic gaps between teacher and student; graduate-level courses that do not address these specific issues would be of little use in bridging these gaps and improving educational outcomes. The notion that the coursework will provide better teachers would be strengthened by a clear definition of "poor perfomance" in the classroom and by additional evidence that the training will address the relevant issues.

Furthermore, the writer assumes that poorly performing teachers currently in the schools have not already met this standard of training. In fact, the writer makes no useful distinction between excellent and inadequate classroom performance in the matter of training. The argument would be strengthened considerably if the writer provided evidence of a direct correlation between teachers' educational backgrounds and their level of effectiveness in the classroom.

Finally, the writer provides no evidence that poorly performing teachers currently working will either stop teaching in the near future or will undergo additional training. In its current form, the argument implies that only brand-new teachers—those not previously certified—will receive the specified training. If this is the case, the bright future that the writer envisions may be decades away. The conclusion requires the support of evidence demonstrating that all teachers in the system will receive the remedial training and will then change their teaching methods accordingly.

The writer would not be wrong to conclude that the state's comprehensive guidelines will potentially lead to some improvement in the educational environment in the public schools. After all, the additional training will certainly not adversely affect classroom performance in any way. But in order to support the current conclusion that the guidelines will, in effect, solve the state's problem, the writer must first define the scope of the problem more clearly and demonstrate a more complete understanding of the need for and benefits of the new requirements.

Sample Argument Essay 2

Although the argument stated above discusses the likelihood that teacher training in the public school system will improve, the reasons given are vague and inconclusive. Simply because the state has imposed guidelines that require teachers to complete a number of graduate credits in education and educational psychology does not automatically improve their classroom performance. The term "poorly performing" may imply a great variety of shortcomings. The types of problems the state could face in achieving its goal are its assumptions that coursework in education will actually improve the teachers' classroom performance, that present bad teachers haven't already met this new standard of training, and that current poor teachers will not be teaching in the future or will get training too. Whether the training will actually address the cause of the problems remains to be seen. Not clear as well is how to either improve or remove the poor teachers now teaching. The writer needs to provide evidence verifying that this training will make better teachers, evidence proving that present bad teachers haven't already had this training, and evidence which suggests why all or many of these inadequate teachers won't still be teaching in the future. Only when such evidence is convincingly presented will the reader feel compelled to accept the argument. The prediction made in the above reasoning is lacking in proper evidence considering its assertions and therefore must be further examined and modified so that conclusion can be properly supported.

Step 5. Proofread.

Save a few minutes to go over your essay and catch any obvious errors.

Assessment of Sample Argument Essay 1: Outstanding, Score of "6"

An outstanding response demonstrates the writer's insightful analytical skills. The introduction notes the prompt's specious reasoning occasioned by unsupported assumptions and a lack of definition and evidence. The writer follows this up with a one-paragraph examination of each of the root flaws in the argument. Specifically, the author exposes these points undermining the argument:

- The assumption that the required courses will make better teachers
- The assumption that poorly performing teachers currently in the schools have not already had the proposed training
- The complete lack of evidence that ineffective teachers currently working will either stop teaching in the future or will successfully adapt the required training to their classroom work

Each point receives thorough and cogent development (given the time constraints) in a smooth and logically organized discourse. In succinct, economical, and error-free writing, sentences vary in length and complexity, while the diction and vocabulary stands out as both precise and expressive.

Assessment of Sample Argument Essay 2: Adequate, Score of "4"

This essay adequately targets the argument's vague and inadequate evidence. The essay identifies and critiques the illogical reasoning that results from misguided assumptions and poorly defined terms that

- requiring educational course credits will address the root of the problem.
- "poorly performing" teachers will actually improve in the classroom.
- teachers currently performing at a below average level have not already met the requirements.

The writer clearly grasps the argument's central weaknesses. But although the ideas are clear, the essay lacks transitional phrases and is not well-organized. While the writer demonstrates a better than adequate control of language and ably conforms to the conventions of written English, this "4" essay suffers from a lack of the more thorough development of a typical "5" response.

KAPLAN'S 22 PRINCIPLES OF EFFECTIVE WRITING

To write an effective analytical essay, there are three main goals you need to meet:

- **Be concise:** waste no words.
- **Be forceful:** make a point.
- **Be correct:** conform to the generally accepted rules of grammar and form.

Let's break down the three broad objectives of conciseness, forcefulness, and correctness into 22 specific principles. (Don't panic—many of them will be familiar to you.) Each principle is illustrated by exercises so that you can immediately practice what you learn; the answers to these exercises are located at the end of this section. Do the exercises and then compare your answers to ours. Make sure you understand what the error was in each sentence. Then use what you learn in this section to help you write and proofread your practice essays.

PRINCIPLE 1: AVOID WORDINESS.

Why use several words when one will do? Many people make the mistake of writing phrases such as *at the present time* or *at this point in time* instead of the simpler *now*, or *take into consideration* instead of simply *consider*, in an attempt to make their prose seem more scholarly or more formal. It won't work. Instead, their prose ends up seeming inflated and pretentious. Don't waste your words or your time.

WORDY: I am of the opinion that the aforementioned managers should be advised that they will be evaluated with regard to the utilization of responsive organizational software for the purpose of devising a responsive network of customers.

CONCISE: We should tell the managers that we will evaluate their use of flexible computerized databases to develop a customer network.

EXERCISE 1: WORDY PHRASES

Improve the following sentences by omitting or replacing wordy phrases.

1. The agency is not prepared to undertake expansion at this point in time.

2. In spite of the fact that she only has a little bit of experience in photography right now, she will probably do well in the future because she has a great deal of motivation to succeed in her chosen profession.

3. Although not untactful, George is a man who says exactly what he believes.

_____

4. Accuracy is a subject that has great importance to English teachers and company presidents alike.

_____

5. Ms. Miller speaks with a high degree of intelligence with regard to many aspects of modern philosophy.

_____

PRINCIPLE 2: DON'T BE REDUNDANT.

Redundancy means that the writer needlessly repeats an idea. It's redundant to speak of _a beginner lacking experience_. The word _beginner_ implies lack of experience by itself. You can eliminate redundant words or phrases without changing the meaning of the sentence.

Here are some common redundancies:

REDUNDANT	CONCISE
refer back	refer
few in number	few
small-sized	small
grouped together	grouped
in my own personal opinion	in my opinion
end result	result
serious crisis	crisis
new initiatives	initiatives

EXERCISE 2: REDUNDANCY

Repair the following sentences by crossing out redundant elements.

1. All of these problems have combined together to create a serious crisis.

_____

2. A staff that large in size needs an effective supervisor who can get the job done.

_____

3. He knows how to follow directions and he knows how to do what he is told.

   _____

4. The writer's technical skill and ability do not mask his poor plot line.

   _____

5. That monument continues to remain a significant tourist attraction.

   _____

6. The recently observed trend of spending on credit has created a middle class that is poorer and more impoverished than ever before.

   _____

7. Those who can follow directions are few in number.

   _____

PRINCIPLE 3: AVOID NEEDLESS QUALIFICATION.

Since the object of your essay is to convince your reader, you will want to adopt a reasonable tone. There will likely be no single, clear-cut "answer" to the essay topic, so don't overstate your case. Occasional use of such qualifiers as *fairly, rather, somewhat,* and *relatively*, and of such expressions as *seems to be, a little*, and *a certain amount of* will let the reader know you are reasonable, but overusing such modifiers weakens your argument. Excessive qualification makes you sound hesitant. Like wordy phrases, qualifiers can add bulk without adding substance.

> WORDY: This rather serious breach of etiquette may possibly shake the very foundations of the corporate world.

> CONCISE: This serious breach of etiquette may shake the foundations of the corporate world.

Just as bad is the overuse of the word *very*. Some writers use this intensifying adverb before almost every adjective in an attempt to be more forceful. If you need to add emphasis, look for a stronger adjective or adverb.

> WEAK: Novak is a very good pianist.
> STRONG: Novak is a virtuoso pianist.
> OR
> Novak plays beautifully.

And don't try to qualify words that are already absolute.

WRONG	CORRECT
more unique	unique
the very worst	the worst
completely full	full

EXERCISE 3: EXCESSIVE QUALIFICATION

Although reasonable qualification benefits an essay, excessive qualification debilitates your argument. Practice achieving conciseness by eliminating needless qualification in the sentences below.

1. She is a fairly excellent teacher.

   _____

2. Ferrara seems to be sort of a slow worker.

   _____

3. It is rather important to pay attention to all the details of a murder trial as well as to the larger picture.

   _____

4. You yourself are the very best person to decide what you should do for a living.

   _____

5. In Italy, I found about the best food I have ever eaten.

   _____

6. Needless to say, children should be taught to cooperate at home and also in school.

   _____

PRINCIPLE 4: DON'T WRITE SENTENCES JUST TO FILL UP SPACE.

This principle suggests several things:

- Don't write a sentence that gets you nowhere.
- Don't ask a question only to answer it.

- Don't merely copy the essay's directions.
- Don't write a whole sentence only to announce that you're changing the subject.

If you have something to say, say it without preamble. If you need to smooth over a change of subject, do so with a transitional word or phrase, rather than with a meaningless sentence.

WORDY: Which idea of the author's is more in line with what I believe? This is a very interesting question.

CONCISE: The author's beliefs are similar to mine.

The author of the wordy example above is just wasting words and time. Get to the point quickly and stay there. Simplicity and clarity win points.

EXERCISE 4: UNNECESSARY SENTENCES

Rewrite each of these two-sentence statements as one concise sentence.

1. In the dawn of the twenty-first century, the Earth can be characterized as a small planet. Advanced technology has made it easy for people who live vast distances from each other to communicate.

   _____

2. What's the purpose of getting rid of the chemical pollutants in water? People cannot safely consume water that contains chemical pollutants.

   _____

3. Napoleon suffered defeat in Russia because most of his troops perished in the cold. Most of his men died because they had no winter clothing to protect them from the cold.

   _____

4. Third, I do not believe those who argue that some of Shakespeare's plays were written by others. There is no evidence that other people had a hand in writing Shakespeare's plays.

   _____

5. Frank Lloyd Wright was a famous architect. He was renowned for his ability to design buildings that blend into their surroundings.

   _____

6. A lot of people find math a difficult subject to master. They have trouble with math because it requires very precise thinking skills.

_____

PRINCIPLE 5: AVOID NEEDLESS SELF-REFERENCE.

Avoid such unnecessary phrases as *I believe, I feel,* and *in my opinion.* There is no need to remind your reader that what you are writing is your opinion. Self-reference is another form of qualifying what you say—a very obvious form.

> WEAK: I am of the opinion that air pollution is a more serious problem than most people realize.
>
> FORCEFUL: Air pollution is a more serious problem than most people realize.

EXERCISE 5: NEEDLESS SELF-REFERENCE

Eliminate needless self-references in these sentences.

1. I feel we ought to pay teachers more than we pay actors.

_____

2. The author, in my personal opinion, is stuck in the past.

_____

3. I do not think this argument can be generalized to most business owners.

_____

4. Although I am no expert, I do not think privacy should be valued more than social concerns.

_____

5. I must emphasize that I am not saying the author does not have a point.

_____

6. If I were a college president, I would implement several specific reforms to combat apathy.

_____

7. It is my belief that either alternative would prove disastrous.

_____

PRINCIPLE 6: USE THE ACTIVE VOICE.

Using the passive voice is a way to avoid accountability. Put verbs in the active voice whenever possible. In the active voice, the subject performs the action (*e.g.,* we write essays). In the passive voice, the subject is the receiver of the action and is often only implied (*e.g.,* essays are written by us).

PASSIVE: The estimate of this year's tax revenues was prepared by the General Accounting Office.

ACTIVE: The General Accounting Office prepared the estimate of this year's tax revenues.

The passive voice creates weak sentences and is usually the product of writing before you think. Avoid this by prewriting. Take a few minutes to find out what you want to say before you say it. To change from the passive to the active voice, ask yourself WHO or WHAT is performing the action. In the sentence above, the General Accounting Office is performing the action; therefore, the the General Accounting Office should be the subject of the sentence.

You should avoid the passive voice EXCEPT in the following cases:

- When you do not know who performed the action: *The letter was opened before I received it.*
- When you prefer not to refer directly to the person who performs the action: *An error has been made in computing this data.*

EXERCISE 6: UNDESIRABLE PASSIVES

Replace passive voice with active wherever possible.

1. The Spanish-American War was fought by brave but misguided men.

   _____

2. The bill was passed in time, but it was not signed by the President until the time for action had passed.

   _____

3. Advice is usually requested by those who need it least; it is not sought out by the truly lost and ignorant.

   _____

4. That building should be relocated where it can be appreciated by the citizens.

   _____

5. Garbage collectors should be generously rewarded for their difficult labors.

   _____

6. The conditions of the contract agreement were ironed out minutes before the strike deadline.

   _____

7. Test results were distributed with no concern for confidentiality.

   _____

PRINCIPLE 7: AVOID WEAK OPENINGS.

Try not to begin a sentence with *there is, there are*, or *it is*. These roundabout expressions usually indicate that you are trying to distance yourself from the position you are taking. Again, weak openings usually result from writing before you think, hedging until you find out what you want to say.

EXERCISE 7: WEAK OPENINGS

Rewrite these sentences to eliminate weak openings.

1. It would be unwise for businesses to ignore the illiteracy problem.

   _____

2. There are several reasons why this plane is obsolete.

   _____

3. It would be of no use to fight a war on poverty without waging a battle against child labor.

   _____

4. There are many strong points in the candidate's favor; intelligence, unfortunately, is not among them.

   _____

5. It is difficult to justify building a more handsome prison.

   _____

6. There seems to be little doubt that Americans like watching television better than conversing.

_____

7. It is obvious that intelligence is a product of environment and heredity.

_____

PRINCIPLE 8: AVOID NEEDLESSLY VAGUE LANGUAGE.

Don't just ramble on when writing your GRE essays. Choose specific, descriptive words. Vague language weakens your writing because it forces the reader to guess what you mean instead of concentrating fully on your ideas and style. The essay topics you'll be given aren't going to be obscure. You will be able to come up with specific examples and concrete information about the topics. Your argument will be more forceful if you stick to this information.

> WEAK: Ms. Brown is highly educated.
> FORCEFUL: Ms. Brown has a master's degree in business administration.
> WEAK: She is a great communicator.
> FORCEFUL: She speaks persuasively.

Notice that sometimes, to be more specific and concrete, you will have to use more words than you might with vague language. This principle is not in conflict with the general objective of conciseness. Being concise may mean eliminating unnecessary words. Avoiding vagueness may mean adding necessary words.

EXERCISE 8: NEEDLESSLY VAGUE LANGUAGE

Rewrite these sentences to replace vague language with specific, concrete language.

1. Water is transformed into steam when the former is heated up to 100°C.

_____

2. The diplomat was required to execute an agreement that stipulated that he would live in whatever country the federal government thought necessary.

_____

3. Arthur is a careless person.

_____

4. She told us that she was going to go to the store as soon as her mother came home.

_____

5. A radar unit is a highly specialized piece of equipment.

_____

6. Thousands of species of animals were destroyed when the last ice age occurred.

_____

7. The secretary was unable to complete the task that had been assigned.

_____

PRINCIPLE 9: AVOID CLICHÉS.

Clichés are overused expressions, expressions that may once have seemed colorful and powerful but are now dull and worn out. Time pressure and anxiety may make you lose focus; that's when clichés may slip into your writing. A reliance on clichés will suggest you are a lazy thinker. Keep them out of your essay.

> WEAK: Performance in a crisis is the acid test for a leader.
>
> FORCEFUL: Performance in a crisis is the best indicator of a leader's abilities.

Putting a cliché in quotation marks in order to indicate your distance from the cliché does not strengthen the sentence. If anything, it just makes weak writing more noticeable. Notice whether or not you use clichés. If you do, ask yourself if you could substitute more specific language for the cliché.

EXERCISE 9: CLICHÉS

Make the following sentences more forceful by replacing clichés with cliché-free formulations.

1. Beyond the shadow of a doubt, Jefferson was a great leader.

_____

2. I have a sneaking suspicion that families spend less time together than they did 15 years ago.

_____

3. The pizza delivery man arrived in the sequestered jury's hour of need.

_____

4. Trying to find the employee responsible for this embarrassing information leak is like trying to find a needle in a haystack.

_____

5. Both strategies would be expensive and completely ineffective, so it's six of one and half a dozen of the other.

_____

6. Older doctors should be required to update their techniques, but you can't teach an old dog new tricks.

_____

PRINCIPLE 10: AVOID JARGON.

Jargon includes two categories of words that you should avoid. First is the specialized vocabulary of a group, such as that used by doctors, lawyers, or baseball coaches. Second is the overly inflated and complex language that burdens many students' essays. You will not impress anyone with big words that do not fit the tone or context of your essay, especially if you misuse them.

If you are not certain of a word's meaning or appropriateness, leave it out. An appropriate word, even a simple one, will add impact to your argument. As you come across words you are unsure of, ask yourself, "Would a reader in a different field be able to understand exactly what I mean from the words I've chosen? Is there any way I can say the same thing more simply?"

> WEAK: The company is not able to bankroll the project.
> FORCEFUL: The company is not able to finance the project.

The following are commonly used jargon words:

assistance	cookie-cutter	input/output	parameter
ballpark	designate	maximize	prioritize
bandwidth	downside	mutually beneficial	target
blindside	face time	ongoing	time frame
bottom line	facilitate	optimize	user-friendly
conceptualize	finalize	originate	utilize

EXERCISE 10: JARGON

Replace the jargon in the following sentences with more appropriate language.

1. The research-oriented person should not be hired for a people-oriented position.

   _____

2. Foreign diplomats should always interface with local leaders.

   _____

3. Pursuant to your being claimed as a dependent on the returns of another taxpayer or resident wage earner, you may not consider yourself exempt if your current income exceeds five hundred dollars.

   _____

4. There is considerable evidentiary support for the assertion that Vienna sausages are good for you.

   _____

5. With reference to the poem, I submit that the second and third stanzas connote a certain despair.

   _____

6. Allow me to elucidate my position: this horse is the epitome, the very quintessence of equine excellence.

   _____

7. In the case of the recent railway disaster, it is clear that governmental regulatory agencies obfuscated in the preparation of materials for release to the public through both the electronic and print media.

   _____

PRINCIPLE 11: PAY ATTENTION TO SUBJECT-VERB AGREEMENT.

A verb must agree with its subject in number regardless of intervening phrases. Do not let the words that come between the subject and the verb confuse you as to the number (singular or plural) of the subject. Usually one word can be pinpointed as the grammatical subject of the sentence. The verb, no matter how far removed, must agree with that subject in number.

INCORRECT: The joys of climbing mountains, especially if one is a novice climber without the proper equipment, escapes me.

CORRECT: The *joys* of climbing mountains, especially if one is a novice climber without the proper equipment, *escape* me.

Watch out for collective nouns like *group*, *audience*, *committee*, or *majority*. These take a singular noun unless the individuals forming the group are to be emphasized.

CORRECT: A *majority* of the committee *have signed* their names to the report. (The individual members of the committee are being emphasized.)

CORRECT: A *majority* of the jury *thinks* that the defendant is guilty. (The collective is being emphasized.)

A subject that consists of two or more nouns connected by the conjunction *and* takes the plural form of the verb.

CORRECT: *Karl*, an expert in cooking Hunan chicken, *and George*, an expert in preparing Hunan spicy duck, *have combined* their expertise to start a new restaurant.

However, when the subject consists of two or more nouns connected by *or* or *nor*, the verb agrees with the CLOSEST noun.

CORRECT: Either the senators or the *President is* misinformed.

CORRECT: Either the President or the *senators are* misinformed.

There are some connecting phrases that look as though they should make a group of words into a plural but actually do not. The only connecting word that can make a series of singular nouns into a plural subject is *and*. In particular, the following connecting words and phrases do NOT result in a plural subject:

along with   as well as   besides   in addition to   together with

INCORRECT: The President, along with the Secretary of State and the Director of the CIA, are misinformed.

CORRECT: The *President*, along with the Secretary of State and the Director of the CIA, *is* misinformed.

You can usually trust your ear to give you the correct verb form. However, subject-verb agreement can be tricky in the following instances:

- When the subject and verb are separated
- When the subject is an indefinite pronoun
- When the subject consists of more than one noun

If a sentence that is grammatically correct still sounds awkward, you should probably rephrase your thought.

EXERCISE 11: SUBJECT-VERB AGREEMENT

Fix or replace the incorrect verbs in the following sentences.

1. The logical structure of his complicated and rather tortuous arguments are always the same.

    _____

2. The majority of the organization's members is over 60 years old.

    _____

3. A case of bananas have been sent to the local distributor in compensation for the fruit that was damaged in transit.

    _____

4. A total of 50 editors read each article, a process that takes at least a week, sometimes six months.

    _____

5. Neither the shipping clerk who packed the equipment nor the truckers who transported it admits responsibility for the dented circuit box.

    _____

6. I can never decide whether to eat an orange or a Belgian chocolate; each of them have their wondrous qualities.

    _____

7. Everyone in the United States, as well as the Canadians, expect the timber agreement to fall through.

    _____

PRINCIPLE 12: PAY ATTENTION TO MODIFICATION.

Modifiers should be placed as close as possible to what they modify. In English, the position of the word within a sentence often establishes the word's relationship to other words in the sentence. If a modifier is placed too far from the word it modifies, the meaning may be lost or obscured. Notice, in the following sentences, the ambiguity that results when the modifying phrases are misplaced in the sentence.

UNCLEAR: Gary and Martha sat talking about the problem in the office.

UNCLEAR: He only threw the ball eight yards.

CLEAR: Gary and Martha sat in the office talking about the problem.

CLEAR: He threw the ball only eight yards.

In addition to misplaced modifiers, watch for dangling modifiers: modifiers whose intended referents are not even present.

INCORRECT: Coming out of context, Peter was startled by Julia's perceptiveness.

CORRECT: Julia's remark, coming out of context, startled Peter with its perceptiveness.

EXERCISE 12: FAULTY MODIFICATION

Rewrite these sentences to put modifiers closer to the words they modify.

1. Mr. Bentley advised him quickly to make up his mind.

   _____

2. The Governor's conference met to discuss student protest in the auditorium.

   _____

3. All of his friends were not able to come, but he decided that he preferred small parties anyway.

   _____

4. Madeleine remembered she had to place a telephone call when she got home.

   _____

5. George told Suzette he did not like to discuss politics as they walked through the museum.

   _____

6. Having worked in publishing for ten years, Spencer's resume shows that he is well qualified.

   _____

7. A politician would fail to serve her constituents without experience in community service.

   _____

PRINCIPLE 13: USE PRONOUNS CAREFULLY.

A pronoun is a word that replaces a noun in a sentence. Every time you write a pronoun—*he, him, his, she, her, it, its, they, their, that,* or *which*—be sure there can be absolutely no doubt what its antecedent is. (An antecedent is the particular noun a pronoun refers to or stands for.) Careless use of pronouns can obscure your intended meaning.

UNCLEAR:	The teacher told the student he was lazy. (Does *he* refer to *teacher* or *student?*)
UNCLEAR:	Sara knows more about history than Irina because she learned it from her father. (Does *she* refer to *Sara* or *Irina?*)

You can usually rearrange a sentence to avoid ambiguous pronoun references.

CLEAR:	The student was lazy, and the teacher told him so.
CLEAR:	The teacher considered himself lazy and told the student so.
CLEAR:	Since Sara learned history from her father, she knows more than Irina does.
CLEAR:	Because Irina learned history from her father, she knows less about it than Sara does.

If you are worried that a pronoun reference will be ambiguous, rewrite the sentence so that there is no doubt. Don't be afraid to repeat the antecedent if necessary:

UNCLEAR:	I would rather settle in Phoenix than in Albuquerque, although it lacks wonderful restaurants.
CLEAR:	I would rather settle in Phoenix than in Albuquerque, although Phoenix lacks wonderful restaurants.

A reader must be able to pinpoint the pronoun's antecedent. Even if you think the reader will know what you mean, do not use a pronoun without a clear and appropriate antecedent.

INCORRECT:	When you are painting, be sure not to get it on the floor. (*It* could only refer to the noun *paint.* But do you see the noun *paint* anywhere in the sentence? Pronouns cannot refer to implied nouns.)
CORRECT:	When you are painting, be sure not to get any paint on the floor.

EXERCISE 13: FAULTY PRONOUN REFERENCE

Correct the pronoun references in the following sentences.

1. Clausen's dog won first place at the show because he was well bred.

2. The critic's review made the novel a commercial success. He is now a rich man.

   _____

3. The military advisor was more conventional than his commander, but he was a superior strategist.

   _____

4. Caroline telephoned her friends in California before going home for the night, which she had not done for weeks.

   _____

5. Although Ricardo hoped and prayed for the job, it did no good. When he called him the next morning, they had hired someone else.

   _____

6. You must pay attention when fishing—otherwise, you might lose it.

   _____

7. Zolsta Karmagi is the better musician, but he had more formal training.

   _____

PRINCIPLE 14: USE PARALLELISM CORRECTLY.

It can be rhetorically effective to use a particular construction several times in succession, in order to provide emphasis. The technique is called parallel construction, and it is effective only when used sparingly.

> EXAMPLE: _As a_ leader, Lincoln inspired a nation to throw off the chains of slavery; _as a_ philosopher, he proclaimed the greatness of the little man; _as a_ human being, he served as a timeless example of humility.

The repetition of the italicized construction provides a strong sense of rhythm and organization to the sentence and alerts the reader to yet another aspect of Lincoln's character.

Matching constructions must be expressed in parallel form. Writers often use a parallel structure incorrectly for dissimilar items.

INCORRECT: They are sturdy, attractive, and cost only a dollar each. (The phrase *They are* makes sense preceding the adjectives *sturdy* and *attractive*, but cannot be understood before *cost only a dollar each*.)

CORRECT: They are sturdy and attractive, and they cost only a dollar each.

Parallel constructions must be expressed in parallel grammatical form: all nouns, all infinitives, all gerunds, all prepositional phrases, or all clauses.

INCORRECT: All business students should learn word processing, accounting, and how to program computers.

CORRECT: All business students should learn word processing, accounting, and computer programming.

This principle applies to any words that might begin each item in a series: either repeat the word before every element in a series or include it only before the first item. (In effect, your treatment of the second element of the series determines the form of all subsequent elements.)

INCORRECT: He invested his money in stocks, in real estate, and a home for retired performers.

CORRECT: He invested his money in stocks, in real estate, and in a home for retired performers.

CORRECT: He invested his money in stocks, real estate, and a home for retired performers.

A number of constructions call for you to always express ideas in parallel form. These constructions include:

X is as _____ as Y.

X is more _____ than Y.

X is less _____ than Y.

Both X and Y...

Either X or Y...

Neither X nor Y...

Not only X but also Y...

X and Y can stand for as little as one word or as much as a whole clause, but in any case the grammatical structure of X and Y must be identical.

INCORRECT: The view from this apartment is as spectacular as from that mountain lodge.

CORRECT: The view from this apartment is as spectacular as the view from that mountain lodge.

Exercise 14: Parallelism

Correct the faulty parallelism in the following sentences.

1. The dancer taught her understudy how to move, how to dress, and how to work with choreographers and deal with professional competition.

   _____

2. Merrill based his confidence on the futures market, the bond market, and on the strength of the president's popularity.

   _____

3. The grocery baggers were ready, able, and were quite determined to do a great job.

   _____

4. The requirements for a business degree are not as stringent as a law degree.

   _____

Principle 15: Do Not Shift Narrative Voice.

True, Principle 5 advised you to avoid needless self-reference. But an occasional self-reference may be appropriate in your GRE essays. You may even call yourself *I* if you want, as long as you keep the number of first-person pronouns to a minimum. Less egocentric ways of referring to the narrator include *we* and *one*. If these more formal ways of writing seem stilted, stay with *I*.

- In my lifetime, I have seen many challenges to the principle of free speech.
- We can see …
- One must admit …

The method of self-reference you select is called the narrative voice of your essay. Any of the above narrative voices are acceptable. Nevertheless, whichever you choose, you must be careful not to shift narrative voice in your essay. If you use *I* in the first sentence, for example, do not use *we* in a later sentence.

INCORRECT: In my lifetime, *I* have seen many challenges to the principle of free speech. *We* can see how a free society can get too complacent when free speech is taken for granted.

It is likewise wrong to shift from *you* to *one*:

INCORRECT: Just by following the news, *you* can readily see how politicians have a vested interest in pleasing powerful interest groups. But *one* should not generalize about this tendency.

EXERCISE 15: SHIFTING NARRATIVE VOICE

Rewrite these sentences to give each a consistent point of view.

1. I am disgusted with the waste we tolerate in this country. One cannot simply stand by without adding to such waste: Living here makes you wasteful.

   _____

2. You must take care not to take these grammar rules too seriously, since one can often become bogged down in details and forget why he is writing at all.

   _____

3. We all must take a stand against waste in this country; or how will one be able to look at oneself in the mirror?

   _____

PRINCIPLE 16: AVOID SLANG AND COLLOQUIALISMS

Conversational speech is filled with slang and colloquial expressions. But you should avoid slang on the GRE. Slang terms and colloquialisms can be confusing to the reader, since these expressions are not universally understood. Even worse, such informal writing may give readers the impression that you are poorly educated or arrogant.

INAPPROPRIATE: He is really into gardening.
CORRECT: He enjoys gardening.
INAPPROPRIATE: She plays a wicked game of tennis.
CORRECT: She excels at tennis.
INAPPROPRIATE: Myra has got to go to Memphis for a week.
CORRECT: Myra must go to Memphis for a week.
INAPPROPRIATE: Joan's been doing science for eight years now.
CORRECT: Joan has been a scientist for eight years now.

EXERCISE 16: SLANG AND COLLOQUIALISMS

Replace the informal elements of the following sentences with more appropriate terms.

1. Cynthia Larson sure knows her stuff.

   _____

2. The crowd was really into watching the fire-eating juggler, but then the dancing horse grabbed their attention.

_____

3. As soon as the personnel department checks out his resume, I'm sure we'll hear gales of laughter issuing from the office.

_____

4. The chef has a nice way with salmon: his sauce was simple but the effect was sublime.

_____

5. Normal human beings can't cope with repeated humiliation.

_____

6. If you want a good cheesecake, you've got to make a top-notch crust.

_____

7. The environmentalists aren't in it for the prestige; they really care about protecting the yellow-throated hornswoggler.

_____

PRINCIPLE 17: WATCH OUT FOR SENTENCE FRAGMENTS AND RUN-ON SENTENCES.

Every sentence in formal expository writing must have an independent clause: a clause that contains a subject and a predicate. A sentence fragment has no independent clause; a run-on sentence has two or more independent clauses that are improperly connected. As you edit your practice essays, check your sentence constructions, noting any tendency toward fragments or run-on sentences.

FRAGMENT: Global warming. That is what the scientists and journalists are worried about this month.

CORRECT: Global warming is the cause of concern for scientists and journalists this month.

FRAGMENT: Seattle is a wonderful place to live. Mountains, ocean, and forests, all within easy driving distance. If you can ignore the rain.

CORRECT: Seattle is a wonderful place to live, with mountains, ocean, and forests all within easy driving distance. However, it certainly does rain often.

FRAGMENT: Why do I think the author's position is preposterous? Because he makes generalizations that I know are untrue.

CORRECT: I think the author's position is preposterous because he makes generalizations that I know are untrue.

Beginning single-clause sentences with coordinate conjunctions—*and, but, or, nor*, and *for*—is acceptable in moderation (although some readers still object to beginning a sentence with *and*).

CORRECT: Most people would agree that indigent patients should receive wonderful health care. But every treatment has its price.

Time pressure may also cause you to write two or more sentences as one. When you proofread your essays, watch out for independent clauses that are not joined with any punctuation at all or are only joined with a comma.

RUN-ON: Current insurance practices are unfair they discriminate against the people who need insurance most.

You can repair run-on sentences in any one of three ways. First, you could use a period to make separate sentences of the independent clauses.

CORRECT: Current insurance practices are unfair. They discriminate against the people who need insurance most.

Second, you could use a semicolon. A semicolon is a weak period. It separates independent clauses but signals to the reader that the ideas in the clauses are related.

CORRECT: Current insurance practices are unfair; they discriminate against the people who need insurance most.

The third method of repairing a run-on sentence is usually the most effective. Use a conjunction to turn an independent clause into a dependent one and to make explicit how the clauses are related.

CORRECT: Current insurance practices are unfair, because they discriminate against the people who need insurance most.

A common cause of run-on sentences is the misuse of adverbs like *however, nevertheless, furthermore, likewise*, and *therefore*.

RUN-ON: Current insurance practices are discriminatory, furthermore they make insurance too expensive for the poor.

CORRECT: Current insurance practices are discriminatory. Furthermore, they make insurance too expensive for the poor.

EXERCISE 17: SENTENCE FRAGMENTS AND RUN-ON SENTENCES

Repair the following by eliminating sentence fragments and run-on sentences.

1. The private academy has all the programs Angie will need. Except the sports program, which has been phased out.

   _____

2. Leadership ability. That is the elusive quality which our current government employees have yet to capture.

   _____

3. Antonio just joined the athletic club staff this year but Barry has been with us since 1975, therefore we would expect Barry to be more skilled with the weight-lifting equipment. What a surprise to find Barry pinned beneath a barbell on the weight-lifting bench with Antonio struggling to lift the three-hundred-pound weight from poor Barry's chest.

   _____

4. However much she tries to act like a Southern belle, she cannot hide her roots. The daughter of a Yankee fisherman, taciturn and always polite.

   _____

5. There is time to invest in property. After one has established oneself in the business world, however.

   _____

6. Sentence fragments are often used in casual conversation, however they should not be used in written English under normal circumstances.

   _____

PRINCIPLE 18: USE COMMAS CORRECTLY.

Use commas to separate items in a series. If more than two items are listed in a series, they should be separated by commas. The final comma—the one that precedes the word *and*—is optional (but be consistent throughout your essays).

CORRECT: My recipe for buttermilk biscuits contains flour,
baking soda, salt, shortening and buttermilk.

CORRECT: My recipe for buttermilk biscuits contains flour,
baking soda, salt, shortening, and buttermilk.

Don't place commas before the first element of a series or after the last element.

INCORRECT: My investment advisor recommended that I construct a portfolio
of, stocks, bonds, commodities futures, and precious metals.

INCORRECT: The elephants, tigers, and dancing bears, were the highlights of
the circus.

Use commas to separate two or more adjectives before a noun, but don't use a comma
after the last adjective in the series.

CORRECT: I can't believe you sat through that long, dull, uninspired movie
three times.

INCORRECT: The manatee is a round, blubbery, bewhiskered, creature whose
continued presence in American waters is endangered by careless
boaters.

Use commas to set off parenthetical clauses and phrases. (A parenthetical expression is
one that is not necessary to the main idea of the sentence.)

CORRECT: Gordon, who is a writer by profession, bakes an excellent
cheesecake.

The main idea is that Gordon bakes an excellent cheesecake. The intervening clause
merely serves to identify Gordon; thus, it should be set off with commas.

Use commas after introductory, participial, or prepositional phrases.

CORRECT: Having watered his petunias every day during the drought, Harold
was very disappointed when his garden was destroyed by insects.

CORRECT: After the banquet, Harold and Martha went dancing.

Use commas to separate independent clauses (clauses that could stand alone as
complete sentences) connected by coordinate conjunctions such as *and, but, yet,* and so on.

CORRECT: Susan's old car has been belching blue smoke from the tailpipe
for two weeks, but it has not broken down yet.

CORRECT: Zachariah's pet frog eats fifty flies a day, yet it has never gotten
indigestion.

INCORRECT: Susan's old car has been belching blue smoke from the tailpipe
for two weeks, but has not broken down yet.

INCORRECT: Zachariah's pet frog eats fifty flies a day, and never gets
indigestion.

EXERCISE 18: COMMAS

Correct the punctuation errors in the following sentences.

1. Peter wants me to bring records games candy and soda to his party.

    _____

2. I need, lumber, nails, a hammer and a saw to build the shelf.

    _____

3. It takes a friendly energetic person to be a successful salesman.

    _____

4. I was shocked to discover that a large, modern, glass-sheathed, office building
    had replaced my old school.

    _____

5. The country club, a cluster of ivy-covered whitewashed buildings was the site of
    the president's first speech.

    _____

6. Pushing through the panicked crowd the security guards frantically searched for
    the suspect.

    _____

7. Despite careful analysis of the advantages and disadvantages of each proposal
    Harry found it hard to reach a decision.

    _____

PRINCIPLE 19: USE SEMICOLONS CORRECTLY.

Use a semicolon instead of a coordinate conjunction such as *and, or*, or *but* to link two
closely related independent clauses. Additionally, use semicolons to separate items in a
series when the items contain commas.

INCORRECT:	Whooping cranes are an endangered species; and they are unlikely to survive if we continue to pollute.
CORRECT:	Whooping cranes are an endangered species; there are only fifty whooping cranes in New Jersey today.
CORRECT:	Whooping cranes are an endangered species; there are only fifty whooping cranes in New Jersey today.
CORRECT:	Three important dates in the history of the company are December 16, 1999; April 4, 2003; and June 30, 2007.

Use a semicolon between independent clauses connected by words like *therefore, nevertheless,* and *moreover.*

CORRECT:	The staff meeting has been postponed until next Thursday; therefore, I will be unable to get approval for my project until then.
CORRECT:	Farm prices have been falling rapidly for two years; nevertheless, the traditional American farm is not in danger of disappearing.

Exercise 19: Semicolons

Correct the punctuation errors in the following sentences.

1. Marcus has five years' experience in karate; but Tyler has even more.

   _____

2. Very few students wanted to take the class in physics, only the professor's kindness kept it from being canceled.

   _____

3. You should always be prepared when you go on a camping trip, however you must avoid carrying unnecessary weight.

   _____

Principle 20: Use Colons Correctly.

In formal writing, the colon is used only as a means of signaling that what follows is a list, definition, explanation, or concise summary of what has gone before. The colon usually follows an independent clause, and it will frequently be accompanied by a reinforcing expression like *the following, as follows,* or *namely,* or by an explicit demonstrative like *this.*

CORRECT: Your instructions are as follows: read the passage carefully, answer the questions on the last page, and turn over your answer sheet.

CORRECT: This is what I found in the refrigerator: a moldy lime, half a bottle of stale soda, and a jar of peanut butter.

Be careful not to put a colon between a verb and its direct object.

INCORRECT: I want: a slice of pizza and a small green salad.

CORRECT: This is what I want: a slice of pizza and a small green salad. (The colon serves to announce that a list is forthcoming.)

CORRECT: I don't want much for lunch: just a slice of pizza and a small green salad. (Here what follows the colon defines what *don't want much* means.)

Context will occasionally make clear that a second independent clause is closely linked to its predecessor, even without an explicit expression like those used above. Here, too, a colon is appropriate, although a period will always be correct too.

CORRECT: We were aghast: the "charming country inn" that had been advertised in such glowing terms proved to be a leaking cabin full of mosquitoes.

EXERCISE 20: COLONS

Edit these sentences so they use colons correctly.

1. I am sick and tired of: your whining, your complaining, your nagging, your teasing, and, most of all, your barbed comments.

   _____

2. The chef has created a masterpiece, the pasta is delicate yet firm, the mustard greens are fresh, and the medallions of veal are melting in my mouth.

   _____

3. In order to write a good essay, you must: practice, get plenty of sleep, and eat a good breakfast.

   _____

PRINCIPLE 21: USE HYPHENS AND DASHES CORRECTLY.

Use a hyphen with the compound numbers twenty-one through ninety-nine, and with fractions used as adjectives.

CORRECT: Sixty-five students constituted a majority.

CORRECT: A two-thirds vote was necessary to carry the measure.

Use a hyphen with the prefixes *ex*, *all*, and *self* and with the suffix *elect*.

> CORRECT: The constitution protects against self-incrimination.
>
> CORRECT: The president-elect was invited to chair the meeting.

Use a hyphen with a compound adjective when it comes before the word it modifies but not when it comes after the word it modifies.

> CORRECT: The no-holds-barred argument continued into the night.
>
> CORRECT: The argument continued with no holds barred.

Use a hyphen with any prefix used before a proper noun or adjective.

> CORRECT: His pro-African sentiments were heartily applauded.
>
> CORRECT: They believed that his accent was un-Australian.

Use a hyphen to separate component parts of a word in order to avoid confusion with other words or to avoid the use of a double vowel.

> CORRECT: The sculptor was able to re-form the clay after the dog knocked over the bust.
>
> CORRECT: The family re-entered their house after the fire marshal departed.

Use a dash to indicate an abrupt change of thought.

> CORRECT: The inheritance must cover the entire cost of the proposal—Gail has no other money to invest.
>
> CORRECT: To get a high score—and who doesn't want to get a high score?—you need to devote yourself to prolonged and concentrated study.

EXERCISE 21: HYPHENS AND DASHES

Edit these sentences so they use hyphens and dashes correctly.

1. The child was able to count from one to ninety nine.

   _____

2. The adults only movie was banned from commercial TV.

   _____

3. It was the first time she had seen a movie that was for adults-only.

   _____

4. John and his ex wife remained on friendly terms.

   _____

5. A two thirds majority would be needed to pass the budget reforms.

      _____

6. The house, and it was the most dilapidated house that I had ever seen was a bargain because the land was so valuable.

      _____

PRINCIPLE 22: USE APOSTROPHES CORRECTLY.

Use an apostrophe in a contraction to indicate that one or more letters have been eliminated. But try to avoid using contractions altogether on the GRE: using the full form of a verb is more appropriate in formal writing.

CONTRACTED: We'd intended to address the question of equal rights, but it's too late to begin the discussion now.

FULL FORM: We had intended to address the question of equal rights, but it is too late to begin the discussion now.

One of the most common errors involving use of the apostrophe is using it in the contraction *you're* or *it's* to indicate the possessive form of *you* or *it*. When you write *you're*, ask yourself whether you mean *you are*. If not, the correct word is *your*. Similarly, are you sure you mean *it is*? If not, use the possessive form *its*.

INCORRECT: You're chest of drawers is ugly.

INCORRECT: The dog hurt it's paw.

CORRECT: *Your* chest of drawers is ugly.

CORRECT: The dog hurt *its* paw.

Use the apostrophe to indicate the possessive form of a noun.

NOUN	POSSESSIVE
the boy	the boy's
Harry	Harry's
the children	the children's
the boys	the boys'

NOTE: The word *boy's* could have one of three meanings:

- The boy's an expert at chess. (contraction: the boy is...)
- The boy's left for the day. (contraction: the boy has...)
- The boy's face was covered with pie. (possessive: the face of the boy)

The word *boys'* can have only one meaning: a plural possessive (the___ of the boys).

CORRECT: Ms. Fox's office is on the first floor. (One person possesses the office.)

CORRECT: The Foxes' apartment has a wonderful view. (There are several people named Fox living in the same apartment. First you must form the plural, then add the apostrophe to indicate possession.)

Possessive pronouns do not use an apostrophe (with the exception of the neutral *one*, which forms its possessive by adding *'s*).

INCORRECT: The tiny cabin had been our's for many years.

CORRECT: The tiny cabin had been *ours* for many years.

EXERCISE 22: APOSTROPHES

Edit these sentences so they use apostrophes correctly.

1. The presidents limousine had a flat tire.

    _____

2. You're tickets for the show will be at the box office.

    _____

3. The opportunity to change ones lifestyle does not come often.

    _____

4. The desks' surface was immaculate, but it's drawers were messy.

    _____

5. The cat on the bed is hers'.

    _____

ANSWERS TO 22 PRINCIPLES EXERCISES

Our answers to these exercises probably won't be indentical to the answers you came up with. That's okay; just make sure you understand how these answers address the errors and weaknesses found in the original sentences.

ANSWERS TO EXERCISE 1: WORDY PHRASES

(1) The agency is not prepared to expand now.

(2) Although she is inexperienced in photography, she will probably succeed because she is motivated.

(3) Although tactful, George says exactly what he believes.

(4) Accuracy is important to English teachers and company presidents alike.

(5) Ms. Miller speaks intelligently about many aspects of modern philosophy.

ANSWERS TO EXERCISE 2: REDUNDANCY

(1) All of these problems have combined to create a crisis.

(2) A staff that large needs an effective supervisor.

(3) He knows how to follow directions.

(4) The writer's technical skill does not mask his poor plot line.

(5) That monument remains a significant tourist attraction.

(6) The recent trend of spending on credit has created a more impoverished middle class.

(7) Few people can follow directions.

ANSWERS TO EXERCISE 3: EXCESSIVE QUALIFICATION

(1) She is an effective teacher.

(2) Ferris is a slow worker.

(3) In a murder trial, it is important to pay attention to the details as well as to the "larger picture."

(4) You are the best person to decide what you should do for a living.

(5) In Italy, I found the best food I have ever eaten.

(6) Children should be taught to cooperate at home and in school.

ANSWERS TO EXERCISE 4: UNNECESSARY SENTENCES

(1) Advanced technology has made it easy for people who live vast distances from each other to communicate.

(2) People cannot safely consume water that contains chemical pollutants.

(3) Napoleon suffered defeat in Russia because most of his troops perished in the cold.

(4) No present evidence suggests that Shakespeare's plays were written by others.

(5) The architect Frank Lloyd Wright was famous for his ability to design buildings that blend into their surroundings.

(6) Many people find math a difficult subject because it requires very precise thinking skills.

ANSWERS TO EXERCISE 5: NEEDLESS SELF-REFERENCE

(1) We ought to pay teachers more than we pay actors.

(2) The author is stuck in the past.

(3) This argument cannot be generalized to most business owners.

(4) Privacy should not be valued more than social concerns.

(5) The author has a point.

(6) College presidents should implement several specific reforms to combat apathy.

(7) Either alternative would prove disastrous.

ANSWERS TO EXERCISE 6: UNDESIRABLE PASSIVES

(1) Brave but misguided men fought the Spanish-American War.

(2) Congress passed the bill in time, but the President did not sign it until the time for action had passed.

(3) Those who need advice least usually request it; the truly lost and ignorant do not seek it.

(4) We should relocate that building where citizens can appreciate it.

(5) City government should generously reward garbage collectors for their difficult labors.

(6) Negotiators ironed out the conditions of the contract agreement minutes before the strike deadline.

(7) The teacher distributed test results with no concern for confidentiality.

ANSWERS TO EXERCISE 7: WEAK OPENINGS

(1) Businesses ignore the illiteracy problem at their own peril.

(2) This plane is obsolete for several reasons.

(3) The government cannot fight a war on poverty effectively without waging a battle against child labor.

(4) The candidate has many strong points; intelligence, unfortunately, is not among them.

(5) The city cannot justify building a more handsome prison.

(6) Americans must like watching television better than conversing.

(7) Intelligence is a product of environment and heredity.

ANSWERS TO EXERCISE 8: VAGUE LANGUAGE

(1) When water is heated to 100°C, it turns into steam.

(2) The diplomat had to agree to live wherever the government sent him.

(3) Arthur often forgets to do his chores.

(4) She told us that she would go to the store when her mother came home.

(5) A radar unit registers the distance to an aircraft.

(6) Thousands of animal species were destroyed in the last ice age.

(7) The secretary was unable to type the document.

ANSWERS TO EXERCISE 9: CLICHÉS

(1) Jefferson was certainly a great leader.

(2) Families probably spend less time together than they did fifteen years ago.

(3) The pizza delivery man arrived just when the sequestered jury most needed him.

(4) Trying to find the employee responsible for this embarrassing information leak may be impossible.

(5) Both strategies would be expensive and completely ineffective: They have an equal chance of failing.

(6) Older doctors should be required to update their techniques, but many seem resistant to changes in technology.

ANSWERS TO EXERCISE 10: JARGON

(1) A person who likes research should not be hired for a position that requires someone to interact with customers all day.

(2) Foreign diplomats should always talk to local leaders.

(3) If someone claims you as a dependent on a tax return, you may still have to pay taxes on your income in excess of five hundred dollars.

(4) Recent studies suggest that Vienna sausages are good for you.

(5) When the poet wrote the second and third stanzas, he must have felt despair.

(6) This is a fine horse.

(7) Government regulatory agencies were not honest in their press releases about the recent railway accident.

ANSWERS TO EXERCISE 11: SUBJECT-VERB AGREEMENT

(1) The logical structure of his complicated and rather tortuous arguments is always the same.

(2) The majority of the organization's members are over 60 years old.

(3) A case of bananas has been sent to the local distributor in compensation for the fruit that was damaged in transit.

(4) A total of 50 editors reads each article, a process that takes at least a week, sometimes six months.

(5) Neither the shipping clerk who packed the equipment nor the truckers who transported it admit responsibility for the dented circuit box.

(6) I can never decide whether to eat an orange or a Belgian chocolate; each of them has its wondrous qualities. (Note that you must also change the possessive pronoun to the singular form.)

(7) Everyone in the United States, as well the Canadians, expects the timber agreement to fall through.

Answers to Exercise 12: Faulty Modification

(1) (*Quickly* is sandwiched between two verbs and could refer to either one.)
Mr. Bentley advised him to make up his mind quickly.

(2) (Was the student protest in the auditorium, or was the conference merely held there?) The Governor's conference met in the auditorium to discuss student protest.

(3) (If none of his friends came, it must have been a small party indeed!) Not all of his friends were able to come, but he decided that he preferred small parties anyway.

(4) (Did she remember when she got home? Or did she have to call when she got home?) When she got home, Madeleine remembered she had to place a telephone call.

(5) (Either he didn't like discussing politics in the museum, or he didn't like discussing it at all.) As they walked through the museum, George told Suzette he did not like to discuss politics.

(6) (Was it Spencer's resume that worked in publishing for ten years?) Spencer, who has worked in publishing for ten years, appears from his resume to be well qualified.

(7) (It is the person holding the job, not the job itself, that requires experience in community service.) A politician without experience in community service would fail to serve her constituents.

Answers to Exercise 13: Faulty Pronoun Reference

(1) (The structure of the sentence might leave us wondering whether Clausen or his dog was well bred. Instead, use the impersonal *it*.) Clausen's dog won first place at the show because it was well bred.

(2) (It's not clear who *he* is: no antecedent exists in the sentence.) The critic's review made the novel a commercial success, and the novelist is now a rich man.

(3) The military advisor was more conventional than his commander, but the advisor was a superior strategist.

(4) (We do not know whether Caroline had not spent the night at home in weeks or whether she had not telephoned her friends in weeks.) Because she had not telephoned her California friends in weeks, Caroline called them before she went home for the night.

(5) (Referring to some ambiguous *they* without identifying who *they* are beforehand is incorrect.) Ricardo wanted the job badly, but when he called the employer the next morning, he found that the company had hired someone else.

(6) (We don't know exactly what *it* is, but we can assume that *it* is a fish.) You must pay attention when fishing—otherwise, you might lose your catch.

(7) Zolsta Karmagi is the better musician, but Sven Wonderup had more formal training.

ANSWERS TO EXERCISE 14: PARALLELISM

(1) The dancer taught her understudy how to move, dress, work with choreographers, and deal with professional competition.

(2) Merrill based his confidence on the futures market, the bond market, and the strength of the President's popularity.

(3) The grocery baggers were ready, able, and quite determined to do a great job.

(4) The requirements for a business degree are not as stringent as those for a law degree.

ANSWERS TO EXERCISE 15: SHIFTING NARRATIVE VOICE

(1) I am disgusted with the waste we tolerate in this country. We cannot simply stand by without adding to such waste: living here makes all of us wasteful.

(2) You must take care not to take these grammar rules too seriously, since you can often become bogged down in details and forget why you are writing at all. (Or use *one* consistently.)

(3) We must all take a stand against waste in this country; or how can we look at ourselves in the mirror? (When using *we*, make sure to use the plural form of verbs and pronouns.)

ANSWERS TO EXERCISE 16: SLANG AND COLLOQUIALISMS

(1) Cynthia Larson is an expert.

(2) The crowd was absorbed in watching the fire-eating juggler, but then the dancing horse caught their attention.

(3) As soon as the personnel department tries to verify his resume, I am sure we will hear gales of laughter issuing from the office.

(4) The chef prepares salmon skillfully: his sauce was simple but the effect was sublime.

(5) Normal human beings cannot tolerate repeated humiliation.

(6) If you want a good cheesecake, you must make a superb crust.

(7) The environmentalists are not involved in the project for prestige; they truly care about protecting the yellow-throated hornswoggler.

ANSWERS TO EXERCISE 17: SENTENCE FRAGMENTS AND RUN-ON SENTENCES

(1) The private academy has all the programs Angie will need, except that the sports program has been phased out.

(2) Leadership ability is the elusive quality that our current government employees have yet to capture.

(3) Antonio just joined the athletic club staff this year, but Barry has been with us since 1975; therefore, we would expect Barry to be more skilled with the weight-lifting equipment. It was quite a surprise to find Barry pinned beneath a barbell on the weight-lifting bench with Antonio struggling to lift the three-hundred-pound weight from poor Barry's chest.

(4) However much she tries to act like a Southern belle, she cannot hide her roots. She will always be the daughter of a Yankee fisherman, taciturn and ever polite.

(5) There is time to invest in property, but only after one has established oneself in the business world.

(6) (Since transitional words like *however* do not subordinate a clause, this is a run-on sentence. You could either change the first comma to a semicolon or separate the clauses with a period.) Sentence fragments are often used in casual conversation. They should not, however, be used in written English under normal circumstances.

ANSWERS FOR EXERCISE 18: COMMAS

(1) Peter wants me to bring records, games, candy, and soda to his party.

(2) I need lumber, nails, a hammer and a saw to build the shelf. (OR: a hammer, and a saw...)

(3) It takes a friendly, energetic person to be a successful salesman.

(4) I was shocked to discover that a large, modern, glass-sheathed office building had replaced my old school.

(5) The country club, a cluster of ivy-covered whitewashed buildings, was the site of the president's first speech.

(6) Pushing through the panicked crowd, the security guards frantically searched for the suspect.

(7) Despite careful analysis of the advantages and disadvantages of each proposal, Harry found it hard to reach a decision.

ANSWERS FOR EXERCISE 19: SEMICOLONS

(1) Marcus has five years' experience in karate, but Tyler has even more.

(2) Very few students wanted to take the class in physics; only the professor's kindness kept it from being canceled.

(3) You should always be prepared when you go on a camping trip; however, you must avoid carrying unnecessary weight.

ANSWERS TO EXERCISE 20: COLONS

(1) I am sick and tired of your whining, your complaining, your nagging, your teasing, and, most of all, your barbed comments.

(2) The chef has created a masterpiece: the pasta is delicate yet firm, the mustard greens are fresh, and the medallions of veal are melting in my mouth.

(3) In order to write a good essay, you must do the following: practice, get plenty of sleep, and eat a good breakfast.

ANSWERS TO EXERCISE 21: HYPHENS AND DASHES

(1) The child was able to count from one to ninety-nine.

(2) The adults-only movie was banned from commercial TV.

(3) It was the first time she had seen a movie that was for adults only.

(4) John and his ex-wife remained on friendly terms.

(5) A two-thirds majority would be needed to pass the budget reforms.

(6) The house—and it was the most dilapidated house that I had ever seen—was a bargain because the land was so valuable.

ANSWERS TO EXERCISE 22: APOSTROPHES

(1) The president's limousine had a flat tire.

(2) Your tickets for the show will be at the box office.

(3) The opportunity to change one's lifestyle does not come often.

(4) The desk's surface was immaculate, but its drawers were messy.

(5) The cat on the bed is hers.

___

SUMMARY

Kaplan's 5-Step Method for GRE Writing is:

Step 1: Take the Issue/Argument Apart.

Step 2: Select the Points You Will Make.

Step 3: Organize Your Thoughts.

Step 4: Type Your Essay.

Step 5: Proofread.

ANALYTICAL WRITING PRACTICE PROMPTS

Now that you've learned the principles behind effective writing, it's time to put what you've learned to good use.

Write an essay on each of the following topics. While writing, pay particular attention to making your essay concise, forceful, and grammatically correct. Allow yourself 45 minutes to complete each Issue essay and 30 minutes to complete each Argument essay.

After you've finished with each essay, proofread to catch your errors. Then evaluate your essay, using the holistic scoring system that was explained at the beginning of this chapter. For this exercise, it's not critical that you assign yourself the "right" grade at the end. It's more important that you understand whether your essays are well written and how well they fulfill the required tasks.

ISSUE PROMPT 1

A country's obsession with celebrity always increases when its citizens need a distraction from the harsh realities of war and economic strife.

_____

_____

_____

ISSUE PROMPT 2

All results of publicly funded scientific studies should be made available to the general public free of charge. Scientific journals that charge a subscription or newsstand price are profiting unfairly.

_____

_____

_____

ARGUMENT PROMPT 1

The following appeared in a memorandum from the owner of the Juniper Café, a small, local coffee shop in the downtown area of a small American city:

"We must reduce overhead here at the café. Instead of opening at 6 A.M. weekdays, we will now open at 8 A.M. On weekends we will only be open from 9 A.M. until 4 P.M. The decrease in hours of operations will help save money because we won't be paying for utilities, employee wages, or other operating costs during the hours we are closed. This is the best strategy for us to save money and remain in business without having to eliminate jobs."

_____

_____

_____

ARGUMENT PROMPT 2

The following appeared in the *Ram*, the Altamonte High School student newspaper:

"65% of Altamonte students polled say they participate in either an intramural, varsity, or community sports team. Being a member of a sports team keeps one fit and healthy and promotes an active lifestyle. Since the majority of students are taking care of their physical fitness after or outside of school, Altamonte High should eliminate all physical education classes and put more resources into the development of the intramural and varsity sports teams."

_____

_____

_____

ANALYTICAL WRITING PRACTICE ESSAYS

What follows are top-scoring sample essays for each of the practice prompts. Note how the authors adhere to Kaplan's 6 basic principles of GRE writing.

ISSUE ESSAY 1

A country's obsession with celebrity always increases when its citizens need a distraction from the harsh realities of war and economic strife.

The United States is one of the most celebrity-obsessed countries in the world. It is easy to see this obsession reflected in all venues of advertising, as well as in the coverage of celebrity lives in tabloids such as *The National Enquirer*; TV shows such as "Entertainment Tonight" and the E! Channel; and magazines such as *People, Us, and Entertainment Weekly*. While other countries may not demonstrate such devoted interest in famous actors or popular athletes, America tends to love her celebrities. In fact, celebrity worship is even more pronounced in periods of high national stress—such as war or recession—since people are looking for escape from their own problems and for a constant in their lives.

Human nature dictates that people look for escape during times of serious economic strife or war. In the Great Depression of the '20s and '30s, for example, the American dream became a nightmare for most people. Because money was scarce during the Depression, people did what they could to distract themselves and make their lives happier. And they could not spend a lot of money doing it. People flocked to see their heroes at baseball games and their screen idols in escapist films such as "Gone with the Wind" and "The Wizard of Oz." It seemed clear that athletes such as Babe Didrikson and Joe Louis and movie stars such as Clark Gable and Bette Davis distracted viewers from worries of job loss and debt. In addition, many newspaper chains were formed in these years, allowing a larger national audience for celebrity photographs and gossip columns.

Admittedly, there were other distractions besides celebrity-watching during the Great Depression. For instance, the golden age of the mystery novel evolved as people escaped into books, reading writers like Agatha Christie, Dashiell Hammett, and Raymond Chandler. Furthermore, millions of people listened to music, news, and serials on the radio every night. Nevertheless, many listeners also tuned in to enjoy their favorite radio personalities, celebrities such as FDR or Burns and Allen.

A second reason for increase in celebrity obsession during times of high national stress is that people need a constant in their lives. With fear and anxiety comes a need for something regular and familiar. Celebrities, as removed as they may seem from "real life," replicate for us that which is the most familiar and the most comforting, since we incorporate them into our daily lives through gossip and news. During wartime, celebrities can soothe people and boost morale. A great example is Bob Hope, who entertained troops hundreds of times over the course of several wars. Hope always included famous actors, athletes, pin-ups, and performers on his famous USO tours. During the current wars in Iraq and Afghanistan, celebrities such as Roger Clemens and Joan Jett visit military bases and hospitals. Household-name celebrities can potentially make anxious soldiers, patients, and their families feel like friends.

It may seem that Americans don't need to rely on celebrities in times of stress because there are enough "average" people who become heroes in extraordinary circumstances. Interestingly, the media and the military recently "created" a celebrity out of an average soldier. Pvt. Jessica Lynch, certainly a brave person, became a celebrity when her capture in Iraq got huge media play. Her rescue was filmed by the military (and fictionalized on several points). Books and a TV movie were made of her story. Lynch left the realm of the ordinary when she was fashioned into a celebrity, and Americans seemed to need her to be a celebrity, even against her will. Lynch's story became a constant in our lives for several weeks, while other frightening and random acts of war were occurring daily.

Celebrities fill both our need for escape and our desire for a sense of constancy. These are two of the major reasons why the American obsession for celebrities increases during times of high national stress, such as war or economic strife.

Issue Essay 2

All results of publicly funded scientific studies should be made available to the general public free of charge. Scientific journals that charge a subscription or newsstand price are profiting unfairly.

Scientific journals that charge a subscription or newsstand price should amend this practice to avail the public of results of publicly funded research. The reasoning here is two-fold: First, the public's taxes have paid for all or a part of the research, and second, scientific results should always be readily accessible to all interested parties.

A publicly funded project means, in effect, that the taxpayers own the research and have a right to the results free of charge. Granted, many research projects are funded by a combination of private contributions, institutional grants, and public funding. Even when this is the case, the public should not be punished for being one part of a coalition that may include profit-making groups. Perhaps the research committee will need to include in its duties finding venues to make research results readily available at no charge.

Of course, the sought-after scientific conclusions may already be available for free in some media forms other than scientific journals. For example, the U.S. Government Printing Office prints all manner of free materials for the public, although people should probably pay a small amount for articles ordered in bulk. These days, research results are often offered online at scientific web sites.

Publishers of scientific journals may argue that they need to make a profit in order to cover their expenses of reporting, printing, handling, and mailing research results. That said, shouldn't the government and private sponsors of a project cover these expenses and include them in their overhead, in the same proportion as their support of the research? Additionally, popular science magazines, using their revenues from advertisers and subscribers, might pay journals to reprint research in their magazines. This practice could also provide funds for making the information available for free to parties not interested in an entire slick magazine with multiple subjects.

Another reason to let the public see results at no charge (besides being totally or partially financially responsible for such research) is that in a larger philosophical view, people should be allowed access to scientific information. Soviet scientists in the former Soviet Union were not allowed to read about scientific endeavors outside of the USSR. This led to decades of wasted money, effort, and time; errors made that shouldn't have been; and a lot of reinventing of the wheel. Furthermore, other scientists, pharmacists, and pharmaceutical companies need professional journals to keep up on the myriad of cutting-edge information released post-research. Ethically speaking, they are charged with nurturing scientific debate and keeping the public safe and informed.

It is supposed that some scientists and government officials will refuse to allow sensitive or secret scientific information to be available to the public for free. But this argument would equally apply to journals and magazines that charge a subscription or newsstand price. It's also probably true that more transparency will promote more international research and more freedom to experiment.

In conclusion, scientific journals that charge a subscription or newsstand price are profiting unfairly when they publish wholly or partially publicly funded research results. These journals need to adjust this practice for the benefit of the public and other professionals. The public's taxes have paid for all or a part of the research, and for ethical reasons, research results must always be readily accessible to all interested parties.

ARGUMENT ESSAY 1

The following appeared in a memorandum from the owner of the Juniper Café, a small, local coffee shop in the downtown area of a small American city:

"We must reduce overhead here at the café. Instead of opening at 6 A.M. weekdays, we will now open at 8 A.M. On weekends we will only be open from 9 A.M. until 4 P.M. The decrease in hours of operations will help save money because we won't be paying for utilities, employee wages, or other operating costs during the hours we are closed. This is the best strategy for us to save money and remain in business without having to eliminate jobs."

In this memo, the owner of the Juniper Café concludes that cutting hours is the "best strategy for us to save money and remain in business without having to eliminate jobs." While the café's employees are undoubtedly grateful for the intent of the memo, they may see that its logic is flawed. First, the memo does not provide enough supporting evidence to prove that money saved by cutting hours would exceed money lost by losing early-morning and weekend clients. Second, the owner does not seem to evaluate other options that would either cut back on overhead or change the café's operation to bring in more revenue.

First, the owner is operating on a false cause fallacy: He concludes that being open too many hours is causing too much overhead expense. There may be other causes, however, such as waste in other areas of management. While it is true that reducing café hours would save money spent on utilities, employee wages, and other operating costs, there is no evidence that those savings would outweigh the café's loss of business. The owner's message fails to give details of operating costs, wages, and utilities saved if the café is closed for the hours suggested by the memo. Perhaps the highest utility expenses are actually incurred between noon and three p.m., when the sun is the hottest and the café's air conditioning and refrigeration are most in use. The owner needs to do more research, including the habits and demography of the town. For example, since the café is located in the downtown area, perhaps *increasing* the number of hours the café is open would be a better solution. Yes, it would cost more in overheard, but doing so might, in fact, make much more money for the café. Say, for instance, the Juniper becomes the only restaurant open on Friday and Saturday date nights, after the football games and movies let out.

Second, the owner of the Juniper Café is not considering that the café serves a small American city. Cutting early-morning hours at a café, in a downtown area, where businesspeople and city workers most likely stop for coffee or breakfast on their way to work, seems very short-sighted and ill-informed. On the other hand, are there one or more other cafés that will gladly steal business from 6 A.M. to 8 A.M. weekdays and that will perhaps win the permanent loyalty of those customers for lunch and dinner? Furthermore, the owner does not seem to have evaluated other options to save the café. Where else might the overhead be cut? Certainly the owner would benefit from a brainstorming session with all employees, to get other ideas on the table. Maybe a new, lower-rent freezer storage facility is nearby. Maybe employees can suggest cutting waste in the purchasing department or dropping services the café doesn't need: "We employees will alternate shoveling the snow and salting the sidewalks instead of your paying Mr. Smith to do so."

What will strengthen the owner's argument is more research, which may affect the hours he chooses to cut. Customer polling could show that few people eat or want coffee in that part of town between 2 P.M. and 5 P.M., and the café could be closed between lunch and dinner, adding flex hours or overlapping shifts for the staff. The memo lacks outlining what other restaurant services are available in the area and how or if they affect the 6 A.M. to 8 A.M. block and weekend hours. The memo as it stands now does not logically prove that reduction in those particular hours will result in financial and future success for the café. Once the marketing research and brainstorming is complete, the owner of the Juniper Café will make a better informed choice for his café's operating hours.

ARGUMENT ESSAY 2

The following appeared in the *Ram*, the Altamonte High School student newspaper:

"65% of Altamonte students polled say they participate in either an intramural, varsity, or community sports team. Being a member of a sports team keeps one fit and healthy and promotes an active lifestyle. Since the majority of students are taking care of their physical fitness after or outside of school, Altamonte High should eliminate all physical education classes and put more resources into the development of the intramural and varsity sports teams."

The *Ram* article falls short of presenting a convincing and logical argument for eliminating all physical education classes at Altamonte High School and putting more resources into the development of intramural and varsity sports. First, the article's statistics are unclear and poorly labeled; they lead to a faulty conclusion. Second, among other things, the article promotes several hasty generalizations, concluding in the very drastic recommendation that "Altamonte High should eliminate all physical education classes."

The statistics in the article are not properly labeled and, therefore, have the potential to be misleading: "65% of Altamonte students polled." How many students does Altamonte High School have? Maybe only 100 out of 2,400 students were polled, which is not a legitimate sampling Who was polled? Maybe only jocks were polled. Maybe only seniors were polled, and seniors tend to have more intramural and varsity members than freshmen. Also, the author overlooks how many of the 65% participate in which (and how many) of the choices: intramural, varsity, and community teams, and that would affect their activity levels. In any case, this part of the argument is an appeal-to-the-majority fallacy: A majority of people do such-and-such, so it must automatically be the best way to go." And, at any rate, is 65% enough of a majority when one is making decisions about the health and future of all our youth?

In addition, the *Ram* article supports a hasty generalization fallacy: "Being a member of a sports team keeps one fit and healthy and promotes an active lifestyle." Just because *some* members of sports teams are fit and healthy, does not logically mean that *all* are. Or maybe not all sports participants are sufficiently active. For example, perhaps some outfielders of the community sports team rarely get to run, catch, or throw and are never selected by their competitive coach for more challenging positions such as pitcher or catcher. In another example, maybe the entire intramural golf team is overweight. In any case, golfing doesn't usually demand aerobic exercise, the kind that is recommended as part of a well-rounded physical education program for high schoolers. Finally, the author fails to note if any of these out-of-school activities teach nutrition, how to make healthy choices, drug abuse and eating disorders, good sportsmanship, and other physical education goals beyond competition and teamwork.

The *Ram* article would be more convincing if the statistics were identified and labeled. Actually, more detail would bolster the conclusion, such as how active the members of the intramural, varsity, and community teams are ("They stretch for 15 minutes and run for 30 minutes during warm-up"). Next, the author should support with detail all of the generalizations the article puts forth. Finally, the author of the article needs to justify why 65%, if a legitimate sampling, is, indeed, a sufficient majority for such a major change in school curriculum.

CHAPTER 6: TAKE CONTROL OF THE TEST

- Learn the basic principles for good test mentality
- Find out how to handle stress leading up to and during the exam
- Review the essentials you'll need to bring with you to the test center

Now that you're familiar with the content that makes up each section of the GRE, and are armed with the strategies and techniques you'll need to tackle all of the question types, you're ready to turn your attention to building the right mentality and attitude that will help you succeed on Test Day. Let's first go over the basic principles of good test mentality.

KAPLAN'S 4 BASIC PRINCIPLES OF GOOD TEST MENTALITY

We've already armed you with the weapons that you need to do well on the GRE. But you must wield those weapons with the right frame of mind and in the right spirit. This involves taking a certain stance toward the entire test, and bolstering your stamina, confidence, and attitude.

TEST AWARENESS

To do your best on the GRE, you must always keep in mind that the test is like no other test you've taken before, both in terms of its content and in terms of its scoring system. If you took a test in high school or college and got a quarter of the questions wrong, you'd probably receive a pretty lousy grade. Not so with the GRE CAT. The test is geared so that only the very best test takers are able to finish every section with time to spare. But even these people rarely get every question right.

KAPLAN

What does this mean for you? Well, just as you shouldn't let one tough Reading Comp passage ruin an entire section, you shouldn't let what you consider to be a subpar performance on one section ruin your performance on the entire test. A lousy performance on one single section will not by itself spoil your score—unless you literally miss almost every question. If you allow that subpar section to rattle you, however, it can have a cumulative negative effect that sets in motion a downward spiral. It's that kind of thing that could potentially do serious damage to your score. Losing a few extra points won't do you in, but losing your head will. Keeping your composure is an important test-taking skill.

Moreover, you may think you are performing poorly on a section when in fact you are doing very well on it. That's just the nature of the GRE CAT. You may think you are doing poorly because one question after another is challenging, leaving you uncertain that you answered several questions correctly. But if the questions seem challenging, that's a good sign! It means you have performed so well that the computer is feeding you one hard question after another. Even if you get a few of these hard questions wrong, you are likely to get a great score on the section.

Also, you should remember that if you feel you've done poorly on a section, it could very well be the experimental section. The experimental section often contains questions that are harder than the questions on the real sections, so you should not let an especially hard section rattle you. Even if it turns out that the section you think you did poorly on was not the experimental section, you still shouldn't sweat it. You'll have time after you've taken the test to think about whether you want to cancel your score. Most likely, you are just underestimating your performance, so try hard to stay confident.

STAMINA

Overall, the GRE is a fairly grueling experience. Remember, you'll likely be taking up to five full-length sections on Test Day (Verbal, Quantitiative, Analytical Writing, Experimental, and Research). Some test takers run out of gas on the final few sections. To avoide this, you must work on your test taking stamina by taking as many full-length Practice Tests as possible in the week or two before the test. If you do this, by Test Day, five sections will seem like a breeze (well, maybe not a breeze, but at least not a hurricane).

When you register for the GRE, ETS will send you a free copy of its POWERPREP® software, including two computer-adaptive Practice Tests. Or if you prefer, you may download the POWERPREP software yourself at **gre.org.**

Another option, if you have enough time left before your exam, would be to take a Kaplan course, either classroom-based or online. You could also set up special one-on-one tutoring sessions with Kaplan experts. If you decide to go this route, visit **kaptest.com,** or call 1-800-KAP-TEST for a Kaplan center location near you.

CONFIDENCE

Confidence feeds on itself, and unfortunately, so does the opposite of confidence—self-doubt. Confidence in your ability leads to quick, sure answers and an ease of concentration that translates into more points. If you lack concentration, you end up reading sentences and answer choices two, three, or four times. This leads to timing difficulties, which only continue the downward spiral, causing anxiety and a tendency to rush.

If you subscribe to the test prep mindset that we've described, however, you'll be ready and able to take control of the test. Learn our techniques and then practice them over and over again. That's the way to score your best on the test.

ATTITUDE

Those who approach the GRE as an obstacle and who rail against the necessity of taking it usually don't fare as well as those who see the GRE as an opportunity to show off the reading and reasoning skills that graduate schools are looking for. Those who look forward to doing battle with the GRE—or, at least, who enjoy the opportunity to distinguish themselves from the rest of the applicant pack—tend to score better than do those who resent or dread it.

It may sound a little dubious, but take our word for it: attitude adjustment is proven to raise points. Here are a few steps you can take to make sure you develop the right GRE attitude:

- Look at the GRE as a challenge, but try not to obsess over it; you certainly don't want to psyche yourself out of the game.
- Remember that, yes, the GRE is obviously important, but, contrary to what some people think, this one test will not single-handedly determine the outcome of your life. In many cases, it's not even the most important piece of your graduate application.
- Try to have fun with the test. Learning how to match your wits against the test makers can be a very satisfying experience, and the reading and thinking skills you'll acquire will benefit you in graduate school as well as in your future career.
- Remember that you're more prepared than most people. You've trained with Kaplan. You have the tools you need, plus the know-how to use those tools.

> **♟ KAPLAN STRATEGY** ————————————————————
>
> Kaplan's basic principles of good test mentality are:
>
> - Be aware of the test and keep your composure even when you are struggling with a difficult question; missing one question won't ruin your score for a section.
>
> - Build your stamina by taking as many Practice Tests as you can.
>
> - Be confident; you are already well on your way to a great score!
>
> - Adjust your attitude; the GRE is an opportunity to show that you can match wits with the test makers.

THE KAPLAN ADVANTAGE™ STRESS-MANAGEMENT SYSTEM

Is it starting to feel as if your whole life is a buildup to the GRE? You've known about it for years, worried about it for months, and now spent at least a few weeks in solid preparation for it. As the test gets closer, you may find that your anxiety is on the rise. You shouldn't worry. Armed with the preparation strategies that you've learned from this book, you're in good shape for Test Day.

To calm any pretest jitters that you may have, however, let's go over a few strategies for the couple of days before the test.

TIPS FOR THE DAYS JUST BEFORE THE EXAM

- The best test takers do less and less as the test approaches. Taper off your study schedule and take it easy on yourself. Give yourself time off, especially the evening before the exam. By that time, if you've studied well, everything you need to know is firmly stored in your memory bank.

- Positive self-talk can be extremely liberating and invigorating, especially as the test looms closer. Tell yourself things such as "I will do well," rather than "I hope things go well"; "I can," rather than "I cannot." Replace any negative thoughts with affirming statements that boost your self-esteem.

- Get your act together sooner rather than later. Have everything (including choice of clothing) laid out in advance. Most important, make sure you know where the test will be held and the easiest, quickest way to get there. You'll have great peace of mind by knowing that all the little details—gas in the car, directions, and so on—are set before Test Day.

- Go to the test site a few days in advance, particularly if you are especially anxious. Better yet, bring some practice material and do at least a section or two.

- Forego any practice on the day before the test. It's in your best interest to marshal your physical and psychological resources for 24 hours or so. Even racehorses are kept in the paddock and treated like princes the day before a race. Keep the test out of your consciousness; go to a movie, take a pleasant hike, or just relax. Don't eat junk food or tons of sugar. And, of course, get plenty of rest the night before—just don't go to bed too early. It's hard to fall asleep earlier than you're used to, and you don't want to lie there worrying about the test.

HANDLING STRESS DURING THE TEST

The biggest stress monster will be the test itself. Fear not; there are methods of quelling your stress during the test.

- Keep moving forward instead of getting bogged down in a difficult question. You don't have to get everything right to achieve a fine score. So, don't linger out of desperation on a question that is going nowhere even after you've spent considerable time on it.

- Don't be thrown if other test takers seem to be working more busily and furiously than you are. Don't mistake the other people's activity as signs of progress and higher scores.

- Breathe! Weak test takers tend to share one major trait: they don't breathe properly as the test proceeds. They might hold their breath without realizing it, or breathe erratically or arrhythmically. Improper breathing hurts confidence and accuracy. Just as important, it interferes with clear thinking.

- Do some quick isometrics during the test—especially if concentration is wandering or energy is waning. Try this: put your palms together and press intensely for a few seconds. Concentrate on the tension you feel through your palms, wrists, forearms, and up into your biceps and shoulders. Then quickly release the pressure. Feel the difference as you let go. Focus on the warm relaxation that floods through the muscles. Now you're ready to return to the task. Or try this one: slowly rotate your head from side to side, turning your head and eyes to look as far back over each shoulder as you can. Feel the muscles stretch on one side of your neck as they contract on the other. Repeat five times in each direction.

TEST DAY

The night before Test Day, gather the following things together:

- ID
- Admission ticket

- A watch
- Bottle of water
- Aspirin or other painkiller, in case you get a headache
- A snack like fruit or an energy bar to keep your energy up for the later sections of the test
- Names of schools you'd like to receive your scores

Test Day should start with a moderate, high-energy breakfast. Cereal, fruit, bagels, or eggs are good. Avoid donuts, danishes, or anything else with a lot of sugar in it. Also, unless you are utterly catatonic without it, it's a good idea to stay away from coffee. Yeah, yeah, you drink two cups every morning and don't even notice it. But it's different during the test. Coffee won't make you alert (your adrenaline will do that much more effectively); it will just give you the jitters. Kaplan has done experiments in which test takers go into one exam having drunk various amounts of coffee and another exam without having drunk coffee. The results indicate that even the most caffeine-addicted test takers will lose their focus midway through the second section if they've had coffee, but report no alertness problems without it.

When you get to the test center, you will be seated at a computer station. Some administrative questions will be asked before the test begins, and once you're done with those—it's showtime. While you're taking the test, a small clock will count down the time you have left in each section. The computer will tell you when you're done with each section, and when you've completed the test.

Here are some last-minute reminders to help guide your work on the test:

- Give all five answer choices a fair shot in Verbal (especially Reading Comp), time permitting. For the Quantitative section, go with the objectively correct answer as soon as you find it, and forget the rest of the answer choices.
- Don't bother trying to figure out which section is unscored. It can't help you, and you might very well be wrong. Instead, just do your best on every section.
- Pay no attention to people who are chattering on their break. Just concentrate on how well prepared you are.
- Dress in layers for maximum comfort. This way, you can adjust to the room's temperature accordingly.
- Take a few minutes now to look back over your preparation and give yourself credit for how far you've come. Confidence is the key. Accentuate the positives and don't dwell on the negatives! Your attitude and outlook are crucial to your performance on the test.
- During the exam, try not to think about how you're scoring. It's like a baseball player who's thinking about the crowd's cheers, the sportswriters, and his contract as he steps up to the plate. It's a great way to strike out. Instead, focus

on the question-by-question task of picking the correct answer choice. After all, the correct answer is there (for the multiple-choice sections, at least). You don't have to come up with it; it's sitting right there in front of you! Concentrate on each question, each passage, each essay prompt—on the mechanics, in other words—and you'll be much more likely to hit a home run.

After all the hard work that you've put in preparing for and taking the GRE, make sure you take time to celebrate afterwards. Plan to get together with friends the evening after the test. Relax, have fun, let loose. After all, you've got a lot to celebrate. You prepared for the test ahead of time. You did your best. You're going to get a great score.

Part Three

FULL-LENGTH PRACTICE TEST

HOW TO TAKE THIS PRACTICE TEST

Before taking this Practice Test, find a quiet place where you can work uninterrupted for three hours and 15 minutes. Make sure you have a comfortable desk and several pencils. Time yourself according to the time limits shown at the beginning of each section. It's okay to take a short break between sections, but for the most accurate results, you should go through all three sections in one sitting. Use the answer grid on the following pages to record your answers to the multiple-choice sections. You'll find the answer key and score converter following the test. Good luck.

Note that the time limits and section lengths for this paper-based Practice Test differ from those of the actual GRE exam. (This compensates for the fact that on the actual exam, the level of difficulty will change based on your previous answers, and you will not be able to skip or return to any questions.) While the interactive test-taking experience is impossible to reproduce in a book, this normed Practice Test is designed to produce an accurate score.

ANSWER SHEET

Remove or photocopy this answer sheet and use it to complete the Verbal and Quantitative sections of the Practice Test. See the answer key at the end of the test to correct your answers when finished.

 ONLINE

Remember to add your Practice Test scores to your online syllabus to track your progress.

SECTION

1

VERBAL

1 Ⓐ Ⓑ Ⓒ Ⓓ Ⓔ	20 Ⓐ Ⓑ Ⓒ Ⓓ Ⓔ	39 Ⓐ Ⓑ Ⓒ Ⓓ Ⓔ	58 Ⓐ Ⓑ Ⓒ Ⓓ Ⓔ
2 Ⓐ Ⓑ Ⓒ Ⓓ Ⓔ	21 Ⓐ Ⓑ Ⓒ Ⓓ Ⓔ	40 Ⓐ Ⓑ Ⓒ Ⓓ Ⓔ	59 Ⓐ Ⓑ Ⓒ Ⓓ Ⓔ
3 Ⓐ Ⓑ Ⓒ Ⓓ Ⓔ	22 Ⓐ Ⓑ Ⓒ Ⓓ Ⓔ	41 Ⓐ Ⓑ Ⓒ Ⓓ Ⓔ	60 Ⓐ Ⓑ Ⓒ Ⓓ Ⓔ
4 Ⓐ Ⓑ Ⓒ Ⓓ Ⓔ	23 Ⓐ Ⓑ Ⓒ Ⓓ Ⓔ	42 Ⓐ Ⓑ Ⓒ Ⓓ Ⓔ	61 Ⓐ Ⓑ Ⓒ Ⓓ Ⓔ
5 Ⓐ Ⓑ Ⓒ Ⓓ Ⓔ	24 Ⓐ Ⓑ Ⓒ Ⓓ Ⓔ	43 Ⓐ Ⓑ Ⓒ Ⓓ Ⓔ	62 Ⓐ Ⓑ Ⓒ Ⓓ Ⓔ
6 Ⓐ Ⓑ Ⓒ Ⓓ Ⓔ	25 Ⓐ Ⓑ Ⓒ Ⓓ Ⓔ	44 Ⓐ Ⓑ Ⓒ Ⓓ Ⓔ	63 Ⓐ Ⓑ Ⓒ Ⓓ Ⓔ
7 Ⓐ Ⓑ Ⓒ Ⓓ Ⓔ	26 Ⓐ Ⓑ Ⓒ Ⓓ Ⓔ	45 Ⓐ Ⓑ Ⓒ Ⓓ Ⓔ	64 Ⓐ Ⓑ Ⓒ Ⓓ Ⓔ
8 Ⓐ Ⓑ Ⓒ Ⓓ Ⓔ	27 Ⓐ Ⓑ Ⓒ Ⓓ Ⓔ	46 Ⓐ Ⓑ Ⓒ Ⓓ Ⓔ	65 Ⓐ Ⓑ Ⓒ Ⓓ Ⓔ
9 Ⓐ Ⓑ Ⓒ Ⓓ Ⓔ	28 Ⓐ Ⓑ Ⓒ Ⓓ Ⓔ	47 Ⓐ Ⓑ Ⓒ Ⓓ Ⓔ	66 Ⓐ Ⓑ Ⓒ Ⓓ Ⓔ
10 Ⓐ Ⓑ Ⓒ Ⓓ Ⓔ	29 Ⓐ Ⓑ Ⓒ Ⓓ Ⓔ	48 Ⓐ Ⓑ Ⓒ Ⓓ Ⓔ	67 Ⓐ Ⓑ Ⓒ Ⓓ Ⓔ
11 Ⓐ Ⓑ Ⓒ Ⓓ Ⓔ	30 Ⓐ Ⓑ Ⓒ Ⓓ Ⓔ	49 Ⓐ Ⓑ Ⓒ Ⓓ Ⓔ	68 Ⓐ Ⓑ Ⓒ Ⓓ Ⓔ
12 Ⓐ Ⓑ Ⓒ Ⓓ Ⓔ	31 Ⓐ Ⓑ Ⓒ Ⓓ Ⓔ	50 Ⓐ Ⓑ Ⓒ Ⓓ Ⓔ	69 Ⓐ Ⓑ Ⓒ Ⓓ Ⓔ
13 Ⓐ Ⓑ Ⓒ Ⓓ Ⓔ	32 Ⓐ Ⓑ Ⓒ Ⓓ Ⓔ	51 Ⓐ Ⓑ Ⓒ Ⓓ Ⓔ	70 Ⓐ Ⓑ Ⓒ Ⓓ Ⓔ
14 Ⓐ Ⓑ Ⓒ Ⓓ Ⓔ	33 Ⓐ Ⓑ Ⓒ Ⓓ Ⓔ	52 Ⓐ Ⓑ Ⓒ Ⓓ Ⓔ	71 Ⓐ Ⓑ Ⓒ Ⓓ Ⓔ
15 Ⓐ Ⓑ Ⓒ Ⓓ Ⓔ	34 Ⓐ Ⓑ Ⓒ Ⓓ Ⓔ	53 Ⓐ Ⓑ Ⓒ Ⓓ Ⓔ	72 Ⓐ Ⓑ Ⓒ Ⓓ Ⓔ
16 Ⓐ Ⓑ Ⓒ Ⓓ Ⓔ	35 Ⓐ Ⓑ Ⓒ Ⓓ Ⓔ	54 Ⓐ Ⓑ Ⓒ Ⓓ Ⓔ	73 Ⓐ Ⓑ Ⓒ Ⓓ Ⓔ
17 Ⓐ Ⓑ Ⓒ Ⓓ Ⓔ	36 Ⓐ Ⓑ Ⓒ Ⓓ Ⓔ	55 Ⓐ Ⓑ Ⓒ Ⓓ Ⓔ	74 Ⓐ Ⓑ Ⓒ Ⓓ Ⓔ
18 Ⓐ Ⓑ Ⓒ Ⓓ Ⓔ	37 Ⓐ Ⓑ Ⓒ Ⓓ Ⓔ	56 Ⓐ Ⓑ Ⓒ Ⓓ Ⓔ	75 Ⓐ Ⓑ Ⓒ Ⓓ Ⓔ
19 Ⓐ Ⓑ Ⓒ Ⓓ Ⓔ	38 Ⓐ Ⓑ Ⓒ Ⓓ Ⓔ	57 Ⓐ Ⓑ Ⓒ Ⓓ Ⓔ	76 Ⓐ Ⓑ Ⓒ Ⓓ Ⓔ

right in Section One

wrong in Section One

SECTION

2

QUANTITATIVE

1 Ⓐ Ⓑ Ⓒ Ⓓ Ⓔ	16 Ⓐ Ⓑ Ⓒ Ⓓ Ⓔ	31 Ⓐ Ⓑ Ⓒ Ⓓ Ⓔ	46 Ⓐ Ⓑ Ⓒ Ⓓ Ⓔ
2 Ⓐ Ⓑ Ⓒ Ⓓ Ⓔ	17 Ⓐ Ⓑ Ⓒ Ⓓ Ⓔ	32 Ⓐ Ⓑ Ⓒ Ⓓ Ⓔ	47 Ⓐ Ⓑ Ⓒ Ⓓ Ⓔ
3 Ⓐ Ⓑ Ⓒ Ⓓ Ⓔ	18 Ⓐ Ⓑ Ⓒ Ⓓ Ⓔ	33 Ⓐ Ⓑ Ⓒ Ⓓ Ⓔ	48 Ⓐ Ⓑ Ⓒ Ⓓ Ⓔ
4 Ⓐ Ⓑ Ⓒ Ⓓ Ⓔ	19 Ⓐ Ⓑ Ⓒ Ⓓ Ⓔ	34 Ⓐ Ⓑ Ⓒ Ⓓ Ⓔ	49 Ⓐ Ⓑ Ⓒ Ⓓ Ⓔ
5 Ⓐ Ⓑ Ⓒ Ⓓ Ⓔ	20 Ⓐ Ⓑ Ⓒ Ⓓ Ⓔ	35 Ⓐ Ⓑ Ⓒ Ⓓ Ⓔ	50 Ⓐ Ⓑ Ⓒ Ⓓ Ⓔ
6 Ⓐ Ⓑ Ⓒ Ⓓ Ⓔ	21 Ⓐ Ⓑ Ⓒ Ⓓ Ⓔ	36 Ⓐ Ⓑ Ⓒ Ⓓ Ⓔ	51 Ⓐ Ⓑ Ⓒ Ⓓ Ⓔ
7 Ⓐ Ⓑ Ⓒ Ⓓ Ⓔ	22 Ⓐ Ⓑ Ⓒ Ⓓ Ⓔ	37 Ⓐ Ⓑ Ⓒ Ⓓ Ⓔ	52 Ⓐ Ⓑ Ⓒ Ⓓ Ⓔ
8 Ⓐ Ⓑ Ⓒ Ⓓ Ⓔ	23 Ⓐ Ⓑ Ⓒ Ⓓ Ⓔ	38 Ⓐ Ⓑ Ⓒ Ⓓ Ⓔ	53 Ⓐ Ⓑ Ⓒ Ⓓ Ⓔ
9 Ⓐ Ⓑ Ⓒ Ⓓ Ⓔ	24 Ⓐ Ⓑ Ⓒ Ⓓ Ⓔ	39 Ⓐ Ⓑ Ⓒ Ⓓ Ⓔ	54 Ⓐ Ⓑ Ⓒ Ⓓ Ⓔ
10 Ⓐ Ⓑ Ⓒ Ⓓ Ⓔ	25 Ⓐ Ⓑ Ⓒ Ⓓ Ⓔ	40 Ⓐ Ⓑ Ⓒ Ⓓ Ⓔ	55 Ⓐ Ⓑ Ⓒ Ⓓ Ⓔ
11 Ⓐ Ⓑ Ⓒ Ⓓ Ⓔ	26 Ⓐ Ⓑ Ⓒ Ⓓ Ⓔ	41 Ⓐ Ⓑ Ⓒ Ⓓ Ⓔ	56 Ⓐ Ⓑ Ⓒ Ⓓ Ⓔ
12 Ⓐ Ⓑ Ⓒ Ⓓ Ⓔ	27 Ⓐ Ⓑ Ⓒ Ⓓ Ⓔ	42 Ⓐ Ⓑ Ⓒ Ⓓ Ⓔ	57 Ⓐ Ⓑ Ⓒ Ⓓ Ⓔ
13 Ⓐ Ⓑ Ⓒ Ⓓ Ⓔ	28 Ⓐ Ⓑ Ⓒ Ⓓ Ⓔ	43 Ⓐ Ⓑ Ⓒ Ⓓ Ⓔ	58 Ⓐ Ⓑ Ⓒ Ⓓ Ⓔ
14 Ⓐ Ⓑ Ⓒ Ⓓ Ⓔ	29 Ⓐ Ⓑ Ⓒ Ⓓ Ⓔ	44 Ⓐ Ⓑ Ⓒ Ⓓ Ⓔ	59 Ⓐ Ⓑ Ⓒ Ⓓ Ⓔ
15 Ⓐ Ⓑ Ⓒ Ⓓ Ⓔ	30 Ⓐ Ⓑ Ⓒ Ⓓ Ⓔ	45 Ⓐ Ⓑ Ⓒ Ⓓ Ⓔ	60 Ⓐ Ⓑ Ⓒ Ⓓ Ⓔ

right in Section Two

wrong in Section Two

Use notebook pages for your essay answers, or type them into a computer.

SECTION

3

ANALYTICAL
WRITING

Essay 1

_____

_____

_____

_____

_____

_____

_____

_____

_____

_____

_____

_____

_____

_____

_____

_____

_____

_____

Essay 2

_____

_____

_____

_____

_____

_____

_____

_____

_____

_____

_____

_____

_____

_____

_____

_____

_____

IF YOU FINISH BEFORE TIME IS CALLED, YOU MAY CHECK YOUR WORK ON
THIS SECTION ONLY. DO NOT TURN TO ANY OTHER SECTION IN THE TEST.

Section One—Verbal
Time—60 minutes 76 questions

Directions: Each of the following questions begins with a sentence that has either one or two blanks. The blanks indicate that a piece of the sentence is missing. Each sentence is followed by five answer choices that consist of words or phrases. Select the answer choice that completes the sentence best.

GO ON TO THE NEXT PAGE

1. The fundamental _____ between dogs and cats is for the most part a myth; members of these species often coexist _____.

   ○ antipathy … amiably

   ○ disharmony … uneasily

   ○ compatibility … together

   ○ relationship … peacefully

   ○ difference … placidly

2. His desire to state his case completely was certainly reasonable; however, his lengthy technical explanations were monotonous and tended to _____ rather than _____ the jury.

   ○ enlighten … inform

   ○ interest … persuade

   ○ provoke … influence

   ○ allay … pacify

   ○ bore … convince

3. In some countries, government restrictions are so _____ that businesses operate with nearly complete impunity.

   ○ traditional

   ○ judicious

   ○ ambiguous

   ○ exacting

   ○ lax

4. The recent Oxford edition of the works of Shakespeare is _____ because it not only departs frequently from the readings of most other modern editions, but also challenges many of the basic _____ of textual criticism.

   ○ controversial … conventions

   ○ typical … innovations

   ○ inadequate … norms

   ○ curious … projects

   ○ pretentious … explanations

5. The early form of writing known as Linear B was _____ in 1952, but no one has yet succeeded in the _____ of the still more ancient Linear A.

   ○ superseded … explanation

   ○ encoded … transcription

   ○ obliterated … analysis

   ○ deciphered … interpretation

   ○ discovered … obfuscation

6. Considering everything she had been through, her reaction was quite normal and even _____; I was therefore surprised at the number of _____ comments and raised eyebrows that her response elicited.

   ○ commendable … complimentary

   ○ odious … insulting

   ○ apologetic … conciliatory

   ○ commonplace … typical

   ○ laudable … derogatory

GO ON TO THE NEXT PAGE ⇨

7. The purpose of the proposed insurance policy is to _____ the burden of medical costs, thereby removing what is for many people a major _____ medical care.

   ◯ augment … problem with

   ◯ eliminate … perquisite of

   ◯ ameliorate … study of

   ◯ assuage … impediment to

   ◯ clarify … explanation for

Directions: Each of the following questions consists of a pair of words or phrases that are separated by a colon and followed by five answer choices. Choose the pair of words or phrases in the answer choices that are most similar to the original pair.

8. NOVEL : BOOK ::

   ◯ epic : poem

   ◯ house : library

   ◯ tale : fable

   ◯ number : page

   ◯ play : theater

9. HUNGRY : RAVENOUS ::

   ◯ thirsty : desirous

   ◯ large : titanic

   ◯ famous : eminent

   ◯ dizzy : disoriented

   ◯ obese : gluttonous

10. BOUQUET : FLOWER ::

    ◯ humidor : tobacco

    ◯ mosaic : tile

    ◯ tapestry : color

    ◯ pile : block

    ◯ sacristy : vestment

11. REALIST : QUIXOTIC ::

    ◯ scholar : pedantic

    ◯ fool : idiotic

    ◯ idler : lethargic

    ◯ tormentor : sympathetic

    ◯ diner : dyspeptic

12. SHARD : GLASS ::

    ◯ grain : sand

    ◯ morsel : meal

    ◯ strand : rope

    ◯ scrap : quilt

    ◯ splinter : wood

13. FILTER : IMPURITY ::

    ◯ expurgate : obscenity

    ◯ whitewash : infraction

    ◯ testify : perjury

    ◯ perform : penance

    ◯ vacuum : carpet

GO ON TO THE NEXT PAGE

14. PARAPHRASE : VERBATIM ::

○ approximation : precise

○ description : vivid

○ quotation : apt

○ interpretation : valid

○ significance : uncertain

15. ONCOLOGY : TUMOR ::

○ chronology : time

○ theology : tenet

○ oral : sound

○ philology : religion

○ taxonomy : classification

16. INTRANSIGENT : FLEXIBILITY ::

○ transient : mobility

○ disinterested : partisanship

○ dissimilar : variation

○ progressive : transition

○ ineluctable : modality

Directions: After each reading passage you will find a series of questions. Select the best choice for each question. Answers are based on the contents of the passage or what the author implies in the passage.

There can be nothing simpler than an elementary particle: it is an indivisible shard of matter, without internal structure and without detectable shape or size. One might expect
(5) commensurate simplicity in the theories that describe such particles and the forces through which they interact; at the least, one might expect the structure of the world to be explained with a minimum number of
(10) particles and forces. Judged by this criterion of parsimony, a description of nature that has evolved in the past several years can be accounted a reasonable success. Matter is built out of just two classes of elementary particles:
(15) the leptons, such as the electron, and the quarks, which are constituents of the proton, the neutron, and many related particles. Four basic forces act between the elementary particles. Gravitation and electromagnetism have long
(20) been familiar in the macroscopic world; the weak force and the strong force are observed only in subnuclear events. In principle this complement of particles and forces could account for the entire observed hierarchy of material structure,
(25) from the nuclei of atoms to stars and galaxies. An understanding of nature at this level of detail is a remarkable achievement; nevertheless, it is possible to imagine what a still simpler theory might be like. The existence of two disparate
(30) classes of elementary particles is not fully satisfying; ideally, one class would suffice.

GO ON TO THE NEXT PAGE ⟹

Similarly, the existence of four forces seems a
needless complication; one force might explain
all the interactions of elementary particles. An
(35)   ambitious new theory now promises at
least a partial unification along these lines.
The theory does not embrace gravitation,
which is by far the feeblest of the forces and
may be fundamentally different from the
(40)   others. If gravitation is excluded, however, the
theory unifies all elementary particles
and forces. The first step in the
construction of the unified theory was the
demonstration that the weak, the strong,
(45)   and the electromagnetic forces could all
described by theories of the same general
kind. The three forces remained distinct,
but they could be seen to operate through
the same mechanism. In the course of this
(50)   development a deep connection was
discovered between the weak force and
electromagnetism, a connection that hinted
at a still grander synthesis. The new theory
is the leading candidate for accomplishing
(55)   the synthesis. It incorporates the leptons
and the quarks into a single family and
provides a means of transforming one kind
of particle into the other. At the same time
the weak, the strong, and the electro-
(60)   magnetic forces are understood as
aspects of a single underlying force. With
only one class of particles and one force (plus
gravitation), the unified theory is a model of
frugality.

17. All of the following are differences between
the two theories described by the author
EXCEPT

○ the second theory is simpler than
the first.

○ the first theory encompasses gravitation
while the second does not.

○ the second theory includes only one
class of elementary particles.

○ the first theory accounts for only part of
the hierarchy of material structure.

○ the second theory unifies forces that the
first theory regards as distinct.

18. The primary purpose of the passage is to

○ correct a misconception in a currently
accepted theory of the nature of matter.

○ describe efforts to arrive at a simplified
theory of elementary particles and
forces.

○ predict the success of a new effort to
unify gravitation with other basic forces.

○ explain why scientists prefer simpler
explanations over more complex ones.

○ summarize what is known about the
basic components of matter.

GO ON TO THE NEXT PAGE ⇨

19. According to the passage, which of the following are true of quarks?

    I. They are the elementary building blocks for neutrons.
    II. Scientists have described them as having no internal structure.
    III. Some scientists group them with leptons in a single class of particles.

    ◯ I only

    ◯ III only

    ◯ I and II only

    ◯ II and III only

    ◯ I, II, and III

20. The author considers which of the following in judging the usefulness of a theory of elementary particles and forces?

    I. The simplicity of the theory
    II. The ability of the theory to account for the largest possible number of known phenomena
    III. The possibility of proving or disproving the theory by experiment

    ◯ I only

    ◯ II only

    ◯ I and II only

    ◯ I and III only

    ◯ II and III only

21. It can be inferred that the author considers the failure to unify gravitation with other forces in the theory he describes to be

    ◯ a disqualifying defect.

    ◯ an unjustified deviation.

    ◯ a needless oversimplification.

    ◯ an unfortunate oversight.

    ◯ an unavoidable limitation.

22. The author organizes the passage by

    ◯ enumerating distinctions among several different kinds of elementary particles.

    ◯ stating a criterion for judging theories of nature, and using it to evaluate two theories.

    ◯ explaining three methods of grouping particles and forces.

    ◯ criticizing an inaccurate view of elemental nature and proposing an alternative approach.

    ◯ outlining an assumption about scientific verification, then criticizing the assumption.

GO ON TO THE NEXT PAGE ▷

23. It can be inferred that the author would be likely to consider a new theory of nature superior to present theories if it were to

   ○ account for a larger number of macroscopic structures than present theories.

   ○ reduce the four basic forces to two more fundamental, incompatible forces.

   ○ propose a smaller number of fundamental particles and forces than current theories.

   ○ successfully account for the observable behavior of bodies due to gravity.

   ○ hypothesize that protons but not neutrons are formed by combinations of more fundamental particles.

   The majority of white abolitionists and the majority of suffragists worked hard to convince their compatriots that the changes they advocated were not revolutionary, that far from
(5) undermining the accepted distribution of power they would eliminate deviations from the democratic principle it was supposedly based on. Non-Garrisonian abolitionists repeatedly disavowed miscegenationist or revolutionary
(10) intentions. And as for the suffragists, despite the presence in the movement of socialists, and in the final years of a few blacks, immigrants, and workers, the racism and nativism in the movement's thinking were not an aberration and
(15) did not conflict with the movement's objective of suffrage. Far from saying, as presentist historians do, that the white abolitionists and suffragists compromised the abiding principles of equality and the equal right of all to life, liberty, and the

(20) pursuit of happiness, I suggest just the opposite: the non-Garrisonian majority of white abolitionists and the majority of suffragists showed what those principles meant in their respective generations, because they traced the
(25) farthest acceptable boundaries around them.

24. The author's main point is that

   ○ the actions of the abolitionist and suffragist movements compromised their stated principles.

   ○ the underlying beliefs of abolitionists and suffragists were closer than is usually believed.

   ○ abolitionists' and suffragists' thinking about equality was limited by the assumptions of their time.

   ○ presentist historians have willfully misrepresented the ideology of abolitionists and suffragists.

   ○ historians should impose their own value systems when evaluating events of the past.

GO ON TO THE NEXT PAGE

25. Which of the following does the author imply about the principle of equality?

   I. It does not have a fixed meaning.
   II. Suffragists applied it more consistently than abolitionists.
   III. Abolitionists and suffragists compromised it to gain their political objectives.

   ○ I only

   ○ II only

   ○ III only

   ○ I and II only

   ○ II and III only

26. The author takes exception to the views of presentist historians by

   ○ charging that they ignore pertinent evidence.

   ○ presenting new information that had not been available before.

   ○ applying a different interpretation to the same set of facts.

   ○ refuting the accuracy of their historical data.

   ○ exposing a logical contradiction in their arguments.

27. Which of the following is suggested about the abolitionist movement?

   ○ Its members disguised their objectives from the public.

   ○ It contained different groupings characterized by varied philosophies.

   ○ It undermined its principles by accommodating public concerns.

   ○ A majority of its members misunderstood its objectives.

   ○ Its progress was hindered by the actions of radical factions within it.

Directions: Each of the following questions begins with a single word in capital letters. Five answer choices follow. Select the answer choice that has the most opposite meaning of the word in capital letters.

Since some of the questions require you to distinguish fine shades of meaning, be sure to consider all the choices before deciding which one is best.

28. UNDERMINE :

   ○ appreciate

   ○ donate

   ○ bolster

   ○ decay

   ○ simplify

GO ON TO THE NEXT PAGE ⇨

29. OBSEQUIOUS :
    - ◯ original
    - ◯ haughty
    - ◯ casual
    - ◯ virtuous
    - ◯ informative

30. BLANCH :
    - ◯ stand
    - ◯ repay
    - ◯ flush
    - ◯ relax
    - ◯ cope

31. DISSIPATED :
    - ◯ temperate
    - ◯ pleased
    - ◯ inundated
    - ◯ encouraged
    - ◯ planned

32. FECUNDITY :
    - ◯ levity
    - ◯ sanity
    - ◯ cowardice
    - ◯ sterility
    - ◯ ventilation

33. ENCUMBER :
    - ◯ animate
    - ◯ inaugurate
    - ◯ bleach
    - ◯ disburden
    - ◯ obliterate

34. DISSEMINATE :
    - ◯ fertilize
    - ◯ ordain
    - ◯ suppress
    - ◯ explain thoroughly
    - ◯ make an impression

35. RESTIVE :
    - ◯ morose
    - ◯ intangible
    - ◯ fatigued
    - ◯ patient
    - ◯ curious

36. SYNCOPATED :
    - ◯ carefully executed
    - ◯ normally accented
    - ◯ brightly illuminated
    - ◯ easily understood
    - ◯ justly represented

GO ON TO THE NEXT PAGE ⟹

37. VITUPERATIVE :

    ○ lethal

    ○ incapacitated

    ○ laudatory

    ○ insulated

    ○ prominent

38. SATURNINE :

    ○ magnanimous

    ○ ebullient

    ○ finicky

    ○ unnatural

    ○ impoverished

Directions: Each of the following questions begins with a sentence that has either one or two blanks. The blanks indicate that a piece of the sentence is missing. Each sentence is followed by five answer choices that consist of words or phrases. Select the answer choice that completes the sentence best.

39. Her concern for the earthquake victims _____ her reputation as a callous person.

    ○ restored

    ○ rescinded

    ○ created

    ○ proved

    ○ belied

40. Due to unforeseen circumstances, the original plans were no longer _____ and were therefore _____ .

    ○ relevant … adaptable

    ○ applicable … rejected

    ○ expedient … adopted

    ○ acceptable … appraised

    ○ capable … allayed

41. The microscopic cross section of a sandstone generally shows a _____ surface, each tiny layer representing an _____ of deposition that may have taken centuries or even millennia to accumulate.

    ○ ridged … enlargement

    ○ multifaceted … angle

    ○ distinctive … area

    ○ stratified … interval

    ○ coarse … episode

42. The convict has always insisted upon his own _____ and now at last there is new evidence to _____ him.

    ○ defensiveness … incarcerate

    ○ culpability … exonerate

    ○ blamelessness … anathematize

    ○ innocence … vindicate

    ○ contrition … condemn

GO ON TO THE NEXT PAGE

43. The theory of plate tectonics was the subject of much _____ when it was first proposed by Alfred Wegener, but now most geophysicists _____ its validity.

   ○ opposition … grant

   ○ consideration … see

   ○ acclamation … boost

   ○ prognostication … learn

   ○ contention … bar

44. Despite her professed _____ , the glint in her eyes demonstrated her _____ with the topic.

   ○ intelligence … obsession

   ○ interest … concern

   ○ obliviousness … confusion

   ○ indifference … fascination

   ○ expertise … unfamiliarity

45. Lacking sacred scriptures or _____ , Shinto is more properly regarded as a legacy of traditional religious practices and basic values than as a formal system of belief.

   ○ followers

   ○ customs

   ○ dogma

   ○ relics

   ○ faith

Directions: Each of the following questions consists of a pair of words or phrases that are separated by a colon and followed by five answer choices. Choice the pair of words or phrases in the answer choices that are most similar to the original pair.

46. IMPECCABLE : FLAW ::

   ○ impeachable : crime

   ○ obstreperous : permission

   ○ impetuous : warning

   ○ moribund : living

   ○ absurd : sense

47. SEISMOGRAPH : EARTHQUAKE ::

   ○ stethoscope : health

   ○ speedometer : truck

   ○ telescope : astronomy

   ○ thermometer : temperature

   ○ abacus : arithmetic

48. GUZZLE : DRINK ::

   ○ elucidate : clarify

   ○ ingest : eat

   ○ boast : describe

   ○ stride : walk

   ○ admonish : condemn

GO ON TO THE NEXT PAGE

49. ORATOR : ARTICULATE ::

   ○ soldier : merciless

   ○ celebrity : talented

   ○ judge : unbiased

   ○ novice : unfamiliar

   ○ dignitary : respectful

50. BADGE : POLICEMAN ::

   ○ placard : demonstrator

   ○ tattoo : sailor

   ○ dog-tag : soldier

   ○ pedigree : dog

   ○ fingerprint : defendant

51. SCRUTINIZE : OBSERVE ::

   ○ excite : pique

   ○ beseech : request

   ○ search : discover

   ○ smile : grin

   ○ dive : jump

52. INDULGE : EPICUREAN ::

   ○ frighten : ugly

   ○ retract : revocable

   ○ hesitate : unproductive

   ○ revenge : vindictive

   ○ understand : comprehensible

53. FLOOD : DILUVIAL ::

   ○ punishment : criminal

   ○ bacteria : biological

   ○ verdict : judicial

   ○ light : candescent

   ○ heart : cardiac

54. SPHINX : PERPLEX ::

   ○ oracle : interpret

   ○ prophet : prepare

   ○ siren : lure

   ○ jester : astound

   ○ minotaur : anger

Directions: After each reading passage you will find a series of questions. Select the best choice for each question. Answers are based on the contents of the passage or what the author implies in the passage.

Although the schooling of fish is a familiar form of animal social behavior, how the school is formed and maintained is only beginning to be understood in detail. It had been thought that
(5)   each fish maintains its position chiefly by means of vision. Our work has shown that, as each fish maintains its position, the lateral line, an organ sensitive to transitory changes in water displacement, is as important as vision. In each
(10) species a fish has a "preferred" distance and angle from its nearest neighbor. The ideal separation and bearing, however, are not maintained rigidly.

GO ON TO THE NEXT PAGE ⟶

The result is a probabilistic arrangement that appears like a random aggregation. The tendency
(15) of the fish to remain at the preferred distance and angle, however, serves to maintain the structure. Each fish, having established its position, uses its eyes and its lateral lines simultaneously to measure the speed of all the other fish in the
(20) school. It then adjusts its own speed to match a weighted average that emphasizes the contribution of nearby fish.

55. According to the passage, the structure of a fish school is dependent upon which of the following?

   I. Rigidly formed random aggregations
   II. The tendency of each fish to remain at a preferred distance from neighboring fish
   III. Measurements of a weighted average by individual fish

   ○ II only

   ○ III only

   ○ I and II only

   ○ I and III only

   ○ II and III only

56. Which of the following best describes the author's attitude toward the theory that the structure of fish schools is maintained primarily through vision?

   ○ Heated opposition

   ○ Careful neutrality

   ○ Considered dissatisfaction

   ○ Cautious approval

   ○ Unqualified enthusiasm

57. The passage suggests that, after establishing its position in the school formation, an individual fish will subsequently

   ○ maintain its preferred position primarily by visual and auditory means.

   ○ rigorously avoid changes that would interfere with the overall structure of the school.

   ○ make continuous sensory readjustments to its position within the school.

   ○ make unexpected shifts in position only if threatened by external danger.

   ○ surrender its ability to make quick, instinctive judgments.

Whether as a result of some mysterious tendency in the national psyche or as a spontaneous reaction to their turbulent historical experience after the breakup of the Mycenaean world, the Greeks felt
(5) that to live with changing, undefined, unmeasured, seemingly random impressions—to live, in short, with what was expressed by the Greek word *chaos*—was to live in a state of constant anxiety.

If the apparent mutability of the physical world
(10) and of the human condition was a source of pain and bewilderment to the Greeks, the discovery of a permanent pattern or an unchanging substratum by which apparently chaotic experience could be measured and explained was a source of
(15) satisfaction, even joy, which had something of a religious nature. For the recognition of order and measure in phenomena did more than simply satisfy their intellectual curiosity or gratify a desire for tidiness; it also served as the basis of a spiritual
(20) ideal. "Measure and commensurability are everywhere identified with beauty and excellence," was Plato's way of putting it in a dialogue in which

GO ON TO THE NEXT PAGE →

measure is identified as a primary characteristic of the ultimate good. Rational definability and

(25) spirituality were never mutually exclusive categories in Greek thought. If the quest for order and clarity was in essence the search for a kind of spiritual ideal, it was not an ideal to be perceived in rapturous emotional mysticism but rather one to

(30) be arrived at by patient analysis.

We see this process at work especially in Greek philosophy, which in various ways was aimed at alleviating the anxiety that is inherent in the more spontaneous expression of lyric poetry. The

(35) Milesian philosophers of the sixth century were interested above all in discovering a primary substance from which all other phenomena could be explained. Neat, clear, and sublimely undisturbed by the social world of humanity,

(40) which took shape and dissolved within the natural order of things, it was an austere ideal, an astringent antidote to the apparent senselessness of life. The person who contemplated it deeply could feel a part of a great system that was impersonal

(45) but predictable, and, like Lucretius, who revived the Milesian attitude in a later age, he or she could derive a peculiar peace from it. As time passed and Greek philosophy developed, the urge to find order in experience was shifted from physics to the realm

(50) of mathematical abstraction by the Pythagoreans, and to the world of human behavior by various thinkers of the later fifth century; and, finally, Plato and Aristotle attempted to weave all these foci of interest into comprehensive pictures of the

(55) relationship between human life and the world as a whole. But in all these epochs the basic quest—the search for a "kosmos"—remained the same.

58. The author's primary purpose is to

○ evaluate conflicting viewpoints.

○ challenge an accepted opinion.

○ question philosophical principles.

○ enumerate historical facts.

○ describe a cultural phenomenon.

59. The author indicates that the discovery of "an unchanging substratum" (line 12) served primarily to

○ alter the Greeks' perception of the mutability of existence.

○ help eradicate severe social problems.

○ alleviate painful memories of national suffering.

○ calm a restless intellectual curiosity.

○ foster a more mystical understanding of the physical world.

60. It can be inferred from the passage that rational thought and spiritual ideals were categories of experience that were

○ unimportant and unfamiliar to most ordinary Greeks.

○ advocated by the Milesians and rejected by the Pythagoreans.

○ neglected by most philosophers before Plato and Aristotle.

○ seen by the Greeks as essentially compatble.

○ embraced mainly by Greek poets.

GO ON TO THE NEXT PAGE ⟶

61. All of the following can be inferred about the Greeks' anxiety over the possibility of "chaos" EXCEPT that it

    ◯ had sources in their national consciousness.

    ◯ was reflected in specific aspects of their religion.

    ◯ was related to their sense of change in the physical world.

    ◯ led to a striving for order in their philosophy.

    ◯ was expressed in their lyric poetry.

62. The author implies that the Milesian philosophers of the sixth century sought relief from worldly anxiety by

    ◯ focusing narrowly on inherently human questions.

    ◯ establishing sharp distinctions between spiritual and rational understanding.

    ◯ focusing primarily on an impersonal natural order.

    ◯ attempting to integrate rational and mystical worldviews.

    ◯ withdrawing from the physical world into the realm of mathematical abstraction.

63. Which of the following best describes the organization of lines 16–26 of the passage ("For the recognition of order … in Greek thought.")?

    ◯ The author summarizes two viewpoints, cites historical evidence, and then declines to support either of the viewpoints.

    ◯ The author makes an observation, admits to evidence that weakens the viewpoint, and then revises his observation.

    ◯ The author specifies two distinct arguments, examines both in detail, then advances a third argument that reconciles the other two.

    ◯ The author clarifies a previous statement, offers an example, and then draws a further conclusion based on these ideas.

    ◯ The author states a thesis, mentions an opposed thesis and cites evidence supporting it, and then restates his original thesis.

GO ON TO THE NEXT PAGE ⟶

64. According to the passage, the Pythagoreans differed from the Milesians primarily in that the Pythagoreans

   ○ focused on mathematical abstractions rather than physical phenomena.

   ○ placed a renewed emphasis on understanding human behavior.

   ○ focused primarily on a rational means to understanding truth.

   ○ attempted to identify a fundamental physical unit of matter.

   ○ stressed concrete reality over formal theory.

65. In the context of the author's overall argument, which of the following best characterizes the Greeks' "search for a 'kosmos'" (line 57)?

   ○ A mystical quest for a strong national identity

   ○ Efforts to replace a sterile philosophical rationalism with revitalized religious values

   ○ Attempts to end conflict among key philosophical schools

   ○ A search for order and measure in an unpredictable world

   ○ A search for an alternative to a narrow preoccupation with beauty and excellence

Directions: Each of the following questions begins with a single word in capital letters. Five answer choices follow. Select the answer choice that has the most opposite meaning of the word in capital letters.

Since some of the questions require you to distinguish fine shades of meaning, be sure to consider all the choices before deciding which one is best.

66. ENMITY :

   ○ friendship

   ○ reverence

   ○ boredom

   ○ stylishness

   ○ awkwardness

67. DILATE :

   ○ enclose

   ○ shrink

   ○ hurry

   ○ inflate

   ○ erase

68. CHARLATAN :

   ○ genuine expert

   ○ powerful leader

   ○ false idol

   ○ unknown enemy

   ○ hardened villain

GO ON TO THE NEXT PAGE ⇒

69. PERIPHERAL :

    ○ civilized

    ○ partial

    ○ central

    ○ unharmed

    ○ stable

70. MERITORIOUS :

    ○ effulgent

    ○ stationary

    ○ uneven

    ○ narrow-minded

    ○ unpraiseworthy

71. DISCHARGE :

    ○ heal

    ○ advance

    ○ enlist

    ○ penalize

    ○ delay

72. MALEDICTION :

    ○ blessing

    ○ preparation

    ○ good omen

    ○ liberation

    ○ pursuit

73. MAWKISH :

    ○ unsentimental

    ○ sophisticated

    ○ graceful

    ○ tense

    ○ descriptive

74. TEMERITY :

    ○ blandness

    ○ caution

    ○ severity

    ○ strength

    ○ charm

75. JEJUNE :

    ○ morose

    ○ natural

    ○ mature

    ○ contrived

    ○ accurate

76. VITIATE :

    ○ deaden

    ○ trust

    ○ rectify

    ○ drain

    ○ amuse

IF YOU FINISH BEFORE TIME IS CALLED, YOU MAY CHECK YOUR WORK ON THIS SECTION ONLY. DO NOT TURN TO ANY OTHER SECTION IN THE TEST.

STOP

Section Two—Quantitative
Time—60 minutes 60 questions

Numbers

All numbers are real numbers.

Figures

The position of points, lines, angles, et cetera, may be assumed to be in the order shown; all lengths and angle measures may be assumed to be positive.

Lines shown as straight may be assumed to be straight.

Figures lie in the plane of the paper unless otherwise stated.

Figures that accompany questions are intended to provide useful information. However, unless a note states that a figure has been drawn to scale, you should solve the problems by using your knowledge of mathematics, and not by estimation or measurement.

Directions

Questions 1–15 each consist of two quantities, one in Column A and one in Column B. You are to compare the two quantities and choose

    ◯ if the quantity in Column A is greater;

    ◯ if the quantity in Column B is greater;

    ◯ if the two quantities are equal; or

    ◯ if the relationship cannot be determined from the information given.

Common Information

In a question, information concerning one or both of the quantities to be compared is centered above the two columns. A symbol that appears in both columns represents the same thing in Column A as it does in Column B.

GO ON TO THE NEXT PAGE ⇨

Column A	Column B

Example 1

3×4 $3 + 4$

Answer: A

Examples 2–4 refer to the figure below.

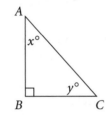

Example 2:

x y

Answer: D
(Because we cannot assume the angles are equal, even though they appear that way.)

Example 3:

$x + y$ 90

Answer: C
Because the sum of the angles is 180°.

Example 4:

x 90

Answer: B
Since $\triangle ABC$ is a right triangle, x is less than 90°.

Column A	Column B
1. 0.0260	0.0256

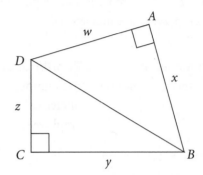

$\triangle ABD$ and $\triangle CDB$ are right triangles.

2. $w^2 + x^2$ $y^2 + z^2$

$$x + 4y = 6$$
$$x = 2y$$

3. x y

---

4. $\sqrt{4^2 + 5^2}$ $\sqrt{3^2 + 6^2}$

GO ON TO THE NEXT PAGE

Column A	Column B

In a certain accounting firm, there are exactly three types of employees: managerial, technical, and clerical. The firm has 120 employees and 25 percent of the employees are managerial.

5. The number of managerial employees | Two-thirds of the number of clerical employees

6. $\dfrac{12 \times 1}{12 + 1}$ | $\dfrac{12 + 1}{12 \times 1}$

7. $(a + 1)(b + 1)$ | $ab + 1$

In the two-digit number jk, the value of the digit j is twice the value of the digit k.

8. k | 6

Column A	Column B

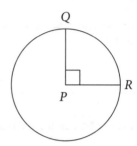

P is the center of the circle and the area of sector PQR is 4.

9. The area of circle P | 4π

Henry purchased x apples and Jack purchased 10 apples fewer than one-third of the number of apples Henry purchased.

10. The number of apples Jack purchased | $\dfrac{x - 30}{3}$

11. The volume of a rectangular solid with a length of 5 feet, a width of 4 feet, and a height of x feet | The volume of a rectangular solid with a length of 10 feet, a width of 8 feet, and a height of y feet

GO ON TO THE NEXT PAGE ⟶

Column A Column B

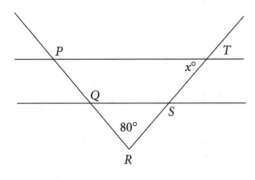

$PQ = ST$

$QR = RS$

12. x 50

_____

$2 \times 16 \times 64 = 2 \times 4n \times 256$

13. n 2

_____

A producer must select a duo, consisting of one lead actor and one supporting actor, from 6 candidates.

14. The number of   30
    possible duos the
    producer could select

_____

The perimeter of isosceles $\triangle ABC$ is 40 and the length of side BC is 12.

15. The length of side AB 14

Directions: Questions 16–30 each have five answer choices. For each of these questions, select the best of the answer choices given.

16. If $\dfrac{p-q}{p} = \dfrac{2}{7}$, then $\dfrac{q}{p} =$

○ $\dfrac{2}{5}$

○ $\dfrac{5}{7}$

○ 1

○ $\dfrac{7}{5}$

○ $\dfrac{7}{2}$

17. Jane must select three different items for each dinner she will serve. The items are to be chosen from among five different vegetarian and four different meat selections. If at least one of the selections must be vegetarian, how many different dinners could Jane create?

○ 30

○ 40

○ 60

○ 70

○ 80

GO ON TO THE NEXT PAGE

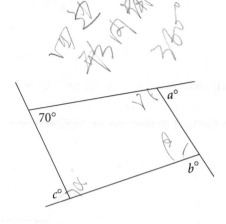

18. In the figure above, what is the value of
    $a + b + c$?

    ○ 110

    ⊕ 250

    ○ 290

    ○ 330

    ○ 430

19. John has four ties, 12 shirts, and three belts.
    If each day he wears exactly one tie, one
    shirt, and one belt, what is the maximum
    number of days he can go without repeating
    a particular combination?

    ○ 12

    ○ 21

    ○ 84

    ○ 108

    ○ 144

20. Which of the following is the greatest?

    ○ $\dfrac{0.00003}{0.0007}$

    ○ $\dfrac{0.0008}{0.0005}$

    ○ $\dfrac{0.007}{0.0008}$

    ○ $\dfrac{0.006}{0.005}$

    ○ $\dfrac{0.01}{0.008}$

Questions 21–25 refer to the charts below.

U.S. PHYSICIANS IN SELECTED SPECIALTIES
BY GENDER, 1986

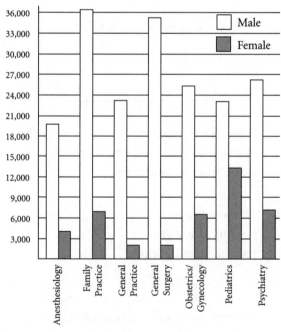

GO ON TO THE NEXT PAGE

GENERAL SURGERY PHYSICIANS BY AGE, 1986

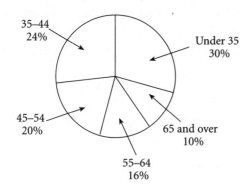

23. In 1986, approximately how many general surgery physicians were between the ages of 45 and 54, inclusive?

   ⬭ 5,440

   ⬭ 6,300

   ⬭ 7,350

   ⬭ 7,800

   ⬭ 8,900

21. Approximately what percent of all general practice physicians in 1986 were male?

   ⬭ 23%

   ⬭ 50%

   ⬭ 75%

   ⬭ 82%

   ⬭ 90%

22. Which of the following physician specialties had the lowest ratio of males to females in 1986?

   ⬭ Family practice

   ⬭ General surgery

   ⬭ Obstetrics/gynecology

   ⬭ Pediatrics

   ⬭ Psychiatry

24. If in 1986 all the family practice physicians represented 7.5 percent of all the physicians in the United States, approximately how many physicians were there total?

   ⬭ 300,000

   ⬭ 360,000

   ⬭ 430,000

   ⬭ 485,000

   ⬭ 570,000

25. If the number of female general surgeon physicians in the under-35 category represented 3.5 percent of all the general surgeon physicians, approximately how many male general surgeon physicians were under 35 years?

   ⬭ 9,200

   ⬭ 9,800

   ⬭ 10,750

   ⬭ 11,260

   ⬭ 11,980

GO ON TO THE NEXT PAGE

26. $|3| + |-4| + |3 - 4| =$

○ 14

○ 8

○ 7

○ 2

○ 0

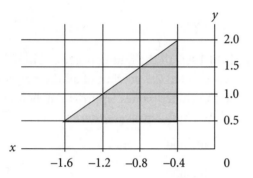

27. What is the area of the shaded region in the figure above?

○ 0.5

○ 0.7

○ 0.9

○ 2.7

○ 4.5

28. A computer can perform 30 identical tasks in six hours. At that rate, what is the minimum number of computers that should be assigned to complete 80 of the tasks within three hours?

○ 6

○ 7

○ 8

○ 12

○ 16

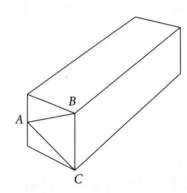

29. The volume of the cube in the figure above is 8. If point A is the midpoint of an edge of this cube, what is the perimeter of $\triangle ABC$?

○ 5

○ $2 + 2\sqrt{3}$

○ $2 + 2\sqrt{5}$

○ 7

○ $6 + \sqrt{5}$

GO ON TO THE NEXT PAGE

30. Which of the following is 850 percent greater than 8×10^3 ?

    ○ 8.5×10^3

    ○ 6.4×10^4

    ○ 6.8×10^4

    ○ 7.6×10^4

    ○ 1.6×10^5

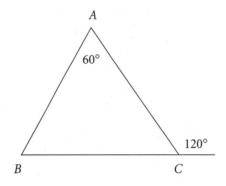

Column A	Column B

$$y = (x + 3)^2$$

31.

The value of y when $x = 1$	9

32.

The number of miles traveled by a car that traveled for four hours at an average speed of 40 miles per hour	The number of miles miles traveled by a train that traveled for two and a half hours at an average speed of 70 miles per hour

33.

The number of cookies in a bag that weighs 3 kilograms	The number of grapes in a bag that weighs 2 kilograms

34.

AB	BC

Column A	Column B

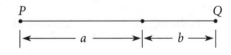

$$8a + 8b = 24$$

35.

The length of segment PQ	2

$$x < y$$

36.

$y - x$	$x - y$

GO ON TO THE NEXT PAGE ▷

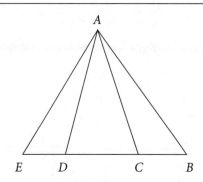

The area of triangular region *ABE* is 75.

37. The area of   The area of
     △*ABC*   △*ADE*

     <u>Column A</u>   <u>Column B</u>

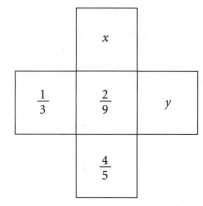

The sum of the numbers in the horizontal row of boxes equals the sum of the numbers in the vertical row of boxes.

38.   *x*   *y*

39. $\dfrac{\frac{1}{3} \times \frac{1}{4}}{\frac{2}{3} \times \frac{1}{2}}$ $\dfrac{\frac{2}{3} \times \frac{1}{2}}{\frac{1}{3} \times \frac{1}{4}}$

Eileen drives due north from town *A* to town *B* for a distance of 60 miles, then drives due east from town *B* to town *C* for a distance of 80 miles.

40.   The distance from   120
      town *A* to town *C*
      in miles

41. $(\sqrt{7} - 2)(\sqrt{7} + 2)$ $(2 - \sqrt{7})(-\sqrt{7} - 2)$

      <u>Column A</u>   <u>Column B</u>

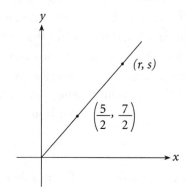

42.   *r*   *s*

x is an integer greater than 0.

43. $1 - \left(\dfrac{1}{4}\right)^{x}$ 0.95

GO ON TO THE NEXT PAGE

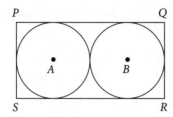

The two circles with centers A and B have the same radius.

44.   The sum of the   The perimeter of
       circumferences of   rectangle $PQRS$
       the two circles

_____

45. $3^{17} + 3^{18} + 3^{19}$ 3^{20}

Directions: Questions 46–60 each have five answer choices. For each of these questions, select the best of the answer choices given.

46. If $4 + y = 14 - 4y$, then $y =$

   ◯ -4

   ◯ 0

   ◯ $\dfrac{5}{8}$

   ◯ $\dfrac{4}{5}$

   ◯ 2

47. $\dfrac{4}{5} + \dfrac{5}{4} =$

   ◯ 1

   ◯ $\dfrac{9}{8}$

   ◯ $\dfrac{6}{5}$

   ◯ $\dfrac{41}{20}$

   ◯ $\dfrac{23}{10}$

48. If $3^m = 81$, then $m^3 =$

   ◯ 9

   ◯ 16

   ◯ 27

   ◯ 54

   ◯ 64

GO ON TO THE NEXT PAGE

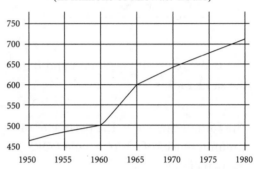

49. In the figure above, there are three square gardening areas. The area of square *A* is 81 square meters and the area of square *B* is 49 square meters. What is the area, in square meters, of square *C* ?

- ◯ 2
- ◯ 4
- ◯ 9
- ◯ 27
- ◯ 32

50. In a certain history class, all except 23 students scored under 85 on a test. If 18 students scored over 85 on this test, how many students are there in this history class?

- ◯ 33
- ◯ 37
- ◯ 39
- ◯ 41
- ◯ It cannot be determined from the information given.

Questions 51–55 refer to the following graphs.

ENERGY USE BY YEAR, COUNTRY *Y*, 1950–1980
(in millions of kilowatt-hours)

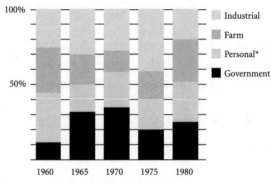

ENERGY USE BY TYPE, COUNTRY *Y*

*Total personal use = population × per-capita personal use

51. In which of the following years was the energy use in country *Y* closest to 650 million kilowatt-hours?

- ◯ 1960
- ◯ 1965
- ◯ 1970
- ◯ 1975
- ◯ 1980

GO ON TO THE NEXT PAGE

52. In 1965, how many of the categories shown had energy use greater than 150 million kilowatt-hours?

○ none

○ one

○ two

○ three

○ four

53. In which of the following years was industrial use of energy greatest in country *Y* ?

○ 1960

○ 1965

○ 1970

○ 1975

○ 1980

54. If the population of country *Y* increased by 20 percent from 1960 to 1965, approximately what was the percent decrease in the per-capita personal use of energy between those two years?

○ 0%

○ 17%

○ 25%

○ 40%

○ It cannot be determined from the information given.

55. Which of the following can be inferred from the graphs?

   I. Farm use of energy increased between 1960 and 1980.
  II. In 1980, industrial use of energy was greater than industrial use of energy in 1965.
 III. More people were employed by the government of country *Y* in 1980 than in 1960.

○ I only

○ II only

○ I and II only

○ II and III only

○ I, II, and III

56. If the average of two numbers is 3*y* and one of the numbers is *y* – *z*, what is the other number, in terms of *y* and *z* ?

○ *y* + *z*

○ 3*y* + *z*

○ 4*y* – *z*

○ 5*y* – *z*

○ 5*y* + *z*

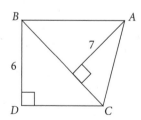

GO ON TO THE NEXT PAGE

57. In the figure above, the area of $\triangle ABC$ is 35. What is the length of DC?

- ○ 6
- ○ 8
- ○ $6\sqrt{2}$
- ○ 10
- ○ $6\sqrt{3}$

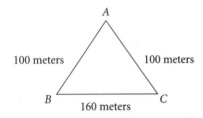

58. In the figure above is a triangular field. What is the minimum distance, in meters, that a person would have to walk to go from point A to a point on side BC?

- ○ 60
- ○ 80
- ○ 100
- ○ 140
- ○ 180

59. If the ratio of $2a$ to b is 8 times the ratio of b to a, then $\dfrac{b}{a}$ could be

- ○ 4.
- ○ 2.
- ○ 1.
- ○ $\dfrac{1}{2}$.
- ○ $\dfrac{1}{4}$.

60. A certain dentist earns n dollars for each filling she puts in, plus x dollars for every 15 minutes she works. If in a certain week she works 14 hours and puts in 21 fillings, how much does she earn for the week, in dollars?

- ○ $\dfrac{7}{2}x + 21n$
- ○ $7x + 14n$
- ○ $14x + 21n$
- ○ $56x + 21n$
- ○ $56x + \dfrac{21}{4}n$

IF YOU FINISH BEFORE TIME IS CALLED, YOU MAY CHECK YOUR WORK ON THIS SECTION ONLY. DO NOT TURN TO ANY OTHER SECTION IN THE TEST.

STOP

Section Three—Analytical Writing
Time—75 minutes 2 questions

Essay 1—Issue

Directions: You will have 45 minutes to plan and write an essay that communicates your perspective on a given topic. Choose one of the two topics provided. No other topics are admissible for this essay.

The topic is a short quotation that expresses an issue of general interest. Write an essay that agrees with, refutes, or qualifies the quotation, and support your opinion with relevant information drawn from your academic studies, reading, observation, or other experiences.

Feel free to consider the issue for a few minutes before you begin writing. Be certain that your ideas are fully developed and organized logically and make sure you have enough time left to review and revise what you've written.

1. "Scientific theories, which most people consider 'fact,' almost invariably prove to be inaccurate. Thus, one should look upon any information described as 'factual' with skepticism since it may well be proven false in the future."

2. "In bygone days, many people received whatever musical education they acquired by singing around the parlor piano. In the age of recorded music and the Internet, people can learn as much by listening as they can by singing."

Essay 2—Argument

Directions: You will have 30 minutes to explain how logically persuasive you find this argument. In discussing your viewpoint, analyze the argument's line of reasoning and its use of evidence. Also explain what, if anything, would make the argument more valid and convincing or help you to better evaluate its conclusion.

The following appeared in a memo written by a member of the booster club at Tusk University:

"Tusk University should build a new recreational facility, both to attract new students and to better serve the needs of our current student body. Tusk projects that enrollment will double over the next ten years, based on current trends. The new student body is expected to reflect a much higher percentage of commuter students than we currently enroll. This will make the existing facilities inadequate. Moreover, the cost of health and recreation club membership in our community has increased rapidly in recent years. Thus, students will find it much more advantageous to make use of the facilities on campus. Finally, an attractive new recreation center would make prospective students, especially athletically gifted ones, more likely to enroll at Tusk."

END OF TEST.

Part Four

PRACTICE TEST ANSWERS AND EXPLANATIONS

ANSWER KEY

SECTION ONE—**VERBAL**

1. A	20. C	39. E	58. E
2. E	21. E	40. B	59. A
3. E	22. B	41. D	60. D
4. A	23. C	42. D	61. B
5. D	24. C	43. A	62. C
6. E	25. A	44. D	63. D
7. D	26. C	45. C	64. A
8. A	27. B	46. E	65. D
9. B	28. C	47. D	66. A
10. B	29. B	48. D	67. B
11. D	30. C	49. C	68. A
12. E	31. A	50. C	69. C
13. A	32. D	51. B	70. E
14. A	33. D	52. D	71. C
15. E	34. C	53. E	72. A
16. B	35. D	54. C	73. A
17. D	36. B	55. E	74. B
18. B	37. C	56. C	75. C
19. E	38. B	57. C	76. C

SECTION TWO—**QUANTITATIVE**

1. A	21. E	41. C
2. C	22. D	42. B
3. A	23. C	43. D
4. B	24. E	44. A
5. D	25. B	45. B
6. B	26. B	46. E
7. D	27. C	47. D
8. B	28. A	48. E
9. A	29. C	49. B
10. C	30. D	50. E
11. D	31. A	51. C
12. C	32. B	52. C
13. B	33. D	53. D
14. C	34. C	54. D
15. D	35. A	55. A
16. B	36. A	56. E
17. E	37. D	57. B
18. B	38. B	58. A
19. E	39. B	59. D
20. C	40. B	60. D

CALCULATE YOUR SCORE

Step 1. Using the Answer Key to check your answers, award yourself one point for each correct answer in the Verbal and Quantitative sections. This is your raw score for each section.

Verbal   Total Correct ☐ (raw score)

Quantitative   Total Correct ☐ (raw score)

Step 2. Find your raw score on the following tables and read across to find your scaled score and your percentile.

Step 3. Use the holistic scoring guide on page 372 to determine your score on the essays. (Also see the sample "6" essays at the end of this section as a basis for comparison.)

VERBAL

Raw Score	Scaled Score	Percentile Rank	Raw Score	Scaled Score	Percentile Rank
0	200	1	39	420	41
1	200	1	40	420	41
2	200	1	41	430	44
3	200	1	42	440	48
4	200	1	43	450	51
5	200	1	44	460	54
6	200	1	45	470	56
7	200	1	46	470	59
8	200	1	47	480	61
9	200	1	48	490	67
10	200	1	49	510	69
11	200	1	50	520	72
12	200	1	51	530	74
13	220	1	52	530	76
14	230	1	53	540	78
15	240	1	54	550	80
16	250	1	55	560	82
17	260	1	56	570	84
18	270	2	57	580	85
19	270	3	58	590	87
20	280	4	59	590	89
21	290	5	60	600	90
22	300	6	61	610	92
23	310	7	62	620	93
24	320	9	63	630	94
25	320	10	64	640	95
26	330	12	65	650	95
27	330	14	66	660	96
28	340	16	67	670	97
29	350	16	68	680	98
30	360	20	69	690	98
31	360	22	70	700	99
32	360	24	71	710	99
33	370	24	72	720	99
34	380	26	73	740	99
35	390	30	74	760	99
36	400	33	75	780	99
37	410	36	76	800	99
38	420	38			

QUANTITATIVE

Raw Score	Scaled Score	Percentile Rank	Raw Score	Scaled Score	Percentile Rank
0	200	1	31	430	24
1	200	1	32	440	26
2	200	1	33	460	28
3	200	1	34	470	32
4	200	1	35	480	35
5	200	1	36	490	37
6	200	1	37	500	40
7	200	1	38	510	42
8	200	1	39	520	45
9	200	1	40	530	48
10	210	1	41	540	49
11	220	1	42	540	51
12	240	1	43	560	57
13	260	1	44	570	59
14	270	1	45	580	61
15	280	2	46	600	66
16	290	2	47	610	68
17	300	3	48	630	72
18	310	4	49	640	74
19	310	5	50	660	78
20	320	5	51	670	80
21	330	6	52	690	84
22	340	7	53	690	86
23	360	9	54	700	89
24	370	10	55	720	92
25	380	13	56	730	94
26	390	14	57	750	97
27	400	16	58	770	97
28	410	18	59	780	97
29	420	20	60	800	97
30	420	22			

ANALYTICAL WRITING

6 and 5.5:   "Outstanding" Essay

- Insightfully presents and convincingly supports an opinion on the issue or a critique of the argument
- Communicates ideas clearly and is generally well organized; connections are logical
- Demonstrates superior control of language: grammar, stylistic variety, and accepted conventions of writing; minor flaws may occur

5 and 4.5:   "Strong" Essay

- Presents well-chosen examples and strongly supports an opinion on the issue or a critique of the argument
- Communicates ideas clearly and is generally well organized; connections are logical
- Demonstrates solid control of language: grammar, stylistic variety, and accepted conventions of writing; minor flaws may occur

4 and 3.5:   "Adequate" Essay

- Presents and adequately supports an opinion on the issue or a critique of the argument
- Communicates ideas fairly clearly and is adequately organized; logical connections are satisfactory
- Demonstrates satisfactory control of language: grammar, stylistic variety, and accepted conventions of writing; some flaws may occur

3 and 2.5:   "Limited" Essay

- Succeeds only partially in presenting and supporting an opinion on the issue or a critique of the argument
- Communicates ideas unclearly and is poorly organized
- Demonstrates less than satisfactory control of language: contains significant mistakes in grammar, usage, and sentence structure

2 and 1.5: "Weak" Essay

- Shows little success in presenting and supporting an opinion on the issue or a critique of the argument
- Struggles to communicate ideas; essay shows a lack of clarity and organization
- Meaning is impeded by many serious mistakes in grammar, usage, and sentence structure

1 and 0.5: "Fundamentally Deficient" Essay

- Fails to present a coherent opinion and/or evidence on the issue or a critique of the argument
- Fails to communicate ideas; essay is seriously unclear and disorganized
- Lacks meaning due to widespread and severe mistakes in grammar, usage, and sentence structure

0: "Unscorable" Essay

- Completely ignores topic
- Attempts to copy the assignments
- Is written in a foreign language or contains undechipherable text

ANSWERS AND EXPLANATIONS

SECTION ONE—VERBAL

1. A

We're told that the fundamental (blank) between cats and dogs is a myth, that the species actually coexist quite (blank). We need a contrast, and we find it in (A)—*antipathy* means aversion or dislike, and *amiably* means agreeably.

In (B), if the members of the species coexisted "uneasily," their "disharmony" wouldn't be a myth. In (C), both *compatibility* and *together* imply that dogs and cats are good friends. In (D), it doesn't make sense to say that the "relationship" between dogs and cats is a myth. In (E), no one could claim that there's no "difference" between dogs and cats.

2. E

The clue is the signal *rather than*: we need a contrast between what the speaker intended and what he achieved. The word *monotonous* clues you into boredom, and *bore* in (E), followed by *convince* makes the contrast we need. In (A), *enlighten* and *inform* are similar. *Interest* and *persuade*, (B), don't show contrast. In (C), *provoke* and *influence* don't express a contrast. *Allay* in (D) means to relieve, which is similar to *pacify*, which means to calm or to make peace. No contrast here, and again, it's (E) for this question.

3. E

The blank is part of a cause-and-effect structure as the keyword *that* indicates. Because government restrictions are so (blank), businesses can operate with nearly complete impunity. There's an absence of restrictions, so we need a word that cancels out restrictions. Would a "traditional" restriction, (A), be canceled out? No. (B), *judicious*, means wise or having sound judgment, but a wise restriction would probably be effective. In (C), *ambiguous* means unclear, but though ambiguity might interfere with the effectiveness of restrictions, it doesn't cancel them out. Choice (D), *exacting*, means very strict, which is the opposite of what we want. Choice (E), *lax*, means loose, careless, or sloppy. This describes restrictions that aren't very strict, and it's correct for this question.

4. A

The first blank describes a book—the recent Oxford edition of the works of Shakespeare is (blank). The word *because* tells us that what follows is an explanation of why this book is whatever it is. The "not only but also" structure tells us that there are *two* reasons why: it departs from the readings of other editions, and it challenges basic (blanks) of textual criticism. In (A), we could say that challenging conventions could make a book "controversial." Conventions are accepted practices, so challenging conventions would make a book controversial. What else have we got? Choice (B) gives us the book is typical because it challenges innovations. *Typical* doesn't fit in with *departs from other editions*. How about (C)? Challenging norms, which are rules or patterns, wouldn't make something "inadequate." Choice (D)—a book that is different might be called curious, but could you call a book curious for challenging projects? Finally, (E) says the book is pretentious because it challenges explanations—no good. So the best answer is (A).

5. D

We learn that an early form of writing, Linear B, was (blank) in 1952. The keyword *but* tells us that Linear A, an older form, met with a contrasting fate, so we'll look for a pair of contrasting words. The words *no one has yet succeeded in* precede the second blank, so instead of a word that is contrasted with the first blank, we need a word that means about the same thing. That leads us to pick **(D)**—the words *deciphered* and *interpretation* are similar since both imply understanding.

The word *superseded* in **(A)** means replaced by something more up to date—not giving an explanation of something. **(B)**—in the context of ancient languages, a *transcription* would probably be a decoded version of something. That would be the opposite of *encoding* something. Choice **(C)**'s *obliterated* and *analysis* imply a contrast—wiping something out is different from figuring it out. In **(E)** *discovered* and *obfuscation* are more at odds than they are alike. *Obfuscation* means confusion, while a discovery usually sheds light on a situation.

6. E

The clue here is the structure "quite normal and even (blank)"—the missing word has a more positive meaning than the word *normal*. Then we get, "I was therefore surprised," which tips us off to look for contrast. *Commendable* and *complimentary* in **(A)** are both positive. In **(B)**, *odious* means hateful, so *odious* and *insulting* are both negative. *Conciliatory* in **(C)** means placating or reconciling, which fits in with *apologetic*. *Commonplace* and *typical* in **(D)** mean the same thing. Only correct choice **(E)** is left—*laudable* means praiseworthy while *derogatory* means belittling or detracting.

7. D

Whatever we're doing to the burden of medical costs is causing the removal of the second blank, signaled by *thereby*. In **(A)**, it doesn't make sense to say that to *augment* or add to the burden would remove a problem—it could make the problem worse. In **(B)**, a *perquisite* is a reward over and above one's salary. But would eliminating a burden remove a perquisite? In **(C)**, to *ameliorate* means to improve, but

you can't talk about removing a major study of medical care. **(D)** is perfect. To *assuage* means to make less severe and an *impediment* is an obstacle. Assuaging the burden would remove an impediment to medical care, so **(D)**'s correct. As for **(E)**, to *clarify* means to explain or make clear, and explaining the burden of medical costs wouldn't remove an explanation.

8. A

A *novel* is a type of *book*. That's an easy bridge. In **(A)**, is an *epic* a type of *poem*? Yes, an epic is a long narrative poem, so **(A)** is right. In **(B)**, a *house* isn't a type of *library*. Choice **(C)** is tempting—*tales* and *fables* are related—but a fable is a kind of tale, not vice versa, so it's not parallel. In **(D)**, a *number* is not a type of *page*, and in **(E)**, a *play* isn't a type of *theater*.

9. B

Ravenous means extremely *hungry*—the second word is an extreme version of the first word. In **(A)**, *desirous* means desiring or wanting something—it's not an extreme form of *thirsty*. Choice **(B)** is perfect—*titanic* is an amplification of *large*. *Titanic* means gigantic, so **(B)** is the answer.

Eminent and *famous* in **(C)** mean the same thing. **(D)**'s *disoriented* and *dizzy* are close in meaning. To be disoriented means to have lost your bearings, and when you're dizzy, you feel as if you're going to fall down. Choice **(E)**'s *obese* and *gluttonous* could be related, but don't have to be. *Gluttonous* comes from *gluttony*—it means excessive eating or drinking. Gluttony doesn't have to result in obesity and it's not an extreme form of it.

10. B

A *bouquet* is an arrangement of *flowers*, so the first word will be an arrangement of the second word. In **(A)**, a *humidor* is a container for *tobacco*—a container for tobacco is not the same as a formal arrangement of it. The next choice, (**B**), is more like it. A *mosaic* is made of *tiles,* just as a bouquet is made up of flowers. That's a good match. In (**C**), a *tapestry* is not made of *color*, it's made of threads woven to make a design. You can't argue that a tapestry is an arrangement of colors. Choice (**D**) also has problems. A *pile* of *blocks* could be an arrangement. But a bouquet isn't just a group of flowers—it's a formal arrangement. In the same way, a mosaic is an orderly arrangement of tiles. A pile isn't a formal arrangement. What about *sacristy* and *vestment* in (**E**)? A sacristy is a room in a church where priests' clothes or vestments are kept, so vestments are stored in a sacristy. The correct answer is (**B**).

11. D

Quixotic means impractical, after the hero of *Don Quixote*. A *realist* is a person who is especially realistic. *Realistic* is the opposite of *quixotic,* so a realist is never quixotic. In (**A**), *pedantic* people show off their learning. Many scholars are pedantic, so this won't work. In (**B**), a *fool* is foolish—a synonym for *idiotic*. The same relationship holds true for (**C**)—an *idler* is a *lethargic* person. Choice (**D**) looks good—a *tormentor* is vicious or cruel. The opposite sort of person would be kinder and more *sympathetic*—a tormentor is never sympathetic. In choice (**E**), *dyspeptic* means suffering from indigestion. A *diner* is someone who eats—some diners get dyspeptic, some don't, so (**D**)'s correct.

12. E

A *shard* is a broken fragment of *glass* or crockery. Glass, when it shatters, creates shards, so a shard is a piece of broken glass. Choice (**E**) shows the same analogy—a *splinter* is a piece of broken *wood*. As for the wrong choices, in (**A**), a *grain* is the basic unit that *sand* comes in, but you can't

talk about breaking sand. Choice (**B**)'s *morsel* means a bit of food, but a *meal* doesn't shatter into morsels. In (**C**), a *rope* is composed of *strands,* and in (**D**), a *quilt* is made from *scraps*. The correct answer is (**E**).

13. A

The word *filter* is used as a verb. When you use a filter, an *impurity* is removed, so you *filter* to remove an *impurity*. The word *expurgate* in (**A**) means to censor, to remove *obscenities*—you *expurgate* to remove an *obscenity*. To *whitewash*, (**B**), is to misrepresent a bad thing to make it look better. An *infraction* isn't removed by *whitewashing* it, it's only covered up, so (**B**) isn't parallel. In (**C**), *perjury* is the crime of lying under oath. To *testify* doesn't mean to remove a false statement. In (**D**), *penance* is something you do to atone for a sin, but you don't *perform* to remove *penance*. And in (**E**), you don't *vacuum* to remove a *carpet*. So (**A**) is correct.

14. A

Paraphrase means restatement of a text using different words. *Verbatim* means word for word or exact. A paraphrase is not verbatim—the words are near opposites. The only choices opposite in meaning are *approximation* and *precise*, in (**A**). An approximation is an estimate, while something that's precise is exact, so an approximation is not precise. A description might or might not be vivid in (**B**). In (**C**), *apt* means appropriate, so a quotation could be apt. There's no relationship in (**D**), *interpretation* and *valid,* or in (**E**), *significance* and *uncertain*. Choice (**A**) is correct.

15. E

Even if you didn't know what *oncology* means, you might have guessed the study of something because of the *ology* ending, and judging from the other word it's probably the study of tumors. The choices look like sciences too. Choice (**A**)'s pairing of *chronology* and *time* looks okay, but not dead on. There's a science called chronology, the science of arranging time into periods. Chronology is not exactly the study of time—it's a science involved with mapping events in time. Likewise, (**B**) is almost there. The *theo* in *theology* comes from the Greek word for god, and *theology* means the study of gods or religious beliefs. *Tenet,* on the other hand, means a particular belief or principle. It's too narrow to say theology is the study of tenets. We can eliminate (**C**) because *aural* is not the study of sound—that would be closer to *acoustics.* In (**D**), *philology* is a field that includes the study of literary history, language history, and systems of writing, not the study of religion. *Taxonomy*, (**E**), is the study of *classification*, the correct answer. *Taxonomy* is also used to refer specifically to the classification of organisms.

16. B

Intransigent means unyielding—the opposite of *flexible.* Our bridge is "a person who is intransigent is lacking in flexibility." The only pair that looks good is (**B**), *disinterested* and *partisanship.* One who's disinterested is unbiased—he doesn't have an interest in either side of a dispute. *Partisan* means partial to a particular party or cause. That's the opposite of disinterested. So partisanship, the quality of being biased, is lacking in a person who could be described as disinterested.

In (**A**), *transient* means transitory, so you wouldn't say that someone transient lacks *mobility.* In (**C**), *dissimilar* means not similar, along the same lines as *variation.* You can't say that something progressive lacks transition, so (**D**) is no good. The word *ineluctable* in (**E**) means inescapable, while *modality* is a longer way of saying mode.

Reading Passage: Questions 17–23

The longer of the two Reading Comp passages appears first. The author's main concern, the aim of science to derive a theory which describes particles and their forces as simply as possible, becomes apparent early in the first paragraph. Simplicity is so important that the author sets it up as a criterion for judging the specific theory of nature. Then the author outlines a recently developed theory that he considers to be a remarkable achievement for its frugality and level of detail. He then asserts that an even simpler theory is conceivable and goes on to mention one that promises at least a partial unification of elementary particles and forces. The last half of the second paragraph and the final paragraph describe this theory in greater detail.

17. D

We need either a choice that describes the similarity between the theories, or one that falsifies information about them. Choice (**D**) should raise your suspicions. The author acknowledged at the end of the first paragraph that the first theory could account for the entire observed hierarchy of material structure. Choice (**D**) is right, but let's look at the others.

Choice (**A**) is a valid difference between the two theories—the second is presented as a simpler alternative to the first. Choice (**B**) is also a real difference. The first theory encompass gravitation and the second unifies three of the four forces, which makes it a better theory, but it doesn't account for gravitation. The first theory includes leptons and quarks, while the second combines these two classes into just one, so (**C**) is valid. In a similar way, the second theory unifies three of the four forces outlined in the first theory, so (**E**) is valid. Again, it's (**D**).

18. B

This question asks for the primary purpose, and we know that the author is concerned with theories that describe, simply and precisely, particles and their forces. The author's primary purpose is to describe attempts to develop a simplified theory of nature. Skimming through the choices, (B) looks good. Choice (E) doesn't fit at all. You might say the author summarizes the theories describing matter, but he doesn't summarize all that is known about matter itself. As for (A), the author doesn't cite a misconception in either of the theories he describes. At most, he mentions ways in which the first could be simplified but this doesn't imply that there's a misconception. The author does refer to the second theory as a leading candidate for achieving unification, but predicting its success, (C), is far from his primary purpose. As for (D), although it's implied that scientists in general do prefer simpler theories, their reasons for this preference are never discussed. Again, it's (B) for Question 18.

19. E

This question is a scattered detail question concerning quarks. In the first paragraph we're told that quarks are constituents of the proton and the neutron. It's reasonable, then, to say that quarks are the elementary building blocks of protons and neutrons, Statement I. Since Statement I is correct, we can eliminate choices which exclude it, (B) and (D). The remaining choices are either I only, I and II only, or I, II, and III. You could skip II and go to III. If you're sure III is right, you can assume that II is also and pick (E). It turns out that III can be easily checked at the end of paragraph three, where the author states that a new theory incorporates the leptons and quarks into a single family or class, so Statement III is correct. For a complete list, let's look at Statement II. In the very first

sentence the author tells us that elementary particles don't have an internal structure and since quarks are elementary particles, Statement II is indeed correct, and (E) is our answer.

20. C

It should be clear that the author has some very definite criteria for judging the usefulness or worth of various theories of nature. As for Statement I, *simplicity* should leap off the page at you—it's what this passage is all about. We can eliminate (B) and (E). The author also takes the theory's completeness into consideration. He commends the first theory he describes because it accounts for the entire observed hierarchy of material structure and therefore Statement II is correct. We know that (C) must be correct because there is no I, II, and III choice. But let's look at III anyway. Does the author ever mention proving either of those two theories he describes? Proof is of no concern to him—there's no mention in the passage of any experiments, or of wanting to find experimental proof. So III is out and (C) it is.

21. E

We've mentioned that the second theory doesn't include gravitation in its attempt to unify the four basic forces. We need the author's opinion about this omission. The author introduces the theory in the second paragraph, describing it as an ambitious theory that promises at least a partial unification of elementary particles and forces. The failure to include gravitation and achieve complete unification doesn't dampen the author's enthusiasm and he seems to suggest that gravitation's omission can't be helped, at least at this stage. So, although the omission is a limitation—it prevents total unification—it is also unavoidable. It looks like (E) does the trick.

You could see the limitation as a defect, (A), but the author never gives the impression that the omission of gravitation disqualifies the theory. As for **(B)**, *deviation* is a funny word—deviation from what? More important, we've already seen that the author doesn't consider the omission to be unjustified. For the same reason, **(C)** can be eliminated. If the omission of gravitation can't be avoided, then it certainly isn't a needless oversimplification. Finally **(D)** is out because there's no way that gravitation's omission could be an oversight. A scientist just forgot about one of the four basic forces when developing a theory of nature? No, the idea is that, for now at least, gravitation just can't be fit in, and **(E)** is correct.

22. B

The passage begins with the author's discussion of the simplicity of elementary particles and the theories which describe them. In the third sentence, the author sets forth simplicity as a standard for judging theories of nature. In the rest of the passage, the author measures two specific theories against this standard. Choice **(B)** summarizes this setup nicely and it's our answer. Choice **(A)** is way off base. Although the author might be said to enumerate distinctions between how the two theories treat elementary particles, he doesn't enumerate distinctions among the particles. Choice **(C)** is easy to eliminate—the author describes only two methods of grouping particles and forces—not three. As for **(D)**, the author doesn't criticize the first theory he describes or call it inaccurate—he commends it. Finally, **(E)** goes overboard. As we mentioned in our discussion of Statement III in Question 20, the author is not interested in scientific verification. Nothing is ever mentioned about proving or verifying either of the theories he describes. Again, **(B)** is correct.

23. C

This question shouldn't be difficult. It asks us to put ourselves in the author's shoes and figure out what sort of theory he would find superior to present theories. We already know—a simpler theory. The author's criteria for judging a theory are its simplicity and its ability to account for the largest possible number of known phenomena. Which choice represents a theory with one or both of these characteristics? Choice **(A)** misrepresents the two theories described in the passage. The author says that the first theory could account for the entire observed hierarchy of material structure. The second does also, even though gravitation must be thrown in as a separate force. A theory that could account for a larger number of structures isn't what's needed. As for **(B)**, why would the author approve of a theory that reduces the four basic forces to two which are incompatible? Choice **(C)** is on the right track. The author would prefer a theory that accounts for all matter with the fewest particles and forces and this is offered by **(C)**, the correct answer. Choice **(D)** is out because it wouldn't represent an improvement on currently existing theories. They account for gravitation, although they haven't yet unified it with the other three forces. Finally, **(E)** represents a step backwards. The current theories hypothesize that both protons and neutrons are formed by combinations of elementary particles. Again, it's **(C)**.

Reading Passage: Questions 24–27

The second passage is short but dense, and the author doesn't arrive at her main point until the last sentence. We see that the author sets herself in opposition to presentist historians, people who believe that white abolitionists and suffragists comprise the abiding principles of equality and the equal right of all to life, liberty, and the pursuit of happiness.

Their evidence is presented in the first three sentences. First, a majority of both groups tried to assure people that the changes they advocated weren't revolutionary and served to support rather than to undermine the status quo. A certain group of abolitionists disclaimed miscegenationist intentions—they were careful to assert that their interest in obtaining freedom for blacks didn't mean they were advocating mixing of races. And finally, suffragists saw no conflict between racism or nativism and their movement's objectives. Presentist historians apparently think that, by denying any revolutionary intentions and miscegenationist intentions, and by justifying nativism and racism, both groups were undermining their own principles. And, because their objectives—the abolition of slavery and voting rights for all—go hand in hand with our present conception of equality, presentist historians think that both groups undermine the principle of equality at the same time. The author uses the same evidence to argue that the actions of both groups served not to show how far these groups deviated from a fixed principle of equality, but to show what the principle meant in their own generations. The author thinks that the principle of equality is not unchanging, but means different things for different generations and that presentist historians err when they judge these movements by our conception of equality.

24. C

We need the author's main point, which we just formulated—the actions of abolitionists and suffragists demonstrate the meaning that equality had in their time. (C) expresses this, and it's the correct answer. Choice (A) is wrong because it's the presentist historians who believe that the actions of the abolitionists and suffragists compromised their principles. Choice (B) has nothing to do with the author's discussion. A comparison of beliefs never occurs. As for (D), the author charges presentist historians with misinterpreting abolitionist and suffragist

ideology, not with willfully misrepresenting it. Finally, (E) constitutes a criticism the author makes about presentist historians—that they impose their own value systems on the past, rather than interpreting actions in the appropriate historical context. Again, it's (C) for this question.

25. A

We can infer something about the author's concept of the principle of equality—it's clear that the author thinks the principle of equality is not abiding. Rather, she thinks, it encompasses different things for people at different times. We can give the nod to Statement I, which eliminates (B), (C), and (E). Since the only choices left include Statement I only or Statements I and II only, Statement III can be eliminated. Statement II—does the author suggest that the suffragists applied the principle of equality more consistently than abolitionists? No, if anything, she implies that they applied it equally consistently. We're left with (A) as our answer. We know Statement III can't be true—presentist historians say that abolitionists and suffragists compromised the principle of equality, not the author, who thinks their actions conform to their generation's conception of equality.

26. C

This question deals with the logical structure of the author's argument, how she argues her case against the presentist historians. She uses the same evidence to support her views that they do, cites the actions of the suffragists and abolitionists, states that the presentist historians knew of these actions, then presents her own interpretation of these same actions. She's applying a different interpretation to the same set of facts, and (C) is our answer. The author doesn't cite any new evidence, so both (A) and (B) can be ruled out. As for (D), the author refutes not the accuracy of the historians' data but the accuracy of their interpretation. Finally, the author doesn't claim that the historians' argument is flawed by a logical contradiction, **(E)**. She claims instead that they erred by assuming that equality is an abiding value and by measuring the actions of past groups against this concept of equality. Again, it's **(C)** for this question.

27. B

We need to know what the author suggests about the abolitionist movement. Well, in her references to this movement, the author mentions the non-Garrisonian abolitionists. If there were non-Garrisonian abolitionists, it seems reasonable to assume that Garrisonian abolitionists existed. Also, the author refers to a majority of white abolitionists who made certain denials. This implies that there was a minority of abolitionists who didn't make such denials and also that there were black abolitionists. In other words, the abolitionist movement was subdivided into different groups and these groups didn't always share identical ideologies. This corresponds closely to **(B)**, the correct answer. As for **(A)**, the passage does state that some abolitionists denied that they had revolutionary or miscegenationist intentions, but these denials don't seem to be an attempt to disguise their real intentions. Choice **(C)** is wrong because the author thinks the abolitionists did live by their principles. As for **(D)**, presentist historians might claim that abolitionists undermined their objectives by making certain disclaimers to the public. But even they wouldn't say that these disclaimers were the result of abolitionists misunderstanding their objectives. Finally, the passage makes no mention of radical factions within the abolitionist movement and the effects of abolitionists' actions on their movement's progress is never discussed, so **(E)** is out. Again, **(B)** is correct.

28. C

Our first word is *undermine,* which means to weaken or cause to collapse, especially by secret means. The opposite would be something like *build up* or make *stronger.* The best choice here is **(C)**, *bolster,* meaning to support. The only other tempting choice is **(A)**, *appreciate,* but a better opposite for appreciate would be *resent.*

29. B

Obsequious means servile or submissive. The opposite of *obsequious* would be something like *snooty* or *arrogant. Haughty,* **(B)**, fits perfectly. A haughty person is overly arrogant while an obsequious person is overly eager to please. None of the other choices comes close.

30. C

The word *blanch* may be familiar to you if you cook. Foods like broccoli are blanched by plunging them in boiling water so they lose color. In the same way, a person might blanch from fear, shock, or dismay. Since *blanch* means to whiten or turn pale, the opposite would be to redden or blush. Choice **(C)**, *flush* is what we need. None of the other answer choices are particularly colorful.

31. A

The word *dissipated* can be a pejorative reference to someone devoted to the pursuit of pleasure—the opposite of dissipation is restraint or moderation. Choice **(A)** is correct because *temperate* means moderate or self-restrained. None of the other answer choices have to do with moderation. *Inundated* means overwhelmed or deluged.

32. D

Fecundity means fertility, the capacity for producing life, whether it be children or vegetation. Clearly the opposite would be **(D)**, *sterility,* which refers to an inability to reproduce.

None of the other choices comes close, and the only unusual word is, (**A**), *levity,* which means silliness or frivolity.

33. D

Encumber means to block or weigh down. A good synonym would be *oppress.* The best opposite is (**D**), *disburden,* which means to free from oppression. *Animate* (**A**), means to make alive—its opposite would be something like deaden. To *inaugurate,* (**B**), is to begin or commence. To *bleach* is to pale or whiten and to *obliterate* means to erase or remove.

34. C

The word *disseminate* isn't easy to figure out if you don't know it—it means to spread widely. Ideas, theories, and beliefs can all be disseminated. The opposite of spreading an idea is *suppressing* it, (**C**). None of the other choices work.

35. D

Restive looks like the word rested, but the two don't mean the same thing at all. Restive can mean stubborn or restless. A mule that won't move is restive, as is a fidgety child. We need something like *obedient, quiet,* or *settled,* and it's *patient,* (**D**). *Morose* in (**A**) means gloomy. *Intangible* means untouchable or elusive. *Fatigued* means tired and the opposite of *curious* would be *indifferent.*

36. B

If you didn't know what *syncopated* means, you might have guessed it had something to do with rhythm from the expression *out of sync.* That would lead you to (**B**), *normally accented.* *Syncopation* refers to a pattern or rhythm in which stress is shifted onto normally unaccented beats.

The opposite of (**A**)'s *carefully executed* would be *haphazard,* and (**C**)'s *brightly illuminated* is the opposite of *dim. Obscure* would be an antonym for (**D**)'s *easily understood. Justly represented,* in

(**E**) isn't easy to match, but even if you couldn't eliminate all the choices, you could have at least narrowed the field.

37. C

Vituperative means verbally abusive. The opposite of defaming someone with vituperative remarks would be praising them—(**C**)'s *laudatory* means expressing praise. As for the other choices, *lethal* means deadly and *incapacitated* means incapable or unfit. In (**D**), *insulated* means protected, as in *insulation,* and *prominent,* (**E**), means famous.

38. B

Saturnine is probably the hardest word in the section. It means heavy, gloomy, sluggish, so its opposite is *cheerful* or *lively.* The answer is (**B**), *ebullient,* which means bubbling with enthusiasm or high spirited. Choice (**A**)'s *magnanimous* means generous or high minded. *Finicky,* (**C**), means fussy or picky. The opposite of (**D**), *unnatural* is natural and (**E**), *impoverished* means poor.

39. E

Callous means unfeeling, uncaring, but if this person has concern for the earthquake victims, her reputation must be an unfounded one, so the correct choice will mean *contradicted* or *proved false.* This is one of the meanings of *belied,* correct choice (**E**). Choice (**B**), *rescinded,* is the second best answer. It means revoked or withdrawn, but you don't say that a reputation is rescinded. Choices (**A**), (**C**), and (**D**) are the opposite of what we're looking for—they don't make sense in this context.

40. B

No longer and *therefore* show strong contrast— something is done with the original plans because they are no longer something else. Choice (**B**) expresses this contrast, *applicable ... rejected,* and if we plug in these words, the plans could no longer be applied so they were tossed aside. In **(A)**, there's no contrast between something being *relevant*, or pertinent, and its being *adaptable*, capable of being changed to fit a new situation. In **(C)**, *expedient* means convenient—it makes no sense for something not expedient to be *adopted* or taken up. In **(D)**, *appraised* means judged or rated, which doesn't follow from no longer being *acceptable*. In **(E)** it doesn't make sense to say that the plans were no longer *capable* or that the plans were *allayed*, or minimized—again, **(B)** is the best choice.

41. D

The second half of the sentence is about each tiny layer of the surface of the cross-section of the sandstone. This must explain what the first part alludes to, so the first blank must mean *layered*—otherwise, what tiny layers is the author talking about? On this basis, **(D)** is the best answer since *stratified* means layered. In **(A)**, a ridge isn't really a layer. In **(B)**, a facet is a face or flat surface, so *multifaceted* can't be right. *Distinctive*, in **(C)** means distinguishing or individual. And *coarse* in **(E)** means rough. Looking at the second blank, *enlargement,* in **(A)**, has nothing to do with the formation of the stone. In **(B)**, if the phrase *angle of deposition* means anything at all, it's an obscure geological term and can't be what we want here. The remaining choices could refer to the time or place in which material is deposited. Since **(D)** has the best answer for the first blank and a possible answer for the second blank, it's correct.

42. D

The phrase *and now* suggests that the second part of the sentence will say something consistent with the first part. Whatever the convict has always insisted upon, the new evidence must support his claim. Choice **(D)** gets this connection right—*innocence ... vindicate.* To vindicate means to clear from an accusation,

to prove innocent. The convict has always insisted upon his own innocence and now at last there is new evidence to vindicate him—this makes perfect sense and it's the answer. In **(A)**, *defensiveness* means a tendency to defend oneself and *incarcerate* means to put in prison. In **(B)**, *culpability* is guilt, as in the word *culprit,* and *exonerate* means to clear from guilt. In **(C)**, to *anathematize* someone means to curse him or pronounce a strong sentence against him but that doesn't go with *blamelessness*. In **(E)** *contrition* is a sense of remorse, while to *condemn* someone means to pass judgment against him. This is probably second best, but it doesn't follow as logically as **(D)**, so **(D)** is correct.

43. A

The word *but* signals a contrast between the opinion of plate tectonics when the theory was first proposed, and the opinion of it now—either people disbelieved the theory at first and believe it now or vice versa. Choice **(A)**, *opposition ... grant* provides the contrast. If most geophysicists now grant its validity, they believe in it. That's the opposite of opposing it, so **(A)** is the answer. In **(B)**, *consideration* is a neutral term—people are thinking about the theory, but it doesn't provide the necessary contrasts with *see,* which implies that physicists now recognize the validity of the theory. In **(C)**, *acclamation* means loud praise and *boost* means to support enthusiastically—no contrast there. In **(D)**, a *prognostication* is a prediction of the future, which doesn't make sense in this context and *learn its validity* doesn't make sense either, so **(D)** isn't a good choice. In **(E)**, *contention* is argument and to *bar* means to exclude or forbid—there is no contrast with this pair. Again, **(A)** is the correct answer.

44. D

Despite clues you in to a contrast between something professed, claimed or pretended, and reality, indicated by the glint in her eyes. A glint in someone's eye is a sign of strong interest, so *obsession* and *fascination,* in (A) and (D) are tempting. We want a contrast with strong interest, so the first word is something like *disinterest.* We find *indifference* in (D) and *obliviousness* in (C). Since both words in (D) fit, it must be correct. None of the others offers the kind of contrasts we need. There's no contrast between *intelligence* and *obsession,* in (A), between *interest* and *concern* in (B), or between *obliviousness* and *confusion* in (C). We get a contrast in (E) between *expertise* and *unfamiliarity,* but the words don't make sense—a glint in someone's eye isn't a sign of unfamiliarity.

45. C
We're looking for something that goes with sacred scriptures and implies a formal system of belief, but something whose absence doesn't rule out a legacy of traditional religious practices and basic values. We can eliminate choices (A), (B), and (E) because if Shinto lacked *followers*, *customs*, or *faith* it wouldn't be a legacy of traditional religious practices and basic values. *Relics*, (D), are sacred objects but relics don't make something a formal system of beliefs. The best choice is (C)—a *dogma* is a formal religious belief.

46. E
Something *impeccable* is perfect, it doesn't have a *flaw*. In (A) *impeachable* means subject to accusation, so something impeachable is not necessarily without *crime*. *Obstreperous*, in (B) means loud or unruly, not without *permission*. *Impetuous,* in (C) means rash or without care, rather than without *warning*. In (D), *moribund* means in the process of dying, so it's inappropriate to use *living*. In (E), *absurd* means without *sense*, so this is the correct answer.

47. D
A *seismograph* is an instrument used to measure an earthquake, so we need another instrument used to measure something. In (A), a *stethoscope* is an instrument used to listen to a patient's chest. Only indirectly can this be used to measure a patient's *health*. In (B), a *speedometer* doesn't measure a *truck*—it measures the speed of any kind of vehicle. In (C), a *telescope* doesn't measure *astronomy*. A telescope is an instrument used to observe far away objects. In (D), a *thermometer* measures *temperature*, so this looks like a promising answer. In (E), an *abacus* is used in *arithmetic* as a calculator but it doesn't measure arithmetic. So (D) is the best answer.

48. D
To *guzzle* is to *drink* very quickly, taking big gulps, so the relationship is one of speed or degree. In (A), *elucidate* and *clarify* mean to make clearer. One doesn't imply greater speed or volume than the other. Similarly, with (B) to *ingest* is to *eat* or drink—it doesn't mean to eat in big bites. In (C), to *boast* and to *describe* are two unrelated ways of talking. In (D), to *stride* is to *walk* quickly, taking big steps, so this may be the answer. In (E), *condemn* is stronger than the first word *admonish,* meaning to rebuke—the opposite of how the stem pair is presented. So (D) is the best answer.

49. C
An *orator* is a public speaker and *articulate* means able to express oneself well. You can form the bridge, "A successful orator is one who is articulate." With that in mind, (A) may seem tempting but the profession of *soldier* isn't defined as aspiring toward being *merciless*. In (B) a *celebrity* is a famous person, not by definition a *talented* one. Choice (C) is good—a good *judge* has to be *unbiased*. It's safe to say that a biased judge is a bad judge in the same way that an inarticulate orator is a bad orator. In (D), a *novice* is a beginner—it wouldn't be unusual for a novice to be *unfamiliar* but that's not what makes

a good novice. In (**E**), a *dignitary* is a person of high rank, and such a person doesn't need to be *respectful*. Choice (**C**) is correct.

50. C

A *badge* is the identification worn by a *policeman*. In (**A**), a *placard* is a sign carried by a *demonstrator*. There's a link here but a placard isn't an official ID and a demonstrator doesn't necessarily carry a placard. Choice (**B**) is wrong because although there is a tradition for a *sailor* to have a *tattoo*, a tattoo isn't an official identification of a sailor. In (**C**), a *soldier* wears a *dog-tag* on his uniform to identify him, so this is plausible. In (**D**), the *pedigree* of a *dog* is the dog's lineage or genealogy, not something worn by the dog as identification. In (**E**), even though a *fingerprint* may be used to identify a *defendant*, everybody has fingerprints. So the best answer is (**C**).

51. B

To *scrutinize* means to *observe* intently, so the relationship is one of degree. In (**A**), to *pique* interest is to *excite* interest. The words mean the same thing. In (**B**), to *beseech* means to *request* with great fervor—this is more like it. In (**C**), to *search* is the process you go through to *discover* something. That's different from the stem pair. In (**D**) to *grin* is to *smile* broadly—this reverses the original pair. And in (**E**), to *dive* means to *jump* in a certain way or under certain conditions, not to jump intently. The best answer is (**B**).

52. D

If you didn't know what *epicurean* means, you might have had trouble here, but you can still eliminate some choices. There must be some relationship between *epicurean* and *indulge*. Could (**A**) have the same relationship? No, because there really is no relationship between *frightened* and *ugly*. Something ugly doesn't

necessarily frighten people. Same with (**C**)—there's no relationship between *hesitate* and *unproductive*. There are good relationships for the other choices but let's see if we can eliminate them. In (**E**), the relationship is that something *comprehensible* can be *understood*. Do you think that something *epicurean* can be *indulged*? That sounds odd—just about everyone and everything can be indulged.

In (**B**), *revocable* means something can be taken back, so the relationship is, "Something *revocable* can be *retracted*." That's the same relationship that we just saw in (**E**), another clue that they must be wrong. If (**B**) and (**E**) share the same relationship, they can't both be right, so they must both be wrong. That leaves us with (**D**), and there our relationship is something like, "someone *vindictive* is likely to *revenge* himself," and that sounds better. In fact, an epicurean person is one who is likely to indulge himself, so (**D**) is correct here.

53. E

Diluvial means having to do with a *flood*. You may have heard the word *antediluvian,* meaning before the flood, Noah's flood, that is—in other words, a long time ago. So our bridge is "having to do with." In (**A**), *criminal* can mean "having to do with crime" but it doesn't mean having to do with *punishment*. In (**B**), *biological* means "having to do with living things." *Bacteria* are living things but to define *biological* as "having to do with bacteria" would be too narrow. In (**C**), *judicial* means "having to do with the administration of justice." A *verdict* is the decision about the guilt or innocence of a defendant, a small part of the judicial process. Choice (**D**)'s *candescent* means "giving off *light*" rather than "having to do with light." This leaves (**E**) and *cardiac* means "having to do with the *heart*," so (**E**) is correct.

54. C

It is in the nature of a *sphinx* to *perplex*. This comes from Greek mythology—the sphinx was a monster that asked a riddle that no one could answer. *Sphinx* can be used to mean anything that is difficult to understand, so our bridge is: "A sphinx is known for perplexing." In (A), an *oracle* is a soothsayer, someone who predicts the future—an oracle doesn't *interpret*. In (B), a *prophet* is someone who foretells the future. This may help someone to *prepare* but you don't say that a prophet is known for preparing. In (C), a *siren* can be a beautiful or a seductive woman who *lures* men. So (C) looks good—a siren lures in the same way that a sphinx perplexes. In (D), the role of a *jester* is to amuse, not necessarily to *astound*. In (E), a *minotaur* is a mythological monster—it didn't, by definition, *anger* someone. So (C) is correct.

Reading Passage: Questions 55–57

This Reading Comp passage is short and it's followed by three questions—the remaining passage will be long with eight questions. The style of this natural science passage is factual, descriptive, and straightforward, although the discussion does get fairly detailed. The topic is clear from the first sentence: our knowledge of how fish schools are formed and how their structure is maintained. The next two sentences get more specific and express the author's main point—that, contrary to the previous theory, the structure of fish schools is not primarily dependent on vision.

The tone is objective, but it's worth noting that since the author is contrasting the new knowledge about lateral lines with older, outdated knowledge, he must be skeptical of the notion that vision is the primary means of forming and maintaining fish schools. The rest of the passage is a more technical report of how the schools are structured, how individual fish actually behave in forming schools—this is detail and the best way to deal with it is to read it attentively but more quickly than the earlier lines.

55. E

This Roman numeral-format question focuses on detail. The stem is asking what the structure of fish schools depends on, and the options focus on the more technical elements in the last half of the passage. The author states that ideal positions of individual fish aren't maintained rigidly and this contradicts Statement I right away. The idea of random aggregation appears: the school formation results from a probabilistic arrangement that appears like a random aggregation, so the idea is that fish are positioned probabilistically, but not rigidly. Statement II is true, repeating the idea in the next sentence that fish school structure is maintained by the preference of fish to have a certain distance from their neighbors. Statement III is true, too. It's a paraphrase of the last two sentences, that each fish uses its vision and lateral line first to measure the speed of the other fish, then to adjust its own speed to conform, based primarily on the position and movements of other fish. So Statements II and III are true and (E) is the right choice.

56. C

You know the primary purpose here is to present new ideas that challenge the emphasis of the old theory. So you're probably safe in assuming that the author's attitude toward the old idea will be at least somewhat negative. You can therefore cross off choices that sound neutral or positive, (B), (D), and (E). The negative choices are (A) and (C). Choice (A) is out because it is much too extreme—the author is not offended or indignant, nor does he or she argue that vision is insignificant—quite the contrary. This leaves

(C), the best choice. The author disagrees with the old theory since it overlooks the role of the lateral line, but the disagreement is tempered by an acknowledgment that the old theory did recognize the role of vision. So it's a qualified or measured disagreement—the adjective *considered* works well here. Again, the correct answer is (C).

57. C

This question involves inference as the word *suggests* in the stem suggests. It refers to the latter, more detailed half of the passage, and that's where correct answer (C) is. It's logically suggested by the last couple of sentences where you're told that once it establishes its position, each fish uses its eyes and lateral line to measure the movements of nearby fish in order to maintain appropriate speed and position. Since the school is moving, each fish's adjustments must be ongoing and continuous, as (C) states. Choice (A) is wrong because auditory organs aren't mentioned. Lateral lines correspond to a sense of touch, not hearing. Choices (B) and (D) both have words that should strike you as improbable. Nothing suggests that each fish rigorously avoids any disruptive movements, (B), or that the fish would make sudden unexpected movements only in the presence of danger, (D). The idea in (E) also isn't mentioned. It's never suggested that a fish, once part of a school, completely loses its ability to act on its own. Again, (C) is our answer for this question.

Reading Passage: Questions 58–65

This passage is divided into three paragraphs. If you figure out what each paragraph covers, you've understood the passage's handful of ideas, plus you've sketched out a rough mental map. In this passage, the first 10 or 15 lines take you through the first paragraph and into the second and if you were careful you picked up the author's broad topic area (ancient Greek social anxiety), the style of the writing (dense and scholarly) and the tone or attitude (expository and neutral).

The second paragraph gives you the central point—what the Greeks apparently succeeded in doing was discovering a way of measuring and explaining chaotic experience so that chaos was no longer so threatening and anxiety producing. This recognition of order in the midst of chaos served as the basis of a spiritual ideal for the Greeks. So by the end of the second paragraph you have the author's central idea plus all the information about style, tone, and topics in the beginning. The first sentence of the last paragraph tells you the search for order and clarity in the midst of chaos is reflected especially in Greek philosophy. The rest of the paragraph is a description of how various philosophers and schools of philosophy offered solutions to the problem of finding order and measure in a disorderly world.

58. E

This kind of primary purpose question is common, and here the right answer is (E). In this case, both the noun and the verb are right on the money. The verb is exactly right for this author's expository neutral tone, and a cultural phenomenon, the Greeks' perception of chaos and their solution to the problem, is what the author is describing. The verbs in (B) and (C), *challenge* and *question* eliminate them right away—no opinion is given but the author's own, and philosophy in (C) is discussed only in the last paragraph. The noun phrase in (A), *conflicting viewpoints* is wrong. Choice (D) is the most tempting—the author is looking at history and mentioning certain facts, but this misses the author's purpose, which is not to simply list facts but rather to describe and define something in the form of a thesis. Again, (E) is the correct answer.

59. A

This is from the first sentence of the second paragraph and it's the central idea that's being focused on, that the discovery of this substratum helped bring a satisfying new sense of order into experience, thus reforming the Greeks' perception of worldly chaos. The choice that paraphrases this point is (A), the perception of constant change was altered by the idea of a permanent principle of order lying underneath it—this is the main point of the passage. Choice (B) is out because severe social problems are never mentioned, at least not in any concrete way. As for (C), it misses the point made in the sentence the question refers to. The passage does refer to pain and bewilderment and to an earlier period of political turbulence, but this choice goes overboard with its notions of painful memories and national humiliation and so on. As for (D), a few lines into the second paragraph the author says directly that the discovery did much more than satisfy intellectual curiosity. And (E) also contradicts the author, distorting a detail at the end of the paragraph. It's not mysticism, but rationality and careful analysis that lead to order and clarity, so it's (A) for this question.

60. D

The author is arguing in the second, third, and fourth sentences that the Greeks identified rational thought and spiritual ideals as inseparable. Rationality, order, measure, and so forth became equivalent to spiritual ideals for the Greeks. Toward the end of the second paragraph the author states that rationality and spirituality are not mutually exclusive. The choice that's most clearly consistent with this is (D). As for (A), the passage never suggests that ordinary Greeks were unfamiliar with or uninterested in the concepts of rational thought and spiritual ideals. The passage suggests quite the contrary.

Choices (B) and (C) are both inconsistent with the passage as well. All the philosophers mentioned accepted the notion that rationality was the key, amounting to an ideal to understanding the world. Choice (E) picks up on the mention of poetry at the beginning of the last paragraph, but the point there is that Greek poetry manifested the sense of cultural anxiety that philosophy tried to alleviate.

61. B

This question is looking for the choice that isn't mentioned as reflecting the Greeks' anxieties about chaos. The one that's never mentioned is (B), that it was reflected in aspects of their religion. We don't actually learn anything about Greek religion in the passage—we just don't know and we certainly can't infer anything about specific aspects. Each of the other choices is mentioned specifically. Choice (A) is implied in the long opening sentence of the first paragraph—the national psyche and historical experience both relate to national consciousness. Choice (C), the sense of change in the physical world, is mentioned at the start of paragraph two. (D), the striving for order and philosophy, is discussed throughout the third paragraph. And finally (E), lyric poetry, is mentioned at the start of the paragraph as one place where the sense of anxiety was expressed directly.

62. C

Your mental map should have taken you straight to the last paragraph—the Milesians are discussed in the first several sentences. Choice (C) encapsulates what the passage says, that Milesians were interested primarily in understanding a fundamental order in nature, outside the disturbing world of human society. Choice (A) gets it backward—the Milesians apparently ignored questions that were inherently human. Choices (B) and (D) contradict the passage. None of the philosophies mentioned did what these choices suggest, either to sharply distinguish between rationality and spirituality, **(B)**, or to integrate rationality and mysticism, **(D)**. Choice **(E)**, finally, describes the approach of the Pythagoreans who were absorbed by the logic and order of mathematics, rather than by attempts to explain physical phenomena.

63. D

You're being asked not the actual content, but the logical progression of the contents. Is he or she making a series of disconnected assertions? Making a point and backing it up with factual evidence, or what? What's the author up to logically in the lines referred to? In the preceding sentence the author is talking about the Greeks' discovery of order and measure, and that it helped them get a secure handle on chaotic experience. The discovery was a relief—its impact was almost religious in nature. In the next sentence, the author says that this recognition, discovery, of order and measure was much more than merely intellectually satisfying—it served as a basic part of their spiritual values. The author quotes Plato to support his point, to give an idea of the significance of measure.

In the last of the three sentences the author finishes up with a statement that pulls the strands of the thesis together and puts the basic point into clear cultural perspective. Rational definability or measure was never regarded by the Greeks as inconsistent with spirituality—**(D)** is the choice that describes things best. The problem with **(A)** is that the author isn't summarizing two viewpoints but discussing one thesis. As for **(B)**, the author neither mentions evidence that weakens his thesis nor revises it. Choice **(C)** is out because the author is not discussing two separate arguments that need to

be reconciled by a third. It's just one argument that's the topic here. **(E)**, finally, is wrong for the same reason—the author discusses one thesis only and never suggests any other.

64. A

We know from our rough map of the structure that except for one reference to Plato in the middle of the second paragraph, philosophy is discussed only in the last paragraph, so that's where you'll find out about the Pythagoreans. The main thing about them was that they concentrated on mathematical abstraction. They shifted the focus in philosophy from the physical realm to the mathematical. The Milesians focused on physical phenomena, and that's the idea you see immediately in **(A)**, the correct choice. Choice **(B)** lists the idea that thinkers who came *after* the Pythagoreans focused on human behavior. Choice **(C)** won't work because both of these schools and all other philosophies mentioned used rationality as the means to truth. Choice **(D)** picks up what characterized the Milesians—we want the Pythagorean side of the contrast. Choice **(E)** gets things backward—the Pythagoreans stressed mathematical theory over physical matter. Again, it's **(A)**.

65. D

The last sentence is saying that in all these various periods of Greek history and philosophy, the basic preoccupation of the Greeks was with the search for a *kosmos*. The term *kosmos* hasn't been used before, but because this sentence is at the end of the passage and because it's phrased as a summary, you should realize that the basic quest here must be the same one the author has been talking about all along. So this refers to the central problem for Greek society—how to find order and measure in a seemingly confusing and disorderly world. This search for a kosmos then is the passage's main idea, and correct choice **(D)** restates it.

Choice **(A)** is out because the word *mystical* is incorrect, since the author states at the end of paragraph two that the Greeks stressed rationalism over mysticism. Choices **(B)** and **(E)** are inconsistent with some major points. In **(B)**, the idea that the Greeks would have regarded rationalism as sterile is completely wrong. And in **(E)**, the ideals of beauty and excellence, as mentioned in paragraph two, are preeminent and fundamental within the Greeks' world view. Finally, **(C)** talks about ending conflict among important schools of philosophy. This last sentence about the search for kosmos is talking about a quest you find in Greek thought as a whole, a much bigger topic than mere conflicts among philosophers.

66. A
Enmity is the state of being an enemy—the opposite is *friendship,* **(A)**. *Reverence,* **(B)**, is great respect, the opposite of contempt. The opposite of *boredom,* **(C)**, is interest. The opposite of **(D)**, *stylishness,* is a lack of style, and the opposite of **(E)**, *awkwardness,* is skillfulness.

67. B
Dilate means expand and widen. The opposite is the word *contract,* so **(B)**, *shrink,* is what we're looking for. Choice **(A)**, *enclose,* means to confine. The opposite of the word *hurry,* **(C)**, is *delay. Inflate,* **(D)**, means to expand or fill with air. The opposite of **(E)**, *erase,* might be *preserve* or *set down.*

68. A
A *charlatan* is a fraud or a quack. Choice **(A)**, *genuine expert,* is a possible answer. The opposite of a *powerful leader,* **(B)**, is a follower or maybe a weak leader. The opposite of a *false idol,* **(C)**, is a true god or a hero. The opposite of an *unknown*

enemy, **(D)**, is a known enemy, an unknown friend or a known friend. The opposite of **(E)**, *hardened villain,* might be an innocent person or first offender. So it's **(A)**.

69. C
Peripheral means having to do with the periphery, the outer edge of something. The opposite of *peripheral* is *central,* **(C)**. The opposite of **(A)**, *civilized,* is *crude* or *savage.* Choice **(B)**, *partial,* means favoring or biased, or incomplete—it has lots of opposites but *peripheral* isn't one of them. *Harmed* is the opposite of *unharmed,* and the opposite of **(E)**, *stable,* is *weak* or *inconstant.* Choice **(C)** is correct.

70. E
Meritorious means full of merit, deserving reward. Its opposite is *unpraiseworthy,* **(E)**, the best choice. *Effulgent,* **(A)**, means shiny—its opposite is *dull.* **(B)**, *stationary,* means not moving. Neither **(C)**, *uneven,* nor **(D)**, *narrowminded,* works, so **(E)** is correct.

71. C
Discharge means to unburden, eject, or exude. However, it has a more specific meaning in military context: to release or remove someone from service. The opposite is to *enlist,* **(C)**. The opposite of **(A)**, *heal,* is *sicken.* The opposite of **(B)**, *advance,* is *retreat.* **(D)** *penalize,* means to punish. The opposite of *delay,* **(E)**, is *hasten.*

72. A
A *malediction* is a curse. We want something like *benediction,* and we find *blessing* in **(A)**. The opposite of *preparation,* **(B)**, is *lack of preparation.* Choice **(C)**, *good omen,* has *bad omen* as its opposite. The opposite of **(D)**, *liberation,* is *captivity.* The opposite of *pursuit,* **(E)**, is tough, but it sure isn't *malediction,* so **(A)** is correct.

73. A

Mawkish means sickeningly sentimental. *Unsentimental,* (**A**), is the answer here. The opposite of (**B**), *sophisticated,* is *naive* or *simple.* The opposite of *graceful,* (**C**), is *clumsy.* The opposite of *tense,* (**D**), is *relaxed.* There are various antonyms to *descriptive,* (**E**), but *mawkish* isn't one.

74. B

Temerity is recklessness or foolish daring. Its opposite is *hesitancy* or *carefulness. Blandness,* (**A**), is a lack of character, not a lack of courage. Choice (**B**), *caution,* fits—one with temerity lacks caution. The opposite of (**C**), *severity,* is *leniency.* The opposite of (**D**), *strength,* is *weakness. Charm,* (**E**), is personal appeal. The best answer is (**B**), caution.

75. C

Jejune can mean immature or sophomoric. The opposite would be *adult* or correct choice (**C**), *mature. Morose,* (**A**), means sad or moody. The opposite of *natural,* (**B**), is *artificial.* (**D**), *contrived,* means deliberately planned. Its opposite is *natural. Accurate,* (**E**), means precise or exact.

76. C

Vitiate means to corrupt, put wrong, spoil, or make worse, and the opposite is *improve* or *correct.* The closest choice is *rectify,* (**C**). Choice (**A**), *deaden,* is way off. The opposite of *trust,* (**B**), is *distrust* or *suspect.* The opposite of *drain,* (**D**), is *fill.* And the opposite of *amuse,* (**E**), is *bore* or *upset.*

SECTION TWO—QUANTITATIVE

1. A

To compare these two quantities, work column by column starting with the decimal point and working to the right. Both have a 0 in the tenths column, so there's no difference there. In the hundredths column, both have a 2, so we go to thousandths. Column A has a 6 and Column B has a 5—there are more thousandths in A than in B, so Column A is larger and (**A**) is the correct answer.

2. C

Right triangles *ABD* and *CDB* share a hypotenuse, segment *DB.* The squared quantities should clue you to use the Pythagorean theorem. See that *w* and *x* are lengths of the legs of right triangle *ABD.* Side *AD* has length *w,* side *AB* has length *x.* Also, *y* and *z* are lengths of the legs of right triangle *CDB.* Side *CD* has length *z,* side *CB* has length *y.* Where *a* and *b* are lengths of the legs of a right triangle, and *C* is the length of the hypotenuse, $a^2 + b^2 = c^2$, so $w^2 + x^2 = $ length BD^2. $y^2 + z^2$ also equals length DB^2, the quantities are equal and the answer is (**C**).

3. A

We have $x + 4y = 6$ and $x = 2y$, and we want to compare *x* and *y,* so substitute $2y$ for *x* in the first equation. Using that information, solve for the other variable. Substitute $2y$ for *x* into $x + 4y = 6$ and get $2y + 4y = 6$ or $6y = 6$. Divide both sides by 6 and we get $y = 1$. If $y = 1$ and $x = 2y$ as the second equation tells us, *x* must equal 2. Since 2 is greater than 1, the quantity in Column A is greater.

4. B

Question 4 looks hard—but you don't have to simplify to find the relationship. With positive numbers, you can square both without changing the relationship. That leaves you with $4^2 + 5^2$ in Column A and $3^2 + 6^2$ in Column B. The product of 4^2 is 16, 5^2 is 25, and 16 + 25 is 41. In Column B we have 3^2, that's 9 + 6^2, that's 36, 9 + 36 is 45. 45 is greater than 41, Column B is greater than Column A, and the answer is (**B**).

5. D

Column A asks for the number of managerial employees—that's easy. There are 120 employees in the firm, and 25 percent of them are managerial. One-fourth of 120 is 30, the value of Column A.

Column B asks for two-thirds of the clerical employees. But we can't figure out how many workers are clerical workers, so we can't find two-thirds of that number. We can't determine a relationship, and the answer is choice (**D**).

6. B

We have 12 × 1 over 12 + 1 in Column A: 12 × 1 is 12 and 12 + 1 is 13. So we have $\frac{12}{13}$ in Column A. In Column B we have 12 + 1 = 13 in the numerator, and 12 × 1 = 12 in the denominator. So $\frac{12}{13}$ in Column A versus $\frac{13}{12}$ in Column B. Of course, $\frac{12}{13}$ is less than 1 while $\frac{13}{12}$ is greater than 1, and the answer is (**B**).

7. D

You might suspect (**D**) because there are no variable restrictions. To make the columns look as much alike as you can, multiply out Column A. You'll get $a \times b$ or ab, plus $1 \times b$, plus $1 \times a$, plus 1×1 or 1. So you get $ab + a + b + 1$. Column B has $ab + 1$. We can subtract ab from both sides, and it won't change the relationship and we have $1 + a + b$ in Column A, and 1 in Column B. Subtract 1 from both sides and we have $a + b$ in Column A and 0 in Column B. But consider that a and b could be negative numbers. Since $a + b$ could be positive, negative, or zero, the answer is (**D**).

8. B

In the two-digit number jk the value of digit j is twice the value of digit k. We have to compare the value of k in Column A with 6 in Column B. If you plug in 6 for k, then go back, you see that the value of digit j is twice digit k. We know that j isn't just a number—it's a digit, which means it's 0, 1, 2, 3, 4, 5, 6, 7, 8, or 9. So 12, twice the value of 6, can't be j. In other words, k has to be

something less than 6, so the answer must be (**B**), the value in Column B is greater.

9. A

We have a circle with right angle QPR as a central angle. The area of sector PQR is 4 and we're asked to compare the area of the circle with 4π. There's a shortcut—the right angle defines the sector, and you have the area of that sector. A 90° angle cuts off one-fourth of the circle. If you multiply by four, you have the area of the circle. So in Column A you have 4 × 4, and in Column B, you have 4π. π is about 3.14, and 4 is bigger than that, so Column A, 4 × 4, must be bigger than 4π, and the answer is (**A**).

10. C

Henry purchased x apples and Jack purchased 10 apples less than one-third the number of apples Henry purchased. *One-third of* means the same as *one-third times* and the number of apples Henry purchased is x. So this boils down to $j = \frac{1}{3}x - 10$. You can plug this in for Column A. We have $\frac{1}{3}x - 10$ in Column A and in Column B we have $\frac{x - 30}{3}$. Now you can clear the fraction in Column B. Let's split Column B to two fractions. $\frac{x}{3} - \frac{30}{3}$. We leave the $\frac{x}{3}$ alone and cancel the factor of 3 from the numerator and denominator of $\frac{30}{3}$ and we're left with $\frac{x}{3} - 10$. What's $\frac{x}{3}$? It's one-third of x, so these two quantities are equal. Column A equals $\frac{1}{3}x - 10$, while Column B also equals $\frac{1}{3}x - 10$, so the answer is (**C**).

11. D

You can suspect (**D**) because there are unrestricted variables. In Column A we have the volume of a rectangular solid with length 5 feet, width 4 feet, and height x feet. The formula is length times width times height, so we have 5 times 4 times x, or $20x$. In Column B we need the volume of rectangular solid with length 10 feet, width 8 feet, and height y feet. 10 times 8 times y gives you a volume of $80y$. Now you may think, I've got $20x$, and $80y$, so $80y$ must be bigger because there are more ys than xs. That would be true if x and y were close together, but the variables are unrestricted, and the answer is (**D**).

12. C

We want to compare 50 with x, one of the angles formed by the intersection of ST and PT. Now angle QRS is labeled 80. We also know PQ and ST have the same length and QR and RS have the same length. If you add PQ and QR, you get PR. If you add ST and RS, you get RT. If you add equals to equals, you get equals, so $PQ + QR$ must be the same as $ST + RS$, which means that PR and RT are the same. You have isoceles triangle PRT and we're given one angle that has measure 80 and the second angle that has measure x. The angle measuring x is opposite equal side PR. That means the other angle must have the same measure, because it's opposite the other equal side. The sum of the interior angles in a triangle always equals 180°. $x + x + 80$ must equal 180, $2x$ must equal 100, $x = 50$. So x and 50 are equal, and the answer is (**C**).

13. B

First we can cancel factors of 2 from $2 \times 16 \times 64$ on the left, and $2 \times 4n \times 256$ on the right. If we cancel a factor of 2 we have 16×64 on the left, $4n \times 256$ on the right. 64 goes into 256 four times, so let's cancel a factor of 64. That leaves us 16 on the left and $4n \times 4$ on the right. We can cancel a factor of 4 and we're left with 4 on the left and $4n$ on the right. If $4 = 4n$, n must equal 1, so we have $n = 1$ for Column A. Column B is 2, so the answer is (**B**).

14. C

For each unordered group of two people selected, there are two ways to arrange the people

(depending on which one is the lead). Hence, this is a permutation problem: order matters. For the lead role, there are 6 people to choose from. For the supporting role, there will be 5. So the number of possible duos is $6 \times 5 = 30$. The columns are equal.

15. D

The perimeter of ABC is 40 and the length of BC is 12, and we want to compare the length of AB with 14. In an isosceles triangle there are two sides with equal length, but we don't know whether side BC is one of those sides or not. If side BC is the unequal side, we have two unknown sides plus 12 and they have a sum of 40, the perimeter. The two remaining sides have a sum of 28, so each is 14. That would mean that AB and AC would have length 14. Then the answer would be (**C**). If BC is one of the equal sides, we have two sides length 12 and a third unknown side, and the sum is 40. $12 + 12$ is 24, so that the third side has length 16. AB could be one of the sides length 12, or the side length 12. There are three possible lengths for side AB—16, 14, and 12—so the answer is (**D**).

16. B

Isolate $\frac{q}{p}$. Multiplying both sides of the equation by p gives $p - q = \frac{2p}{7}$. Subtracting p from both sides gives $-q = \frac{2p}{7} - p = \frac{2p}{7} - \frac{7p}{7} = -\frac{5p}{7}$. So $-q = -\frac{5p}{7}$, or $q = \frac{5p}{7}$. Dividing both sides by p gives $\frac{q}{p} = \frac{5}{7}$.

17. E

The question asks for the number of different dinners Jane could make. Since the order of the selections in the dinner doesn't matter, this presents itself as a combination problem. But it involves three possible combination types: Veg, Meat, Meat; Veg, Veg, Meat; or Veg, Veg, Veg. We must calculate the possibilities for each type of combination and then add the results to find the total number of different combinations possible.

Let V represent vegetarian and M represent meat.

Then with V, M, M, she has 5 choices for the vegetarian and she must choose 1, times 4 choices for meat among which she must choose 2.

For V, V, M, she will choose 2 from among 5 for the vegetarian, and 1 among 4 for the meat.

If she goes with V, V, V, the all-vegetarian menu, she will choose a subgroup of 3 from among 5 vegetarian choices (or 5 choose 3).

If n and k are positive integers where $n \geq k$, then the number of different subgroups consisting of k objects that can be selected from a group consisting of n different objects, denoted by $_nC_k$, is given by the formula

$$_nC_k = \frac{n!}{k!(n-k)!}$$

Here the total number of different possible servings for a plate is $(_5C_1)(_4C_2) + (_5C_2)(_4C_1) + (_5C_3)$.

Now $_5C_1$ represents choosing 1 type of vegetable selection from 5 different types, so $_5C_1 = 5$. The formula also gives this result.

$$_4C_2 = \frac{4}{2!(4-2)!} = \frac{4!}{2! \times 2!} = \frac{4 \times 3 \times 2 \times 1}{2 \times 1 \times 2 \times 1} = 6$$

$$_5C_2 = \frac{5!}{2!(5-2)!} = \frac{5!}{2! \times 3!} = \frac{5 \times 4 \times 3 \times 2 \times 1}{2 \times 1 \times 3 \times 2 \times 1} = 10$$

Here $_4C_1$ corresponds to choosing 1 type of meat selection from 4 different types, so $_4C_1 = 4$.

$$_5C_3 = \frac{5!}{3!(5-3)!} = \frac{5!}{3! \times 2!} = \frac{5 \times 4 \times 3 \times 2 \times 1}{3 \times 2 \times 1 \times 2 \times 1} = 10$$

So the number of different possible servings that can be made for a plate is 5 × 6 + 10 × 4 + 10 = 80.

18. B

We need the value of $a + b + c$. We know that a, b, and c are exterior angles of our quadrilateral in the diagram and there's a fourth exterior angle, which isn't labeled. But the measure of the interior angle next to it is given to us—it's 70°. The sum of the exterior angles of any figure is always 360°. So we can figure out the measure of the missing angle, then subtract it from 360 and get the sum of the other three. The unlabeled angle must be 110°. Now we know $110 + a + b + c = 360$, we subtract to get the sum of a, b, and c and we get 250, **(B)** as the correct answer.

19. E

John has four ties, 12 shirts, and three belts, and we need the number of days he can go without repeating. So we multiply the number of ties times the number of shirts times the number of belts. Four ties, 12 shirts—48 combinations. Multiply by three choices of belt, and you get 3 × 48 or 144 combinations, **(E)**.

20. C

Move the decimal points to the right until they disappear—but keep track of how many places you move the decimal. In **(A)** we have 0.00003 in the numerator. Move five places to the right to change it to 3. Then we change from 0.0007 to 70 in the denominator and we end up with $\frac{3}{70}$. In **(B)** we have 0.0008 on top, 0.0005 on the bottom—we get $\frac{8}{5}$. We have $\frac{70}{8}$ for **(C)**, equaling 8.75. In **(D)**, we end up with $\frac{60}{50}$ and $\frac{10}{8}$ in **(E)**. Clearly **(C)**, 8.75, is the largest value.

Graphs: Questions 21–25

21. E

The bar graph doesn't give us the total number of general practice physicians, but if we add the number of males to the number of females, we get the total number of g.p. physicians. To find the percent who are male, we take the number of males and put it over the total number and that will give us our percent. We have about 2,000 women and about 23,000 men, making the total about 25,000. Well, if there are around 25,000 g.p. physicians altogether and 2,000 to 3,000 of them are female, that's what percent of 25,000? It's around 10 percent. About 22,500 are male, which gives us 90 percent, **(E)**.

22. D

We're looking for the lowest ratio of males to females so we have to get the smallest number of males and the largest number of females. Skimming the bar graphs, we can see that in pediatrics the female graph and the male graph are closer than any of the others. Pediatrics **(D)** is the correct answer.

23. C

To refer to ages of physicians, we need to find the slice of the pie that goes from 45 to 54. It's 20 percent, but 20 percent of what? We're not looking for a percent, we're looking for a number of doctors. For general surgery the male bar goes up to about 35,000 and the female bar goes up to about 2,000—about 37,000 total. So 20 percent of 37,000 is the number of general surgery physicians between ages 45 and 54, inclusive. What's 20 percent of 37,000, or $\frac{1}{5}$ of 37,000? Well, $\frac{1}{5}$ of 35,000 is 7,000, $\frac{1}{5}$ of 2,000 is 400, making 7,400. Choice **(C)** is 7,350, the correct answer.

24. E

We'll have to find the total number of family practice physicians, which represents 7.5 percent of all the physicians in the United States, then we can find 100 percent of that number. The male bar of family practice physicians goes just

over 36,000, so we'll say it's 36,000 plus. The number of females goes just over 6,000 so we'll call that 6,000 plus, so we have about 43,000 all together. This is 7.5 percent of all the physicians. 7.5 percent is awkward—it's three-quarters of 10 percent, which is $\frac{3}{4} \times \frac{1}{10}$, or $\frac{3}{40}$. So 43,000 is $\frac{3}{40}$ of the total number of doctors. To change 43,000 into the number of total physicians, we multiply it by $\frac{40}{3}$. Think of it this way: We have an equation now, $\frac{3}{40}$ of the number we're looking for, we'll call it N, the number of physicians, equals 43,000. We want to get N by itself, so we have to get rid of that $\frac{3}{40}$. So we multiply by the reciprocal, $\frac{40}{3}$, and that leaves us N by itself on the left. But the hard part is multiplying $\frac{40}{3} \times$ 43,000. What's $\frac{40}{3}$? It's $13\frac{1}{3}$ and that's easier to multiply. $13 \times 43 = 559$, so $13 \times 43,000 = $ 559,000—you can look at your choices and estimate. Only one is close to 559,000—**(E)**, 570,000, and we're going to add on to that, so **(E)** is the correct answer.

25. B

How many male general surgeon physicians were under 35 years old? The pie chart breaks down general surgery physicians by age, so we'll be working with it. And, since we're looking for a number of general surgery physicians, we know that we're going to have to find the total number of general surgery physicians, then break it down according to the percentages on the pie chart.

We're told the number of female general surgery physicians in the under-35 category represented 3.5 percent of all the general surgery physicians. What this does is break that slice of the pie for under-35 into two smaller slices, one for men under 35 and one for women under 35. Now we know that the whole slice for under-35-year-olds is 30 percent of the total and we've just been told that the number of females under 35 is 3.5 percent of the total. So the difference between 30 percent and 3.5 percent must be the men in the under-35 category, which leaves 26.5 percent, which we have to multiply by the total number of general surgery physicians.

We figured out in Question 23 that there were 37,000 total general surgery physicians, and 26.5 percent of those are men under 35. What's 26.5 percent of 37,000? One-quarter of 37,000 is 9,250 and that's very close to (**A**), but remember we've still got another 1.5 percent to go. One percent of 37,000 is 370 and half of that, or 0.5 percent will be 185, so if you add 370 and 185 to 9,250 you end up with a total of 9,805 which is very close to (**B**), the correct answer.

26. B

We want to find the sum of the absolute value of three, the absolute value of –4 and the absolute value of 3 – 4. Well, the absolute value of 3 is 3, the absolute value of –4 is 4. What's the absolute value of 3 – 4? Do the subtraction inside the absolute value sign first, and we get –1. What's the absolute value of –1? It's 1, so we have 3 + 4 + 1 or 8 as our sum for Question 26, (**B**).

27. C

This looks like a right triangle on a coordinate grid, but it's not a normal coordinate grid—the lines on the grid don't represent integer units, they represent units of less than an integer. Going up on the y-axis, we have 0.5, 1.0, 1.5, and 2.0, so the lines each represent half an integer and, going to the left, the lines are labeled –0.4, –0.8, –1.2, so these each represent 0.4, and yet the diagram's not drawn to scale. Going left to right, the vertical lines are actually farther apart than the horizontal lines, which represent more value on the number line. Now, to find the

area of the shaded region, a triangle, we need a base and a height. This is a right triangle because its base lies on the horizontal line on our grid and its height, the side to the right, lies right on a vertical line on the grid. What's the length of the bottom side? The far right end point is at –0.4 and the far left end point is at –1.6, and the difference is 1.2 units, so the base is 1.2. The lower right vertex has value 0.5 and the upper right vertex has value 2.0—the difference is 1.5, so that's the height. The base is 1.2 and the height is 1.5, and the formula for the area of a right triangle is one half base times height. We have 1.2 as our base, we can call that $\frac{6}{5}$, 1.5 is $\frac{3}{2}$ so the area is $\frac{1}{2} \times \frac{6}{5} \times \frac{3}{2}$—that's $\frac{9}{10}$ or 0.9, choice (**C**).

28. A

You could find the number of tasks per hour from one computer, but that would add extra steps, because you want to find out how many computers you need to do a certain number of tasks in three hours. Well, if it can do 30 tasks in six hours, it can do 15 tasks in three hours. So, if you have two computers, that's 30 tasks, three is 45, four is 60, five is 75, six is 90. You can't get by with five because you have to get 80 tasks done, so you'll need six computers, (**A**).

29. C

One side of triangle ABC is an edge of our cube, segment BC. But segments AB and AC aren't lengths of the edge of the cube or fractions of a length of an edge of the cube. Well, let's find the length of an edge of the cube. If the cube has volume 8, that's the length of an edge to the third power. Since 2 cubed is 8, the length of an edge of this cube is 2. We need AB and AC, and so we have to concentrate on smaller right triangles on the same face of the cube that includes triangle ABC.

On the upper left, directly above point A is an unlabeled vertex—let's call that point Y—and down below point A is an unlabeled vertex—we'll call that point X. Look at triangle AXC. It's a right triangle because angle AXC is one of the angles formed by two edges of a cube—and AC is its hypotenuse. AX is half an edge of the cube because point A's the midpoint of edge XY. That means that AX has length 1 and XC is an edge of the cube, so it has length 2 . The legs of this right triangle are 1 and 2, so we can use the Pythagorean theorem to find the length of AC. AX^2 is 1^2, XC^2 is 2^2, 1^2 is 1, 2^2 is 4, the sum of 1 and 4 is 5, AC^2 is 5 and AC has length $\sqrt{5}$. AB is identical to AC because triangle AYB is identical to triangle AXC, so AB also has length $\sqrt{5}$ and the perimeter of ABC is $2 + 2\sqrt{5}$, choice (**C**).

30. D

The catch here is that it's not which of the following is 850 percent *of* 8×10^3, it's which of the following is 850 percent *greater than* 8×10^3. Well, what's bigger, 850 percent of 1 or a number that's 850 percent greater than 1? Eight hundred and fifty percent of 1 is 8.5×1 or $8\frac{1}{2}$. But a number that's 850 percent greater than 1 is $1 + 850$ percent of 1, it's $1 + 8.5$ or 9.5. So the number we want is $9.5 \times 8 \times 10^3$. And $9.5 \times 8 = 76$, so the answer is 76×10^3, or 7.6×10^4, in scientific notation.

31. A

We have to plug 1 in for x and solve the equation for y. Well, $x + 3$ is $1 + 3$—that's what's inside the parentheses and we do that first. We have $1 + 3 = 4$ inside the parentheses. $y = 4^2$, 4^2 is 16, and 16 is greater than 9, so the answer is (**A**).

32. B

In both columns we'll use the basic formula: rate × time = distance. In Column A, 40 mph × 4 hours traveled gives you 160 miles. In Column B, 70 mph × $2\frac{1}{2}$ hours, $2 \times 70 = 140$, half of 70 is 35,

and $140 + 35 = 175$ miles in Column B. And 175 is greater than 160, so the answer is (**B**).

33. D

This is intended to conjure up a picture of heavy cookies in one bag and light grapes in the other, but you can't assume that because cookies are usually bigger than grapes, these cookies weigh more than these grapes. Since you don't know how much each cookie and each grape weighs, you can't find the number of cookies or grapes, so it's (**D**).

34. C

Here we have triangle ABC—base BC has been extended on one side so we have an exterior angle drawn in and labeled 120°. We want to compare side lengths AB and BC—in any triangle, the largest side will be opposite the largest angle, so we want to see which of these sides is opposite a larger angle. Since angle A is labeled 60°, is angle C less than, equal to, or greater than 60? Notice that the adjacent angle is 120°—the two together form a straight line, so their sum is 180°. And $180 - 120 = 60$, so angle C is a 60° angle. Since the angles are equal, the sides are equal, and the answer is (**C**).

35. A

Notice the way the diagram is set up—$a + b$ is the same as PQ. Our equation is $8a + 8b = 24$. Divide by 8. We end up with $a + b = 3$. PQ is 3 and since 3 is greater than 2, the answer is (**A**).

36. A

All we know is that x is less than y, but though we don't know their values, we may know enough to determine a relationship. In Column A we have $y - x$, the larger number minus the smaller number, so you must get a positive difference, even if both numbers are negative. In Column B you have the smaller number minus the larger number—the difference is the same except this time it is negative. So you can determine a relationship—you know the answer is (**A**), the quantity in Column A is always greater than the quantity in Column B.

37. D

Remember, area equals $\frac{1}{2}$ × base × height. Both triangles have the same height, because they have the same apex point A and each of them has as its base a part of line EB. So the one with the larger base has the larger area. Which is bigger, CB or DE? We have no way to figure it out. We are not given any relationships or lengths for any of those segments, so the answer is (**D**).

38. B

There's one box that's in both rows—the one in the middle with value $\frac{2}{9}$. In fact, we have $\frac{1}{3}$ + $\frac{2}{9}$ + y in the horizontal row, $x + \frac{2}{9} + \frac{4}{5}$ in the vertical row, and we are comparing x and y. Since $\frac{2}{9}$ is part of both rows, we can throw it out. So we have $\frac{1}{3} + y = \frac{4}{5} + x$. We have $\frac{1}{3} + y$ and that is the same as $\frac{4}{5} + x$. Since $\frac{4}{5}$ is greater than $\frac{1}{3}$, the number we add to $\frac{4}{5}$ has to be less than the number we add to $\frac{1}{3}$ for the sums to be the same. Since $\frac{4}{5}$ is greater than $\frac{1}{3}$, x must be less than y. The answer is (**B**).

39. B

Looking at the fraction in Column A we have $\frac{1}{3} \times \frac{1}{4}$ in the numerator, $\frac{2}{3} \times \frac{1}{2}$ in the denominator. We can cancel the factor of $\frac{1}{3}$ from the numerator and denominator, right? Cancel a $\frac{1}{3}$ from each and you end up with $1 \times \frac{1}{4}$ in the numerator, $2 \times \frac{1}{2}$ in the denominator. Using the same approach, we can cancel a factor of $\frac{1}{4}$, so we're left with 1×1 in the numerator and 2×2

in the denominator, so the value of Column A is $\frac{1}{4}$. Now take a look at Column B. It's the reciprocal of the value in Column A. You have $\frac{2}{3} \times \frac{1}{2}$ in the numerator and $\frac{1}{3} \times \frac{1}{4}$ in the denominator. So you have $\frac{4}{1}$ as your value for Column B. With 4 in Column B and $\frac{1}{4}$ in Column A, the answer is (**B**).

40. B

Make a map—if you have trouble with geometry, this will make it much easier. Eileen drives due north from town A to town B for 60 miles. Start at a point and draw a line straight up. Label the point you started at A and the point above it, B. Label 60 as the length of the distance from A to B. Next she drives due east from town B to town C for a distance of 80 miles. Start at point B, draw a line straight over to the right, call the right endpoint C, and label as 80 the distance BC. You have a right angle, angle ABC. Well, the distance from town A to town C is the hypotenuse of a right triangle if you draw line AC. The two legs are 60 and 80 and this is one of our Pythagorean ratios. It is a 6–8–10 triangle except this time it is 60–80–100. So the distance from A to C is 100 miles, the same as our value for Column A, so the answer is (**B**).

41. C

Let's see if we can do something to make these look more alike by getting both sets of binomials so the $\sqrt{7}$s are in the front. We have $\sqrt{7} - 2$. Is that a positive or negative quantity? And 2^2 is 4, 3^2 is 9 so $\sqrt{7}$ is between 2 and 3. We have $\sqrt{7} - 2$, that is positive, times $\sqrt{7} + 2$, that is positive again. Two positives in Column A and the product of two positives is always positive. What do we have in Column B? Two $- \sqrt{7}$, that is, a negative number times negative $\sqrt{7} - 2$. And $-\sqrt{7}$ is a negative, -2 is negative, that quantity is negative. You have the product of two negatives in Column B, but a product of two negatives is positive also, so you can't tell which is greater. Let's see if we can make these quantities look more alike. With the last one on the right, $-\sqrt{7} - 2$, if we divide the whole thing by -1, we're left with a positive $\sqrt{7}$ and a positive 2, $\sqrt{7} + 2$. On the right in Column B we have $(2 - \sqrt{7}) \times (-1) \times (\sqrt{7} + 2)$, and $(\sqrt{7} + 2)$ is also in Column A, so we can cancel. Those two factors are the same, right? We have $-1 \times (2 - \sqrt{7})$. Let's distribute again. What is -1×2? It's -2. What is $-1 \times -\sqrt{7}$? It's $+\sqrt{7}$ so we end up with $+\sqrt{7} + -2$ or $\sqrt{7} - 2$. It's exactly the same as the factor in Column A. So the quantities are equal and the answer is **(C)**.

42. B

We can see from our diagram that r and s are the coordinates of a point on our line. We have a line on the graph with one point with coordinates $\left(\frac{5}{2}, \frac{7}{2}\right)$. The line also goes through the origin $(0, 0)$, so what can we figure out about this line? Well, draw in the line $x = y$, a line which makes a 45° angle with the x-axis that goes from the lower left to the upper right—you notice that it goes through the point $\left(\frac{5}{2}, \frac{5}{2}\right)$, because any point on line $x = y$ has the same x-coordinate and y-coordinate. Point $\left(\frac{5}{2}, \frac{7}{2}\right)$ falls above point $\left(\frac{5}{2}, \frac{5}{2}\right)$, because the y-coordinate is greater, it's above the $x = y$ line. Similarly, point (r, s) lies above the $x = y$ line so the y-coordinate is greater than the x-coordinate and the y-coordinate of that point is s. Where we have coordinates (r, s), r is the x-coordinate, s is the y-coordinate; s is greater than r in this case. The answer is **(B)**, the quantity in Column B is greater.

43. D

We have $1 - \left(\frac{1}{4}\right)$ to the x power in Column A and we have 0.95 in Column B. That's a bizarre comparison, isn't it? Converting Column B, 0.95 into fraction form, $0.95 = \frac{95}{100} = \frac{19}{20}$. What do we have in Column A if $x = 1$? We have $1 - \frac{1}{4}$ or $\frac{3}{4}$. $\frac{19}{20}$ is greater than $\frac{3}{4}$. What happens if we have $x = 2$? Column A becomes $1 - \left(\frac{1}{4}\right)^2$. $\frac{1^2}{4}$ is $\frac{1}{4} \times \frac{1}{4}$ or $1 - \frac{1}{16}$ is $\frac{15}{16}$. So what's bigger, $\frac{15}{16}$ or $\frac{19}{20}$? Still $\frac{19}{20}$, but as x gets larger and we multiply $\frac{1}{4}$ times itself more times, the amount that we're taking away from 1 is going to get smaller and we'll be taking less than $\frac{1}{20}$ away from 1 as soon as we get to $x = 3$. $\frac{1}{4}$ to the third power is $\frac{1}{64}$ and at that point Column A becomes $\frac{63}{64}$. What is bigger, $\frac{19}{20}$ or $\frac{63}{64}$? Well, $\frac{63}{64}$ is bigger, it is closer to 1, and there are two possible relationships here. If x is 1 or 2, Column B is greater. If x is 3 or larger, Column A is greater. The answer is choice **(D)**.

44. A

If you draw in some diameters in the circles, you will see that PS is equal to one diameter, and PQ is equal to two diameters. Let one diameter be d. The perimeter of $PQRS$ is then $PS + PQ + SR + QR = 6d$. The circumference of a circle is πd, where d is a diameter. Since we have two circles, the combined circumferences is $2 \times \pi d = 2\pi d$. Since π is greater than 3 (it's about 3.14), the value in Column A is greater than $6d$ in Column B.

45. B

Hopefully you didn't try to figure out the exact values of each of these. Instead, if you look at Column B and Column A, they look sort of alike because they both have 3 in terms of a power. What is 3^{20}? It's 3×3^{19} right? So we can have $3^{19} + 3^{19} + 3^{19}$ in Column B. In Column A we have $3^{17} + 3^{18} + 3^{19}$. We can subtract 3^{19} from both sides and we're left with $3^{17} + 3^{18}$ in Column A and

$3^{19} + 3^{19}$ in Column B. We know that 3^{19} is bigger than 3^{17} or 3^{18} so we know that $3^{19} + 3^{19}$ is bigger than $3^{17} + 3^{18}$. The answer is (**B**), the quantity in Column B is greater.

46. E

We have $4 + y = 14 - 4y$ and we want to solve for y. We can isolate the ys on one side of the equal sign by adding $4y$ to both sides, giving us $4 + 5y = 14$. Subtracting the 4 from both sides we get $5y = 10$. Divide both sides by 5 and get $y = 2$, (**E**).

47. D

Let's go the quickest, most obvious route and use the common denominator method. With $\frac{4}{5}$ and $\frac{5}{4}$, the denominator that we will use is easy to find; just use 5×4 or 20. $\frac{4}{5}$ is $\frac{16}{20}$ and $\frac{5}{4}$ is $\frac{25}{20}$. $\frac{16}{20} + \frac{25}{20}$ is $\frac{41}{20}$, which is (**D**).

48. E

First we need to find m. We are told that $3m$ is 81. Well, 81 is 9×9. 9 is 3^2. So we have $3^2 \times 3^2 = 81$ or $3 \times 3 \times 3 \times 3 = 81$. How many factors of 3 are there in 81? There are 4, so m has the value 4. Now 4^3 is 4×4 is 16. And 16×4 is 64. So (**E**) is correct, 64 is m^3.

49. B

We are looking for the area in square meters of square C. Now notice we have one side of square B butted up against one side of square A—they're not the same length, but the difference in their lengths is made up by the length of a side of square C. One side of square B + one side of square C = one side of square A. We can figure out the length of the side of A and length of the side of B, which will let us figure out the length of side of square C. That is what we need to figure out the area of square C. The area of a square is its side squared. The area of square A is 81, so it has a side of $\sqrt{81} = 9$. The area of square B is 49, so it has sides of length $\sqrt{49} = 7$.

So $9 = 7 + C$, so C must have length 2. So we have 2 as the length of the side of square C, 2^2 is 4, there are 4 square meters in gardening area C, and the answer is (**B**).

50. E

We can figure out how many students scored exactly 85. Twenty-three scored 85 or over, and 18 scored over 85. So $23 - 18$ or 5 students scored exactly 85 on the exam, but that's no help. How many students scored less than 85? We don't know—we can't answer this question. It's (**E**), it can't be determined.

51. C

We're asked in which year the energy use in country Y was closest to 650 million kilowatt hours, so we just have to follow the jagged line, which represents energy use from left to right until we encounter a vertical line representing a year in which we're close to 650 million. The one year in which this is true is 1970. In no other year are we as close, so (**C**), 1970, is our answer.

52. C

In order to find how many categories had energy use greater than 150 million kilowatts, you have to find out how many total kilowatts were used in that year using the line graph. You see that there were 600 million kilowatts used in 1965. What is the relationship of 150 million kilowatts to 600 million kilowatts? It's 25 percent of 600 million kilowatts, so we're looking for categories with more than 25 percent of the energy use for 1965. How many categories exceeded 25 percent? Just two, government and industrial. So our answer is (**C**).

53. D

We can estimate quite a bit from our graph. If we look at our line chart, we can see that as time goes on, energy use goes up pretty steadily. It went up sharply between 1960 and 1965, then more gradually from 1965 to 1980. Because in more recent years the overall use was much greater, if the percent of industrial use was about the same over all the years, then as the overall use increases, the amount used for industrial purposes will increase also. Let's take a quick look at the bar graph and see if that is the case. Was the percent being used for industrial use about the same? Well, it didn't fluctuate much from 1960 to 1970, but in 1975 industrial use jumped significantly as a percent of the total, then shrank significantly going to 1980. The most likely answer is 1975, and if you find 40 percent of 690 million, your amount for 1975, you get 276 million kilowatt hours. Then if you find 20 percent of 710 million, your amount for 1980, you only get 142 million kilowatt hours, so **(D)**, 1975, is the correct answer.

54. D

What we are going to do for 1960 and 1965 is find the per capita personal use, then find the percent decrease from 1960 to 1965. To do that, we have to plug in a value for the population of country Y for 1960. Let's use 100 million for the '60s population. The per capita use in 1960 is the total personal use, which is 30 percent of 500 million, that's 150 million. We know that 150 million, the total personal use, equals 100 million, the population × the per capita use. The per capita use is $\frac{3}{2}$ or 1.5. Going on to 1965, we are told the population increased by

20 percent, so in 1965 the population was 120 million people. What was the total personal use of energy? It was a little bit less than 20 percent of our total 600 million so we'll call it 20 percent of 600 million, or 120 million. If total personal use is 120 million and we have 120 million people, that's one kilowatt hour per person. What's the percent decrease? It's a decrease of $\frac{1}{3}$, $33\frac{1}{3}$ percent. But remember, in 1965, they were

using a little more energy for personal use than we figured. The correct answer must be a little greater than $33\frac{1}{3}$ percent, so 40 percent, **(D)**, is the correct answer.

55. A

Statement I says farm use of energy increased between 1960 and 1980. In 1960, 500 million kilowatt hours were used. In 1980, 710 million kilowatt hours were used. What was the percent of farm use in 1960? It was 30 percent of the total in 1960 and a little bit less than 30 percent, around 28 percent, in 1980. The percent is very close together while the whole has become much larger from 1960 to 1980, so 30 percent of 500 million is less than 28 percent of 710 million. Farm use of energy did go up in that 20-year period and Statement I is going to be part of our answer. That eliminates two answer choices, **(B)** and **(D)**.

Statement II is harder. It says that in 1980, industrial use of energy was greater than industrial use of energy in 1965. But what was it in 1965? Industrial use of energy in 1965 was 30 percent of 600 million. We got the percent from the bar graph, the total from the line chart. Okay, 30 percent of 600 million is 180 million. But what about 1980? In 1980 industrial use of energy was 20 percent of a larger whole, 710 million kilowatt hours. Well, 20 percent of 710 is 142 million. That's less than 180 million, isn't it? In fact, industrial use of energy went down from 1965 to 1980, so this can't be inferred from the graph and it's not part of our answer. That cuts out **(C)** and **(E)**, leaving choice **(A)**, I only. Statement III is another easy one to eliminate because it says more people were employed by the government of country Y in 1980 than in 1960. These graphs deal only with energy use, not with employment, so it's irrelevant and we can eliminate it. Only Statement I can be inferred, and (**A**) is correct.

56. E

The average is $\dfrac{\text{The sum of terms}}{\text{The number of terms}}$. Here we have $y - z$ and the other number, which we will call x. The average of x and $y - z$ is $3y$, so $3y = \dfrac{x + y - z}{2}$. Multiplying both sides by 2 gives $6y = x + y - z$. Subtracting $y - z$ from both sides gives $5y + z = x$. So the other number, x, is $5y + z$, answer choice (**E**).

57. B

We're told that the area of triangle ABC is 35 and in our diagram we're given a height for triangle ABC. If we use BC as the base of the triangle, the perpendicular distance from segment BC up to point A is 7, so we can find the length of BC. When we find the length BC, the base of triangle ABC, what do we have? We have the hypotenuse of right triangle BDC. Given the hypotenuse and the length of leg BD, which is given in the diagram as 6, we'll be able to find the third leg of the triangle, side DC, which is what we're looking for. Okay, going back to triangle ABC where we started, the area is 35 and the height is 7. The area of a triangle is $\dfrac{1}{2}$ base × height, so $\dfrac{1}{2}$ base × height is 35, $\dfrac{1}{2} \times 7 \times$ length BC is 35. That means $7 \times$ length BC is 70, so BC must have length 10. Now we can look at right triangle BDC. Here is a right triangle with one leg of length 6, the hypotenuse of length 10, and the third side unknown; what we have is a 6-blank-10 right triangle. That's one of our famous Pythagorean ratios—it's a 6-8-10 triangle. So DC must have length 2×4, or 8, (**B**).

58. A

We're trying to find the shortest distance in meters a person would have to walk to go from point A to a point on side BC of the triangular field represented in our diagram. In order to get the shortest distance from side BC up to point A, we want to draw a perpendicular line from point A down to side BC. That will divide up the triangular field into right triangles. Let's draw in the path from point A down to segment BC and call the new vertex we make point D. We just created two smaller right triangles, ADC and ADB. Now our diagram tells us that length BC is 160 meters and AB is 100 meters—AC is also 100 meters. Now each of these two right triangles has 100 meters as the length of its hypotenuse. What does that tell you about triangle ABC? AB and AC have the same lengths, so this is an isosceles triangle. That means that when you drew in the perpendicular distance from A down to D, you split that isosceles triangle into two identical right triangles. Length BD is the same as length BC. So each of them is half of 160 meters, or 80 meters each. We have right triangles with hypotenuses of length 100 meters each and one leg of each these right triangles is 80 meters. This is a 3–4–5 right triangle, with each member of the ratio multiplied by 80. So AD must have length 60, and the minimum distance is 60 meters, (**A**).

59. D

We're told the ratio of $2a$ to b is eight times the ratio of b to a. That's awkward to keep track of in English—it's a little easier to write fractions. The ratio of $2a{:}b$ equals $2\dfrac{b}{a}$. So $2\dfrac{a}{b} = 8\left(\dfrac{b}{a}\right)$. We're asked to find what $\dfrac{b}{a}$ could be; that may tell you there's more than one possible value for $\dfrac{b}{a}$, but let's start with the equation we just put together using translation and isolate $\dfrac{b}{a}$. To do that, we'll divide both sides of the equation by 8, which is the same as multiplying by $\dfrac{1}{8}$. So now we have

$\frac{1}{8} \times 2\frac{b}{a} = \frac{b}{a}$. Well, what is $\frac{1}{8} \times 2\frac{b}{a}$? It's $\frac{a}{4b}$.

So $\frac{a}{4b} = \frac{b}{a}$. We need to multiply both sides of the equation right now on both sides by $\frac{b}{a}$. It'll be more complicated on the right side but simpler on the left because the as and bs on the left side will cancel out, and you'll be left with $\frac{1}{4}$. On the right you have $\frac{b}{a} \times \frac{b}{a} = \frac{b^2}{a^2}$. So we have $\frac{1}{4} = \frac{b^2}{a^2}$. So $\frac{b}{a}$ could represent positive or negative $\frac{1}{2}$.

60. D

A dentist earns n dollars for each filling plus x dollars for every 15 minutes. So the money is figured in two different ways; dollars for each filling and dollars per hour, represented in terms of 15 minutes. Our result will be a two-part answer choice. If you can figure out one part, it will let you eliminate some choices. She put in 21 fillings. She makes n dollars for each, so she gets $21n$ dollars for fillings. You can eliminate **(B)** and **(E)** because **(B)** has only $14n$ in it, and **(E)** has $\frac{21}{4}n$ dollars in it. That narrows our choices to **(A)**, **(C)**, and **(D)**.

How about the hourly rate? The dentist works 14 hours in a week. Does that mean she makes $14x$ dollars? No, because the rate is dollars for every 15 minutes. Now if she makes x dollars for every 15 minutes and 15 minutes is $\frac{1}{4}$ of an hour, then we have to multiply that rate by 4 to get the rate per hour, it's $4x$ dollars per hour. Well, $4x$ times 14 hours is $56x$, so **(D)**, $56x + 21n$, is correct.

SECTION THREE—ANALYTICAL WRITING

Present Your Perspective on an Issue

Sample Essay Response to prompt 1

At face value, the belief that "one should look upon any information described as 'factual'

with skepticism since it may well be proven false in the future," seems ludicrous almost to the point of threatening anarchy. Yet not only does this belief prove well justified, it also amounts to the linchpin around which our complex, highly technical society creates and consolidates its advances.

Science itself provides the best evidence and example in support of this statement. One need look no further than contemporary medicine to see how far we have come from the days when illness was perceived as a sign of moral weakness or as a punishment from on high. In fact, the most outstanding characteristic of what we call "the scientific method" amounts to endless questioning of received theory in search of a more comprehensive explanation of what we perceive to be true. This inquiry extends even to the nature of perception itself. It demands the kind of creative madness perhaps epitomized in the rejoinder Nobel prize–winning physicist Enrico Fermi offered to fellow laureate Nils Bohr who had questioned Fermi on whether a new theory the Italian was presenting went far enough in its skepticism to meet the test of new science. "But think, Enrico, is this crazy enough?" demanded Bohr. "Maybe," proffered Fermi, "but not really."

Furthermore, the advances made through constant questioning are not limited to the scientific arena: The skeptical attitudes of ancient Greek philosophers, as well as those of Renaissance mariners, 19th-century suffragists, and 20th-century civil rights activists, have left the world a richer and more hopeful place. By refusing to accept the world as explained by contemporary "fact," these doubters helped give birth to societies and cultures in which human potential and accomplishment have been enabled to an unprecedented degree.

In contrast, those societies that cultivate adherence to received belief and a traditional nonskeptical approach have advanced very little over the centuries. In Tibet, for instance, the prayer wheels spin endlessly around a belief system as secure and unquestioning as the Himalayas themselves. While there may very well be things worth learning from such a society, Tibet has proven to lack adaptability and expansiveness and prefers to turn inward, away from the modern world. Such introspection has not given Tibet immunity nor an array of defenses in the face of contemporary medical, social, and political problems.

It seems clear from the above discussion that a healthy skepticism remains the hallmark of Western faith and hope as we face the future. As the basis of our resiliency and creativity, this attitude offers the most positive prognosis for a society that revels in the solution of conundrums that its own constant questioning brings continually into view.

Analyze an Argument

Sample Essay Response

While it may prove to be a worthy project, the argument that Tusk University should build a new recreational facility to attract new students and to better serve the needs of its current student body appears to rely upon assumptions that lack conclusive supporting evidence. The writer would be well advised to address these issues in order to make the point of the argument more cogent and convincing.

First and foremost, the writer assumes, without providing any evidence, that recreational facilities will be a significant factor in attracting and serving students interested in Tusk. This begs the question of the role of recreation and/or athletic facilities in the matriculation and retention of students in institutions of higher learning. In the absence of any reference to the academic mission of the University, or even of the role that the facility might have in attracting, retaining, or helping to fund areas more central to that mission, the writer's conclusion appears unsupported.

Secondly, the writer assumes, again without citing specific evidence, that the projected doubling of enrollment will by itself lead to an increase in demand and presumably in use for the new recreational facilities proposed. Even if the facilities would indeed be attractive relative to those available off-campus, the author has provided no proof that a substantial part of the increased or even current enrollment would be inclined to consider the new facilities an asset to their education. Suppose for a moment that this enlarged commuter-based enrollment turns out to be largely made up of part-time students with jobs and family demands away from the campus. Would such a student body see the new facility as a priority? Would the schedules of such students allow them to take advantage of the improvement?

Finally, the author fails to describe what specific services, programs, and amenities the proposed new facility will provide, how and at what cost relative to facilities available elsewhere these will be made available to the university community, and how the financial burden of both building and operating the new center will be offset. Beyond these issues endemic to the campus setting, the writer presents no overview of the environmental, social, and public relations aspects of the project in a larger context, either intra- or extracollegiate.

The issues raised here could easily be addressed by the provision of evidence that backs up the author's claim. By assembling sufficient and specific demographic and economic evidence to support the argument's questionable assumptions, the writer may not only be able to overcome the limitations of the present argument, but provide a rationale for the proposal beyond the terms offered here.

Part Five

GETTING INTO GRAD SCHOOL

CHAPTER 7: **WHERE AND WHEN TO APPLY**

- Find the right kind of school for you
- Review the key criteria for selecting a program
- Assess your chances of getting in
- Learn how to set up an application schedule
- Keep track of important deadlines

You probably know what you want to study as a graduate student; but where will you apply? This question is usually a two-part question. First: which graduate programs should you consider, regardless of your chances? And second: which of these programs can you actually get into? This chapter will help you answer these questions—and many more you may have about the process of choosing an institution for postgraduate study.

WHAT PROGRAMS YOU SHOULD CONSIDER

Once you've made the decision to pursue graduate studies, the decision about where to go to school shouldn't be taken lightly. It will have a major influence on your daily life for the next several years and will influence your academic and career paths for years to come. Many students allow themselves to be influenced by a professor or mentor or school rankings, then find that they're unhappy in a certain program because of its location, workload, cost, or some unforeseen factor. With that said, remember: this is for your own good! Some hard work today will help to ensure that you'll be happy in your choice tomorrow. Let's take a look at some of the factors that you'll need to consider when choosing a school.

 **READ MORE**

For more tips on getting into grad school, pick up a copy of Kaplan's *Get Into Graduate School.*

YOUR GOALS

It's important to keep your goals in mind when evaluating graduate programs. Before you take the leap, it's key that you have a pretty clear idea where your interests really lie, what grad school life is like, and whether you are compatible with a particular program and its professors. Armed with this information, you should be able to successfully apply to the right programs, get accepted, and use your graduate school time to help you get a head start on the postgraduation job search.

Students decide to enter master's and doctoral degree programs for a variety of reasons. Some want to pursue a career in academia. To teach at two-year colleges, you'll need at least a master's degree; to teach and do research at four-year colleges, universities, and graduate programs, you'll need a doctorate. Others need graduate education to meet national and state licensing requirements in fields such as social work, engineering, and architecture. Some students want to change careers, while for others, an advanced degree opens up new opportunities in their current field.

Most master's programs are two years long, and master's students are generally one of two types: those on the academic track, where the degree programs focus on classical research and scholarship, and those on the practical track, where the degree program is actually a professional training program that qualifies them to enter or advance in a field such as social work or education.

Other options to consider if you're pursuing a master's degree are cooperative, joint, and interdisciplinary programs. In cooperative programs, you apply to, answer to, and graduate from one school, but you have access to classes, professors, and facilities at a cooperating school as part of the program. In joint- or dual-degree programs you work toward two degrees simultaneously, either within the same school or at two neighboring schools. Interdisciplinary programs are generally run by a faculty committee from a number of different departments. You apply to, register with, and are graduated by only one of the departments; you and your faculty committee design your curriculum.

Doctoral programs are designed to create scholars capable of independent research that will add new and significant knowledge in their fields. From the first, you will be regarded as an apprentice in your field. Your first year or two in the program will be spent on coursework, followed by "field" or "qualifying" exams. Once you've passed those exams, demonstrating that you have the basic factual and theoretical knowledge of your field down cold, you will then be permitted to move on to independent research, in the form of your doctoral dissertation. During most of this time you can get financial aid in the form of teaching or research assistantships; in exchange for assisting professors in the classroom or the lab, you get a small stipend and/or tuition remission.

If you want to get a doctoral degree, you can get a master's and reapply to Ph.D. programs, or enter directly into the doctoral program. The first method gives you flexibility but generally takes longer, costs more in the long run, and means reliving the application process.

PROGRAM REPUTATION

Although you shouldn't place too much stock in the school and program rankings, you should consider a program's overall reputation. When you assess a program's reputation, don't just consider its national ranking, but think about whether it fits your goals and interests. You can get information from a variety of sources, formal and informal.

Each year, various groups publish rankings of graduate programs: *U.S. News and World Report* on American graduate programs, *Maclean's* on Canadian programs, and many others. These rankings can give you a general sense of the programs in your field and may include profiles of distinguished professors, but they tell you nothing about departmental politics, job placement records, or financial aid possibilities.

You should find out which programs are highly regarded in the areas that interest you. You can learn about such details through professional associations (such as the American Psychological Association), comprehensive commercial directories of graduate programs (available through school or local libraries), and via the Internet.

Don't forget to contact schools and departments directly. Most departments have a chairperson who is also the admissions contact; he or she can put you in touch with current students and alumni who are willing to discuss the program with you. The chair is usually willing to answer questions as well.

Try to speak to at least one current student and one alumnus from each program you're seriously considering. You'll find that many graduate students are quite outspoken about the strengths and weaknesses of their professors, programs, and the state of the job market in their field.

If you're an undergraduate, or still have contacts from your undergraduate experience, ask your professors for their take on the various graduate programs. You'll often find that they have a great deal of inside information on academic and research trends, impending retirements, intellectual rivalries, and rising stars.

Remember, a program's reputation isn't everything, but the higher your school is regarded in the marketplace, the better your job prospects are likely to be upon graduation.

LOCATION

The two key questions that you should consider regarding a school's location are: how will it affect the overall quality of your graduate school experience, and how will it affect your employability? Some students prefer an urban setting. Others prefer a more rustic environment. Cost of living can also be a factor.

Geography may be an important criterion for you. Perhaps your geographical choices are limited by a spouse's job or other family obligations. Or perhaps you already know where you want to live after graduation. If you're planning on a career in academia, you'll probably want to choose a nationally known program, regardless of where it's located. If, on the other hand, your program involves a practical dimension (psychology, social work, education, or some interdisciplinary programs), you may want to concentrate your school search on the area in which you hope to live and work, at least initially.

CURRICULUM

To maximize the value of your graduate school experience, be sure that a department's areas of concentration match up with your own interests. Knowing a program's particular theoretical bent and practical selling points can help ensure that you choose a school that reflects your own needs and academic leanings. Does one school of thought, one style of research, predominate? If so, is there anyone else working in the department with a different theoretical framework? Will you have opportunities to work within a variety of theories and orientations? What special opportunities are available? How well are research programs funded? Do the professors have good records at rounding up grants? In field or clinical work, what are the options? Are programs available in your area of interest?

Find the environment that works best for you. Don't put yourself in a situation in which you don't have access to the courses or training you're seeking. It's your education. Your time. Your energy. Your investment in your future. By being proactive, you can help guarantee that you maximize your graduate school experience.

FACULTY

One of the most important decisions you make in your graduate school career will be your choice of adviser. This one person will help you with course selection, clinical, research, or field education opportunities, and can make or break the thesis/dissertation process. So when you investigate a department, look for a faculty member whose interests and personality are compatible with yours. Since this single person (your "dream adviser") may not be available, be sure to also look for a couple of other professors who, although their interests may not coincide exactly with yours, could work with you if you need them.

If one of your prime motivations in attending a certain program is to take classes from specific professors, make sure that you will have that opportunity. At the master's level, access to prominent professors is often limited to large, foundation-level lecture courses, where papers and exams are graded by the professor's graduate assistants or tutors. At the doctoral level, professors are generally much more accessible.

Is the department stable or changing? Find out whether the faculty is nearing retirement age. Impending retirements may not affect you in a two-year master's program, but this is a serious consideration in doctoral programs, which can (and often do) stretch on for over five years. If you have hopes of working with a distinguished professor, will he or she even be available for that time—and longer, if you are delayed? Will the department be large and stable enough to allow you to put together a good thesis or dissertation committee? Also try to find out whether younger members of the department are established. Do they get sufficient funding? Have they settled into the institution enough that there are not likely to be political controversies?

PLACEMENT

Although some people attend graduate school for the love of knowledge, most want to enhance their career prospects in some way. When you graduate with your hard-won degree, what are your chances of getting your desired job?

You'll want to ask what kind of track record a given program has in placing its alums. With today's highly competitive job market, it's especially important to find out when and where graduates have found work. If you're considering work in business, industry, local agencies, schools, health care facilities, or the government, find out whether these employers visit the campus to recruit. Major industries may visit science programs to interview prospective graduates. Some will even employ graduate students over the summers or part time. If you're going into academia, find out whether recent grads have been able to find academic posts, how long the search took, and where they are working. Are they getting tenure-track positions at reasonably prestigious departments, or are they shifting from temporary appointment to temporary appointment with little hope of finding a stable position?

Don't just look at the first jobs that a school's graduates take. Where are they in 5, 10, and even 25 years? Your career is more like a marathon than a sprint. So take the long view. A strong indicator of a program's strength is the accomplishments of its alumni.

STUDENT BODY

Some graduate catalogs contain profiles of or statements by current master's and Ph.D. students. Sometimes this is an informal blurb on a few students—it's really marketing material—and sometimes it's a full listing of graduate students. Use this as a resource both to find out what everyone else in the program is up to, and to find current students you can interview about the school and the program.

Because much of your learning will come from your classmates, consider the makeup of your class. A school with a geographically, professionally, and ethnically diverse student body will expose you to far more viewpoints than will a school with a more homogeneous group. If you're an older applicant, ask yourself how you will fit in with a predominantly younger group of students. For many, the fit is terrific, but for others, the transition can be tougher. The answer depends on you, but it's something to consider.

The student body, as well as the faculty, will have varied philosophical and political orientations. The theories and perspectives considered liberal in one program can be deemed conservative in another, and where you fit among your peers can have a great deal of influence on your image and your opportunities in your department. If you plan on an academic career, remember that your student colleagues will someday be your professional colleagues.

NETWORKING

Forging relationships—with your classmates, your professors and, in a larger sense, all the alumni—is a big part of the graduate school experience. One of the things that you'll take with you when you graduate, aside from an education, a diploma, and debt, is that network. And whether you thrive on networking or consider it a four-letter word, it's a necessity. At some point it may help you advance your career, in academia or outside.

QUALITY OF LIFE

Your graduate school experience will extend far beyond your classroom learning, particularly for full-time students. That's why it's so important to find out as much as you can about the schools that interest you. For example, what activities would you like to take part in? Perhaps convenient recreational facilities or an intramural sports program is appealing. If you'd like to be involved in community activities, perhaps there's a school volunteer organization. Regardless of your interests, your ability to maintain balance in your life in the face of a rigorous academic challenge will help you keep a healthy outlook.

Housing is another quality-of-life issue to consider. Is campus housing available? Is off-campus housing convenient? Is it affordable? Where do most of the students live?

Quality of life is also an important consideration for spouses and significant others, especially if school requires a move to a new city. When graduate school takes over your life, your spouse may feel left out. Find out what kind of groups and activities there are for partners. For example, are there any services to help your spouse find employment? Is child care available? Is there a good school system in the area?

FULL-TIME VERSUS PART-TIME

In a full-time program, you can focus your energy on your studies to maximize your learning. You're also likely to meet more people and forge closer relationships with your classmates. Many programs are oriented toward the full-time student and many top-tier programs don't offer part-time programs. A part-time schedule may also make it difficult for you to take classes with the best professors.

There are, however, many compelling reasons why attending part time may make sense for you. It may just not be economically feasible for you to attend full time. Or you may wish to continue gaining professional experience while earning the degree that will allow you to move on to the next level. If there is a possibility that you will have to work while you are in school, particularly while you're in the coursework stage, check out the flexibility of any program that interests you. Are there night/weekend classes? When is the library open? What about the lab? Talk to students who are currently in the program, especially those who work. Part-time programs often are slow, which can be discouraging, especially when licensure or salary increases are at stake.

Although many students in full-time graduate programs support themselves with part-time work, their primary allegiance is to the graduate degree. It will become the focus of your life, but if there is any way that you can manage full-time, or nearly full-time, studies at the higher levels, do it. You can graduate quicker and start picking up the financial pieces that much sooner—and often with a more secure base for your job search in the form of good support from your adviser.

Most master's programs are flexible about part-time studies, but doctoral programs are less so. Many doctoral programs expect a minimum amount of time "in residence"— that is, enrolled as a full-time student for a certain number of consecutive semesters. This requirement is usually listed in the catalog.

PROGRAM COSTS

Some graduate programs charge "per credit" or "per hour," meaning that your tuition bill is calculated by the number of credits you take each semester. Other programs charge per semester or per year with a minimum and maximum number of credits you can take per semester for that flat fee. In general, per credit makes sense for part-time students while per semester makes sense for full-time students.

Generally speaking, the most expensive kind of graduate program (per semester) will be a master's degree at a private school. Loans are available to master's-level students, but grants, scholarships, and other forms of "free" financial assistance are harder to find. Furthermore, most private schools apply the same tuition rate to in-state and out-of-state residents. State colleges and universities usually give in-state residents a tuition break. Other forms of savings can come from finding the cheapest living and housing expenses and from working your way through the program as quickly as possible.

At the doctoral level, tuition remission (you don't pay any of it) and grants or stipends (they pay you) are common. Percentages of doctoral students in a program receiving full tuition remission plus stipend/grant money can range anywhere from 0 percent (although students in these programs may be receiving either tuition remission or stipend/grant money) to 100 percent—every student in the program pays no tuition and receives some grant or stipend. In these programs the major financial burden is living expenses over the years of coursework, language requirements, qualifying and field exams, research, and the dissertation.

WHERE YOU CAN GET IN

Now that you've developed a list of schools that meet your needs, you should take an objective look at your chances of getting into them.

ASSESSING YOUR CHANCES

A good way to get a sense of how graduate schools will perceive you is to make up a fact sheet with your GRE scores (or projected scores), your overall grade point average (GPA) as well as your GPA in your major, and your work experience. Outside activities and your personal statement will contribute to the overall "score" that admissions officers will use to evaluate you, but let's stick with the raw data for now.

The next step is to find a current source of information about graduate school programs. There are several guides published every year that provide data about acceptance rates for given years, median GPA, and GRE scores. You also can request this information directly from a given department. The school of your dreams may not care very much about your GPA, but it might be very interested in your GRE scores. Make sure you find out what your target school prioritizes in its search for worthy applicants.

One of the best ways to gauge whether you're in contention for a certain program is to compare your numbers to theirs. And remember that you needn't hit the nail on the head. Median means average, so some applicants do better or worse than the GRE scores or GPA cited. And, remember all those other factors that add up to make you a desirable applicant. Comparing numbers is merely a good way to get a preliminary estimate of your compatibility with the schools of your choice.

"SAFETY" SCHOOLS

Now that you have some idea of where you fall in the applicant pool, you can begin to make decisions about your application strategy. No matter what your circumstances, it's wise to choose at least one school that is likely to accept you, a "safety" school. Make sure it's one that fits your academic goals and your economic circumstances. If your GRE scores and GPA are well above a school's median scores, and you don't anticipate any problems with other parts of your record or application, you've probably found your safety school.

TOP CHOICE SCHOOLS

If your ideal program is one that you don't seem qualified for, apply to your "dream school" anyway. You may be surprised! GPA and GRE scores are not the only two criteria by which applications are judged, and you may discover that you are admitted in spite of your academic background, on the merits of your personal statement, work samples, or other criteria. It's always worth a try. Some people underestimate their potential and only apply to safety schools. This can often lead to disappointment when they end up at one of these schools and discover that it doesn't provide the rigorous training that they want.

WHEN TO APPLY

With the number of graduate school applications received by institutions of higher learning on the rise, the issue of when to apply for admission has become very important. There are perfect times to begin and end the application process. You should begin at least a year before you plan to enter school (sooner if you're a nontraditional candidate or are changing fields). Find out the following essential dates as early as possible and incorporate them into your own personal application schedule:

- Standardized test registration deadlines
- Transcript deadlines (some schools send out transcripts only on particular dates)
- Letters of recommendation due dates
- Application deadlines (submit your application as early as possible to ensure that you get a fair and comprehensive review)
- Financial aid forms (federal/state programs, universities, and independent sources of aid all have definite deadlines)

SETTING UP AN APPLICATION SCHEDULE

The following "seasonal" schedule is organized to help you understand how to proceed through the admissions process.

Winter (18–20 months prior to start date)
- If you're a nontraditional applicant or plan to switch fields, begin investigating program requirements. Take courses to make up any missing portion of your background.

Spring (16–18 months prior to start date)
- Browse through program catalogs and collect information on different grants and loans. Create your own graduate school library.

Summer
- Request applications from schools. If they're not available yet, ask for last year's so you can get a feel for the questions you'll have to answer.
- Write a draft of your personal statement and show it to trusted friends and/or colleagues for feedback.

- Consider registering for the GRE in the fall. This will give you plenty of time to submit your scores with your application.
- Research your options for test preparation. Take the test included in this book to give you a good idea of where you stand with regard to the GRE.

Early Fall

- Ask for recommendations. Make sure that your recommenders know enough about you to write a meaningful letter. Once your recommenders have agreed to write a recommendation, let them know when deadlines will be, so you can avoid any timing conflicts.

Late Fall

- Take the GRE.
- Request applications from schools, if you haven't already done so.
- Request institutional, state, and federal financial-aid materials from school aid offices.
- Request information on independent grants and loans.
- Order transcripts from your undergraduate (and any graduate) institution(s).

Winter

- Fill out applications. Mail them as early as possible.
- Fill out financial-aid applications. Mail these early as well.
- Make sure your recommendation writers have the appropriate forms and directions for mailing. Remind them of deadline dates.

Spring

- Sit back and relax (if you can). Most schools indicate how long they will take to inform you of their decision. This is also a crucial time to solidify your financial plans as you begin to receive offers of aid (with any luck).

The timing described here is rough, and you needn't follow it exactly. The most important thing for you to do is make yourself aware of strict deadlines well in advance, so that you'll be able to devote plenty of quality time to your application. In the next chapter, we'll go over the application process in detail.

CHAPTER 8: HOW TO APPLY

- Find out what graduate schools look for
- Learn how to assemble a winning application
- Ace your application essay and interview

Your first step is to order the application forms from the various schools that you've selected. You can do it by mail, but the quickest way is to call the admissions offices around July and have them put you on their mailing lists. Once the applications begin arriving you'll notice one thing quickly: no two applications are exactly alike. Some ask you to write one essay or personal statement, and others may ask for three or more essays on various subjects. Some have very detailed forms requiring extensive background information; others are satisfied with your name and address and little else.

Despite these differences, most applications follow a general pattern with variations on the same kinds of questions. So read this section with the understanding that, although not all of it is relevant to every application, these guidelines will be valuable for just about any graduate school application you'll encounter.

HOW SCHOOLS EVALUATE APPLICANTS

Each graduate school has its own admissions policies and practices, but all programs evaluate your application on a range of objective and subjective criteria. Regardless of which schools you are pursuing, understanding how admissions officers judge your candidacy can give you a leg up on the competition.

Generally, all admissions officers use the application process to measure your intellectual abilities, aptitude in your field of study, and personal characteristics. When you submit your application, admissions officers will evaluate the total package. Most admissions officers look for reasons to admit candidates, not for reasons to reject them. Your challenge, therefore, is to distinguish yourself positively from the other candidates.

INTELLECTUAL ABILITY

To assess your intellectual ability, admissions officers look at two key factors: your academic record and your GRE score.

Academic Record

Your grade point average (GPA) is important, but it's just part of your academic profile. Admissions officers will consider the reputation of your undergraduate institution and the difficulty of your courses. Admissions officers are well aware that comparing GPAs from different schools and even different majors from the same school is like comparing apples and oranges. So they'll look closely at your transcript. Do your grades show an upward trend? How did you perform in your major? How did you fare in courses related to the program you're applying to?

Admissions officers focus primarily on your undergraduate performance, but they will consider graduate studies and nondegree coursework that you have completed. Be sure to submit those transcripts. Generally, the GPA of applicants who are about to complete or have recently completed undergraduate school is given much more weight than that of applicants returning to school after several years.

If you have a poor academic record, it will be tougher to get into a top school, but it is by no means impossible. Your challenge is to find other ways to demonstrate your intellectual horsepower. High GRE scores, an intelligently written personal statement, and strong recommendations will help.

The GRE

You are already familiar with the GRE and are armed with strategies to score higher on the test. An integral part of the admissions process at virtually all schools, the GRE measures general verbal, quantitative, and analytical writing skills. Some programs, particularly in psychology and the sciences, require you to take one or more GRE Subject Tests as well. In addition to or instead of the GRE, some programs require the Miller Analogies Test (MAT). Be sure to check with the programs you're considering to see which tests they require.

When admissions officers review your GRE scores, they'll look at your Verbal, Quantitative, and Writing scores separately, particularly if they have any questions about your abilities in a certain area. Different programs give varying weight to each score. If you've taken the GRE more than once, schools will generally credit you with your highest score, though some may average the scores or take the most recent.

Used by itself, the GRE may not be a great predictor of academic performance, but it is the single best one available. The GRE does not measure your intelligence, nor does it measure the likelihood of your success in your field. As with any standardized test, by preparing properly for the GRE, you can boost your score significantly.

The GRE's Analytical Writing section includes two essays: one requiring you to express and support a position on a given issue, and one requiring you to critique the logic of a given argument. The essays you type into the computer are graded on a 1 to 6 scale and sent to the schools you designate along with your traditional 200–800 scores for the Verbal and Quantitative sections. The Analytical Writing section is designed to provide schools with information about your communications skills that is not otherwise captured on the GRE.

Essentially, the Analytical Writing section is another tool that schools can use to evaluate you. Graduate schools have recognized that the writing section provides you with an opportunity to demonstrate your ability to think critically and communicate complex ideas in a very limited time period. For that reason, admissions officers will be as interested in reading your Analytical Writing samples as they are in relying on your other GRE scores.

Even though the Analytical Writing section is scored separately from the multiple-choice sections, you should prepare for it with the same intensity that you put into preparing for the rest of the GRE. Outstanding writing samples can help you stand out from the crowd. Conversely, seriously flawed essays can reduce your admissions chances.

Fellowships and assistantships

Some graduate programs award fellowships and assistantships partly on the basis of GRE scores. Since most programs have limited funds and therefore limited positions to offer, the awards process can be quite competitive. Not only should you take your scores seriously, you should also confirm the submission deadline with your department. The financial aid deadline is usually earlier than the application deadline.

Relevant Experience and Skills

When evaluating your application, admissions officers look at work experience and other activities related to the program in question. In fields like psychology, social work, and health, your research and practical experience will play a role in the admissions decision. If you're applying to film, writing, or other arts programs, you'll be asked to submit samples of your work. And if you're planning on an academic career, your research and publications will be of particular interest to the admissions committee. The way you present yourself and your achievements should be tailored to the programs you're applying to.

You can communicate some of your abilities through the straightforward "data" part of your application. Be sure to describe your job and internship responsibilities. Don't list your title and assume that an admissions officer knows what you do or the level of your responsibilities.

If you are working and applying to a graduate program in the same field, admissions officers will look at your overall career record. How have you progressed? Have you been an outstanding performer? What do your recommendation writers say about your performance? Have you progressed to increasingly higher levels of responsibility? If you have limited work experience, you will not be expected to match the accomplishments of an applicant with 10 years' experience, but you will be expected to demonstrate your abilities.

Extracurricular activities and community involvement also present opportunities for you to highlight your skills. For younger applicants, college activities play a more significant role than for more-seasoned applicants. Your activities say a lot about who you are and what's important to you. Were you a campus leader? Did your activities require discipline and commitment? Did you work with a team? What did you learn from your involvement?

Active community involvement provides a way for you to demonstrate your skills and to impress admissions officers with your personal character. In fact, many applications ask directly about community activities. If you are contemplating getting involved in your community, here's a chance to do something worthwhile and enhance your application in the process.

Personal Characteristics

The third, and most subjective, criterion on which schools evaluate you is your personal character. Admissions officers judge you in this area primarily through your personal statement (and essays, if applicable), recommendations, and personal interview (if applicable). Although different schools emphasize different qualities, most seek candidates who demonstrate maturity, integrity, responsibility, and a clear sense of how they fit into their chosen field. The more competitive programs place special emphasis on these criteria because they have many qualified applicants for each available spot in the class.

Who Evaluates Applicants

At most schools, the board includes professional admissions officers and/or faculty from the department you're applying to. At some schools, the authority to make admissions decisions lies with the Graduate School itself, that is, with the central administration. At others, it lies with individual departments.

What Decisions Do They Make?

Upon reviewing your application, the admissions board may make any number of decisions, including:

- *Admit*: Congratulations, you're in. But read the letter carefully. The board may recommend or, in some cases, require you to do some preparatory coursework to ensure that your quantitative or language skills are up to speed.

- *Reject*: At the top schools, there are far more qualified applicants than there are spaces in the class. Even though you were rejected, you can reapply at a later date. However, if you are considering reapplying, you need to understand why you were rejected and whether you have a reasonable chance of being admitted the next time around. Some schools will speak with you about your application, but they often wait for the end of the admissions season, by which time you may have accepted another offer.

- *Waiting list*: Schools use the waiting list—the educational equivalent of purgatory—to manage class size. The good news is that you wouldn't be on the list if you weren't considered a strong candidate. The bad news is there is no way to know with certainty whether you'll be accepted. Be aware, though, that schools do tend to look kindly upon wait-listed candidates who reapply in a subsequent year.

- *Request for an interview*: Schools at which an interview is not required may request that you interview prior to making their final decision. Your application may have raised some specific issues that you can address in an interview, or perhaps the board feels your personal statement did not give them a complete enough picture to render a decision. Look at this as a positive opportunity to strengthen your case.

PREPARING YOUR APPLICATION

A key part of getting into the graduate school of your choice is to develop a basic application strategy so you can present yourself in the best light.

YOUR APPLICATION AS A MARKETING TOOL

When it comes to applying to graduate school, you are the product. Your application is your marketing document. Marketing yourself doesn't mean that you should lie or even embellish; it just means that you need to make a tight presentation of the facts. Everything in your application should add up to a coherent whole and underscore the fact that you are not only qualified to be in the program but that you should be in it.

Many application forms have a certain tone, one that's comforting and accepting. Why would you like to come to our program, they seem to be asking. They do want an answer to that question, but what's even more important—the subtext for the whole application process—is a bigger question: why should we accept you? This is the question that your application will answer. And with some effective marketing strategies, your answer will be clear, concise, coherent, and strong.

MAXIMIZING THE VARIOUS PARTS OF YOUR APPLICATION

Let's take a close look at how you should approach the specific parts of your application.

PERSONAL STATEMENT

Your personal statement is a critical part of your application. The personal statement is where you can explain why you're applying to graduate school, what interests you about this program, and what your future goals are. The situations you choose to write about and the manner in which you present them can have a major bearing on the strength of your candidacy.

Writing an effective personal statement requires serious self-examination and sound strategic planning. What are the major personal and professional events that have shaped you? What accomplishments best demonstrate your abilities? Remember, admissions officers are interested in getting to know you as a complete person. What you choose to write about sends clear signals about what's important to you and what your values are. You want the readers to put your essay down and think, 'Wow! that was really interesting and memorable,' and, 'Wow! this person really knows why she's going into this program and has real contributions to make to the field.'

Personal Statement Topics

Here are some recent personal-statement topics we found in graduate school catalogs:

UCLA

Please state your purpose in applying for graduate study, your particular area of specialization with the major field, your plans for future occupation or profession, and any additional information that may aid the selection committee in evaluating your preparation and your aptitude for graduate study at UCLA. Attach an additional sheet if necessary.

Bank Street College of Education

Select and describe those experiences and relationships in your background which seem to you to have been significant for your development and as a person going into the field of education. What connections can you make between those experiences and your ideas about children and youth, parents, your own dominant patterns of actions, your plans for graduate study, and your future career? You may include more recent experiences which you consider especially significant for the development of new insights into yourself.

Carnegie Mellon University (Engineering)

Type or print a one- or two-page concise statement that includes the following information:

(1) A brief statement of your primary educational and research interests.

(2) An outline of your research experience and a list of any publications.

(3) A description of your background in engineering and allied fields that is particularly relevant to your objectives—include any relevant industrial or work experience and any academic honors.

Creating Your Statement

Your statement should demonstrate the pattern in your life that has led you to apply for the program. Part of demonstrating why you are right for the program involves demonstrating that you understand what the program is and where it will lead you. A personal statement requires honesty and distinctiveness. If you are heading to graduate school straight from undergraduate school, what has made you so certain that you know what you want to do with your life? If you are returning to school, particularly if you are changing fields, what has led you to this decision? You can use vignettes from your personal history, academic life, work life, and extracurricular activities to explain. If you are applying to a doctoral program, indicate which ideas, fields of research, or problems intrigue you. It's always a good idea to demonstrate familiarity with the field you want to enter.

You should start compiling information for your statement three or four months before you fill out your application. Write a draft once you've narrowed your list of potential topics. Have it edited by someone who knows you well. After rewriting, have someone whose opinion and writing skills you trust read your final draft, make suggestions, and above all, help you proofread.

General Personal Statement Tips

Once you've determined what you plan to write for your statement, keep the following tips in mind:

- *Length*: Schools are pretty specific about how long they want your statement to be. Adhere to their guidelines.

- *Spelling/typos/grammar*: Remember, your application is your marketing document. What would you think of a product that's promoted with sloppy materials containing typos, spelling errors, and grammatical mistakes?

- *Write in the active voice*: Candidates who write well have an advantage in the application process because they can state their case in a concise, compelling manner. Less-effective writers commonly write "passively." For example:

  Passive voice: The essays were written by me.

  Active voice: I wrote the essays.

  Strong writing will not compensate for a lack of substance, but poor writing can torpedo an otherwise impressive candidate.

- *Tone*: On the one hand, you want to tout your achievements and present yourself as a poised, self-confident applicant. On the other hand, arrogance and self-importance do not go over well with admissions officers. Before you submit your application, be sure that you're comfortable with the tone as well as the content.

- *Creative approaches*: If you choose to submit a humorous or creative application, you are employing a high-risk, high-reward strategy. If you're confident you can pull it off, go for it. Be aware, though, that what may work for one admissions officer may fall flat with another. Admissions officers who review thousands of essays every year may consider your approach gimmicky or simply find it distracting. Remember, your challenge is to stand out in the applicant pool in a positive way. Don't let your creativity obscure the substance of your application.

Making Your Statement Distinctive

Depending on the amount of time you have and the amount of effort you're willing to put in, you can write a personal statement that will stand out from the crowd. One of the first mistakes that some applicants make is in thinking that "thorough" and "comprehensive" are sufficient qualities for their personal statement. They try to include as much information as possible, without regard for length limitations or strategic intent. Application readers dread reading these bloated personal statements. So how do you decide what to include? There are usually clear length guidelines, and admissions officers prefer that you adhere to them. So, get rid of the idea of "comprehensive" and focus more on "distinctive."

Unless they ask for it, don't dwell on your weak points. A strong personal statement, for example, about how much you learned in your current position and how the experience and knowledge you've gained inspired you to apply to graduate school will give readers what they want—a quick image of who you are, how you got that way, and why you want to go to their school. One of the best ways to be distinctive is to sell your image briefly and accurately, including real-life examples to back up your points.

"Distinctive" means that your statement should answer the questions that admissions officers think about while reading personal statements: what's different about this applicant? Why should we pick this applicant over others? Authentic enthusiasm can be a plus, and writing about parts of your life or career that are interesting and relevant help grab a reader's attention.

THE INTERVIEW

In some programs, an interview with the department is conducted at the applicant's discretion: if you want one, you're welcome to ask. In other programs, only the most promising applicants get invited to interviews. Whether or not a department can pay your travel expenses depends on its financial picture. If you have the opportunity, definitely go to interview at your first-choice departments. There's no substitute for face-to-face contact with your potential colleagues, and by visiting the school you can check out the city or town where it is located. You should investigate cost of living and transportation options during your visit.

As you prepare for an interview, here are some tips.

- *Review your application.* If you've submitted your application prior to the interview, your interviewer is likely to use it as a guide and may ask specific questions about it. Be sure you remember what you wrote.

- *Be ready to provide examples and specifics.* Professionally trained interviewers are more likely to ask you about specific situations than they are to ask broad open-ended questions. They can learn more by asking what you've done in situations than by asking what you think you'd do. Here are a few situations an interviewer may ask you to discuss: "Tell me about a recent accomplishment." "Discuss a recent situation in which you demonstrated leadership." "Give me an example of a situation where you overcame difficult circumstances." As you think about these situations, be prepared to discuss specifics—what you did and why you did it that way. You do not need to "script" or over-rehearse your responses, but you should go into the interview confident that you can field any question.

- *Be open and honest.* Don't struggle to think of "right" answers. The only right answers are those that are right for you. By responding openly and honestly, you'll find the interview less stressful, and you'll come across as a more genuine, attractive candidate.

- *Ask questions.* The interview is as much an opportunity for you to learn about the school as for the school to learn about you. Good questions demonstrate your knowledge about a particular program and your thoughtfulness about the entire process.

- *Follow proper professional decorum.* Be on time, dress appropriately, and follow up with thank-you letters. Treat the process as you would a job interview, which in many respects it is.

- *Watch your nonverbal cues.* Nonverbal communication is much more important than people realize. Maintain eye contact, keep good posture, sustain positive energy, and avoid nervous fidgeting. It will help you come across as confident, poised, and mature.

- *Be courteous to the administrative staff.* These people are colleagues of the board members, and how you treat them can have an impact, either positive or negative.

- *Relax and have fun.* Interviews are naturally stressful. But by being well prepared, you can enhance your prospects for admission, learn about the school, and enjoy yourself in the process.

RECOMMENDATIONS

Graduate schools will require at least three recommendations. Choose recommenders who can write meaningfully about your strengths. One of the more common mistakes is to sacrifice an insightful recommendation from someone who knows you well for a generic recommendation from a celebrity or a prominent professor. Admissions officers are not impressed by famous names. So unless that individual knows you and can write convincingly on your behalf, it's not a strategy worth pursuing. Good choices for recommenders include current and past supervisors, professors, academic and nonacademic advisers, and people you work with in community activities.

Many schools will specifically request an academic recommendation. Professors in your major are ideal recommenders, as they can vouch for your ability to study at the graduate level. If you don't have a professor who can recommend you, use a TA who knows your work well. Similarly, if requesting a recommendation from your employer would create an awkward situation, look for someone else who can comment on your skills. Your recommendations will confirm your strengths and in some cases help you overcome perceived weaknesses in your application.

If you wish to submit an extra recommendation, it's generally not a problem. Most schools will include the letter in your file, and those that don't will not penalize you for it. You should, however, send a note explaining why you have requested an additional recommendation so it does not appear that you can't follow instructions. It's a good idea to check with the admissions department before submitting an extra recommendation.

Asking for Recommendations

There are two fundamental rules of requesting recommendations: ask early and ask nicely. As soon as you decide to go to graduate school, you should start sizing up potential recommendation writers and let them know that you may ask them for a recommendation. This will give them plenty of time to think about what to say. Once they've agreed, let them know about deadlines well in advance to avoid potential scheduling conflicts. The more time they have, the better the job they'll do recommending you. As for asking nicely, you should let these people know you think highly of their opinion and you'd be happy and honored if they would consider writing you a letter of recommendation. You can help your recommenders by scheduling brief appointments with them to discuss your background, providing any forms required by the program, supplying stamped, addressed envelopes, and following up with them.

BEFORE YOU SUBMIT YOUR APPLICATION

When you've completed your personal statement and you're ready to submit your application, take two more steps to ensure that your application is as strong as it can be.

- Be sure to read your personal statement in the context of your entire application. Does the total package make sense? Does it represent you favorably? Is everything consistent? Have you demonstrated your intellectual ability, relevant experience and skills, and personal characteristics? Most importantly, do you feel good about the application? After all, you don't want to be rejected with an application that you don't believe represents the real you.

- Have someone you trust and respect review your application. Someone who has not been involved in writing the application may pick up spelling or grammatical errors that you've overlooked. In addition, because your application is an intensely personal document that requires significant self-examination, you may not be able to remain objective. Someone who knows you and can be frank will tell you whether your application has "captured" you most favorably.

  Some schools prohibit you from using any outside help on your application. A last-minute once-over from a friend or family member is probably within reason, but you may want to ask the school directly what is permissible.

PUTTING IT ALL TOGETHER

There are no magic formulas that automatically admit you to, or reject you from, the school of your choice. Rather, your application is like a jigsaw puzzle. Each component—GPA, GRE scores, professional experience, school activities, recommendations—is a different piece of the puzzle.

Outstanding professional experience and personal characteristics may enable you to overcome a mediocre academic record. Conversely, outstanding academic credentials will not ensure your admission to a top-tier program if you do not demonstrate strong relevant skills and experience, as well as solid personal character. Your challenge in preparing your application is to convince the admissions board that all of the pieces in your background fit together to form a substantial and unique puzzle.

CONGRATULATIONS!

You have all of the tools you need to put together a stand-out application package, including a top GRE score. Best of luck, and remember, your Kaplan training will be with you each step of the way.

A SPECIAL NOTE FOR INTERNATIONAL STUDENTS

About a quarter million international students pursue advanced academic degrees at the master's or Ph.D. level at U.S. universities each year. This trend of pursuing higher education in the United States, particularly at the graduate level, is expected to continue. Business, management, engineering, and the physical and life sciences are popular areas of study for students coming to the United States from other countries. Along with these academic options, international students are also taking advantage of opportunities for research grants, teaching assistantships, and practical training or work experience in U.S. graduate departments.

If you are not from the United States, but are considering attending a graduate program at a university in the United States, here is what you'll need to get started.

- If English is not your first language, start there. You will probably need to take the Test of English as a Foreign Language (TOEFL) or show some other evidence that you're proficient in English prior to gaining admission to a graduate program. Graduate programs will vary on what is an acceptable TOEFL score. For degrees in business, journalism, management, or the humanities, a minimum TOEFL score of 600 (250 on the computer-based TOEFL) or better is expected. For the hard sciences and computer technology, a TOEFL score of 550 (213 on the computer-based TOEFL) is a common minimum requirement.

- You may also need to take the GRE® (Graduate Record Exam). The strategies in this book are designed to help you maximize your score on the computer-adaptive GRE exam. However, most sites outside the United States and Canada offer only the paper-and-pencil version of the GRE exam. For paper-and-pencil strategies, see chapter 2.

- Since admission to many graduate programs is quite competitive, you may want to select three or four programs you would like to attend and complete applications for each program.

- Selecting the correct graduate school is very different from selecting a suitable undergraduate institution. You should research the qualifications and interests of faculty members teaching and doing research in your chosen field. Look for professors who share your specialty.

- You need to begin the application process at least a year in advance. Be aware that many programs offer only August or September start dates. Find out application deadlines and plan accordingly.

- Finally, you will need to obtain an 1–20 Certificate of Eligibility in order to obtain an F-1 Student Visa to study in the United States.

Kaplan English Programs*

If you need more help with the complex process of graduate school admissions, assistance preparing for the TOEFL or GRE, or help building your English language skills in general, you may be interested in Kaplan's programs for international students.

---

* Kaplan is authorized under federal law to enroll nonimmigrant alien students.
Kaplan is accredited by ACCET (Accrediting Council for Continuing Education and Training).

Kaplan English Programs were designed to help students and professionals from outside the United States meet their educational and career goals. At locations throughout the United States, international students take advantage of Kaplan's programs to help them improve their academic and conversational English skills, raise their scores on the TOEFL, GRE, and other standardized exams, and gain admission to the schools of their choice. Our staff and instructors give international students the individualized instruction they need to succeed. Here is a brief description of some of Kaplan's programs for international students:

General Intensive English

Kaplan's General Intensive English course is the fastest and most effective way for students to improve their English. This full-time program integrates the four key elements of language learning—listening, speaking, reading, and writing. The challenging curriculum and intensive schedule are designed for both the general language learner and the academically bound student.

TOEFL and Academic English

Our world-famous TOEFL course prepares you for the TOEFL and also teaches you the academic language and skills needed to succeed in a university. Designed for high-intermediate to advanced-level English speakers, our course includes TOEFL-focused reading, writing, listening, speaking, vocabulary, and grammar instruction.

General English

Our General English course is a semi-intensive program designed for students who want to improve their listening and speaking skills without the time commitment of an intensive program. With morning class time and flexible computer lab hours throughout the week, our General English course is perfect for every schedule.

GRE FOR INTERNATIONAL STUDENTS

The GRE is required for admission to many graduate programs in the United States. Nearly one-half million people take the GRE each year. A high score can help you stand out from other test takers. This course, designed especially for non-native English speakers, includes the skills you need to succeed on each section of the GRE, as well as access to Kaplan's exclusive computer-based practice materials and extra Verbal practice.

OTHER KAPLAN PROGRAMS

Since 1938, more than 3 million students have come to Kaplan to advance their studies, prepare for entry to American universities, and further their careers. In addition to the above programs, Kaplan offers courses to prepare for the SAT, GMAT, LSAT, MCAT, DAT, USMLE, NCLEX, and other standardized exams at locations throughout the United States.

APPLYING TO KAPLAN ENGLISH PROGRAMS

To get more information, or to apply for admission to any of Kaplan's programs for international students and professionals, contact us at:

Kaplan English Programs
700 South Flower, Suite 2900
Los Angeles, CA 90017, USA
Phone (if calling from within the United States): 800-818-9128
Phone (if calling from outside the United States): 213-452-5800
Fax: 213-892-1364
Website: kaplanenglish.com
Email: world@kaplan.com

GRE
RESOURCES

KAPLAN'S WORD GROUPS

The following lists contain a lot of common GRE words grouped together by meaning. Make flashcards from these lists and look over your cards a few times a week from now until the day of the test. Look over the word group lists once or twice a week for 30 seconds every week until the test. If you don't have much time until the exam date, look over your lists more frequently. Then, by the day of the test, you should have a rough idea of what most of the words on your lists mean.

Note: The categories in which these words are listed are *general* and should *not* be interpreted as the exact definitions of the words.

ABBREVIATED COMMUNICATION

abridge
compendium
cursory
curtail
syllabus
synopsis
terse

ACT QUICKLY

apace
abrupt
headlong
impetuous
precipitate

ASSIST

abet
advocate
ancillary
bolster
corroborate
countenance
espouse
mainstay
munificent
proponent
stalwart
sustenance

BAD MOOD

bilious
dudgeon
irascible
pettish
petulant
pique
querulous
umbrage
waspish

BEGINNER/AMATEUR

dilettante
fledgling
neophyte
novitiate

proselyte
tyro

BEGINNING/YOUNG

burgeoning
callow
engender
inchoate
incipient
nascent

BITING (AS IN WIT OR TEMPERAMENT)

acerbic
acidulous
acrimonious
asperity
caustic
mordacious
mordant
trenchant

BOLD

audacious
courageous
dauntless

BORING

banal
fatuous
hackneyed
insipid
mundane
pedestrian
platitude
prosaic
quotidian
trite

CAROUSAL

bacchanalian
debauchery
depraved
dissipated
iniquity
libertine
libidinous

licentious
reprobate
ribald
salacious
sordid
turpitude

CHANGING QUICKLY

capricious
mercurial
volatile

COPY

counterpart
emulate
facsimile
factitious
paradigm
precursor
quintessence
simulated
vicarious

CRITICIZE/CRITICISM

aspersion
belittle
berate
calumny
castigate
decry
defamation
denounce
deride/derisive
diatribe
disparage
excoriate
gainsay
harangue
impugn
inveigh
lambaste
objurgate
obloquy
opprobrium
pillory
rebuke
remonstrate

reprehend
reprove
revile
tirade
vituperate

DEATH/MOURNING
bereave
cadaver
defunct
demise
dolorous
elegy
knell
lament
macabre
moribund
obsequies
sepulchral
wraith

DENYING OF SELF
abnegate
abstain
ascetic
spartan
stoic
temperate

DICTATORIAL
authoritarian
despotic
dogmatic
hegemonic (hegemony)
imperious
peremptory
tyrannical

DIFFICULT TO UNDERSTAND
abstruse
ambiguous
arcane
bemusing
cryptic
enigmatic
esoteric

inscrutable
obscure
opaque
paradoxical
perplexing
recondite
turbid

DISGUSTING/OFFENSIVE
defile
fetid
invidious
noisome
odious
putrid
rebarbative

EASY TO UNDERSTAND
articulate
cogent
eloquent
evident
limpid
lucid
pellucid

ECCENTRIC/DISSIMILAR
aberrant
anachronism
anomalous
discrete
eclectic
esoteric
iconoclast

EMBARRASS
abash
chagrin
compunction
contrition
diffidence
expiate
foible
gaucherie
rue

EQUAL
equitable
equity
tantamount

FALSEHOOD
apocryphal
canard
chicanery
dissemble
duplicity
equivocate
erroneous
ersatz
fallacious
feigned
guile
mendacious/mendacity
perfidy
prevaricate
specious
spurious

FAMILY
conjugal
consanguine
distaff
endogamous
filial
fratricide
progenitor
scion

FAVORING/NOT IMPARTIAL
ardor/ardent
doctrinaire
fervid
partisan
tendentious
zealot

FORGIVE
absolve
acquit
exculpate
exonerate
expiate

palliate
redress
vindicate

Funny

chortle
droll
facetious
flippant
gibe
jocular
levity
ludicrous
raillery
riposte
simper

Gaps/Openings

abatement
aperture
fissure
hiatus
interregnum
interstice
lull
orifice
rent
respite
rift

Generous/Kind

altruistic
beneficent
clement
largess
magnanimous
munificent
philanthropic
unstinting

Greedy

avaricious
covetous
mercenary
miserly
penurious

rapacious
venal

Hardhearted

asperity
baleful
dour
fell
malevolent
mordant
sardonic
scathing
truculent
vitriolic
vituperation

Harmful

baleful
baneful
deleterious
inimical
injurious
insidious
minatory
perfidious
pernicious

harsh-sounding

cacophony
din
dissonant
raucous
strident

Hatred

abhorrence
anathema
antagonism
antipathy
detestation
enmity
loathing
malice
odium
rancor

Healthy

beneficial
salubrious
salutary

Hesitate

dither
oscillate
teeter
vacillate
waver

Hostile

antithetic
churlish
curmudgeon
irascible
malevolent
misanthropic
truculent
vindictive

Innocent/Inexperienced

credulous
gullible
ingenuous
naive
novitiate
tyro

Insincere

disingenuous
dissemble
fulsome
ostensible
unctuous

Investigate

appraise
ascertain
assay
descry
peruse

Lazy/Sluggish

indolent
inert

lackadaisical
languid
lassitude
lethargic
phlegmatic
quiescent
slothful
torpid

LUCK

adventitious
amulet
auspicious
fortuitous
kismet
optimum
portentous
propitiate
propitious
providential
talisman

NAG

admonish
cavil
belabor
enjoin
exhort
harangue
hector
martinet
remonstrate
reproof

NASTY

fetid
noisome
noxious

NOT A STRAIGHT LINE

askance
awry
careen
carom
circuitous
circumvent
gyrate

labyrinth
meander
oblique
serrated
sidle
sinuous
undulating
vortex

OVERBLOWN/WORDY

bombastic
circumlocution
garrulous
grandiloquent
loquacious
periphrastic
prolix
rhetoric
turgid
verbose

PACIFY/SATISFY

ameliorate
appease
assuage
defer
mitigate
mollify
placate
propitiate
satiate
slake
sooth

PLEASANT-SOUNDING

euphonious
harmonious
melodious
sonorous

POOR

destitute
esurient
impecunious
indigent

PRAISE

acclaim
accolade
aggrandize
encomium
eulogize
extol
fawn
laud/laudatory
venerate/veneration

PREDICT

augur
auspice
fey
harbinger
portentous
presage
prescient
prognosticate

PREVENT/OBSTRUCT

discomfort
encumber
fetter
forfend
hinder
impede
inhibit
occlude

SMART/LEARNED

astute
canny
erudite
perspicacious

SORROW

disconsolate
doleful
dolor
elegiac
forlorn
lament
lugubrious
melancholy
morose

plaintive
threnody

Stubborn

implacable
inexorable
intractable
intransigent
obdurate
obstinate
recalcitrant
refractory
renitent
untoward
vexing

Terse

compendious
curt
laconic
pithy
succinct
taciturn

Time/Order/Duration

anachronism
antecede
antedate
anterior
archaic
diurnal
eon
ephemeral
epoch
fortnight
millennium
penultimate
synchronous
temporal

Timid/Timidity

craven
diffident
pusillanimous
recreant
timorous
trepidation

Truth

candor/candid
fealty
frankness
indisputable
indubitable
legitimate
probity
sincere
veracious
verity

Unusual

aberration
anomaly
iconoclast
idiosyncrasy

Walking About

ambulatory
itinerant
peripatetic

Wandering

discursive
expatiate
forage
itinerant
peregrination
peripatetic
sojourn

Weaken

adulterate
enervate
exacerbate
inhibit
obviate
stultify
undermine
vitiate

Wisdom

adage
aphorism
apothegm
axiom
bromide
dictum
epigram
platitude
sententious
truism

Withdrawal/Retreat

abeyance
abjure
abnegation
abortive
abrogate
decamp
demur
recant
recidivism
remission
renege
rescind
retrograde

KAPLAN'S ROOT LIST

Kaplan's Root List can boost your knowledge of GRE-level words, and that can help you get more questions right. No one can predict exactly which words will show up on your test, but there are certain words that the test makers favor. The Root List gives you the component parts of many typical GRE words. Knowing these words can help you because you may run across them on your GRE. Also, becoming comfortable with the types of words that pop up will reduce your anxiety about the test.

Knowing roots can help you in two more ways. First, instead of learning one word at a time, you can learn a whole group of words that contain a certain root. They'll be related in meaning, so if you remember one, it will be easier for you to remember others. Second, roots can often help you decode an unknown GRE word. If you recognize a familiar root, you could get a good enough grasp of the word to answer the question.

A: WITHOUT

amoral: neither moral nor immoral
atheist: one who does not believe in God
atypical: not typical
anonymous: of unknown authorship or origin
apathy: lack of interest or emotion
atrophy: the wasting away of body tissue
anomaly: an irregularity
agnostic: one who questions the existence of God

AB/ABS: OFF, AWAY FROM, APART, DOWN

abduct: to take by force
abhor: to hate, detest
abolish: to do away with, make void
abstract: conceived apart from concrete realities, specific objects, or actual instances
abnormal: deviating from a standard
abdicate: to renounce or relinquish a throne
abstinence: forbearance from any indulgence of appetite
abstruse: hard to understand; secret, hidden

AC/ACR: SHARP, BITTER

acid: something that is sharp, sour, or ill natured
acute: sharp at the end; ending in a point
acerbic: sour or astringent in taste; harsh in temper
acrid: sharp or biting to the taste or smell
acrimonious: caustic, stinging, or bitter in nature
exacerbate: to increase bitterness or violence; aggravate

ACT/AG: TO DO; TO DRIVE; TO FORCE; TO LEAD

agile: quick and well-coordinated in movement; active, lively
agitate: to move or force into violent, irregular action
litigate: to make the subject of a lawsuit
prodigal: wastefully or recklessly extravagant
pedagogue: a teacher
synagogue: a gathering or congregation of Jews for the purpose of religious worship

AD/AL: TO, TOWARD, NEAR

adapt: adjust or modify fittingly
adjacent: near, close, or contiguous; adjoining

addict: to give oneself over, as to a habit or pursuit
admire: to regard with wonder, pleasure, and approval
address: to direct a speech or written statement to
adhere: to stick fast; cleave; cling
adjoin: to be close or in contact with
advocate: to plead in favor of

AL/ALI/ALTER: OTHER, ANOTHER

alternative: a possible choice
alias: an assumed name; another name
alibi: the defense by an accused person that he was verifiably elsewhere at the time of the crime with which he is charged
alien: one born in another country; a foreigner
alter ego: the second self; a substitute or deputy
altruist: a person unselfishly concerned for the welfare of others
allegory: figurative treatment of one subject under the guise of another

AM: LOVE

amateur: a person who engages in an activity for pleasure rather than financial or professional gain
amatory: of or pertaining to lovers or lovemaking
amenity: agreeable ways or manners
amorous: inclined to love, esp. sexual love
enamored: inflamed with love; charmed; captivated
amity: friendship; peaceful harmony
inamorata: a female lover
amiable: having or showing agreeable personal qualities
amicable: characterized by exhibiting good will

AMB: TO GO; TO WALK

ambient: moving freely; circulating
ambitious: desirous of achieving or obtaining power
preamble: an introductory statement
ambassador: an authorized messenger or representative
ambulance: a wheeled vehicle equipped for carrying sick people, usually to a hospital

ambulatory: of, pertaining to, or capable of
walking

ambush: the act of lying concealed so as to attack
by surprise

perambulator: one who makes a tour of inspection
on foot

AMBI/AMPH: BOTH, MORE THAN ONE, AROUND

ambiguous: open to various interpretations

amphibian: any cold-blooded vertebrate, the
larva of which is aquatic, and the adult of
which is terrestrial; a person or thing having a
twofold nature

ambidextrous: able to use both hands
equally well

ANIM: OF THE LIFE, MIND, SOUL, SPIRIT

unanimous: in complete accord

animosity: a feeling of ill will or enmity

animus: hostile feeling or attitude

equanimity: mental or emotional stability,
especially under tension

magnanimous: generous in forgiving an insult
or injury

ANNUI/ENNI: YEAR

annual: of, for, or pertaining to a year; yearly

anniversary: the yearly recurrence of the date of
a past event

annuity: a specified income payable at stated
intervals

perennial: lasting for an indefinite amount of time

annals: a record of events, esp. a yearly record

ANTE: BEFORE

anterior: placed before

antecedent: existing, being, or going before

antedate: precede in time

antebellum: before the war
(especially the American Civil War)

antediluvian: belonging to the period before the
biblical flood; very old or old-fashioned

ANTHRO/ANDR: MAN, HUMAN

anthropology: the science that deals with the
origins of mankind

android: robot; mechanical man

misanthrope: one who hates humans or mankind

philanderer: one who carries on flirtations

androgynous: being both male and female

androgen: any substance that promotes
masculine characteristics

anthropocentric: regarding man as the central
fact of the universe

ANTI: AGAINST

antibody: a protein naturally existing in blood
serum, that reacts to overcome the toxic
effects of an antigen

antidote: a remedy for counteracting the effects
of poison, disease, etcetera

antiseptic: free from germs; particularly clean
or neat

antipathy: aversion

antipodal: on the opposite side of the globe

APO: AWAY

apology: an expression of one's regret or sorrow
for having wronged another

apostle: one of the 12 disciples sent forth by
Jesus to preach the gospel

apocalypse: revelation; discovery; disclosure

apogee: the highest or most distant point

apocryphal: of doubtful authorship or
authenticity

apostasy: a total desertion of one's religion,
principles, party, cause, etcetera

ARCH/ARCHI/ARCHY: CHIEF, PRINCIPAL, RULER

architect: the devisor, maker, or planner of
anything

archenemy: chief enemy

monarchy: a government in which the supreme
power is lodged in a sovereign

anarchy: a state or society without government
or law

oligarchy: a state or society ruled by a select
group

AUTO: SELF

automatic: self-moving or self-acting

autocrat: an absolute ruler

autonomy: independence or freedom

BE: TO BE; TO HAVE A PARTICULAR QUALITY; TO EXIST

belittle: to regard something as less impressive than it apparently is

bemoan: to express pity for

bewilder: to confuse or puzzle completely

belie: to misrepresent; to contradict

BEL/BEL: WAR

antebellum: before the war

rebel: a person who resists authority, control, or tradition

belligerent: warlike, given to waging war

BEN/BON: GOOD

benefit: anything advantageous to a person or thing

benign: having a kindly disposition

benediction: act of uttering a blessing

benevolent: desiring to do good to others

bonus: something given over and above what is due

bona fide: in good faith; without fraud

BI: TWICE, DOUBLE

binoculars: involving two eyes

biennial: happening every two years

bilateral: pertaining to or affecting two or both sides

bilingual: able to speak one's native language and another with equal facility

bipartisan: representing two parties

CAD/CID: TO FALL; TO HAPPEN BY CHANCE

accident: happening by chance; unexpected

coincidence: a striking occurrence of two or more events at one time, apparently by chance

decadent: decaying; deteriorating

cascade: a waterfall descending over a steep surface

recidivist: one who repeatedly relapses, as into crime

CANT/CENT/CHANT: TO SING

accent: prominence of a syllable in terms of pronunciation

chant: a song; singing

enchant: to subject to magical influence; bewitch

recant: to withdraw or disavow a statement

incantation: the chanting of words purporting to have magical power

incentive: that which incites action

CAP/CIP/CEPT: TO TAKE; TO GET

capture: to take by force or stratagem

anticipate: to realize beforehand; foretaste or foresee

susceptible: capable of receiving, admitting, undergoing, or being affected by something

emancipate: to free from restraint

percipient: having perception; discerning; discriminating

precept: a commandment or direction given as a rule of conduct

CAP/CAPIT/CIPIT: HEAD, HEADLONG

capital: the city or town that is the official seat of government

disciple: one who is a pupil of the doctrines of another

precipitate: to hasten the occurrence of; to bring about prematurely

precipice: a cliff with a vertical face

capitulate: to surrender unconditionally or on stipulated terms

caption: a heading or title

CARD/CORD/COUR: HEART

cardiac: pertaining to the heart

encourage: to inspire with spirit or confidence

concord: agreement; peace, amity

discord: lack of harmony between persons or things

concordance: agreement, concord, harmony

CARN: FLESH

carnivorous: eating flesh

carnage: the slaughter of a great number of people

carnival: a traveling amusement show

reincarnation: rebirth of a soul in a new body

incarnation: a being invested with a bodily form

CAST/CHAST: CUT

cast: to throw or hurl; fling

caste: a hereditary social group, limited to people of the same rank

castigate: to punish in order to correct

chastise: to discipline, esp. by corporal
  punishment
chaste: free from obscenity; decent

CED/CEED/CESS: TO GO; TO YIELD; TO STOP

antecedent: existing, being, or going before
concede: to acknowledge as true, just, or proper;
  admit
predecessor: one who comes before another in an
  office, position, etcetera
cessation: a temporary or complete
  discontinuance
incessant: without stop

CENTR: CENTER

concentrate: to bring to a common center;
  to converge, to direct toward one point
eccentric: off center
concentric: having a common center, as in circles
  or spheres
centrifuge: an apparatus that rotates at high speed
  that separates substances of different densities
  using centrifugal force
centrist: of or pertaining to moderate political or
  social ideas

CERN/CERT/CRET/CRIM/CRIT: TO SEPARATE; TO JUDGE; TO DISTINGUISH; TO DECIDE

discrete: detached from others, separate
ascertain: to make sure of; to determine
certitude: freedom from doubt
discreet: judicious in one's conduct of speech,
  esp. with regard to maintaining silence about
  something of a delicate nature
hypocrite: a person who pretends to have beliefs
  that she does not
criterion: a standard of judgment or criticism

CHRON: TIME

synchronize: to occur at the same time or agree
  in time
chronology: the sequential order in which past
  events occurred
anachronism: an obsolete or archaic form
chronic: constant, habitual
chronometer: a time piece with a mechanism to
  adjust for accuracy

CIRCU: AROUND, ON ALL SIDES

circumference: the outer boundary of a
  circular area
circumstances: the existing conditions or state of
  affairs surrounding and affecting an agent
circuit: the act of going or moving around
circumambulate: to walk about or around
circuitous: roundabout, indirect

CIS: TO CUT

scissors: cutting instrument for paper
precise: definitely stated or defined
exorcise: to seek to expel an evil spirit by ceremony
incision: a cut, gash, or notch
incisive: penetrating, cutting

CLA/CLO/CLU: SHUT, CLOSE

conclude: to bring to an end; finish; to terminate
claustrophobia: an abnormal fear of enclosed
  places
disclose: to make known, reveal, or uncover
exclusive: not admitting of something else;
  shutting out others
cloister: a courtyard bordered with covered walks,
  esp. in a religious institution
preclude: to prevent the presence, existence, or
  occurrence of

CLAIM/CLAM: TO SHOUT; TO CRY OUT

exclaim: to cry out or speak suddenly and
  vehemently
proclaim: to announce or declare in an
  official way
clamor: a loud uproar
disclaim: to deny interest in or connection with
reclaim: to claim or demand the return of a right
  or possession

CLI: TO LEAN TOWARD

decline: to cause to slope or incline downward
recline: to lean back
climax: the most intense point in the development
  of something
proclivity: inclination, bias
disinclination: aversion, distaste

CO/COL/COM/CON: WITH, TOGETHER

connect: to bind or fasten together
coerce: to compel by force, intimidation, or
   authority
compatible: capable of existing together in
   harmony
collide: to strike one another with a forceful
   impact
collaborate: to work with another, cooperate
conciliate: to placate, win over
commensurate: suitable in measure,
   proportionate

COUR/CUR: RUNNING; A COURSE

recur: to happen again
curriculum: the regular course of study
courier: a messenger traveling in haste who bears
   news
excursion: a short journey or trip
cursive: handwriting in flowing strokes with the
   letters joined together
concur: to accord in opinion; agree
incursion: a hostile entrance into a place, esp.
   suddenly
cursory: going rapidly over something; hasty;
   superficial

CRE/CRESC/CRET: TO GROW

accrue: to be added as a matter of periodic gain
creation: the act of producing or causing to exist
increase: to make greater in any respect
increment: something added or gained; an
   addition or increase
accretion: an increase by natural growth

CRED: TO BELIEVE; TO TRUST

incredible: unbelievable
credentials: anything that provides the basis
   for belief
credo: any formula of belief
credulity: willingness to believe or trust too readily
credit: trustworthiness

CRYP: HIDDEN

crypt: a subterranean chamber or vault
apocryphal: of doubtful authorship or
   authenticity

cryptology: the science of interpreting secret
   writings, codes, ciphers, and the like
cryptography: procedures of making and using
   secret writing

CUB/CUMB: TO LIE DOWN

cubicle: any small space or compartment that is
   partitioned off
succumb: to give away to superior force; yield
incubate: to sit upon for the purpose of hatching
incumbent: holding an indicated position
recumbent: lying down; reclining; leaning

CULP: BLAME

culprit: a person guilty for an offense
culpable: deserving blame or censure
inculpate: to charge with fault
mea culpa: through my fault; my fault

DAC/DOC: TO TEACH

doctor: someone licensed to practice medicine;
   a learned person
doctrine: a particular principle advocated, as of
   a government or religion
indoctrinate: to imbue a person with learning
docile: easily managed or handled; tractable
didactic: intended for instruction

DE: AWAY, OFF, DOWN, COMPLETELY, REVERSAL

descend: to move from a higher to a lower place
decipher: to make out the meaning; to interpret
defile: to make foul, dirty, or unclean
defame: to attack the good name or reputation of
deferential: respectful; to yield to judgment
delineate: to trace the outline of; sketch or trace
   in outline

DEM: PEOPLE

democracy: government by the people
epidemic: affecting at the same time a large
   number of people, and spreading from person
   to person
endemic: peculiar to a particular people or
   locality
pandemic: general, universal
demographics: vital and social statistics of
   populations

DI/DIA: APART, THROUGH

dialogue: conversation between two or more
  persons
diagnose: to determine the identity of something
  from the symptoms
dilate: to make wider or larger; to cause to expand
dilatory: inclined to delay or procrastinate
dichotomy: division into two parts, kinds, etcetera

DIC/DICT/DIT: TO SAY; TO TELL; TO USE WORDS

dictionary: a book containing a selection of the
  words of a language
predict: to tell in advance
verdict: judgment, decree
interdict: to forbid; prohibit

DIGN: WORTH

dignity: nobility or elevation of character;
  worthiness
dignitary: a person who holds a high rank
  or office
deign: to think fit or in accordance with one's
  dignity
condign: well deserved; fitting; adequate
disdain: to look upon or treat with contempt

DIS/DIF: AWAY FROM, APART, REVERSAL, NOT

disperse: to drive or send off in various directions
disseminate: to scatter or spread widely;
  promulgate
dissipate: to scatter wastefully
dissuade: to deter by advice or persuasion
diffuse: to pour out and spread, as in a fluid

DOG/DOX: OPINION

orthodox: sound or correct in opinion or
  doctrine
paradox: an opinion or statement contrary to
  accepted opinion
dogma: a system of tenets, as of a church

DOL: SUFFER, PAIN

condolence: expression of sympathy with one
  who is suffering
indolence: a state of being lazy or slothful
doleful: sorrowful, mournful
dolorous: full of pain or sorrow, grievous

DON/DOT/DOW: TO GIVE

donate: to present as a gift or contribution
pardon: kind indulgence, forgiveness
antidote: something that prevents or counteracts
  ill effects
anecdote: a short narrative about an
  interesting event
endow: to provide with a permanent fund

DUB: DOUBT

dubious: doubtful
dubiety: doubtfulness
indubitable: unquestionable

DUC/DUCT: TO LEAD

abduct: to carry off or lead away
conduct: personal behavior, way of acting
conducive: contributive, helpful
induce: to lead or move by influence
induct: to install in a position with formal
  ceremonies
produce: to bring into existence; give cause to

DUR: HARD

endure: to hold out against;
  to sustain without yielding
durable: able to resist decay
duress: compulsion by threat, coercion
dour: sullen, gloomy
duration: the length of time something exists

DYS: FAULTY, ABNORMAL

dystrophy: faulty or inadequate nutrition or
  development
dyspepsia: impaired digestion
dyslexia: an impairment of the ability to read due
  to a brain defect
dysfunctional: poorly functioning

E/EF/EX: OUT, OUT OF, FROM, FORMER, COMPLETELY

evade: to escape from, avoid
exclude: to shut out; to leave out
extricate: to disentangle, release
exonerate: to free or declare free from blame
expire: to come to an end, cease to be valid
efface: to rub or wipe out; surpass, eclipse

EPI: UPON

epidemic: affecting at the same time a large number of people, and spreading from person to person

epilogue: a concluding part added to a literary work

epidermis: the outer layer of the skin

epigram: a witty or pointed saying tersely expressed

epithet: a word or phrase, used invectively as a term of abuse

EQU: EQUAL, EVEN

equation: the act of making equal

adequate: equal to the requirement or occasion

equidistant: equally distant

iniquity: gross injustice; wickedness

ERR: TO WANDER

err: to go astray in thought or belief, to be mistaken

error: a deviation from accuracy or correctness

erratic: deviating from the proper or usual course in conduct

arrant: downright, thorough, notorious

ESCE: BECOMING

adolescent: between childhood and adulthood

obsolescent: becoming obsolete

incandescent: glowing with heat, shining

convalescent: recovering from illness

reminiscent: reminding or suggestive of

EU: GOOD, WELL

euphemism: pleasant-sounding term for something unpleasant

eulogy: speech or writing in praise or commendation

eugenics: improvement of qualities of race by control of inherited characteristics

euthanasia: killing a person painlessly, usually one who has an incurable, painful disease

euphony: pleasantness of sound

EXTRA: OUTSIDE, BEYOND

extraordinary: beyond the ordinary

extract: to take out, obtain against a person's will

extradite: to hand over (person accused of crime) to state where crime was committed

extrasensory: derived by means other than known senses

extrapolate: to estimate (unknown facts or values) from known data

FAB/FAM: SPEAK

fable: fictional tale, esp. legendary

affable: friendly, courteous

ineffable: too great for description in words; that which must not be uttered

famous: well known, celebrated

defame: attack good name of

FAC/FIC/FIG/FAIT/FEIT/FY: TO DO; TO MAKE

factory: building for manufacture of goods

faction: small dissenting group within larger one, esp. in politics

deficient: incomplete or insufficient

prolific: producing many offspring or much output

configuration: manner of arrangement, shape

ratify: to confirm or accept by formal consent

effigy: sculpture or model of person

counterfeit: imitation, forgery

FER: TO BRING; TO CARRY; TO BEAR

offer: to present for acceptance, refusal, or consideration

confer: to grant, bestow

referendum: to vote on political question open to the entire electorate

proffer: to offer

proliferate: to reproduce; produce rapidly

FERV: TO BOIL; TO BUBBLE

fervor: passion, zeal

fervid: ardent, intense

effervescent: with the quality of giving off bubbles of gas

FID: FAITH, TRUST

confide: to entrust with a secret

affidavit: written statement on oath

fidelity: faithfulness, loyalty

fiduciary: of a trust; held or given in trust

infidel: disbeliever in the supposed true religion

FIN: END

final: at the end; coming last
confine: to keep or restrict within certain limits;
   imprison
definitive: decisive, unconditional, final
infinite: boundless; endless
infinitesimal: infinitely or very small

FLAG/FLAM: TO BURN

flammable: easily set on fire
flambeau: a lighted torch
flagrant: blatant, scandalous
conflagration: a large destructive fire

FLECT/FLEX: TO BEND

deflect: to bend or turn aside from a purpose
flexible: able to bend without breaking
inflect: to change or vary pitch of
reflect: to throw back
genuflect: to bend knee, esp. in worship

FLU/FLUX: TO FLOW

fluid: substance, esp. gas or liquid, capable of
   flowing freely
fluctuation: something that varies, rising and
   falling
effluence: flowing out of (light, electricity, etc.)
confluence: merging into one
mellifluous: pleasing, musical

FORE: BEFORE

foresight: care or provision for future
foreshadow: be warning or indication of
   (future event)
forestall: to prevent by advance action
forthright: straightforward, outspoken, decisive

FORT: CHANCE

fortune: chance or luck in human affairs
fortunate: lucky, auspicious
fortuitous: happening by luck

FORT: STRENGTH

fortify: to provide with fortifications; strengthen
fortissimo: very loud
forte: strong point; something a person does well

FRA/FRAC/FRAG/FRING: TO BREAK

fracture: breakage, esp. of a bone
fragment: a part broken off
fractious: irritable, peevish
refractory: stubborn, unmanageable, rebellious
infringe: to break or violate (law, etcetera)

FUS: TO POUR

profuse: lavish, extravagant, copious
fusillade: continuous discharge of firearms or
   outburst of criticism
suffuse: to spread throughout or over from within
diffuse: to spread widely or thinly
infusion: infusing; liquid extract so obtained

GEN: BIRTH, CREATION, RACE, KIND

generous: giving or given freely
genetics: study of heredity and variation among
   animals and plants
gender: classification roughly corresponding to
   the two sexes and sexlessness
carcinogenic: producing cancer
congenital: existing or as such from birth
progeny: offspring, descendants
miscegenation: interbreeding of races

GN/GNO: KNOW

agnostic: person who believes that the existence
   of God is not provable
ignore: to refuse to take notice of
ignoramus: a person lacking knowledge,
   uninformed
recognize: to identify as already known
incognito: with one's name or identity concealed
prognosis: to forecast, especially of disease
diagnose: to make an identification of disease or
   fault from symptoms

GRAD/GRESS: TO STEP

progress: forward movement
aggressive: given to hostile act or feeling
degrade: to humiliate, dishonor, reduce to
   lower rank
digress: to depart from main subject
egress: going out; way out
regress: to move backward, revert to an
   earlier state

GRAT: PLEASING

grateful: thankful

ingratiate: to bring oneself into favor

gratuity: money given for good service

gracious: kindly, esp. to inferiors; merciful

HER/HES: TO STICK

coherent: logically consistent; having waves in phase and of one wavelength

adhesive: tending to remain in memory; sticky; an adhesive substance

inherent: involved in the constitution or essential character of something

adherent: able to adhere; believer or advocate of a particular thing

heredity: the qualities genetically derived from one's ancestors and the transmission of those qualities

(H)ETERO: DIFFERENT

heterosexual: of or pertaining to sexual orientation toward members of the opposite sex; relating to different sexes

heterogeneous: of other origin: not originating in the body

heterodox: different from acknowledged standard; holding unorthodox opinions or doctrines

(H)OM: SAME

homogeneous: of the same or a similar kind of nature; of uniform structure of composition throughout

homonym: one of two or more words spelled and pronounced alike but different in meaning

homosexual: of, relating to, or exhibiting sexual desire toward a member of one's own sex

anomaly: deviation from the common rule

homeostasis: a relatively stable state of equilibrium

HYPER: OVER, EXCESSIVE

hyperactive: excessively active

hyperbole: purposeful exaggeration for effect

hyperglycemia: an abnormally high concentration of sugar in the blood

HYPO: UNDER, BENEATH, LESS THAN

hypodermic: relating to the parts beneath the skin

hypochondriac: one affected by extreme depression of mind or spirits often centered on imaginary physical ailments

hypocritical: affecting virtues or qualities one does not have

hypothesis: assumption subject to proof

IDIO: ONE'S OWN

idiot: an utterly stupid person

idiom: a language, dialect, or style of speaking particular to a people

idiosyncrasy: peculiarity of temperament; eccentricity

IM/IN/EM/EN: IN, INTO

embrace: to clasp in the arms; to include or contain

enclose: to close in on all sides

intrinsic: belonging to a thing by its very nature

influx: the act of flowing in; inflow

implicit: not expressly stated; implied

incarnate: given a bodily, esp. a human, form

indigenous: native; innate, natural

IM/IN: NOT, WITHOUT

inactive: not active

innocuous: not harmful or injurious

indolence: showing a disposition to avoid exertion; slothful

impartial: not partial or biased; just

indigent: deficient in what is requisite

INTER: BETWEEN, AMONG

interstate: connecting or jointly involving states

interim: a temporary or provisional arrangement; meantime

interloper: one who intrudes in the domain of others

intermittent: stopping or ceasing for a time

intersperse: to scatter here and there

JECT: TO THROW; TO THROW DOWN

inject: to place (quality, etc.) where needed in something

dejected: sad, depressed

eject: to throw out, expel

conjecture: formation of opinion on incomplete
    information
abject: utterly hopeless, humiliating, or wretched

JOIN/JUNCT: TO MEET; TO JOIN

junction: the act of joining; combining
adjoin: to be next to and joined with
subjugate: to conquer
rejoinder: to reply, retort
junta: (usually military) clique taking power after
    a *coup d'état*

JUR: TO SWEAR

perjury: willful lying while on oath
abjure: to renounce on oath
adjure: to beg or command

LAV/LUT/LUV: TO WASH

lavatory: a room with equipment for washing hands
    and face
dilute: to make thinner or weaker by the
    addition of water
pollute: to make foul or unclean
deluge: a great flood of water
antediluvian: before the biblical flood;
    extremely old
ablution: act of cleansing

LECT/LEG: TO SELECT, TO CHOOSE

collect: to gather together or assemble
elect: to choose; to decide
select: to choose with care
eclectic: selecting ideas, etcetera from various
    sources
predilection: preference, liking

LEV: LIFT, LIGHT, RISE

relieve: to mitigate; to free from a burden
alleviate: to make easier to endure, lessen
relevant: bearing on or pertinent to information
    at hand
levee: embankment against river flooding
levitate: to rise in the air or cause to rise
levity: humor, frivolity, gaiety

LOC/LOG/LOQU: WORD, SPEECH

dialogue: conversation, esp. in a literary work
elocution: art of clear and expressive speaking
prologue: introduction to poem, play, etc.
eulogy: speech or writing in praise of someone
colloquial: of ordinary or familiar conversation
grandiloquent: pompous or inflated in language
loquacious: talkative

LUC/LUM/LUS: LIGHT

illustrate: to make intelligible with examples
    or analogies
illuminate: to supply or brighten with light
illustrious: highly distinguished
translucent: permitting light to pass through
lackluster: lacking brilliance or radiance
lucid: easily understood, intelligible
luminous: bright, brilliant, glowing

LUD/LUS: TO PLAY

allude: to refer casually or indirectly
illusion: something that deceives by producing a
    false impression of reality
ludicrous: ridiculous, laughable
delude: to mislead the mind or judgment of,
    deceive
elude: to avoid capture or escape defection by
prelude: a preliminary to an action, event, etc.

MAG/MAJ/MAX: BIG

magnify: to increase the apparent size of
magnitude: greatness of size, extent, or
    dimensions
maximum: the highest amount, value, or degree
    attained
magnate: a powerful or influential person
magnanimous: generous in forgiving an insult
    or injury
maxim: an expression of general truth or principle

MAL/MALE: BAD, ILL, EVIL, WRONG

malfunction: failure to function properly
malicious: full of or showing malice
malign: to speak harmful untruths about,
    to slander
malady: a disorder or disease of the body
maladroit: clumsy, tactless

malapropism: humorous misuse of a word

malfeasance: misconduct or wrongdoing often committed by a public official

malediction: a curse

MAN: HAND

manual: operated by hand

manufacture: to make by hand or machinery

emancipate: to free from bondage

manifest: readily perceived by the eye or the understanding

mandate: an authoritative order or command

MIN: SMALL

minute: a unit of time equal to one-sixtieth of an hour, or sixty seconds

minutiae: small or trivial details

miniature: a copy or model that represents something in greatly reduced size

diminish: to lessen

diminution: the act or process of diminishing

MIN: TO PROJECT, TO HANG OVER

eminent: towering above others; projecting

imminent: about to occur; impending

prominent: projecting outward

preeminent: superior to or notable above all others

minatory: menacing, threatening

MIS/MIT: TO SEND

transmit: to send from one person, thing, or place to another

emissary: a messenger or agent sent to represent the interests of another

intermittent: stopping and starting at intervals

remit: to send money

remission: a lessening of intensity or degree

MISC: MIXED

miscellaneous: made up of a variety of parts or ingredients

miscegenation: the interbreeding of races, esp. marriage between white and nonwhite persons

promiscuous: consisting of diverse and unrelated parts or individuals

MON/MONIT: TO REMIND; TO WARN

monument: a structure, such as a building, tower, or sculpture, erected as a memorial

monitor: one that admonishes, cautions, or reminds

summon: to call together; convene

admonish: to counsel against something; caution

remonstrate: to say or plead in protect, objection, or reproof

premonition: forewarning, presentiment

MORPH: SHAPE

amorphous: without definite form; lacking a specific shape

metamorphosis: a transformation, as by magic or sorcery

anthropomorphism: attribution of human characteristics to inanimate objects, animals, or natural phenomena

MORT: DEATH

immortal: not subject to death

morbid: susceptible to preoccupation with unwholesome matters

moribund: dying, decaying

MUT: CHANGE

commute: to substitute; exchange; interchange

mutation: the process of being changed

transmutation: the act of changing from one form into another

permutation: a complete change; transformation

immutable: unchangeable, invariable

NAT/NAS/NAI: TO BE BORN

natural: present due to nature, not to artificial or man-made means

native: belonging to one by nature; inborn; innate

naive: lacking worldliness and sophistication; artless

cognate: related by blood; having a common ancestor

renaissance: rebirth, esp. referring to culture

nascent: starting to develop

NIC/NOC/NOX: HARM

innocent: uncorrupted by evil, malice, or wrongdoing
noxious: injurious or harmful to health or morals
obnoxious: highly disagreeable or offensive
innocuous: having no adverse effect; harmless

NOM: RULE, ORDER

astronomy: the scientific study of the universe beyond the earth
economy: the careful or thrifty use of resources, as of income, materials, or labor
gastronomy: the art or science of good eating
taxonomy: the science, laws, or principles of classification
autonomy: independence, self-governance

NOM/NYM/NOUN/NOWN: NAME

synonym: a word having a meaning similar to that of another word of the same language
anonymous: having an unknown or unacknowledged name
nominal: existing in name only; negligible
nominate: to propose by name as a candidate
nomenclature: a system of names; systematic naming
acronym: a word formed from the initial letters of a name

NOUNC/NUNC: TO ANNOUNCE

announce: to proclaim
pronounce: to articulate
renounce: to give up, especially by formal announcement

NOV/NEO/NOU: NEW

novice: a person new to any field or activity
renovate: to restore to an earlier condition
innovate: to begin or introduce something new
neologism: a newly coined word, phrase, or expression
neophyte: a recent convert
nouveau riche: one who has lately become rich

OB/OC/OF/OP: TOWARD, TO, AGAINST, OVER

obese: extremely fat, corpulent
obstinate: stubbornly adhering to an idea, inflexible
obstruct: to block or fill with obstacles

oblique: having a slanting or sloping direction
obstreperous: noisily defiant, unruly
obtuse: not sharp, pointed, or acute in any form
obfuscate: to render indistinct or dim; darken
obsequious: overly submissive

OMNI : ALL

omnibus: an anthology of the works of one author or of writings on related subjects
omnipresent: everywhere at one time
omnipotent: all powerful
omniscient: having infinite knowledge

PAC/PEAC: PEACE

appease: to bring peace to
pacify: to ease the anger or agitation of
pacifier: something or someone that eases the anger or agitation of
pact: a formal agreement, as between nations

PAN: ALL, EVERYONE

panorama: an unobstructed and wide view of an extensive area
panegyric: formal or elaborate praise at an assembly
panoply: a wide-ranging and impressive array or display
pantheon: a public building containing tombs or memorials of the illustrious dead of a nation
pandemic: widespread, general, universal

PAR: EQUAL

par: an equality in value or standing
parity: equally, as in amount, status, or character
apartheid: any system or caste that separates people according to race, etc.
disparage: to belittle, speak disrespectfully about
disparate: essentially different

PARA: NEXT TO, BESIDE

parallel: extending in the same direction
parasite: an organism that lives on or within a plant or animal of another species, from which it obtains nutrients
parody: to imitate for purposes of satire
parable: a short, allegorical story designed to illustrate a moral lesson or religious principle

paragon: a model of excellence

paranoid: suffering from a baseless distrust of others

PAS/PAT/ PATH: FEELING, SUFFERING, DISEASE

sympathy: harmony or agreement in feeling

empathy: the identification with the feelings or thoughts of others

compassion: a feeling of deep sympathy for someone struck by misfortune, accompanied by a desire to alleviate suffering

dispassionate: devoid of personal feeling or bias

impassive: showing or feeling no emotion

sociopath: a person whose behavior is antisocial and who lacks a sense of moral responsibility

pathogenic: causing disease

PAU/PO/POV/PU: FEW, LITTLE, POOR

poverty: the condition of being poor

paucity: smallness of quantity; scarcity; scantiness

pauper: a person without any personal means of support

impoverish: to deplete

pusillanimous: lacking courage or resolution

puerile: childish, immature

PED: CHILD, EDUCATION

pedagogue: a teacher

pediatrician: a doctor who primarily has children as patients

pedant: one who displays learning ostentatiously

encyclopedia: book or set of books containing articles on various topics, covering all branches of knowledge or of one particular subject

PED/POD: FOOT

pedal: a foot-operated lever or part used to control

pedestrian: a person who travels on foot

expedite: to speed up the progress of

impede: to retard progress by means of obstacles or hindrances

podium: a small platform for an orchestra conductor, speaker, etcetera

antipodes: places diametrically opposite each other on the globe

PEN/PUN: TO PAY; TO COMPENSATE

penal: of or pertaining to punishment, as for crimes

penalty: a punishment imposed for a violation of law or rule

punitive: serving for, concerned with, or inflicting punishment

penance: a punishment undergone to express regret for a sin

penitent: contrite

PEND/PENS: TO HANG; TO WEIGHT; TO PAY

depend: to rely; to place trust in

stipend: a periodic payment; fixed or regular pay

compensate: to counterbalance, offset

indispensable: absolutely necessary, essential, or requisite

appendix: supplementary material at the end of a text

appendage: a limb or other subsidiary part that diverges from the central structure

PER: COMPLETELY

persistent: lasting or enduring tenaciously

perforate: to make a way through or into something

perplex: to cause to be puzzled or bewildered over what is not understood

peruse: to read with thoroughness or care

perfunctory: performed merely as routine duty

pertinacious: resolute

perspicacious: shrewd, astute

PERI: AROUND

perimeter: the border or outer boundary of a two-dimensional figure

periscope: an optical instrument for seeing objects in an obstructed field of vision

peripatetic: walking or traveling about; itinerant

PET/PIT: TO GO; TO SEEK; TO STRIVE

appetite: a desire for food or drink

compete: to strive to outdo another for acknowledgment

petition: a formally drawn request soliciting some benefit

centripetal: moving toward the center

impetuous: characterized by sudden or rash action or emotion

petulant: showing sudden irritation, esp. over some annoyance

PHIL: LOVE

philosophy: the rational investigation of the truths and principles of being, knowledge, or conduct

philatelist: one who loves or collects postage stamps

philology: the study of literary texts to establish their authenticity and determine their meaning

bibliophile: one who loves or collects books

PLAC: TO PLEASE

placid: pleasantly calm or peaceful

placebo: a substance with no pharmacological effect which acts to placate a patient who believes it to be a medicine

implacable: unable to be pleased

complacent: self-satisfied, unconcerned

complaisant: inclined or disposed to please

PLE: TO FILL

complete: having all parts or elements

deplete: to decrease seriously or exhaust the supply of

supplement: something added to supply a deficiency

implement: an instrument, tool, or utensil for accomplishing work

replete: abundantly supplied

plethora: excess, overabundance

PLEX/PLIC/PLY: TO FOLD, TWIST, TANGLE, OR BEND

complex: composed of many interconnected parts

replica: any close copy or reproduction

implicit: not expressly stated, implied

implicate: to show to be involved, usually in an incriminating manner

duplicity: deceitfulness in speech or conduct, double-dealing

supplicate: to make humble and earnest entreaty

PON/POS/POUND: TO PUT; TO PLACE

component: a constituent part, elemental ingredient

expose: to lay open to danger, attack, or harm

expound: to set forth in detail

juxtapose: to place close together or side by side, esp. for contract

repository: a receptacle or place where things are deposited

PORT: TO CARRY

import: to bring in from a foreign country

export: to transmit abroad

portable: easily carried

deportment: conduct, behavior

disport: to divert or amuse oneself

importune: to urge or press with excessive persistence

POST: AFTER

posthumous: after death

posterior: situated at the rear

posterity: succeeding in future generations collectively

post facto: after the fact

PRE: BEFORE

precarious: dependent on circumstances beyond one's control

precocious: unusually advanced or mature in mental development or talent

premonition: a feeling of anticipation over a future event

presentiment: foreboding

precedent: an act that serves as an example for subsequent situations

precept: a commandment given as a rule of action or conduct

PREHEND/PRISE: TO TAKE; TO GET; TO SEIZE

surprise: to strike with an unexpected feeling of wonder or astonishment

enterprise: a project undertaken

reprehensible: deserving rebuke or censure

comprise: to include or contain

reprisals: retaliation against an enemy

apprehend: to take into custody

PRO: MUCH, FOR, A LOT

prolific: highly fruitful

profuse: spending or giving freely

prodigal: wastefully or recklessly extravagant

prodigious: extraordinary in size, amount, or extent

proselytize: to convert or attempt to recruit

propound: to set forth for consideration

provident: having or showing foresight

PROB: TO PROVE; TO TEST

probe: to search or examine thoroughly

approbation: praise, consideration

opprobrium: the disgrace incurred by shameful conduct

reprobate: a depraved or wicked person

problematic: questionable

probity: honesty, high-mindedness

PUG: TO FIGHT

pugnacious: to quarrel or fight readily

impugn: to challenge as false

repugnant: objectionable or offensive

pugilist: a fighter or boxer

PUNC/PUNG/POIGN: TO POINT; TO PRICK

point: a sharp or tapering end

puncture: the act of piercing

pungent: caustic or sharply expressive

compunction: a feeling of uneasiness for doing wrong

punctilious: strict or exact in the observance of formalities

expunge: to erase, eliminate completely

QUE/QUIS: TO SEEK

acquire: to come into possession of

exquisite: of special beauty or charm

conquest: vanquishment

inquisitive: given to research, eager for knowledge

query: a question, inquiry

querulous: full of complaints

perquisite: a gratuity, tip

QUI: QUIET

quiet: making little or no sound

disquiet: lack of calm or peace

tranquil: free from commotion or tumult

acquiesce: to comply, give in

quiescence: the condition of being at rest, still, inactive

RID/RIS: TO LAUGH

riddle: a conundrum

derision: the act of mockery

risible: causing laughter

ROG: TO ASK

interrogate: to ask questions of, esp. formally

arrogant: making claims to superior importance or rights

abrogate: to abolish by formal means

surrogate: a person appointed to act for another

derogatory: belittling, disparaging

arrogate: to claim unwarrantably or presumptuously

SACR/SANCT/SECR: SACRED

sacred: devoted or dedicated to a deity or religious purpose

sacrifice: the offering of some living or inanimate thing to a deity in homage

sanctify: to make holy

sanction: authoritative permission or approval

execrable: abominable

sacrament: something regarded as possessing sacred character

sacrilege: the violation of anything sacred

SAL/SIL/SAULT/SULT: TO LEAP, TO JUMP

insult: to treat with contemptuous rudeness

assault: a sudden or violent attack

somersault: to roll the body end over end, making a complete revolution

salient: prominent or conspicuous

resilient: able to spring back to an original form after compression

insolent: boldly rude or disrespectful

exult: to show or feel triumphant joy

desultory: at random, unmethodical

SCI: TO KNOW

conscious: aware of one's own existence

conscience: the inner sense of what is right or wrong, impelling one toward right action unconscionable: unscrupulous

omniscient: knowing everything

prescient: having knowledge of things before they happen

SCRIBE/SCRIP: TO WRITE

scribble: to write hastily or carelessly

describe: to tell or depict in words

script: handwriting

postscript: any addition or supplement

proscribe: to condemn as harmful or odious

ascribe: to credit or assign, as to a cause or course

conscription: draft

transcript: a written or typed copy

circumscribe: to draw a line around

SE: APART

select: to choose in preference to another

separate: to keep apart, divide

seduce: to lead astray

segregate: to separate or set apart from others

secede: to withdraw formally from an association

sequester: to remove or withdraw into solitude or retirement

sedition: incitement of discontent or rebellion against a government

SEC/SEQU: TO FOLLOW

second: next after the first

prosecute: to seek to enforce by legal process

sequence: the following of one thing after another

obsequious: fawning

non sequitur: an inference or a conclusion that does not follow from the premises

SED/SESS/SID: TO SIT; TO BE STILL; TO PLAN; TO PLOT

preside: to exercise management or control

resident: a person who lives in a place

sediment: the matter that settles to the bottom of a liquid

dissident: disagreeing, as in opinion or attitude

residual: remaining, leftover

subsidiary: serving to assist or supplement

insidious: intended to entrap or beguile

assiduous: diligent, persistent, hardworking

SENS/SENT: TO FEEL; TO BE AWARE

sense: any of the faculties by which humans and animals perceive stimuli originating outside the body

sensory: of or pertaining to the senses or sensation

sentiment: an attitude or feeling toward something

presentiment: a feeling that something is about to happen

dissent: to differ in opinion, esp. from the majority

resent: to feel or show displeasure

sentinel: a person or thing that stands watch

insensate: without feeling or sensitivity

SOL: TO LOOSEN; TO FREE

dissolve: to make a solution of, as by mixing in a liquid

soluble: capable of being dissolved or liquefied

resolution: a formal expression of opinion or intention made

dissolution: the act or process of dissolving into parts or elements

dissolute: indifferent to moral restraints

absolution: forgiveness for wrongdoing

SPEC/SPIC/SPIT: TO LOOK; TO SEE

perspective: one's mental view of facts, ideas, and their interrelationships

speculation: the contemplation or consideration of some subject

suspicious: inclined to suspect

spectrum: a broad range of related things that form a continuous series

retrospective: contemplative of past situations

circumspect: watchful and discreet, cautious

perspicacious: having keen mental perception and understanding

conspicuous: easily seen or noticed; readily observable

specious: deceptively attractive

STA/STI: TO STAND; TO BE IN PLACE

static: of bodies or forces at rest or in equilibrium

destitute: without means of subsistence

obstinate: stubbornly adhering to a purpose, opinion, or course of action

constitute: to make up

stasis: the state of equilibrium or inactivity caused by opposing equal forces

apostasy: renunciation of an object of one's previous loyalty

SUA: SMOOTH

suave: smoothly agreeable or polite

persuade: to encourage; to convince

dissuade: to deter

assuage: to make less severe, ease, relieve

SUB/SUP: BELOW

submissive: inclined or ready to submit

subsidiary: serving to assist or supplement

subliminal: existing or operating below the threshold of confidence

subtle: thin, tenuous, or rarefied

subterfuge: an artifice or expedient used to evade a rule

supposition: the act of assuming

SUPER/SUR: ABOVE

surpass: to go beyond in amount, extent, or degree

superlative: the highest kind or order

supersede: to replace in power, as by another person or thing

supercilious: arrogant, haughty, condescending

superfluous: extra, more than necessary

surmount: to get over or across, to prevail

surveillance: a watch kept over someone or something

TAC/TIC: TO BE SILENT

reticent: disposed to be silent or not to speak freely

tacit: unspoken understanding

taciturn: uncommunicative

TAIN/TEN/TENT/TIN: TO HOLD

detain: to keep from proceeding

pertain: to have reference or relation

tenacious: holding fast

abstention: the act of refraining voluntarily

tenure: the holding or possessing of anything

tenable: capable of being held, maintained, or defended

sustenance: nourishment, means of livelihood

pertinacious: persistent, stubborn

TEND/TENS/TENT/TENU: TO STRETCH; TO THIN

tension: the act of stretching or straining

tentative: of the nature of, or done as a trial, attempt

tendentious: having a predisposition towards a point of view

distend: to expand by stretching

attenuate: to weaken or reduce in force

extenuating: making less serious by offering excuses

contentious: quarrelsome, disagreeable, belligerent

THEO: GOD

atheist: one who does not believe in a deity or divine system

theocracy: a form of government in which a deity is recognized as the supreme ruler

theology: the study of divine things and the divine faith

apotheosis: glorification, glorified ideal

TRACT: TO DRAG; TO PULL; TO DRAW

tractor: a powerful vehicle used to pull farm machinery

attract: to draw either by physical force or by an appeal to emotions or senses

contract: a legally binding document

detract: to take away from, esp. a positive thing

abstract: to draw or pull away, remove

tractable: easily managed or controlled

protract: to prolong, draw out, extend

TRANS: ACROSS

transaction: the act of carrying on or conduct to a conclusion or settlement

transparent: easily seen through, recognized, or detected

transition: a change from one way of being to another

transgress: to violate a law, command, or moral code

transcendent: going beyond ordinary limits

intransigent: refusing to agree or compromise

US/UT: TO USE

abuse: to use wrongly or improperly
usage: a customary way of doing something
usurp: to seize and hold
utilitarian: efficient, functional, useful

VEN/VENT: TO COME OR TO MOVE TOWARD

convene: to assemble for some public purpose
venturesome: showing a disposition to undertake risks
intervene: to come between disputing factions, mediate
contravene: to come into conflict with
adventitious: accidental

VER: TRUTH

verdict: any judgment or decision
veracious: habitually truthful
verity: truthfulness
verisimilitude: the appearance or semblance of truth
aver: to affirm, to declare to be true

VERD: GREEN

verdant: green with vegetation; inexperienced
verdure: fresh, rich vegetation

VERS/VERT: TO TURN

controversy: a public dispute involving a matter of opinion
revert: to return to a former habit
diverse: of a different kind, form, character
aversion: dislike
introvert: a person concerned primarily with inner thoughts and feelings
extrovert: an outgoing person
inadvertent: unintentional
covert: hidden, clandestine
avert: to turn away from

VI: LIFE

vivid: strikingly bright or intense
vicarious: performed, exercised, received, or suffered in place of another
viable: capable of living
vivacity: the quality of being lively, animated, spirited

joie de vivre: joy of life (French expression)
convivial: sociable

VID/VIS: TO SEE

evident: plain or clear to the sight or understanding
video: the elements of television pertaining to the transmission or reception of the image
adviser: one who gives counsel
survey: to view in a general or comprehensive way
vista: a view or prospect

VIL: BASE, MEAN

vilify: to slander, to defame
revile: to criticize with harsh language
vile: loathsome, unpleasant

VOC/VOK: TO CALL

vocabulary: the stock of words used by or known to a particular person or group
advocate: to support or urge by argument
equivocate: to use ambiguous or unclear expressions
vocation: a particular occupation
avocation: something one does in addition to a principle occupation
vociferous: crying out noisily
convoke: to call together
invoke: to call on a deity

VOL: TO WISH

voluntary: undertaken of one's own accord or by free choice
malevolent: characterized by or expressing bad will
benevolent: characterized by or expressing goodwill
volition: free choice, free will; act of choosing

VOR: TO EAT

voracious: having a great appetite
carnivorous: meat-eating
omnivorous: eating or absorbing everything

TOP GRE WORDS IN CONTEXT

The GRE tests the same kinds of words over and over again. Here you will find the most popular GRE words with their definitions in context to help you to remember them. If you see a word that's unfamiliar to you, take a moment to study the definition and, most importantly, reread the sentence with the word's definition in mind.

Remember: learning vocabulary words in context is one of the best ways for your brain to retain the words' meanings. A broader vocabulary will serve you well on all four GRE Verbal question types and will also be extremely helpful in the Analytical Writing section.

ABATE: TO REDUCE IN AMOUNT, DEGREE, OR SEVERITY

As the hurricane's force ABATED, the winds dropped and the sea became calm.

ABSCOND: TO LEAVE SECRETLY

The patron ABSCONDED from the restaurant without paying his bill by sneaking out the back door.

ABSTAIN: TO CHOOSE NOT TO DO SOMETHING:

She ABSTAINED from choosing a mouthwatering dessert from the tray.

ABYSS: AN EXTREMELY DEEP HOLE

The submarine dove into the ABYSS to chart the previously unseen depths.

ADULTERATE: TO MAKE IMPURE

The restaurateur made his ketchup last longer by ADULTERATING it with water.

ADVOCATE: TO SPEAK IN FAVOR OF

The vegetarian ADVOCATED a diet containing no meat.

AESTHETIC: CONCERNING THE APPRECIATION OF BEAUTY

Followers of the AESTHETIC Movement regarded the pursuit of beauty as the only true purpose of art.

AGGRANDIZE: TO INCREASE IN POWER, INFLUENCE, AND REPUTATION

The supervisor sought to AGGRANDIZE himself by claiming that the achievements of his staff were actually his own.

ALLEVIATE: TO MAKE MORE BEARABLE

Taking aspirin helps to ALLEVIATE a headache.

AMALGAMATE: TO COMBINE; TO MIX TOGETHER

Giant Industries AMALGAMATED with Mega Products to form Giant-Mega Products Incorporated.

AMBIGUOUS: DOUBTFUL OR UNCERTAIN; ABLE TO BE INTERPRETED SEVERAL WAYS

The directions she gave were so AMBIGUOUS that we disagreed on which way to turn.

AMELIORATE: TO MAKE BETTER; TO IMPROVE

The doctor was able to AMELIORATE the patient's suffering using painkillers.

ANACHRONISM: SOMETHING OUT OF PLACE IN TIME

The aged hippie used ANACHRONISTIC phrases like *groovy* and *far out* that had not been popular for years.

ANALOGOUS: SIMILAR OR ALIKE IN SOME WAY; EQUIVALENT TO

In a famous argument for the existence of God, the universe is ANALOGOUS to a mechanical timepiece, the creation of a divinely intelligent "clockmaker."

ANOMALY: DEVIATION FROM WHAT IS NORMAL

Albino animals may display too great an ANOMALY in their coloring to attract normally colored mates.

ANTAGONIZE: TO ANNOY OR PROVOKE TO ANGER

The child discovered that he could ANTAGONIZE the cat by pulling its tail.

ANTIPATHY: EXTREME DISLIKE

The ANTIPATHY between the French and the English regularly erupted into open warfare.

APATHY: LACK OF INTEREST OR EMOTION

The APATHY of voters is so great that less than half the people who are eligible to vote actually bother to do so.

ARBITRATE: TO JUDGE A DISPUTE BETWEEN TWO OPPOSING PARTIES

Since the couple could not come to agreement, a judge was forced to ARBITRATE their divorce proceedings.

ARCHAIC: ANCIENT, OLD-FASHIONED

Her ARCHAIC Commodore computer could not run the latest software.

ARDOR: INTENSE AND PASSIONATE FEELING

Bishop's ARDOR for landscape was evident when he passionately described the beauty of the scenic Hudson Valley.

ARTICULATE: ABLE TO SPEAK CLEARLY AND EXPRESSIVELY

She is such an ARTICULATE defender of labor that unions are among her strongest supporters.

ASSUAGE: TO MAKE SOMETHING UNPLEASANT LESS SEVERE

Serena used aspirin to ASSUAGE her pounding headache.

ATTENUATE: TO REDUCE IN FORCE OR DEGREE; TO WEAKEN

The Bill of Rights ATTENUATED the traditional power of government to change laws at will.

AUDACIOUS: FEARLESS AND DARING

Her AUDACIOUS nature allowed her to fulfill her dream of skydiving.

AUSTERE: SEVERE OR STERN IN APPEARANCE; UNDECORATED

The lack of decoration makes Zen temples seem AUSTERE to the untrained eye.

BANAL: PREDICTABLE, CLICHÉD, BORING

He used BANAL phrases like *Have a nice day*, or *Another day, another dollar.*

BOLSTER: TO SUPPORT; TO PROP UP

The presence of giant footprints BOLSTERED the argument that Sasquatch was in the area.

BOMBASTIC: POMPOUS IN SPEECH AND MANNER

The dictator's speeches were mostly BOMBASTIC; his boasting and outrageous claims had no basis in fact.

CACOPHONY: HARSH, JARRING NOISE

The junior high orchestra created an almost unbearable CACOPHONY as they tried to tune their instruments.

CANDID: IMPARTIAL AND HONEST IN SPEECH

The observations of a child can be charming since they are CANDID and unpretentious.

CAPRICIOUS: CHANGING ONE'S MIND QUICKLY AND OFTEN

Queen Elizabeth I was quite CAPRICIOUS; her courtiers could never be sure which of their number would catch her fancy.

CASTIGATE: TO PUNISH OR CRITICIZE HARSHLY

Americans are amazed at how harshly the authorities in Singapore CASTIGATE perpetrators of what would be considered minor crimes in the United States.

CATALYST: SOMETHING THAT BRINGS ABOUT A CHANGE IN SOMETHING ELSE

The imposition of harsh taxes was the CATALYST that finally brought on the revolution.

CAUSTIC: BITING IN WIT

Dorothy Parker gained her reputation for CAUSTIC wit from her cutting, yet clever, insults.

CHAOS: GREAT DISORDER OR CONFUSION

In most religious traditions, God created an ordered universe from CHAOS.

CHAUVINIST: SOMEONE PREJUDICED IN FAVOR OF A GROUP TO WHICH HE OR SHE BELONGS

The attitude that men are inherently superior to women and therefore must be obeyed is common among male CHAUVINISTS.

CHICANERY: DECEPTION BY MEANS OF CRAFT OR GUILE

Dishonest used car salesmen often use CHICANERY to sell their beat-up old cars.

COGENT: CONVINCING AND WELL REASONED

Swayed by the COGENT argument of the defense, the jury had no choice but to acquit the defendant.

CONDONE: TO OVERLOOK, PARDON, OR DISREGARD

Some theorists believe that failing to prosecute minor crimes is the same as CONDONING an air of lawlessness.

CONVOLUTED: INTRICATE AND COMPLICATED

Although many people bought *A Brief History of Time*, few could follow its CONVOLUTED ideas and theories.

CORROBORATE: TO PROVIDE SUPPORTING EVIDENCE

Fingerprints CORROBORATED the witness's testimony that he saw the defendant in the victim's apartment.

CREDULOUS: TOO TRUSTING; GULLIBLE

Although some four-year-olds believe in the Easter Bunny, only the most CREDULOUS nine-year-olds also believe in him.

CRESCENDO: STEADILY INCREASING VOLUME OR FORCE

The CRESCENDO of tension became unbearable as Evel Knievel prepared to jump his motorcycle over the school buses.

DECORUM: APPROPRIATENESS OF BEHAVIOR OR CONDUCT; PROPRIETY

The countess complained that the vulgar peasants lacked the DECORUM appropriate for a visit to the palace.

DEFERENCE: RESPECT, COURTESY

The respectful young law clerk treated the Supreme Court justice with the utmost DEFERENCE.

DERIDE: TO SPEAK OF OR TREAT WITH CONTEMPT; TO MOCK

The awkward child was often DERIDED by his "cooler" peers.

DESICCATE: TO DRY OUT THOROUGHLY

After a few weeks of lying on the desert's baking sands, the cow's carcass became completely DESICCATED.

DESULTORY: JUMPING FROM ONE THING TO ANOTHER; DISCONNECTED

Diane had a DESULTORY academic record; she had changed majors 12 times in three years.

DIATRIBE: AN ABUSIVE, CONDEMNATORY SPEECH

The trucker bellowed a DIATRIBE at the driver who had cut him off.

DIFFIDENT: LACKING SELF-CONFIDENCE

Steve's DIFFIDENT manner during the job interview stemmed from his nervous nature and lack of experience in the field.

DILATE: TO MAKE LARGER; TO EXPAND

When you enter a darkened room, the pupils of your eyes DILATE to let in more light.

DILATORY: INTENDED TO DELAY

The congressman used DILATORY measures to delay the passage of the bill.

DILETTANTE: SOMEONE WITH AN AMATEURISH AND SUPERFICIAL INTEREST IN A TOPIC

Jerry's friends were such DILETTANTES that they seemed to have new jobs and hobbies every week.

DIRGE: A FUNERAL HYMN OR MOURNFUL SPEECH

Melville wrote the poem "A DIRGE for James McPherson" for the funeral of a Union general who was killed in 1864.

DISABUSE: TO SET RIGHT; TO FREE FROM ERROR

Galileo's observations DISABUSED scholars of the notion that the Sun revolved around the Earth.

DISCERN: TO PERCEIVE; TO RECOGNIZE

It is easy to DISCERN the difference between butter and butter-flavored topping.

DISPARATE: FUNDAMENTALLY DIFFERENT; ENTIRELY UNLIKE

Although the twins appear to be identical physically, their personalities are DISPARATE.

DISSEMBLE: TO PRESENT A FALSE APPEARANCE; TO DISGUISE ONE'S REAL INTENTIONS OR CHARACTER

The villain could DISSEMBLE to the police no longer—he admitted the deed and tore up the floor to reveal the body of the old man.

DISSONANCE: A HARSH AND DISAGREEABLE COMBINATION, OFTEN OF SOUNDS

Cognitive DISSONANCE is the inner conflict produced when long-standing beliefs are contradicted by new evidence.

DOGMA: A FIRMLY HELD OPINION, OFTEN A RELIGIOUS BELIEF

Linus's central DOGMA was that children who believed in the Great Pumpkin would be rewarded.

DOGMATIC: DICTATORIAL IN ONE'S OPINIONS

The dictator was DOGMATIC—he, and only he, was right.

DUPE: TO DECEIVE; A PERSON WHO IS EASILY DECEIVED

Bugs Bunny was able to DUPE Elmer Fudd by dressing up as a lady rabbit.

ECLECTIC: SELECTING FROM OR MADE UP FROM A VARIETY OF SOURCES

Budapest's architecture is an ECLECTIC mix of eastern and western styles.

EFFICACY: EFFECTIVENESS

The EFFICACY of penicillin was unsurpassed when it was first introduced; the drug completely eliminated almost all bacterial infections for which it was administered.

ELEGY: A SORROWFUL POEM OR SPEECH

Although Thomas Gray's "ELEGY Written in a Country Churchyard" is about death and loss, it urges its readers to endure this life, and to trust in spirituality.

ELOQUENT: PERSUASIVE AND MOVING, ESPECIALLY IN SPEECH

The Gettysburg Address is moving not only because of its lofty sentiments but also because of its ELOQUENT words.

EMULATE: TO COPY; TO TRY TO EQUAL OR EXCEL

The graduate student sought to EMULATE his professor in every way, copying not only how she taught, but also how she conducted herself outside of class.

ENERVATE: TO REDUCE IN STRENGTH

The guerrillas hoped that a series of surprise attacks would ENERVATE the regular army.

ENGENDER: TO PRODUCE, CAUSE, OR BRING ABOUT

His fear and hatred of clowns was ENGENDERED when he witnessed the death of his father at the hands of a clown.

ENIGMA: A PUZZLE; A MYSTERY

Speaking in riddles and dressed in old robes, the artist gained a reputation as something of an ENIGMA.

ENUMERATE: TO COUNT, LIST, OR ITEMIZE

Moses returned from the mountain with tablets on which the commandments were ENUMERATED.

EPHEMERAL: LASTING A SHORT TIME

The lives of mayflies seem EPHEMERAL to us, since the flies' average life span is a matter of hours.

EQUIVOCATE: TO USE EXPRESSIONS OF DOUBLE MEANING IN ORDER TO MISLEAD

When faced with criticism of his policies, the politician EQUIVOCATED and left all parties thinking he agreed with them.

ERRATIC: WANDERING AND UNPREDICTABLE

The plot seemed predictable until it suddenly took a series of ERRATIC turns that surprised the audience.

ERUDITE: LEARNED, SCHOLARLY, BOOKISH

The annual meeting of philosophy professors was a gathering of the most ERUDITE, well-published individuals in the field.

ESOTERIC: KNOWN OR UNDERSTOOD BY ONLY A FEW

Only a handful of experts are knowledgeable about the ESOTERIC world of particle physics.

ESTIMABLE: ADMIRABLE

Most people consider it ESTIMABLE that Mother Teresa spent her life helping the poor of India.

EULOGY: SPEECH IN PRAISE OF SOMEONE

His best friend gave the EULOGY, outlining his many achievements and talents.

EUPHEMISM: USE OF AN INOFFENSIVE WORD OR PHRASE IN PLACE OF A MORE DISTASTEFUL ONE

The funeral director preferred to use the EUPHEMISM "sleeping" instead of the word "dead."

EXACERBATE: TO MAKE WORSE

It is unwise to take aspirin to try to relieve heartburn; instead of providing relief, the drug will only EXACERBATE the problem.

EXCULPATE: TO CLEAR FROM BLAME; PROVE INNOCENT

The adversarial legal system is intended to convict those who are guilty and to EXCULPATE those who are innocent.

EXIGENT: URGENT; REQUIRING IMMEDIATE ACTION

The patient was losing blood so rapidly that it was EXIGENT to stop the source of the bleeding.

EXONERATE: TO CLEAR OF BLAME

The fugitive was EXONERATED when another criminal confessed to committing the crime.

EXPLICIT: CLEARLY STATED OR SHOWN; FORTHRIGHT IN EXPRESSION

The owners of the house left a list of EXPLICIT instructions detailing their house-sitters' duties, including a schedule for watering the house plants.

FANATICAL: ACTING EXCESSIVELY ENTHUSIASTIC; FILLED WITH EXTREME, UNQUESTIONED DEVOTION

The stormtroopers were FANATICAL in their devotion to the Emperor, readily sacrificing their lives for him.

FAWN: TO GROVEL

The understudy FAWNED over the director in hopes of being cast in the part on a permanent basis.

FERVID: INTENSELY EMOTIONAL; FEVERISH

The fans of Maria Callas were unusually FERVID, doing anything to catch a glimpse of the great opera singer.

FLORID: EXCESSIVELY DECORATED OR EMBELLISHED

The palace had been decorated in an excessively FLORID style; every surface had been carved and gilded.

FOMENT: TO AROUSE OR INCITE

The protesters tried to FOMENT feeling against the war through their speeches and demonstrations.

FRUGALITY: A TENDENCY TO BE THRIFTY OR CHEAP

Scrooge McDuck's FRUGALITY was so great that he accumulated enough wealth to fill a giant storehouse with money.

GARRULOUS: TENDING TO TALK A LOT

The GARRULOUS parakeet distracted its owner with its continuous talking.

GREGARIOUS: OUTGOING, SOCIABLE

She was so GREGARIOUS that when she found herself alone she felt quite sad.

GUILE: DECEIT OR TRICKERY

Since he was not fast enough to catch the roadrunner on foot, the coyote resorted to GUILE in an effort to trap his enemy.

GULLIBLE: EASILY DECEIVED

The con man pretended to be a bank officer so as to fool GULLIBLE bank customers into giving him their account information.

HOMOGENOUS: OF A SIMILAR KIND

The class was fairly HOMOGENOUS, since almost all of the students were senior journalism majors.

ICONOCLAST: ONE WHO OPPOSES ESTABLISHED BELIEFS, CUSTOMS, AND INSTITUTIONS

His lack of regard for traditional beliefs soon established him as an ICONOCLAST.

IMPERTURBABLE: NOT CAPABLE OF BEING DISTURBED

The counselor had so much experience dealing with distraught children that she seemed IMPERTURBABLE, even when faced with the wildest tantrums.

IMPERVIOUS: IMPOSSIBLE TO PENETRATE; INCAPABLE OF BEING AFFECTED

A good raincoat will be IMPERVIOUS to moisture.

IMPETUOUS: QUICK TO ACT WITHOUT THINKING

It is not good for an investment broker to be IMPETUOUS, since much thought should be given to all the possible options.

IMPLACABLE: UNABLE TO BE CALMED DOWN OR MADE PEACEFUL

His rage at the betrayal was so great that he remained IMPLACABLE for weeks.

INCHOATE: NOT FULLY FORMED; DISORGANIZED

The ideas expressed in Nietzsche's mature work also appear in an INCHOATE form in his earliest writing.

INGENUOUS: SHOWING INNOCENCE OR CHILDLIKE SIMPLICITY

She was so INGENUOUS that her friends feared that her innocence and trustfulness would be exploited when she visited the big city.

INIMICAL: HOSTILE, UNFRIENDLY

Even though the children had grown up together they were INIMICAL to each other at school.

INNOCUOUS: HARMLESS

Some snakes are poisonous, but most species are INNOCUOUS and pose no danger to humans.

INSIPID: LACKING INTEREST OR FLAVOR

The critic claimed that the painting was INSIPID, containing no interesting qualities at all.

INTRANSIGENT: UNCOMPROMISING; REFUSING TO BE RECONCILED

The professor was INTRANSIGENT on the deadline, insisting that everyone turn the assignment in at the same time.

INUNDATE: TO OVERWHELM; TO COVER WITH WATER

The tidal wave INUNDATED Atlantis, which was lost beneath the water.

IRASCIBLE: EASILY MADE ANGRY

Attila the Hun's IRASCIBLE and violent nature made all who dealt with him fear for their lives.

LACONIC: USING FEW WORDS

She was a LACONIC poet who built her reputation on using words as sparingly as possible.

LAMENT: TO EXPRESS SORROW; TO GRIEVE

The children continued to LAMENT the death of the goldfish weeks after its demise.

LAUD: TO GIVE PRAISE; TO GLORIFY

Parades and fireworks were staged to LAUD the success of the rebels.

LAVISH: TO GIVE UNSPARINGLY (V.); EXTREMELY GENEROUS OR EXTRAVAGANT (ADJ.)

She LAVISHED the puppy with so many treats that it soon became overweight and spoiled.

LETHARGIC: ACTING IN AN INDIFFERENT OR SLOW, SLUGGISH MANNER

The clerk was so LETHARGIC that, even when the store was slow, he always had a long line in front of him.

LOQUACIOUS: TALKATIVE

She was naturally LOQUACIOUS, which was a problem in situations in which listening was more important than talking.

LUCID: CLEAR AND EASILY UNDERSTOOD

The explanations were written in a simple and LUCID manner so that students were immediately able to apply what they learned.

LUMINOUS: BRIGHT, BRILLIANT, GLOWING

The park was bathed in LUMINOUS sunshine which warmed the bodies and the souls of the visitors.

MALINGER: TO EVADE RESPONSIBILITY BY PRETENDING TO BE ILL

A common way to avoid the draft was by MALINGERING—pretending to be mentally or physically ill so as to avoid being taken by the Army.

MALLEABLE: CAPABLE OF BEING SHAPED

Gold is the most MALLEABLE of precious metals; it can easily be formed into almost any shape.

METAPHOR: A FIGURE OF SPEECH COMPARING TWO DIFFERENT THINGS; A SYMBOL

The METAPHOR "a sea of troubles" suggests a lot of troubles by comparing their number to the vastness of the sea.

METICULOUS: EXTREMELY CAREFUL ABOUT DETAILS

To find all the clues at the crime scene, the investigators METICULOUSLY examined every inch of the area.

MISANTHROPE: A PERSON WHO DISLIKES OTHERS

The character Scrooge in *A Christmas Carol* is such a MISANTHROPE that even the sight of children singing makes him angry.

MITIGATE: TO SOFTEN; TO LESSEN

A judge may MITIGATE a sentence if she decides that a person committed a crime out of need.

MOLLIFY: TO CALM OR MAKE LESS SEVERE

Their argument was so intense that is was difficult to believe any compromise would MOLLIFY them.

MONOTONY: LACK OF VARIATION

The MONOTONY of the sound of the dripping faucet almost drove the research assistant crazy.

NAIVE: LACKING SOPHISTICATION OR EXPERIENCE

Having never traveled before, the hillbillies were more NAIVE than the people they met in Beverly Hills.

OBDURATE: HARDENED IN FEELING; RESISTANT TO PERSUASION

The president was completely OBDURATE on the issue, and no amount of persuasion would change his mind.

OBSEQUIOUS: OVERLY SUBMISSIVE AND EAGER TO PLEASE

The OBSEQUIOUS new associate made sure to compliment her supervisor's tie and agree with him on every issue.

OBSTINATE: STUBBORN, UNYIELDING

The OBSTINATE child could not be made to eat any food that he disliked.

OBVIATE: TO PREVENT; TO MAKE UNNECESSARY

The river was shallow enough to wade across at many points, which OBVIATED the need for a bridge.

OCCLUDE: TO STOP UP; TO PREVENT THE PASSAGE OF

A shadow is thrown across the Earth's surface during a solar eclipse, when the light from the sun is OCCLUDED by the moon.

ONEROUS: TROUBLESOME AND OPPRESSIVE; BURDENSOME

The assignment was so extensive and difficult to manage that it proved ONEROUS to the team in charge of it.

OPAQUE: IMPOSSIBLE TO SEE THROUGH; PREVENTING THE PASSAGE OF LIGHT

The heavy buildup of dirt and grime on the windows almost made them OPAQUE.

OPPROBRIUM: PUBLIC DISGRACE

After the scheme to embezzle the elderly was made public, the treasurer resigned in utter OPPROBRIUM.

OSTENTATION: EXCESSIVE SHOWINESS

The OSTENTATION of the Sun King's court is evident in the lavish decoration and luxuriousness of his palace at Versailles.

PARADOX: A CONTRADICTION OR DILEMMA

It is a PARADOX that those most in need of medical attention are often those least able to obtain it.

PARAGON: MODEL OF EXCELLENCE OR PERFECTION

She is the PARAGON of what a judge should be: honest, intelligent, hardworking, and just.

PEDANT: SOMEONE WHO SHOWS OFF LEARNING

The graduate instructor's tedious and excessive commentary on the subject soon gained her a reputation as a PEDANT.

PERFIDIOUS: WILLING TO BETRAY ONE'S TRUST

The actress's PERFIDIOUS companion revealed all of her intimate secrets to the gossip columnist.

PERFUNCTORY: DONE IN A ROUTINE WAY; INDIFFERENT

The machinelike bank teller processed the transaction and gave the waiting customer a PERFUNCTORY smile.

PERMEATE: TO PENETRATE

This miraculous new cleaning fluid is able to PERMEATE stains and dissolve them in minutes!

PHILANTHROPY: CHARITY; A DESIRE OR EFFORT TO PROMOTE GOODNESS

New York's Metropolitan Museum of Art owes much of its collection to the PHILANTHROPY of private collectors who willed their estates to the museum.

PLACATE: TO SOOTHE OR PACIFY

The burglar tried to PLACATE the snarling dog by saying, "Nice doggy," and offering it a treat.

PLASTIC: ABLE TO BE MOLDED, ALTERED, OR BENT

The new material was very PLASTIC and could be formed into products of vastly different shape.

PLETHORA: EXCESS

Assuming that more was better, the defendant offered the judge a PLETHORA of excuses.

PRAGMATIC: PRACTICAL AS OPPOSED TO IDEALISTIC

While daydreaming gamblers think they can get rich by frequenting casinos, PRAGMATIC gamblers realize that the odds are heavily stacked against them.

PRECIPITATE: TO THROW VIOLENTLY OR BRING ABOUT ABRUPTLY; LACKING DELIBERATION

Upon learning that the couple married after knowing each other only two months, friends and family members expected such a PRECIPITATE marriage to end in divorce.

PREVARICATE: TO LIE OR DEVIATE FROM THE TRUTH

Rather than admit that he had overslept again, the employee PREVARICATED and claimed that heavy traffic had prevented him from arriving at work on time.

PRISTINE: FRESH AND CLEAN; UNCORRUPTED

Since concerted measures had been taken to prevent looting, the archeological site was still PRISTINE when researchers arrived.

PRODIGAL: LAVISH, WASTEFUL

The PRODIGAL son quickly wasted all of his inheritance on a lavish lifestyle devoted to pleasure.

PROLIFERATE: TO INCREASE IN NUMBER QUICKLY

Although he only kept two guinea pigs initially, they PROLIFERATED to such an extent that he soon had dozens.

PROPITIATE: TO CONCILIATE; TO APPEASE

The management PROPITIATED the irate union by agreeing to raise wages for its members.

PROPRIETY: CORRECT BEHAVIOR; OBEDIENCE TO RULES AND CUSTOMS

The aristocracy maintained a high level of PROPRIETY, adhering to even the most minor social rules.

PRUDENCE: WISDOM, CAUTION, OR RESTRAINT

The college student exhibited PRUDENCE by obtaining practical experience along with her studies, which greatly strengthened her résumé.

PUNGENT: SHARP AND IRRITATING TO THE SENSES

The smoke from the burning tires was extremely PUNGENT.

QUIESCENT: MOTIONLESS

Many animals are QUIESCENT over the winter months, minimizing activity in order to conserve energy.

RAREFY: TO MAKE THINNER OR SPARSER

Since the atmosphere RAREFIES as altitudes increase, the air at the top of very tall mountains is too thin to breathe.

REPUDIATE: TO REJECT THE VALIDITY OF

The old woman's claim that she was Russian royalty was REPUDIATED when DNA tests showed she was of no relation to them.

RETICENT: SILENT, RESERVED

Physically small and RETICENT in her speech, Joan Didion often went unnoticed by those upon whom she was reporting.

RHETORIC: EFFECTIVE WRITING OR SPEAKING

Lincoln's talent for RHETORIC was evident in his beautifully expressed Gettysburg Address.

SATIATE: TO SATISFY FULLY OR OVERINDULGE

His desire for power was so great that nothing less than complete control of the country could SATIATE it.

SOPORIFIC: CAUSING SLEEP OR LETHARGY

The movie proved to be so SOPORIFIC that soon loud snores were heard throughout the theater.

SPECIOUS: DECEPTIVELY ATTRACTIVE; SEEMINGLY PLAUSIBLE BUT FALLACIOUS

The student's SPECIOUS excuse for being late sounded legitimate, but was proved otherwise when her teacher called her home.

STIGMA: A MARK OF SHAME OR DISCREDIT

In *The Scarlet Letter*, Hester Prynne was required to wear the letter "A" on her clothes as a public STIGMA for her adultery.

STOLID: UNEMOTIONAL; LACKING SENSITIVITY

The prisoner appeared STOLID and unaffected by the judge's harsh sentence.

SUBLIME: LOFTY OR GRAND

The music was so SUBLIME that it transformed the rude surroundings into a special place.

TACIT: DONE WITHOUT USING WORDS

Although not a word had been said, everyone in the room knew that a TACIT agreement had been made about which course of action to take.

TACITURN: SILENT, NOT TALKATIVE

The clerk's TACITURN nature earned him the nickname "Silent Bob."

TIRADE: LONG, HARSH SPEECH OR VERBAL ATTACK

Observers were shocked at the manager's TIRADE over such a minor mistake.

TORPOR: EXTREME MENTAL AND PHYSICAL SLUGGISHNESS

After surgery, the patient experienced TORPOR until the anesthesia wore off.

TRANSITORY: TEMPORARY, LASTING A BRIEF TIME

The reporter lived a TRANSITORY life, staying in one place only long enough to cover the current story.

VACILLATE: TO SWAY PHYSICALLY; TO BE INDECISIVE

The customer held up the line as he VACILLATED between ordering chocolate chip or rocky road ice cream.

VENERATE: TO RESPECT DEEPLY

In a traditional Confucian society, the young VENERATE their elders, deferring to the elders' wisdom and experience.

VERACITY: FILLED WITH TRUTH AND ACCURACY

She had a reputation for VERACITY, so everyone trusted her description of events.

VERBOSE: WORDY

The professor's answer was so VERBOSE that his student forgot what the original question had been.

VEX: TO ANNOY

The old man who loved his peace and quiet was VEXED by his neighbor's loud music.

VOLATILE: EASILY AROUSED OR CHANGEABLE; LIVELY OR EXPLOSIVE

His VOLATILE personality made it difficult to predict his reaction to anything.

WAVER: TO FLUCTUATE BETWEEN CHOICES

If you WAVER too long before making a decision about which testing site to register for, you may not get your first choice.

WHIMSICAL: ACTING IN A FANCIFUL OR CAPRICIOUS MANNER; UNPREDICTABLE

The ballet was WHIMSICAL, delighting the children with its imaginative characters and unpredictable sets.

ZEAL: PASSION, EXCITEMENT

She brought her typical ZEAL to the project, sparking enthusiasm in the other team members.

COMMONLY CONFUSED WORDS

Already—by this or that time, previously
He already completed his work.

All ready—completely prepared
The students were all ready to take their exam.

Altogether—entirely, completely
I am altogether certain that I turned in my homework.

All together—in the same place
She kept the figurines all together on her mantle.

Capital—a city containing the seat of government, the wealth or funds owned by a business or individual, resources
Atlanta is the capital of Georgia.
The company's capital gains have diminished in recent years.

Capitol—the building in which a legislative body meets.
Our trip included a visit to the Capitol building in Washington, D.C.

Coarse—rough, not smooth; lacking refinement
The truck's large wheels enabled it to navigate the coarse, rough terrain.
His coarse language prevented him from getting hired for the job.

Course—path, series of classes or studies.
James's favorite course is biology.
The doctor suggested that Amy rest and let the disease run its course.

Here—in this location.
George Washington used to live here.

Hear—to listen to or to perceive by the ear
Did you hear the question?

Its—a personal pronoun that shows possession
Please put the book back in its place.

It's—the contraction of it is
It's snowing outside.

Lead—to act as a leader, to go first, or to take a superior position
The guide will lead us through the forest.

Led—past tense of lead
The guide led us through the forest.

Lead—a metal
It is dangerous to inhale fumes from paint containing lead.

Loose—free, to set free, not tight
She always wears loose clothing when she does yoga.

Lose—to become without
Use a bookmark so you don't lose your place in your book.

Passed—the past tense of pass
We passed by her house on Sunday.

Past—that which has gone by or elapsed in time, by
In the past, Abby never used to study.
We drove past her house.

Principal—the head of a school, main or important
The quarterback's injury is the principal reason the team lost.
The principal of the school meets with parents regularly.

Stationary—fixed, not moving
Thomas rode a stationary bicycle at the gym.

Stationery—paper used for letter writing
The principal's stationery has the school's logo on the top.

Their—possessive of they
Pau and Ben studied for their test together.

There—a place, in that matter or respect
There are several question types on the GRE.
Please hang up your jacket over there.

They're—contraction of they are
Be careful of the bushes as they're filled with thorns.

MATH REFERENCE

The math on the GRE covers a lot of ground—from basic algebra to symbol problems to geometry. Don't let yourself be intimidated.

We've highlighted the 100 most important concepts that you need to know and divided them into three levels. The GRE Quantitative section tests your understanding of a relatively limited number of mathematical concepts, all of which you will be able to learn.

Level 1 is the most basic. You can't answer any GRE math questions if you don't know Level 1 math. Most people preparing to take the GRE are already pretty good at Level 1 math but look over the Level 1 list just to make sure you're comfortable with the basics.

Level 2 where most people start their review of math. Level 2 skills and formulas come into play quite frequently on the GRE, especially in the medium and hard questions.

Level 3 is the hardest math you'll find on the GRE. Don't spend a lot of time on Level 3 if you still have gaps in Level 2; but once you've mastered Level 2, tackling Level 3 can put you over the top.

LEVEL 1 (Math You Probably Already Know)

1. How to add, subtract, multiply, and divide **WHOLE NUMBERS**

2. How to add, subtract, multiply, and divide **FRACTIONS**

3. How to add, subtract, multiply, and divide **DECIMALS**

4. How to convert **FRACTIONS TO DECIMALS** and **DECIMALS TO FRACTIONS**

5. How to add, subtract, multiply, and divide **POSITIVE AND NEGATIVE NUMBERS**

6. How to plot points on the **NUMBER LINE**

7. How to plug a number into an **ALGEBRAIC EXPRESSION**

8. How to **SOLVE** a simple **EQUATION**

9. How to add and subtract **LINE SEGMENTS**

10. How to find the **THIRD ANGLE** of a **TRIANGLE**, given the other two angles

LEVEL 2 (Math You Might Need to Review)

11. **How to use PEMDAS**

When you're given an ugly arithmetic expression, it's important to know the order of operations. Just remember PEMDAS (as in "Please excuse my dear Aunt Sally"). What PEMDAS means is this: Clean up **Parentheses** first; then deal with **Exponents**; then do the **Multiplication** and **Division** together, going from left to right; and finally do the **Addition** and **Subtraction** together, again going from left to right.

Example: $9 - 2 \times (5 - 3)^2 + 6 \div 3 =$

Begin with the parentheses:
$$9 - 2 \times (2)^2 + 6 \div 3$$

Then do the exponent:
$$9 - 2 \times 4 + 6 \div 3$$

Now do multiplication and division from left to right:
$$9 - 8 + 2$$

Finally, do addition and subtraction from left to right:
$$9 - 8 + 2 = 1 + 2 = 3$$

12. How to use the PERCENT FORMULA

Identify the part, the percent, and the whole.

$$Part = percent \times whole$$

Find the part.

Example: What is 12 percent of 25?

Setup: $Part = \dfrac{12}{100} \times 25 = 3$

Find the percent.

Example: 45 is what percent of 9?

Setup: $45 = Percent \times 9$

$Percent = \dfrac{45}{9} = 5 = 5 \times 100\% = 500\%$

Find the whole.

Example: 15 is $\dfrac{3}{5}$ percent of what number?

Setup: $15 = \dfrac{3}{5}\left(\dfrac{1}{100}\right) \times whole$

$15 = \dfrac{3}{500} \times whole$

$whole = 15\left(\dfrac{500}{3}\right) = 5(500) = 2,500$

13. How to use the PERCENT INCREASE/DECREASE FORMULAS

Identify the original whole and the amount of increase/decrease.

$$Percent\ increase = \frac{amount\ of\ increase}{original\ whole} \times 100\%$$

$$Percent\ decrease = \frac{amount\ of\ decrease}{original\ whole} \times 100\%$$

Example: The price goes up from $80 to $100. What is the percent increase?

Setup: $Percent\ increase = \dfrac{20}{80} \times 100\% = 25\%$

14. How to predict whether a sum, difference, or product will be ODD or EVEN

Don't bother memorizing the rules. Just take simple numbers like 1 and 2 and see what happens.

Example: If m is even and n is odd, is the product mn odd or even?

Setup: Say $m = 2$ and $n = 1$.

2×1 is even, so mn is even.

15. How to recognize MULTIPLES OF 2, 3, 4, 5, 6, 9, 10, and 12

2: Last digit is even

3: Sum of digits is a multiple of 3

4: Last two digits are a multiple of 4

5: Last digit is 5 or 0

6: Sum of digits is a multiple of 3 and last digit is even

9: Sum of digits is a multiple of 9

10: Last digit is 0

12: Sum of digits is a multiple of 3 and last two digits are a multiple of 4

16. How to find a COMMON FACTOR

Break both numbers down to their prime factors to see what they have in common. Then multiply the shared prime factors to find all common factors.

Example: What factors greater than 1 do 135 and 225 have in common?

Setup: First find the prime factors of 135 and 225; $135 = 3 \times 3 \times 3 \times 5$, and $225 = 3 \times 3 \times 5 \times 5$. The numbers share $3 \times 3 \times 5$ in common. Thus, aside from 3 and 5, the remaining common factors can be found by multiplying 3, 3, and 5 in every possible combination: $3 \times 3 = 9$, $3 \times 5 = 15$, and $3 \times 3 \times 5 = 45$.

17. How to find a COMMON MULTIPLE

The product is the easiest common multiple to find. If the two numbers have any factors in common, you can divide them out of the product to get a lower common multiple.

Example: What is the least common multiple of 28 and 42?

Setup: The product of 28 × 42 = 1,176 is a common multiple, but not the least. 28 = 2 × 2 × 7, and 42 = 2 × 3 × 7. They share a 2 and a 7, so divide the product by 2 and then by 7. 1,176 ÷ 2 = 588. 588 ÷ 7 = 84. The least common multiple is 84.

18. How to find the AVERAGE

$$Average = \frac{Sum\ of\ terms}{Number\ of\ terms}$$

Example: What is the average of 3, 4, and 8?

Setup: $Average = \dfrac{3+4+8}{3} = \dfrac{15}{3} = 5.$

19. How to use the AVERAGE to find the SUM

$Sum = (Average) \times (Number\ of\ terms)$

Example: 17.5 is the average (arithmetic mean) of 24 numbers. What is the sum?

Setup: Sum = 17.5 × 24 = 420

20. How to find the AVERAGE of CONSECUTIVE NUMBERS

The average of evenly spaced numbers is simply the average of the smallest number and the largest number. The average of all the integers from 13 to 77, for example, is the same as the average of 13 and 77:

$$\frac{13+77}{2} = \frac{90}{2} = 45$$

21. How to COUNT CONSECUTIVE NUMBERS

The number of integers from A to B inclusive is $B - A + 1$.

Example: How many integers are there from 73 through 419, inclusive?

Setup: 419 − 73 + 1 = 347

22. How to find the SUM OF CONSECUTIVE NUMBERS

$Sum = (Average) \times (Number\ of\ terms)$

Example: What is the sum of the integers from 10 through 50, inclusive?

Setup: Average = (10 + 50) ÷ 2 = 30
Number of terms = 50 − 10 + 1 = 41
Sum = 30 × 41 = 1,230

23. How to find the MEDIAN

Put the numbers in numerical order and take the middle number. (If there's an even number of numbers, the average of the two numbers in the middle is the median.)

Example: What is the median of 88, 86, 57, 94, and 73?

Setup: Put the numbers in numerical order and take the middle number:

57, 73, 86, 88, 94

The median is 86. (If there's an even number of numbers, take the average of the two in the middle.)

24. How to find the MODE

Take the number that appears most often. For example, if your test scores were 88, 57, 68, 85, 98, 93, 93, 84, and 81, the mode of the scores is 93 because it appears more often than any other score. (If there's a tie for most often, then there's more than one mode.)

25. How to find the RANGE

Simply take the positive difference between the highest and lowest values. Using the previous example, if your test scores were 88, 57, 68, 85, 98, 93, 93, 84, and 81, the range of the scores is 41, the highest value minus the lowest value (98 – 57 = 41).

26. How to use actual numbers to determine a RATIO

To find a ratio, put the number associated with *of* on the top and the word associated with *to* on the bottom.

$$Ratio = \frac{of}{to}$$

The ratio of 20 oranges to 12 apples is $\frac{20}{12}$, or $\frac{5}{3}$.

27. How to use a ratio to determine an ACTUAL NUMBER

Set up a proportion.

Example: The ratio of boys to girls is 3 to 4. If there are 135 boys, how many girls are there?

Setup: $\frac{3}{4} = \frac{135}{x}$

$3 \times x = 4 \times 135$

$x = 180$

28. How to use actual numbers to determine a RATE

Identify the quantities and the units to be compared. Keep the units straight.

Example: Anders typed 9,450 words in $3\frac{1}{2}$ hours. What was his rate in words per minute?

Setup: First convert $3\frac{1}{2}$ hours to 210 minutes. Then set up the rate with words on top and minutes on bottom:

$\frac{9{,}450 \text{ words}}{210 \text{ minutes}} = 45$ words per minute

29. How to deal with TABLES, GRAPHS, AND CHARTS

Read the question and all labels extra carefully. Ignore extraneous information and zero in on what the question asks for. Take advantage of the spread in the answer choices by approximating the answer whenever possible.

30. How to count the NUMBER OF POSSIBILITIES

In most cases, you won't need to apply the combination and permutation formulas on the GRE. The number of possibilities is generally so small that the best approach is just to write them out systematically and count them.

Example: How many three-digit numbers can be formed with the digits 1, 3, and 5 used only once?

Setup: Write them out. Be systematic so you don't miss any: 135, 153, 315, 351, 513, 531. Count them: six possibilities.

31. How to calculate a simple PROBABILITY

$$Probability = \frac{Number\ of\ favorable\ outcomes}{Total\ number\ of\ possible\ outcomes}$$

Example: What is the probability of throwing a 5 on a fair six-sided die?

Setup: There is one favorable outcome—throwing a 5. There are 6 possible outcomes—one for each side of the die.

Probability = $\frac{1}{6}$

32. How to work with new SYMBOLS

If you see a symbol you've never seen before, don't freak out: it's a made-up symbol. Everything you need to know is in the question stem. Just follow the instructions.

33. How to SIMPLIFY POLYNOMIALS

First multiply to eliminate all parentheses. Each term inside one parentheses is multiplied by each term inside the other parentheses. All like terms are then combined.

Example: $(3x^2+5x)(x-1) =$
$3x^2(x-1) + 5x(x-1) =$
$3x^3 - 3x^2 + 5x^2 - 5x =$
$3x^3 + 2x^2 - 5x$

34. How to FACTOR certain POLYNOMIALS

Learn to spot these classic factorables:

$$ab + ac = a(b + c)$$

$$a^2 + 2ab + b^2 = (a + b)^2$$

$$a^2 - 2ab + b^2 = (a - b)^2$$

$$a^2 - b^2 = (a - b)(a + b)$$

35. How to solve for one variable IN TERMS OF ANOTHER

To find x "in terms of" y: isolate x on one side, leaving y as the only variable on the other.

36. How to solve an INEQUALITY

Treat it much like an equation—adding, subtracting, multiplying, and dividing both sides by the same thing. Just remember to reverse the inequality sign if you multiply or divide by a negative quantity.

Example: Rewrite $7 - 3x > 2$ in its simplest form

Setup: $7 - 3x > 2$.
Subtract 7 from both sides:
$7 - 3x - 7 > 2 - 7$
So $-3x > -5$. Now divide both sides by -3, and remember to reverse the inequality sign:
$$x < \frac{5}{3}$$

37. How to handle ABSOLUTE VALUES

The *absolute value* of a number n, denoted by $|n|$, is defined as n if $n \geq 0$ and $-n$ if $n < 0$. The absolute value of a number is the distance from zero to the number on the number line:

$|-5| = 5$
If $|x| = 3$, then x could be 3 or -3.

Example: If $|x - 3| < 2$, what is the range of possible values for x?

Setup: $|x - 3| < 2$, so $(x - 3) < 2$ and $-(x - 3) < 2$
So $x - 3 < 2$ and $x - 3 > -2$
So $x < 2 + 3$ and $x > -2 + 3$
So $x < 5$ and $x > 1$
So $1 < x < 5$

38. How to TRANSLATE ENGLISH INTO ALGEBRA

Look for the key words and systematically turn phrases into algebraic expressions and sentences into equations.

Here's a table of key words that you may have to translate into mathematical terms:

Operation	Key Words
Addition	sum, plus, and, added to, more than, increased by, combined with, exceeds, total, greater than
Subtraction	difference between, minus, subtracted from, decreased by, diminished by, less than, reduced by
Multiplication	of, product, times, multiplied by, twice, double, triple, half
Division	quotient, divided by, per, out of, ratio of __ to __
Equals	equals, is, was, will be, the result is, adds up to, costs, is the same as

39. How to find an ANGLE formed by INTERSECTING LINES

Vertical angles are equal. Adjacent angles add up to 180°.

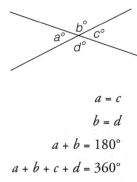

$$a = c$$
$$b = d$$
$$a + b = 180°$$
$$a + b + c + d = 360°$$

40. How to find an angle formed by a TRANSVERSAL across PARALLEL LINES

All the acute angles are equal. All the obtuse angles are equal. An acute plus an obtuse equals 180°.

Example:

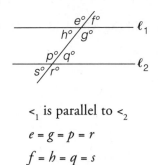

ℓ_1 is parallel to ℓ_2

$$e = g = p = r$$
$$f = h = q = s$$
$$e + q = g + s = 180°$$

41. How to find the AREA of a TRIANGLE

$$Area = \frac{1}{2}(base)(height)$$

Example:

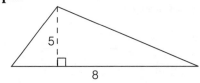

Setup: $Area = \frac{1}{2}(8)(5) = 20$

42. How to work with ISOSCELES TRIANGLES

Isosceles triangles have two equal sides and two equal angles. If a GRE question tells you that a triangle is isoceles, you can bet that you'll need to use that information to find the length of a side or a measure of an angle.

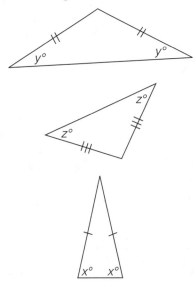

43. How to work with EQUILATERAL TRIANGLES

Equilateral triangles have three equal sides and three 60° angles. If a GRE question tells you that a triangle is equilateral, you can bet that you'll need to use that information to find the length of a side or a measure of an angle.

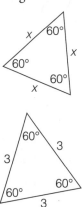

44. How to work with SIMILAR TRIANGLES

In similar triangles, corresponding angles are equal and corresponding sides are proportional. If a GRE question tells you that triangles are similar, you'll probably need that information to find the length of a side or the measure of an angle.

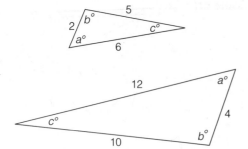

45. How to find the HYPOTENUSE or a LEG of a RIGHT TRIANGLE

Pythagorean theorem: $a^2 + b^2 = c^2$

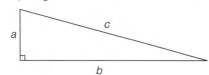

46. How to spot SPECIAL RIGHT TRIANGLES

3-4-5

5-12-13

30-60-90

45-45-90

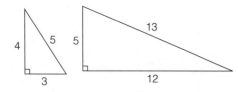

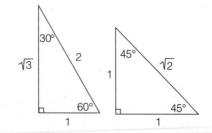

47. How to find the PERIMETER of a RECTANGLE

Perimeter = 2(length + width)

Example:

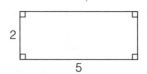

Setup: Perimeter = 2(2 + 5) = 14

48. How to find the AREA of a RECTANGLE

Area = (length)(width)

Example:

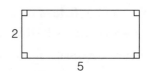

Setup: Area = 2 × 5 = 10

49. How to find the AREA of a SQUARE

Area = (side)²

Example:

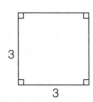

Setup: Area = 3² = 9

50. How to find the AREA of a PARALLELOGRAM

Area = (base)(height)

Example:

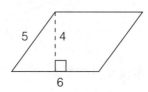

Setup: Area = 6 × 4 = 24

51. How to find the AREA of a TRAPEZOID

A trapezoid is a quadrilateral having only two parallel sides. You can always drop a line or two to break the figure into a rectangle and a triangle or two triangles. Use the area formulas for those familiar shapes. You could also apply the general formula for the area of a trapezoid:

Area = (Average of parallel sides) × (height)

Example:

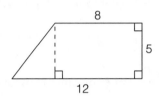

Setup: Area of rectangle = 8 × 5 = 40
Area of triangle = $\frac{1}{2}$(4 × 5) = 10
Area of trapeziod = 40 + 10 = 50

52. How to find the CIRCUMFERENCE of a CIRCLE

Circumference = 2πr

Example:

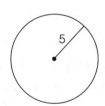

Setup: Circumference = 2π(5) = 10π

53. How to find the AREA of a CIRCLE

Area = πr²

Example:

Setup: Area = π × 5² = 25π

54. How to find the DISTANCE BETWEEN POINTS on the coordinate plane

If two points have the same *x*s or the same *y*s— that is, they make a line segment that is parallel to an axis—all you have to do is subtract the numbers that are different.

Example: What is the distance from (2, 3) to (–7, 3)?

Setup: The *y*s are the same, so just subtract the *x*s. 2 –(–7) = 9

If the points have different *x*s and different *y*s, make a right triangle and use the Pythagorean theorem.

Example: What is the distance from (2, 3) to (–1, –1)?

Setup:

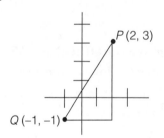

It's a 3-4-5 triangle!
PQ = 5

55. How to find the SLOPE of a LINE

$$Slope = \frac{rise}{run} = \frac{change\ in\ y}{change\ in\ x}$$

Example: What is the slope of the line that contains the points (1, 2) and (4, –5)?

Setup: $Slope = \frac{-5-2}{4-1} = \frac{-7}{3}$

LEVEL 3 (Math You Might Find Difficult)

56. How to determine COMBINED PERCENT INCREASE/DECREASE

Start with 100 and see what happens.

Example: A price rises by 10 percent one year and by 20 percent the next. What's the combined percent increase?

Setup: Say the original price is $100.

Year one:
$100 + (10% of 100) = 100 + 10 = 110.

Year two:
110 + (20% of 110) = 110 + 22 = 132.

From 100 to 132—That's a 32 percent increase.

57. How to find the ORIGINAL WHOLE before percent increase/decrease

Think of a 15 percent increase over x as $1.15x$ and set up an equation.

Example: After decreasing by 5 percent, the population is now 57,000. What was the original population?

Setup: $0.95 \times$ (Original Population) = 57,000
Original Population = $57,000 \div 0.95 = 60,000$

58. How to solve a SIMPLE INTEREST problem

With simple interest, the interest is computed on the principal only and is given by:

interest = (principal) × (interest rate*) × (time**)

* expressed as a decimal
** expressed in years

Example: If $12,000 is invested at 6 percent simple annual interest, how much interest is earned after 9 months?

Setup: $(12{,}000) \times (0.06) \times \left(\dfrac{9}{12}\right) = \$540$

59. How to solve a COMPOUND INTEREST problem

If interest is compounded, the interest is computed on the principal as well as on any interest earned. To compute compound interest:

$$(\textit{final balance}) = (\textit{principal}) \times \left(1 + \frac{\textit{interest rate}}{C}\right)^{(\textit{time})(C)}$$

where C = the number of times compounded annually

Example: If $10,000 is invested at 8 percent annual interest, compounded semiannually, what is the balance after 1 year?

Setup: Final balance.

$$= (10{,}000) \times \left(1 + \frac{0.08}{2}\right)^{(1)(2)}$$
$$= (10{,}000) \times (1.04)^2$$
$$= \$10{,}816$$

60. How to solve a REMAINDERS problem

Pick a number that fits the given conditions and see what happens.

Example: When n is divided by 7, the remainder is 5. What is the remainder when $2n$ is divided by 7?

Setup: Find a number that leaves a remainder of 5 when divided by 7. A good choice would be 12. If $n = 12$, then $2n = 24$, which, when divided by 7, leaves a remainder of 3.

61. How to solve a DIGITS problem

Use a little logic—and some trial and error.

Example: If *A*, *B*, *C*, and *D* represent distinct digits in the addition problem below, what is the value of *D*?

$$\begin{array}{r} AB \\ +BA \\ \hline CDC \end{array}$$

Setup: Two 2-digit numbers will add up to at most something in the 100s, so *C* = 1. *B* plus *A* in the units' column gives a 1, and since it can't simply be that *B* + *A* = 1, it must be that *B* + *A* = 11, and a 1 gets carried. In fact, *A* and *B* can be any pair of digits that add up to 11 (3 and 8, 4 and 7, etcetera), but it doesn't matter what they are, they always give you the same thing for *D*:

$$\begin{array}{r} 47 \\ +74 \\ \hline 121 \end{array} \qquad \begin{array}{r} 83 \\ +38 \\ \hline 121 \end{array}$$

62. How to find a WEIGHTED AVERAGE

Give each term the appropriate "weight."

Example: The girls' average score is 30. The boys' average score is 24. If there are twice as many boys as girls, what is the overall average?

Setup:

$$\text{Weighted Avg.} = \frac{1 \times 30 + 2 \times 24}{3} = \frac{78}{3} = 26$$

HINT: Don't just average the averages.

63. How to find the NEW AVERAGE when a number is added or deleted

Use the sum of the terms of the old average to help you find the new average.

Example: Michael's average score after four tests is 80. If he scores 100 on the fifth test, what's his new average?

Setup: Find the original sum from the original average:

Original sum = 4 × 80 = 320

Add the fifth score to make the new sum:

New sum = 320 + 100 = 420

Find the new average from the new sum:

$$\text{New average} = \frac{420}{5} = 84$$

64. How to use the ORIGINAL AVERAGE and NEW AVERAGE to figure out WHAT WAS ADDED OR DELETED

Use the sums.

Number added = (new sum) – (original sum)

Number deleted = (original sum) – (new sum)

Example: The average of five numbers is 2. After one number is deleted, the new average is –3. What number was deleted?

Setup: Find the original sum from the original average:

Original sum = 5 × 2 = 10

Find the new sum from the new average:

New sum = 4 × (–3) = –12

The difference between the original sum and the new sum is the answer.

Number deleted = 10 – (–12) = 22

65. How to find an AVERAGE RATE

Convert to totals.

$$Average\ A\ per\ B = \frac{Total\ A}{Total\ B}$$

Example: If the first 500 pages have an average of 150 words per page, and the remaining 100 pages have an average of 450 words per page, what is the average number of words per page for the entire 600 pages?

Setup: Total pages = 500 + 100 = 600
Total words = $500 \times 150 + 100 \times 450 = 120,000$

$$Average\ words\ per\ page = \frac{120,000}{600} = 200$$

To find an average speed, you also convert to totals.

$$Average\ speed = \frac{Total\ distance}{Time}$$

Example: Rosa drove 120 miles one way at an average speed of 40 miles per hour and returned by the same 120-mile route at an average speed of 60 miles per hour. What was Rosa's average speed for the entire 240-mile round trip?

Setup: To drive 120 miles at 40 mph takes 3 hours. To return at 60 mph takes 2 hours. The total time, then, is 5 hours.

$$Average\ speed = \frac{240\ miles}{5\ hours} = 48\ mph$$

66. How to solve a WORK PROBLEM

In a work problem, you are given the rate at which people or machines perform work individually, and asked to compute the rate at which they work together (or vice versa). The work formula states: The inverse of the time it would take everyone working together equals the sum of the inverses of the times it would take each working individually. In other words:

$$\frac{1}{r} + \frac{1}{s} = \frac{1}{t}$$

where r and s are, for example, the number of hours it would take Rebecca and Sam, respectively to complete a job working by themselves, and t is the number of hours it would take the two of them working together.

Example: If it takes Joe 4 hours to paint a room and Pete twice as long to paint the same room, how long would it take the two of them, working together, to paint the same room, if each of them works at his respective individual rate?

Setup: Joe takes 4 hours, so Pete takes 8 hours; thus:

$$\frac{1}{4} + \frac{1}{8} = \frac{1}{t}$$

$$\frac{2}{8} + \frac{1}{8} = \frac{1}{t}$$

$$\frac{3}{8} = \frac{1}{t}$$

$$t = \frac{1}{\left(\frac{3}{8}\right)} = \frac{8}{3}$$

So it would take them $\frac{8}{3}$ hours, or 2 hours 40 minutes, to paint the room together.

67. How to determine a COMBINED RATIO

Multiply one or both ratios by whatever you need to in order to get the terms they have in common to match.

Example: The ratio of a to b is 7:3. The ratio of b to c is 2:5. What is the ratio of a to c?

Setup: Multiply each member of $a:b$ by 2 and multiply each member of $b:c$ by 3 and you get $a:b = 14:6$ and $b:c = 6:15$. Now that the bs match, you can just take a and c and say $a:c = 14:15$.

68. How to solve a DILUTION or MIXTURE problem

In dilution or mixture problems, you have to determine the characteristics of the resulting mixture when substances with different characteristics are combined. Or, alternatively, you have to determine how to combine substances with different characteristics to produce a desired mixture. There are two approaches to such problems—the straightforward setup and the balancing method.

Example: If 5 pounds of raisins that cost $1 per pound are mixed with 2 pounds of almonds that cost $2.40 per pound, what is the cost per pound of the resulting mixture?

Setup: The straightforward setup: ($1)(5) + ($2.40)(2) = $9.80
The cost per pound is $n = \$\dfrac{9.80}{7} =$ $1.40

Example: How many liters of a solution that is 10 percent alcohol by volume must be added to 2 liters of a solution that is 50 percent alcohol by volume to create a solution that is 15 percent alcohol by volume?

Setup: The balancing method: Make the weaker and stronger (or cheaper and more expensive, etc.) substances balance. That is: (percent/price difference between the weaker solution and the desired solution) × (amount of weaker solution) = (percent/price difference between the stronger solution and the desired solution) × (amount of stronger solution).

In this case: $n(15 - 10) = 2(50 - 15)$

$$n \times 5 = 2(35)$$
$$n = \frac{70}{5} = 14$$

So 14 liters of the 10 percent solution must be added.

69. How to solve a GROUP problem involving BOTH/NEITHER

Some GRE word problems involve two groups with overlapping members, and possibly elements that belong to neither group. It's easy to identify this type of question because the words "both" and/or "neither" appear in the question. These problems are quite easy if you just memorize the following formula:

Group 1 + Group 2 + Neither – Both = Total

Example: Of the 120 students at a certain language school, 65 are studying French, 51 are studying Spanish, and 53 are studying neither language. How many are studying both French and Spanish?

Setup: 65 + 51 + 53 – Both = 120
169 – Both = 120
Both = 49

70. How to solve a GROUP problem involving EITHER/OR CATEGORIES

Other GRE word problems involve groups with distinct "either/or" categories (male/female, blue collar/white collar, etc.). The key to solving this type of problem is to organize the information in a grid.

Example: At a certain professional conference with 130 attendees, 94 of the attendees are doctors and the rest are dentists. If 48 of the attendees are women, and $\frac{1}{4}$ of the dentists in attendance are women, how many of the attendees are male doctors?

Setup: To complete the grid, each row and column adds up to the corresponding total:

	Doctors	Dentists	Total
Male	55	27	82
Female		9	48
Total	94	36	130

After you've filled in the information from the question, simply fill in the remaining boxes until you get the number you are looking for—in this case, that 55 of the attendees are male doctors.

71. How to work with FACTORIALS

You may see a problem involving factorial notation. If n is an integer greater than 1, then n factorial, denoted by $n!$, is defined as the product of all the integers from 1 to n. In other words:

$2! = 2 \times 1 = 2$

$3! = 3 \times 2 \times 1 = 6$

$4! = 4 \times 3 \times 2 \times 1 = 24$, etc.

By definition, $0! = 1! = 1$.

Also note: $6! = 6 \times 5! = 6 \times 5 \times 4!$, etc. Most GRE factorial problems test your ability to factor and/or cancel.

Example: $\dfrac{8!}{6! \times 2!} = \dfrac{8 \times 7 \times 6!}{6! \times 2 \times 1} = 28$

72. How to solve a PERMUTATION problem

Factorials are useful for solving questions about permutations, i.e., the number of ways to arrange elements sequentially. For instance, to figure out how many ways there are to arrange 7 items along a shelf, you would multiply the number of possibilities for the first position times the number of possibilities remaining for the second position, and so on—in other words: $7 \times 6 \times 5 \times 4 \times 3 \times 2 \times 1$, or $7!$.

If you're asked to find the number of ways to arrange a smaller group that's being drawn from a larger group, you can either apply logic or you can use the permutation formula:

$$_nP_k = \frac{n!}{(n-k)!}$$

where n = (# in the larger group) and k = (# you're arranging).

Example: Five runners run in a race. The runners who come in first, second, and third place will win gold, silver, and bronze medals respectively. How many possible outcomes for gold, silver, and bronze medal winners are there?

Setup: Any of the 5 runners could come in first place, leaving 4 runners who could come in second place, leaving 3 runners who could come in third place, for a total of $5 \times 4 \times 3 = 60$ possible outcomes for gold, silver, and bronze medal winners. Or, using the formula:

$$_5P_3 = \frac{5!}{(5-3)!} = \frac{5!}{2!} = 5 \times 4 \times 3 = 60$$

73. How to solve a COMBINATION problem

If the order or arrangement of the smaller group that's being drawn from the larger group does NOT matter, you are looking for the numbers of combinations, and a different formula is called for:

$$_nC_k \frac{n!}{k!(n-k)!}$$

Where n = (# in the larger group) and k = (# you're choosing)

> **Example:** How many different ways are there to choose 3 delegates from 8 possible candidates?
>
> **Setup:** $_8C_3 = \frac{8!}{3! \times 5!} = \frac{8 \times 7 \times 6 \times 5!}{3 \times 2 \times 1 \times 5!} = 56$

So there are 56 different possible combinations.

74. How to solve PROBABILITY problems where probabilities must be multiplied

Suppose that a random process is performed. Then there is a set of possible outcomes that can occur. An event is a set of possible outcomes. We are concerned with the probability of events.

When all the outcomes are all equally likely, the basic probability formula is:

$$Probability = \frac{Number\ of\ desired\ outcomes}{Number\ of\ possible\ outcomes}$$

Many hard probability questions involve finding the probability that several events occur. Let's consider first the case of the probability that two events occur. Call these two events A and B. The probability that both events occur is the probability that event A occurs multiplied by the probability that event B occurs given that event A occurred. The probability that B occurs given that A occurs is called the conditional probability that B occurs given that A occurs. Except when events A and B do not depend on one another, the probability that B occurs given that A occurs is not the same as the probability that B occurs.

The probability that three events A, B, and C occur is the probability that A occurs multiplied by the conditional probability that B occurs given that A occurred multiplied by the conditional probability that C occurs given that both A and B have occurred.

This can be generalized to n events, where n is a positive integer greater than 3.

> **Example:** If 2 students are chosen at random to run an errand from a class with 5 girls and 5 boys, what is the probability that both students chosen will be girls?
>
> **Setup:** The probability that the first student chosen will be a girl is $\frac{5}{10} = \frac{1}{2}$, and since there would be girls and 5 boys left out of 9 students, the probability that the second student chosen will be a girl (given that the first student chosen is a girl) is $\frac{4}{9}$. Thus the probability that both students chosen will be girls is $\frac{1}{2} \times \frac{4}{9} = \frac{2}{9}$.

Let's consider another example where a random process is repeated.

> **Example:** If a fair coin is tossed 4 times, what's the probability that at least 3 of the 4 tosses will be heads?
>
> **Setup:** There are 2 possible outcomes for each toss, so after 4 tosses there are $2 \times 2 \times 2 \times 2 = 16$ possible outcomes.

We can list the different possible sequences where at least 3 of the 4 tosses are heads. These sequences are

> HHHT
>
> HHTH
>
> HTHH
>
> THHH
>
> HHHH

Thus, the probability that at least 3 of the 4 tosses will come up heads is:

$$\frac{\text{Number of favorable outcomes}}{\text{Number of possible outcomes}} = \frac{5}{16}$$

We could have also solved this question using the combinations formula. The probability of a head is $\frac{1}{2}$ and the probability of a tail is $\frac{1}{2}$. The probability of any particular sequence of heads and tails resulting from 4 tosses is $\frac{1}{2} \times \frac{1}{2} \times \frac{1}{2} \times \frac{1}{2}$, which is $\frac{1}{16}$.

Suppose that the result each of the four tosses is recorded in each of the four spaces.

____ ____ ____ ____

Thus, we would record an H for head or a T for tails in each of the 4 spaces.

The number of ways of having exactly 3 heads among the 4 tosses is the number of ways of choosing 3 of the 4 spaces above to record an H for heads.

The number of ways of choosing 3 of the 4 spaces is

$$_4C_3 = \frac{4!}{3!(4-3)!} = \frac{4!}{3!(1)!} = \frac{4 \times 3 \times 2 \times 1}{3 \times 2 \times 1 \times 1} = 4.$$

The number of ways of having exactly 4 heads among the 4 tosses is 1.

If we use the combinations formula, using the definition that $0! = 1$, then

$$_4C_4 = \frac{4!}{4!(4-4)!} = \frac{4!}{4!(0)!} = \frac{4!}{4!(0)!}$$

$$= \frac{4 \times 3 \times 2 \times 1}{4 \times 3 \times 2 \times 1 \times 1} = 1.$$

Thus, $_4C_3 = 4$ and $_4C_4 = 1$. So the number of different sequences containing at least 3 heads is $4 + 1 = 5$.

The probability of having at least 3 heads is $\frac{5}{16}$.

75. How to deal with STANDARD DEVIATION

Like mean, mode, median, and range, standard deviation is a term used to describe sets of numbers. Standard deviation is a measure of how spread out a set of numbers is (how much the numbers deviate from the mean). The greater the spread, the higher the standard deviation. You'll never actually have to calculate the standard deviation on Test Day, but here's how it's calculated:

- Find the average (arithmetic mean) of the set.
- Find the differences between the mean and each value in the set.
- Square each of the differences.
- Find the average of the squared differences.
- Take the positive square root of the average.

Although you won't have to calculate standard deviation on the GRE, you may be asked to compare standard deviations between sets of data, or otherwise demonstrate that you understand what standard deviation means.

Example: High temperatures, in degrees Fahrenheit, in 2 cities over 5 days:

September	1	2	3	4	5
City A	54	61	70	49	56
City B	62	56	60	67	65

For the 5-day period listed, which city had the greater standard deviation in high temperatures?

Setup: Even without trying to calculate them out, one can see that City A has the greater spread in temperatures, and therefore the greater standard deviation in high temperatures. If you were to go ahead and calculate the standard deviations following the steps described above, you would find that the standard deviation in

high temperatures for City A = $A = \sqrt{\frac{254}{5}} \approx 7.1$,

while the standard deviation for City $B = \sqrt{\frac{74}{5}} \approx 3.8$.

76. How to MULTIPLY/DIVIDE POWERS

Add/subtract the exponents.

Example: $x^a \times x^b = x^{a+b}$
$2^3 \times 2^4 = 2^7$

Example: $\frac{x^c}{x^d} = x^{c-d}$

$\frac{5^6}{5^2} = 5^4$

77. How to RAISE A POWER TO A POWER TO AN EXPONENT

Multiply the exponents.

Example: $(x^a)^b = x^{ab}$
$(3^4)^5 = 3^{20}$

78. How to handle POWERS with a base of ZERO and POWERS with an EXPONENT of ZERO

Zero raised to any nonzero exponent equals zero.

Example: $0^4 = 0^{12} = 0^1 = 0$
Any nonzero number raised to the exponent 0 equals 1.

Example: $3^0 = 15^0 = (0.34)^0 = -345^0 = \pi^0 = 1$
The lone exception is 0 raised to the 0 power, which is *undefined*.

79. How to handle NEGATIVE POWERS

A number raised to the exponent $-x$ is the reciprocal of that number raised to the exponent x.

Example: $5^{-3} = \frac{1}{5^3} = \frac{1}{5 \times 5 \times 5} = \frac{1}{125}$

$n^{-1} = \frac{1}{n}, n^{-2} = \frac{1}{n^2}$, and so on.

80. How to handle FRACTIONAL POWERS

Fractional exponents relate to roots. For instance, $x^{\frac{1}{2}} = \sqrt{x}$.
Likewise, $x^{\frac{1}{3}} = \sqrt[3]{x}, x^{\frac{2}{3}} = \sqrt[3]{x^2}$, and so on.

Example: $4^{\frac{1}{2}} = \sqrt{4} = 2$

$(x^{-2})^{\frac{1}{2}} = x^{(-2)\left(\frac{1}{2}\right)} = x^{-1} = \frac{1}{x}$

81. How to handle CUBE ROOTS

The cube root of x is just the number that multiplied by itself 3 times (i.e., cubed) gives you x. Both positive and negative numbers have one and only one cube root, denoted by the symbol $\sqrt{3}$, and the cube root of a number is always the same sign as the number itself.

Example: $(-5) \times (-5) \times (-5) = -125$, so $\sqrt[3]{-125}$

$= -5$

$\frac{1}{2} \times \frac{1}{2} \times \frac{1}{2} = \frac{1}{8}$, so $\sqrt[3]{\frac{1}{8}} = \frac{1}{2}$

82. How to ADD, SUBTRACT, MULTIPLY, and DIVIDE ROOTS

You can add/subtract roots only when the parts inside the $\sqrt{}$ are identical.

Example: $\sqrt{2} + 3\sqrt{2} = 4\sqrt{2}$

$\sqrt{2} - 3\sqrt{2} = -2\sqrt{2}$

$\sqrt{2} + \sqrt{3}$ cannot be combined.

To multiply/divide roots, deal with what's inside the $\sqrt{}$ and outside the $\sqrt{}$ separately.

Example: $(2\sqrt{3})(7\sqrt{5}) = (2 \times 7)(\sqrt{3 \times 5}) = 14\sqrt{15}$

$$\frac{10\sqrt{21}}{5\sqrt{3}} = \frac{10}{5}\sqrt{\frac{21}{3}} = 2\sqrt{7}$$

83. How to SIMPLIFY A RADICAL

Look for perfect squares (4, 9, 16, 25, 36…) inside the $\sqrt{}$. Factor them out and "unsquare" them.

Example: $\sqrt{48} = \sqrt{16} \times \sqrt{3} = 4\sqrt{3}$

$\sqrt{180} = \sqrt{36} \times \sqrt{5} = 6\sqrt{5}$

84. How to solve certain QUADRATIC EQUATIONS

Forget the quadratic formula. Manipulate the equation (if necessary) into the "_____ = 0" form, factor the left side, and break the quadratic into two simple equations.

Example:
$$x^2 + 6 = 5x$$
$$x^2 - 5x + 6 = 0$$
$$(x - 2)(x - 3) = 0$$
$$x - 2 = 0 \text{ or } x - 3 = 0$$
$$x = 2 \text{ or } 3$$

Example:
$$x^2 = 9$$
$$x = 3 \text{ or } -3$$

85. How to solve MULTIPLE EQUATIONS

When you see two equations with two variables on the GRE, they're probably easy to combine in such a way that you get something closer to what you're looking for.

Example: If $5x - 2y = -9$ and $3y - 4x = 6$, what is the value of $x + y$?

Setup: The question doesn't ask for x and y separately, so don't solve for them separately if you don't have to. Look what happens if you just rearrange a little and "add" the equations:

$$5x - 2y = -9$$
$$\underline{-4x + 3y = 6}$$
$$x + y = -3$$

86. How to solve a SEQUENCE problem

The notation used in sequence problems scares many test takers, but these problems aren't as bad as they look. In a sequence problem, the nth term in the sequence is generated by performing an operation, which will be defined for you, on either n or on the previous term in the sequence. Familiarize yourself with sequence notation and you should have no problem.

Example: What is the positive difference between the fifth and fourth terms in the sequence 0, 4, 18, … whose nth term is $n^2(n - 1)$?

Setup: Use the operation given to come up with the values for your terms:

$$n_5 = 5^2(5 - 1) = 25(4) = 100$$
$$n_4 = 4^2(4 - 1) = 16(3) = 48$$

So the positive difference between the fifth and fourth terms is $100 - 48 = 52$.

87. How to solve a FUNCTION problem

You may see classic function notation on the GRE. An algebraic expression of only one variable may be defined as a function, f or g, of that variable.

Example: What is the minimum value of the function $f(x) = x^2 - 1$?

Setup: In the function $f(x) = x^2 - 1$, if x is 1, then $f(1) = 1^2 - 1 = 0$. In other words, by inputting 1 into the function, the output $f(x) = 0$. Every number inputted has one and only one output (although the reverse is not necessarily true). You're asked to find the minimum value, so how would you minimize the expression $f(x) = x^2 - 1$? Since x^2 cannot be negative, in this case $f(x)$ is minimized by making $x = 0$: $f(0) = 0^2 - 1 = -1$, so the minimum value of the function is -1.

88. How to handle GRAPHS of FUNCTIONS

You may see problem that involves a function graphed onto the xy-coordinate plane, often called a "rectangular coordinate system" on the GRE. When graphing a function, the output, $f(x)$, becomes the y-coordinate. For example, in the previous example, $f(x) = x^2 - 1$, you've already determined 2 points, $(1, 0)$ and $(0, -1)$. If you were to keep plugging in numbers to determine more points and then plotted those points on the xy-coordinate plane, you would come up with something like this:

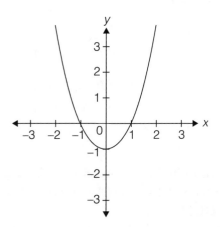

This curved line is called a *parabola*. In the event that you should see a parabola on the GRE (it could be upside down or more narrow or wider than the one shown), you will most likely be

asked to choose which equation the parabola is describing. These questions can be surprisingly easy to answer. Pick out obvious points on the graph, such as $(1, 0)$ and $(0, -1)$ above, plug these values into the answer choices, and eliminate answer choices that don't jibe with those values until only one answer choice is left.

89. How to handle LINEAR EQUATIONS

You may also encounter linear equations on the GRE. A linear equation is often expressed in the form

$y = mx + b$, where:
- m = the slope of the line = $\dfrac{rise}{run}$.

For instance, a slope of 3 means that the line rises 3 steps for every 1 step it makes to the right. A positive slope slopes up from left to right. A negative slope slopes down from left to right. A slope of zero (e.g., $y = 5$) is a flat line.

- b = the y-intercept (where the line passes the y-axis).

Example: The graph of the linear equation

$$y = -\frac{3}{4}x + 3 \text{ is:}$$

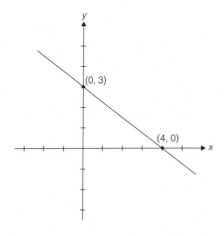

Note: The equation above could also be written in the form $3x + 4y = 12$.

To get a better handle on an equation written in this form, you can solve for y to write it in its more familiar form. Or, if you're asked to choose which equation the line is describing, you can pick obvious points such as (0, 3) and (4, 0) above, and use these values to eliminate answer choices until only one answer is left.

90. How to find the x- and y-INTERCEPTS of a line

The x-intercept of a line is the value of x where the line crosses the x-axis. In other words, it's the value of x when $y = 0$. Likewise, the y-intercept is the value of y where the line crosses the y-axis, i.e., the value of y when $x = 0$. The y-intercept is also the value b when the equation is in the form: $y = mx + b$. For instance, in the line shown in the previous example, the x-intercept is 4 and the y-intercept is 3.

91. How to find the MAXIMUM and MINIMUM lengths for a SIDE of a TRIANGLE

If you know n = the lengths of two sides of a triangle, you know that the third side is between the positive difference and the sum.

Example: The length of one side of a triangle is 7. The length of another side is 3. What is the range of possible lengths for the third side?

Setup: The third side is greater than the difference (7 − 3 = 4) and less than the sum (7 + 3 = 10).

92. How to find one angle or the sum of all the ANGLES of a REGULAR POLYGON

Sum of the interior angles in a polygon with n sides =

$(n - 2) \times 180$

Degree measure of one angle in a regular polygon with

n sides $= \dfrac{(n - 2) \times 180}{n}$.

Example: What is the measure of one angle of a regular pentagon?

Setup: Plug $n = 5$ into the formula:
Degree measure of one angle =
$\dfrac{(5 - 2) \times 180}{5} = \dfrac{540}{5} = 108$

93. How to find the LENGTH of an ARC

Think of an arc as a fraction of the circle's circumference.

$$\text{Length of } arc = \dfrac{n}{360} \times 2\pi r$$

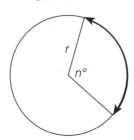

94. How to find the AREA of a SECTOR

Think of a sector as a fraction of the circle's area.

$$\text{Area of } sector = \dfrac{n}{360} \times \pi r^2$$

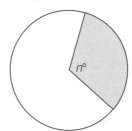

95. How to find the dimensions or area of an INSCRIBED or CIRCUMSCRIBED FIGURE

Look for the connection. Is the diameter the same as a side or a diagonal?

Example: If the area of the square is 36, what is the circumference of the circle?

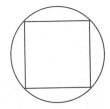

Setup: To get the circumference, you need the diameter or radius. The circle's diameter is also the square's diagonal, which (the diagonal creates two 45-45-90 triangles!) is $6\sqrt{2}$.

Circumference = π(diameter) = $6\pi\sqrt{2}$

96. How to find the VOLUME of a RECTANGULAR SOLID

Volume = length × width × height

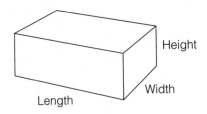

97. How to find the SURFACE AREA of a RECTANGULAR SOLID

To find the surface area of a rectangular solid, you have to find the area of each face and add them together. Here's the formula:

Surface area = 2(length × width + length × height + width × height)

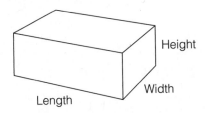

98. How to find the DIAGONAL of a RECTANGULAR SOLID

Use the Pythagorean theorem twice, unless you spot "special" triangles.

Example: What is the length of *AG*?

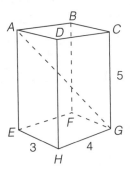

Setup: Draw diagonal *AC*.

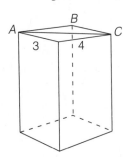

ABC is a 3-4-5 triangle, so *AC* = 5. Now look at triangle *ACG*:

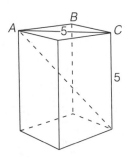

ACG is another special triangle, so you don't need to use the Pythagorean theorem. *ACG* is a 45-45-90, so *AG* = $5\sqrt{2}$.

99. How to find the VOLUME of a CYLINDER

Volume = $\pi r^2 h$

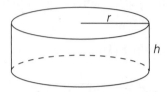

100. How to find the VOLUME of a SPHERE

Volume = $\dfrac{4}{3}\pi r^3$

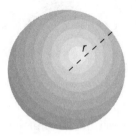